Value Creation
The Power of Brand Equity

William Neal – Ron Strauss

SOUTH-WESTERN
CENGAGE Learning

Australia • Brazil • Japan • Korea • Mexico • Singapore • Spain • United Kingdom • United States

Value Creation: The Power of Brand Equity

William Neal, Ron Strauss

COPYRIGHT © 2008 by Texere, an imprint of Cengage Learning/South-Western, a part of The Cengage Learning Corporation. The Cengage trademark used herein is under license.

Composed by: ICC Macmillan Inc.

Printed in the United States of America by
RR Donnelley—Crawfordsville
1 2 3 4 5 11 10 09 08
This book is printed on acid-free paper.

ISBN 1-587-99204-3

Library of Congress Cataloging in Publication Number is available. See page 354 for details.

For more information about our products, contact us at:

Cengage Learning Academic
Resource Center
1-800-423-0563

Cengage Learning
5191 Natorp Boulevard
Mason, Ohio 45040
USA

TABLE OF CONTENTS

"The power of the fish is in the water."
—Zimbabwean proverb

ACKNOWLEDGEMENTS

The authors readily acknowledge that we stand on the shoulders of those who have contributed to the body of knowledge on business, marketing and branding. If this book has any merit, it is due to the people who we each reference below, as well as many who have impacted our lives and thoughts but who we have not formally acknowledged.

The folks at the SouthWestern Learning division of Cengage (formerly Thomson) have been very patient and helpful throughout the writing and production process - our thanks to Elizabeth Lowry, Jennifer Zeigler, and Sarah Greber. Thanks also to Mary Reed, publicist. And a special thanks to Steve Momper who initiated this project at Thomson before becoming director of Darden Business Publishing at the Darden Graduate School of Business at the University of Virginia.

Thanks also to folks at the American Marketing Association, co-publishers of this book. Especially to Francesca van Gorp Cooley, Director of Professional Publications.

The authors assume all responsibility for mistakes, incorrect information, or points-of-view that the reader may disagree with. We welcome your comments and suggestions for future editions.

Bill Neal

First and foremost, I wish to acknowledge my wife and soul mate, Carolyn Pollard Neal. Her long term support and advice have been invaluable. I want to especially thank her for cajoling me into reviewing so many quality articles submitted to *Marketing Management,* the magazine she has been managing since 1990.

Without the support and collaboration of my long time business partner, David Feldman, and the staff at SDR Consulting, past and present, this book would have not been possible. I thank you all from the bottom of my heart.

I would like to particularly acknowledge a special group of marketing practitioners and academics who have, over many years, consistently contributed to improving the practice of marketing research through their many publications, their presentations, and especially their participation in practitioner conferences. Those who have personally had a great influence on me and my research include, in no particular order, Richard Johnson, Paul Green, Gary Mullet, Phil Kotler, Frank Bass, Jag Sheth, Don Schultz, Fred Webster, Naresh Malhotra, Chuck Chakrapani, John Wurst, and Greg Allenby. Over the years and in many different ways you gentlemen have forced me to study more and think harder about new concepts and approaches. You have all been great teachers. Thank you.

Ron Strauss

My family taught me the value of values. My father Jerry taught me and my sisters Gale, Linda and Barbara to work for what we wanted, and to respect others. My mother Pearl taught us to value education, perseverance, and living within our means. We learned character is an intangible asset that creates the greatest value of all – self-respect.

Friends, business associates, and clients who influenced this book in ways in which they are likely unaware include: Ed Mitchell and Bob Fowler (founders of ITHACO, now part of GE), Dick Athey, Ron Seichrist; Harry Burker, Thomas J Mallot, Tom McCausland of Siemens; Gordon Bailey, Al Schoelles, Gudjon B. Olafsson, Del Thomas, Bill Dahlberg, Jag Sheth, and many, many others.

Vistage has had a powerful impact on my thinking. Bud Carter served as chair of my first Vistage group. This book reflects the wisdom of many Vistage speakers, including: Jim Bleech, Peter Schutz, Don Schmincke, Morris Schectman, Lee Thayer, Kraig Kramers, Max Cary, James Cecil, Harry Dent, Jr., Mardy Grothe, Frank Maguire, Frank Chamberlain, Duane Lakin, Chuck Reaves, and others.

My Vistage group's members have provided valuable counsel for many years. Jansen Chazanof, our group's chair, has made many helpful comments that have improved this book.

My final thank you is to my wife Deana. Deana heads up the strategic planning department at JWT communications, entertainment and technology and has been a constant source of encouragement, support and ideas. Deana models the values of respect and caring for others with intelligence and integrity. Without her this book would not have been possible. She is my love and my inspiration.

"LET'S TALK ABOUT IT OVER LUNCH . . ."

Sometimes, the best things begin by accident. Two marketing professionals, joined by a shared interest in brand practice and measurement, started to meet over lunch to informally discuss the issues that they felt were frustrating other marketing professionals, other business leaders, and themselves.
5 There's nothing like hot food and cold beer to lubricate a conversation.

The issues we discussed concerned the lack of measurement that plagued the marketing arena. We bemoaned the lack of in-depth understanding of the role and power of brand. We worried about many practitioners' focus on tactics rather than strategy. But most of all, we talked about the incredible
10 waste of resources and potential within many companies being reported daily in the press.

Now, things could have stayed there. Two guys with decades of business, management, and marketing experience who could see that things could be better, but just talking about what was 'wrong', and like most people, letting
15 things end there. These conversations were cathartic, in their own way, but soon just describing the problem wasn't enough. So, we began to explore solutions.

The more we talked, the more we began to develop what seemed to be some interesting 'outside-the-box' answers. Those answers then suggested
20 some other issues. And on it went - until we had the makings of a compelling business book. We realized **this book would set a new standard for leadership and management practices in the creation and measurement of value.**
It would become a valued resource to the investment and accounting communities. And it would help marketing service providers (ad agencies, PR
25 firms, consultants) redefine their role in bringing objective counsel to their clients. Best of all, these ideas would be generally applicable across industries and markets.

Each author brings a wealth of experience to this area. Bill Neal is founder and Senior Partner of SDR Consulting, Inc., a professional services and
30 consulting firm specializing in advanced marketing research methods and technologies. His firm has provided consulting and project management services to more than 1000 organizations. SDR is widely recognized as one of the nation's leading firms in the application of advanced statistical modeling and analysis techniques.

35   Bill has authored over 60 articles, tutorials and seminars on marketing research spanning such diverse topics as market segmentation, product positioning, product optimization, brand value analysis, and brand equity measurement.

Over the years Bill has been very active in the American Marketing
40 Association, serving as Chairman of the Board of Directors in 1992–93 and several other positions prior to that, including Director of AMA's Marketing Research Division, Regional Vice President, and President of the Atlanta Chapter.

Bill initiated AMA's Marketing Research Tutorial Series now offered at
45 every AMA research conference. He has served as an instructor in that program since its' beginning. He also started several new conferences for the AMA including the annual Advanced Research Techniques Forum.

He has previously served on the Boards of Advisors for all four of the university Masters in Marketing Research degree programs in the US.
50 Bill was one of the two co-developers (with Dr. Malcolm McNiven) of the worldwide standard for basic training in the field of marketing research-the Principles of Marketing Research Online Certificate Course. This program is offered through the University of Georgia's Center for Continuing Education and endorsed by the leading marketing and marketing research
55 professional societies, worldwide.

Currently Bill serves on the editorial review boards of Marketing Management and Marketing Research magazines.

Bill was the fourth person to receive AMA's Lifetime Achievement Award for service to the Profession of Marketing Research.
60 Recognizing his long-term contributions to the profession of marketing research, the Marketing Research Association awarded Bill with an Honorary Lifetime Membership.

In 2001 Bill was elected to receive the Charles Coolidge Parlin Award-the oldest and most prestigious award in Marketing Research.
65 Bill received a Bachelor of Science degree in Commerce and Engineering from Drexel University and a Master of Science in Industrial Management with a specialization in Operations Research and Systems Analysis from Georgia Tech.

Bill served and an officer in the United States Army and was on active
70 duty from 1966 through 1977, attaining the rank of Major.

Ron Strauss is Founder and President of Brandzone, a brand consulting firm, and previously Executive Vice President of Gordon Bailey & Associates, Inc. and GBA/The Business Generation Company® with more than

30 years experience advising clients. Programs he's worked on for Siemens, Land O' Lakes, Mobil, Best Products, Anheuser-Busch Companies, Iceland Seafood Corporation and many others have won CLIO, One Show, AMY and other awards; and have been featured in textbooks and magazines.

A Cornell University alumnus, Ron is former President of the Atlanta Chapter of the Business Marketing Association; recipient of the BMA Atlanta Chapter President's Award and a Certified Business Communicator (CBC). Ron is Chair of the American Marketing Association's online Brand Strategy and Management Special Interest Group; and conducts their national workshop - 'Brand Measurement: Its Purpose, Potential, and New Approaches.' Ron regularly speaks to Vistage (an international organization of more than 14,000 CEO's) on the topic of 'Values-driven Branding.'

The authors view this book as the first step in the creation of a new way to look at leadership and management in the 21st century. We're confident readers will find new ideas and concepts that they can use to accelerate value creation for their clients and customers, employees, channels and strategic partners, investors, and other key stakeholders.

INTRODUCTION

Our first fundamental premise: Brands are the most valuable assets that a corporation owns. Brands are the key source of sustainable competitive advantage. Brands are the 'invisible hand' of management, telling employees the right things to do. Top management understanding of the company's corporate, product and service brands and how they create value is key to long-term success. If a company has weak brands, it is automatically at a competitive disadvantage – price competition and cost cutting will dominate management thinking and actions; employee morale will suffer.

On the other hand, strong brands allow the owner to exert more control over margin and/or share in their targeted markets. Strong brands provide a platform for efficient new product launches. Strong brands reduce marketing and selling costs per sales unit. Strong brands, managed correctly, create pricing and margin advantages in the near term, build and protect near and long term enterprise market value for stakeholders including investors, owners, employees, suppliers, and the community.

We believe brands should dominate the thinking and actions of those charged with improving long-term stakeholder value. Brands are the one defensible long-term asset a company owns. Competitors can quickly replicate your product or service performance. They can meet or beat your prices. They can match your channels and enter any market they wish. In today's globally competitive world, there are no naturally stable or protected markets.

If one accepts our premise, then it spawns a fundamental shift in the way corporations are managed. Decisions are driven by what improves the brand asset value of the firm. Assessing how investments will improve the total value of the firm's brand assets drives investment priorities. The inevitable financial trade-offs that corporate managers face becomes driven by a different question: How, and by how much, will this investment improve the asset value of our brands?

This, in turn, directly impacts the way the stock market values public companies, and the way private companies are valued as well. This book will show the role that brands play as intangible assets, how intangible assets are becoming a greater share of a firm's market value, and how investors associate brands with a firm's intrinsic market value. In fact, we show the role that brands play in helping investors assign P/E multiples when they value a stock.

At this point, you're probably thinking something like: "If you guys are so smart, why haven't we seen this happen already?" The answer is simple. Brand asset value is not reported by any of the numbers you have available in the corporate suite. Although brands clearly influence unit sales, profitability, cash flow, and ultimately, stock price, none of these numbers can be partitioned to reveal the specific contribution of the various component parts of brand value.

That leads us to our second fundamental premise: Only when the asset value of brands can be measured, will they be effectively managed to improve stockholder value. That is the underlying centerpiece of this book – a framework for brand value measurement that will allow senior management to understand and rationally invest in brands. And once that begins to happen, most corporate processes will need to become realigned and corporate leadership will have a new way to focus the entire organization on improving stakeholder value. Measurement will legitimize the role of brand as organizing principle for the enterprise.

When corporate leadership focuses on building brand asset value, the entire organization is affected - not just marketing, but also sales, human resources, research and development, finance, customer relationships, and distribution. Sales personnel and front-line contact personnel are hired and evaluated based on their alignment with and contribution to the brand. New product development is driven by the concept of brand value creation and enhancement. Financial resources are allocated based on their contribution to enhancing brand asset value or on building new brand platforms. Customers are segmented into groups based on their alignment with, and perceptions of, brand value. And channels are supported based on their alignment with the brand's promise. In a nutshell, a focus on brand asset value is a focus on corporate leadership. We call it Values Driven Leadership & Management.

This book establishes the framework for developing Values Driven Leadership. We identify the issues and provide a solution – one that we know works. We will provide a measurement system for assessing and reporting brand value and brand equity, show you how to implement that measurement system, and how to use it to lead your firm into a full-court focus on improving brand asset value, and therefore long-term stakeholders' value. Along the way, we show you proven methods for creating and improving brand asset value, and segmenting customers to enhance growth and profitability. We'll show you how to avoid Jag Sheth's 20/80/50 rule - 20% of your customers generate 80% of your profits, and the remaining 80% of customers cut those profits by 50%. Jag Sheth has told us that no citation is necessary beyond mentioning his name.

How to use this book

Of course, we would like you to read the entire book. But recognizing that not all audiences are keen on investing that amount of time, here is a quick primer based on your perspective.

We believe everyone one should read Chapters 1 and 2 – they set the stage and provide the vision of what we think can be a revolution in management focus. In those two chapters we identify the problem and set the framework for the solution.

Chapter 2 begins a parable that tells the story of a CEO who is in trouble – and the issues at hand. It introduces the role of using outside resources to help diagnose the problem. It suggests many of the ideas that will prove successful. While this chapter is fictional in form, it contains a powerful story.[1]

Chapter 3 is a review of elements that comprise a brand, and terms associated with brand. This chapter is a basic primer on brand. However, it also introduces new ways of thinking about what a brand is, and the role of brand. A particularly good chapter for non-marketing people. If you are really up to speed on those topics, skip this.

Chapter 4 makes the case for brands as key assets of the firm and provides the rationale for tying brand asset value to Financial Accounting Standards (FAS) Rule 142. Unless you are up to speed on FAS 142, we recommend you read this chapter. If you want to better understand the link between brand value, market value, EVA[2] and stock price – this chapter is for you.

Chapter 5: Value Creation/Value Destruction demonstrates on a more granular level how brand value is created and how it is depreciated or destroyed. Here we demonstrate how management actions can grow strong brands into powerhouses of profitability. We also demonstrate how misalignment of values can severely depreciate a brand's asset value over both the short term and the long term. The relationship of Brand to the Business

---

[1] Note: Chapters 2 and 15 make use of parable, a form of fictional storytelling. Except for occasional quotes from Jack F. Eli's fictional character, first introduced in chapter 2, all the other chapters, information and people are real and non-fictional. Vistage International, Inc. the organization used in chapters 2 and 15, however, is a real organization headquartered in San Diego, CA., and the meeting format accurately reflects the organizations' methods and procedures, although the names and characters used in these chapters are fictitious.

[2] EVA and Economic Value Added are trademarks of Stewart, Stern & Company.

Model, Values (based on Discipline of Market Leaders), Quality, and LCV (Lifetime Customer Value) is discussed. There are plenty of examples. Everyone should at least cruise over this chapter.

In Chapter 6, The Current State of Brand Measurement, we establish the criteria for a comprehensive brand value measurement system then demonstrate why all of the more popular measurement systems aren't meeting that criteria. It's not necessary for all readers, but certainly worthwhile if you are currently using a brand value measurement system.

Everyone should read the first half of Chapter 7. That's where we establish how a brand creates value (brand value) and equity (brand equity), the definition of each term, why they are different, and why they are important to the firm and its shareholders. We introduce the conceptual (and visual) model of total brand value and its component parts, including brand equity We continue this chapter with the conceptual framework for measuring the components of total brand value, including brand equity, and demonstrate the model – including how to use the information for pricing. In a separate section we discuss how to apply two-stage choice modeling to implement the model. If you are not familiar with trade-off models, you can skip that section.

In Chapter 8, Brand Loyalty and Brand Performance, we more deeply explore the connections between Brand Value and Brand Equity, and how they work over time to create loyalty among customers, employees, and suppliers. The chapter addresses the salient differences between attitudinal loyalty and behavioral loyalty, and the implications for brand performance and value creation. Brand performance is discussed in terms of how EVA, DCF or other measures of added value are created and grown. It's a "must" chapter for every reader.

Chapter 9, What is Branding? This chapter discusses branding - the process of creating and maintaining a brand as a corporate asset. The chapter expands on some of the precepts introduced in Chapters 4 and 5 in terms of a quality-based process. It discusses some of the realities of controlling the branding process. We also look at how branding standards are set and who sets them. The 'Who', 'What', 'Why', 'Where' and 'When' of Branding are examined. The process of continuous improvement (CQI) is compared to the Branding process, and discussed as a template for that process. It's a "must" chapter for the serious reader – anyone in a leadership, management or advisory position.

Chapter 10, Brand Success Profiles, presents real-life examples of successful applications of some of the principles we have discussed in previous chapters. We examine how the organization's values create brand value and equity, and where appropriate, the key drivers of the equity. This chapter reinforces what we have covered. Skip it if you are on a fast read.

Chapter 11 addresses Values-Based Market Segmentation. One of the most powerful questions every enterprise should ask and answer is: "Who should be our customer, and why?" We demonstrate how derivation of the Brand Value Model naturally leads to a powerful values-based segmentation scheme. We show how that segmentation scheme is superior to any others for deeply understanding market structure and uncovering your best target markets. We also discuss a powerful choice simulator for 'what if' scenarios. We think this chapter is really important for effective strategic implementation of Values Based Management.

In Chapter 12, Leveraging the Brand Value Model and Brand Performance, we discuss practical ways to apply measures of brand performance to different audiences – senior corporate leaders, chief financial officers, senior brand managers, the sales force, and employees. We tie the metrics to share of choice, pricing premium, share of served segments, and Economic Value Added (EVA). This chapter is primarily for the implementer of the program.

Chapter 13: Salient Lessons for Marketing Service Providers, also discusses 'how to' apply the lessons discussed in the rest of the book for service brands. It also includes requirements and pitfalls to be aware of in a service provider organization, including ad agencies, pr firms, and professional services firms. If it applies to you, read it.

In Chapter 14, The Value Creation Process, we visit some of the practical issues that impact the application of branding practices within most companies and organizations. 'Pull Thinking' is reviewed. The roles of HR, IT, Sales, Marketing, Customer Service and Finance are discussed. CRM and SFA are discussed. Internal branding to employees is addressed. Examples are provided. This chapter is of particular value to CEO's in terms of 'harmonizing' the various departments of the enterprise.

Chapter 15, The Solution, is the companion parable to chapter 2. We lay out the steps that are necessary to begin applying the ideas in the book. The framework begins with an assessment of the culture of the organization and its values, then extends out to the brand and branding structure in terms of positioning and discipline, then the organizational levers (segmentation, recruiting practices, compensation, recognition, communications, training, etc.), the operating results, and finally, the financial outcomes. A must read if you are serious about implementing our approach.

CHAPTER 1

THE NEED

There is a story of a new CEO spending his first day at the office. The recently "retired" outgoing CEO stopped by and said to him, "I've put three envelopes in the top center drawer of your desk. If you ever get into trouble trying to do this job, open the first envelope and it will tell you what to do."

Sure enough, after a few months in office, the new CEO, feeling some pressure, and knowing that things were not going well, looked in the desk drawer, took out envelope #1, opened it and read:

"Blame everything on me. Good luck. And if things don't improve, open envelope #2."

The letter was signed by the previous CEO.

The new CEO blamed everything on his predecessor, and things seemed to settle down, with everyone saying, "Yes, if only so-and-so had done blah, blah, blah." And morale appeared to lift, at least for a while…

After another few months, conditions worsened. Last quarter's results missed forecast, and the next quarter looked equally dim. New product introductions had bogged down. There were serious channel conflicts. Warranty costs were up. And employee morale was back at rock bottom. The stock price had taken a series of hits. The few Wall Street analysts that covered the stock pegged it as a lukewarm "hold".

This was happening despite the CEO working 75–80 hour weeks, meeting with all the business unit heads, getting everyone focused on increasing customer satisfaction, communicating incessantly with Wall Street analysts, appearing on business shows, flying the flag at industry events, working diligently to cut costs while trying to accelerate new initiatives.

So, the CEO opened his desk drawer, found the remaining two envelopes, and pulled out envelope #2. Quickly opening it he read,

"Blame everything on the poor economy, overseas competition and the strong/weak (pick one) dollar. If things still don't improve, then, as a last resort only, open envelope #3."

Letter #2 was also signed by the previous CEO.

The new CEO blamed the economy, overseas competitors and the dollar. And the Board seemed to be mollified. At least for a while…

Unfortunately, the situation did not improve. The quality improvement initiatives, the cost cutting, the downsizing, the new strategic plan, the new ad campaign, nothing seemed to help the stock price. The Board became increasingly impatient and short-tempered. So the CEO went to his desk drawer, pulled out envelope #3, tore it open, unfolded the letter, and read the following message,

"Prepare three envelopes."[1]

This story, no doubt apocryphal, does serve to highlight the pressures that chief executive officers and other C-level executives are experiencing. And it's not only C-level executives. These pressures are reverberating throughout companies, from executive suites to local sales offices, to plant floors and call centers. No industry is immune, from foodservice to financial services, from media to pharmaceuticals, from retail to transportation. Succeeding in a company, large or small, public or private, is more challenging than ever before.

To Be, Or Not To Be

One sign of this "challenge" is fewer people want to be CEOs. A survey by New York-based global consultancy Burson-Marsteller found 64 percent of the most senior executives at North American Fortune 1,000 companies have no desire to be promoted to CEO.[2] That's more than twice the 27 percent who had no desire to be CEO in 2001, an incredible change in a short time. Seventy-three percent of 369 CEOs answered yes to the question "Do you think about quitting your job?"[3]

In 2005, 1,228 chief executives left their jobs, more than in any other year—doubling the level of departures experienced in 2004, and surpassing even the dot-com exodus of 2000; turnover among top management in general has picked up too, according to a study conducted by outplacement firm Challenger, Gray & Christmas.[4]

The risk/reward ratio is not sufficient to help them decide to be CEO. The Sarbanes-Oxley law, passed in response to the Enron debacle, requires painful reporting for companies, and holds the CEO accountable for reported numbers, under the threat of prison. That increases the risk. "We believe the current (higher) annual rate of CEO turnover is the 'new normal'," notes Paul Kocourek, a senior vice president of Booz Allen Hamilton. "Today's typical CEO knows that he will remain in office only as long as

---

[1] Thanks to Vistage (formerly The Executive Committee) Chair, Jansen Chazanof, for sharing this story with us.
[2] Burson-Marsteller with the Economist Intelligence Unit (EIU), *The 2005 CEO Capital Survey*.
[3] Burson-Marsteller, *Building CEO Capital Survey*, 2003.
[4] CFO.com, *Record for CEO Turnover in 2005*, CFO Publishing Corporation, November 8, 2005.

performance for investors is acceptable. The CEO's insider allies are typically gone, or less powerful. No longer can a CEO expect to prolong his career by managing the board."[5]

"Due to shortened CEO tenure and intense media scrutiny, executives are more wary of the corner office," said Patrick Ford, chair of Burson-Marsteller's Corporate/Financial Practice. "Executives know that CEO decisions and actions are examined 24 hours a day."

Boards are judging CEO performance more harshly. CEOs who were dismissed in 2000 generated median, regionally adjusted shareholder returns 13.5 percent lower than retiring CEOs; in 2001 it took a 11.9 percent shortfall to prompt a firing, and in 2002 it took a 6.2 percent shortfall.[6] In three short years the CEO's margin for error was just about cut in half.

A study of 1,000 individual investors and 24 Wall Street analysts and portfolio managers showed that the typical individual investor, one who owns stock outside of a 401K or IRA portfolio, will give a new CEO about 17.5 months on average to make a difference. Wall Street professionals are less forgiving, with CEOs having an average tenure of only 14 months to demonstrate results.[7]

In Burson-Marsteller's 2003 *Building CEO Capital*[TM] survey, conducted with RoperASW, 1,040 "business influencers" shared their opinions on the leadership issues that determine CEO success. These business influencers now grant new CEOs about 18 months to prove themselves—about two months longer than they gave CEOs in 1999. The following is the timeline for other goals:[8]

	Months
Win the board's confidence	8.49
Win employee support	8.57
Develop a strategic vision	9.18
Develop a quality management team	13.91
Execute promises made in first 100 days	13.93
Earn credibility with Wall Street	17.93
Increase share price	21.06
Turn company around	22.10
Reinvent how company does business	22.74

[5] Booz Allen Hamilton, *Global CEO Turnover Set New Record in 2005*, May 18, 2006.

[6] Booz Allen Hamilton, *CEO Succession 2002: Deliver or Depart*, June 2003.

[7] Ketchum Reputation Laboratory, "Who Wants to Be a CEO Anymore?" *Forum*, April 2003.

[8] Burson-Marsteller, *Building CEO Capital Survey*, 2003.

According to Booz Allen Hamilton, the frequency of CEO "succession events" (the departure of one CEO and the accession of another) nearly doubled, from 6 percent of the largest global 2,500 companies per year in 1995 to 15.3 percent in 2005.[9] For many CEOs, these are not "the good old days."

The situation is summed up in this statement by Charles Lucier, senior vice president Emeritus of Booz Allen Hamilton, "Business leaders are enduring scrutiny and pressure unseen since the Great Depression. The CEO mystique has all but evaporated, and director activism has replaced crony capitalism in the boardroom."

Misery Loves Company

CEOs and other C-level executives, feeling the pressure for performance, are energetically passing it on. Understandably, employees, key suppliers, channel partners, and others feel the heat.

CRMGuru.com reports that within the high tech community, marketing vice presidents experienced a 75 percent turnover rate between 2002 and 2003. Many organizations with revenues between $15 and $50 million have eliminated every single marketing position. Software Product Marketing, a volunteer group with a charter to help out-of-work software marketers find jobs, has more than 3,500 members.[10]

This reflects an overall trend by business to get lean and mean. And that often entails gutting middle management. It's simply marketing's turn.

Executive recruiting firm Spencer Stuart reports the average CMO (Chief Marketing Officer) tenure only lasts 23 months. In the food industry, tenure is only 12 months.[11] By the time this person's business cards show up, the food industry CMO may already be gone.

Marketing management, in turn, is looking to their most trusted advisors and suppliers to help them show the worth of every investment made in marketing. This is impacting advertising, PR, design, naming and identity, research and other marketing service provider firms. The mantra, "If you *can't* measure it, don't do it" has never been more true—and, for many firms—more feared.

Ad agencies are receiving RFPs (Requests For Proposals) from prospective client companies that contain strong requirements for credible information

---

[9] Booz Allen Hamilton, *Global CEO Turnover Set New Record in 2005*, May 18, 2006.
[10] Scott Santucci, "The Marketing and Sales Divide," CRMGuru.com, May 2004.
[11] Greg Welch, "CMO Tenure: Slowing Down The Revolving Door." SpencerStuart.com, July 2004.

on how the ad agency will measure results and demonstrate a return on investment. Agencies are being asked to share case histories of how they've helped other clients measure ROI. Ad agencies and other key suppliers and vendors are being asked to justify their value and their existence.

For these service provider firms, the questions of "What is the ROI from your activities and programs?" and "How do they contribute to an increase in shareholder value?" need to be urgently answered.

Measurement alone, however, is not the answer. As the late, great management guru Peter Drucker told us, "Efficiency is doing things right; effectiveness is doing the right things."[12] Measurement of the "right things" gives us the best of both worlds. Measurement, therefore, must provide answers that are credible and germane to the firm's value drivers.

Why Is This Happening?

Pressure for performance affects all businesses, but not all businesses fail to perform. Many businesses find ways to control costs, expand revenues and margins, and continue to grow profits. What's the difference between those businesses and the ones that are in trouble?

Can it be explained by the type of industry they're in? Not likely, since most industries contain a mix of leaders, "middle-of-the-roaders" and laggards—even though the industry may be ascending or declining in importance.

That also knocks out other reasons, like technological change. Seems some companies are better than others at adapting to technological and other types of change; whether it's gradual or discontinuous doesn't seem to matter. In fact, there's a positive correlation between the pace of change and the appearance of new business units and start-ups trying to capitalize on change by applying technology to improve products or develop new products for current and new markets.

The investment community views innovation as a hallmark of companies that create shareholder value. So innovation, or lack thereof, or inability to translate innovation into shareholder value may be an area that can explain CEO and executive churn. This gives us another clue: Innovation is an intangible asset.

However, the track record of innovation being converted into shareholder value is not very good. Let's look at innovation via the application of new

---

[12] Peter F. Drucker, *The Effective Executive*, Revised 2002.

technology: Morgan Stanley estimates that between 2000 and 2002, U.S. companies wasted $130 billion on unneeded technology, according to its study of 25 years of tech spending. Separately, analysts at Gartner Group have estimated that $75 billion is wasted annually on failed technology initiatives in the United States alone. Using financial analysis to measure the total impact, this $75 billion translates into a staggering trillion-dollar figure in lost market value for U.S. companies. What were the implications and outcomes of that loss of market value in terms of shareholders and boards demanding that CEOs be held accountable—and for executive churn?

Baruch Lev, in his insightful book *Intangibles—Management, Measurement and Reporting* wrote, "Wealth and growth in today's economy are driven primarily by intangible (intellectual) assets."[13] When you look at the stock market value of publicly traded companies, the value of intangible assets represents well over 50 percent of overall firm value. This varies from a low in heavy industries like petro-chemicals to a high (over 90 percent) in some consumer and luxury goods.

Most corporations are run with standard cost-accounting systems that don't measure and report on intangible assets in a way that gives executives useful insight into how value creation works in their enterprise. Leading and managing an enterprise by using standard cost accounting system-provided data is like trying to drive a car by only looking in the rear view mirror. Sooner or later, you're sure to encounter a nasty surprise.

This lack of forward-looking information, especially in the area of what creates brand value, results in under-investment of resources in some parts of the organization and over-investment in other parts, misalignment of processes designed to create loyal customers, and the attendant disappointing outcomes.

The National Institute of Standards and Technology estimates that not incorporating customer requirements costs U.S. corporations nearly $100 billion a year in failed projects. There's another $1.25 trillion in potential market value that goes unrealized.

Adding to the need is the difference between what company leaders and managers think the brand asset and other value creators are, and the perception of investors, employees, suppliers and customers as to the most important sources of value. If there is a gap between the different perceptions, then company leaders and managers may think they are effectively

---

[13] Baruch Lev, *Intangibles – Management, Measurement, and Reporting*, 2001.

communicating, when, in fact, they are not.[14] They may be focused on the wrong "drivers," and they may be communicating the wrong information, at the wrong time, in the wrong way. This may encourage employees to focus on the wrong issues. This may lead investors to incorrectly assess the value of intangible assets like brands, intellectual property, and other forms of innovation, thus leading them to either undervalue or overvalue firms, with the subsequent poor allocation of capital. This may also send the wrong signals to the company's board and to the media and generate negative pressure, perhaps incorrectly and prematurely, on the company's leadership.

PricewaterhouseCoopers surveyed hundreds of institutional investors and sell-side analysts in 14 countries—only 19 percent of the investors and 27 percent of the analysts found financial reports very useful in communicating the true value of companies. Only 38 percent of executives in the United States felt their reports were very useful. In high-tech companies, the results are even worse.[15]

Can the pressure on companies be explained by the transition to a service economy, using knowledge workers in flatter, less hierarchal organizations? Seems there are plenty of companies out there that are doing very well in this environment. However, one of the conditions associated with knowledge workers is often an inability to be effective—due to not doing the right things in the right way at the right time.[16] This may be another clue to poor company performance and CEO malaise.

Many companies are organized under a system that borrows liberally from the military's old WWII "command and control" model. This model worked well when people were relatively inexpensive cogs in an expensive machine (the factory) during the Industrial Age and needed to be carefully monitored and controlled.

Today, however, knowledge workers largely control themselves. The old model of command and control does not work with knowledge workers. What's needed is a system that nurtures self-directed workers, often operating within teams, with the flexibility to change on the fly as market needs dictate, within the parameters set by management. Leadership and management need to operate with their "ears close to the ground," so they can anticipate the needs of their knowledge workers and the markets they serve. They need to create "closed-loop feedback" processes. The brand concept

---

[14] Robert G. Eccles, Robert H. Herz, E. Mary Kegan, David M. H. Phillips, *The Value Reporting Revolution*, 2001.
[15] Ibid.
[16] Peter F. Drucker, *The Effective Executive*, Revised 2002.

can serve this need, but only when the definition of brand practice moves beyond its traditional media links, and expands to include the enterprises' internal operational processes.

Perhaps part of the answer to why there's so much pressure on management is due to the rapid pace of change in today's world.

The Nature of Value Creation

However, rapid change may not be the only answer to why this is happening. We've gone through periods of rapid change before. And every period of rapid transformation, from an agrarian to an industrial to a service to a knowledge economy created winners and losers. The answer most likely lies in the nature of what now creates value within the firm.

The industrial economy of the last century taught us that scale and scope were vital to competitiveness, and, therefore, the ability to create value. And the constraint to scale and scope was capital. Massive amounts of capital were needed to build huge steel, transportation, warehousing, manufacturing and other industrial concerns and infrastructure. Only then could goods be mass-produced cheaply, driving share growth and profits.

Financial and standard cost-accounting systems were fine-tuned to provide information that could be used to manage in this environment.

In most markets, there was an irresistible push to become the biggest vertically integrated provider, so that costs could be driven down through mass purchasing power, and per unit costs could be minimized, thus enhancing pricing power and the ability to drive share. This created a competitive cycle that resulted in most industries going through a series of consolidations that eventually produced about three main market survivors, with a bunch of small niche players. That was a mass market model. In the post WWII era this model worked well as consumers were hungry for any kinds of goods and services in most product categories. Since most consumers had relatively low levels of disposable income compared to today, price was an important consideration in many product categories. During this era, brands were associated with a certain level of quality, each at a price point, and brands acted as an implied warranty.

Capital is no longer the key constraint. As the late Peter Drucker observed, ". . . there is an enormous amount of surplus capital in the world for which there is no productive investment. The supply greatly exceeds the demand."[17] It is certainly necessary for enterprises to have access to capital

---

[17] Schlender, *Fortune Magazine* interview, "Peter Drucker Still Battling at 94", January 2004.

and the use of it, but the availability or the cost to use capital is not sufficient to describe today's constraints on a firm's ability to generate value.

In the second half of the twentieth century, the economy changed dramatically from a manufacturing-based economy to the service and knowledge-based economy that we have today. As economies have advanced the world over, the percentage of U.S. jobs in manufacturing has declined. The Department of Labor forecasts that goods-producing employment in the United States will drop from 23 percent of the non-farm labor force in 1990 to 18 percent by 2010, while the share of services employment will rise from 77 percent in 1990 to 82 percent in 2010. Jobs of all kinds are also requiring more knowledge.

Today's constraints seem more tied into people, information, organization, and process. Of those four, people are the most important. Human capital, properly motivated, is the most powerful force on earth. Today, people are expensive cogs within increasingly decentralized, flattened, less capital-intensive organizations. People are expensive to educate, hire, train, support, and replace. What is it that is limiting the power of people within some organizations to be keenly competitive, while in others the people are driving the organization to be wildly successful?

People Power Drives Value Creation Via Innovation

With the right support in place (access to information, flexible team-based structures, feedback, funding, and proper goals) people power will drive value creation through innovation. Often, several companies combine their talents and create "network effects" as they generate value for their served markets. The "Win-tel" combination of Microsoft Windows®-based software providers and compatible Intel-based computers created a virtuous cycle that met the needs of corporate and personal computer users while increasing product functionality and reducing prices. That set the stage for other players, such as Google® and eBay®, to further amplify the network effect in other applications and markets. Network effects enabled rapid scalability and increases in scope.

The innovation that created the personal computer and the chips that powered them created opportunities to develop industries and serve new markets. However, accompanying these opportunities were risks. The opportunity/risk continuum was subject to company leadership and management selecting the right value creators in order to realize the opportunity while reducing the risk. Innovation was required to create virtual companies via networks, thus more quickly realizing opportunity while limiting (or at least spreading out) the risks. However, who owns the "Win-tel" brand? How do the various players partition the value of the network?

The greater the difference between what company leaders and managers think the value creators are, and the perception of investors, employees, suppliers, and customers as to what are the most important creators of value, the greater the chances that success will be illusory. If there is a gap between the different perceptions, then company leaders and managers may think they are effectively communicating, when, in fact, they are not. These "value perception" and "value reporting" gaps make for frustration and disappointment on the part of many of the key players.[18] And that leads to changes in the executive suite. We need to develop a new language of values and value that is understood by all the players and encompasses both tangible and intangible assets.

Perhaps another way of explaining why there is turmoil in the executive suite is the information explosion. The information explosion, as evidenced by the Internet and by the proliferation of customer information databases within companies, coupled with concerns about how that information is used and disseminated, has created an environment where customers are looking for seamless interactions, respect of their privacy, and confidentiality in the way their information is handled. The revelations of security breaches and the misappropriation of consumers' information for use in identity theft scams have created this concern. This is an opportunity.

At the same time, the customer has changed. The customer of today enjoys relatively high levels of disposable income. The customer of today often values time over money. Another outcome of the information explosion—easy access to information—has made consumers more savvy and sophisticated than ever. And, in an increasingly time-constrained world, this fast access to information has value. "Not your father's Oldsmobile" has taken on greater significance with the demise of the Oldsmobile brand—and helps to underscore the changes in customers' relationships with their brands. To appreciate why this is important, let's take a look at what's changed in the overall economy.

In the economy of the last century, the producer held pricing power. Goods were relatively scarce, and information about them was provided most often by the producer, via mass media, other forms of advertising, and at the point of sale. Today, while those tools are still in use, the Internet makes product and pricing information easily available to most consumers. This

---

[18] Robert G. Eccles, Robert H. Herz, E. Mary Kegan, David M. H. Phillips, *The Value Reporting Revolution*, 2001.

IN THIS CRISIS FOR THE FIRST EVER
TIME IN A LONG LONG TIME -
MONEY IS VALUED OVER TIME.

[handwritten at top: Is your communication seamless — that is, consistent across all multiple channel forms of media]

information is often made available by third parties, and may not be what the producer of the goods or services would have presented. Comparisons can be made instantly. Chat rooms and blogs make getting information about user experiences of actual consumers of a product or service easier than ever before. Producer claims and brand promises must deliver. If they don't, the word gets out far and wide—at the speed of light. The Internet has created transparency. Or, as some wag has observed: "Either no one knows the secret, or everyone knows the secret."

The experience of engaging with the brand over multiple channels (Internet, retail location, catalog, and so on) must be made seamless and optimized from the customer's perspective. This has become critical. According to Forrester Research, 65 percent of all shoppers now shop and browse both on and off-line. Fifty-one percent of shoppers characterize themselves as active cross-channel shoppers.[19] ShopLocal.com reported that 83.4 million consumers made in-store purchases during the 2004 holiday season after researching the purchase online. That's up 20 percent over 2003.[20]

This phenomenon is not limited to retail. GM and AIG, two of the top ten Fortune 500 companies, sell services and provide customer information through several channels. AIG connects with customers through brick-and-mortar offices, printed materials, a contact center, and a Web site. Pfizer, Merck, and other pharmaceutical companies don't sell directly to consumers, but they do provide products and information to physicians via sales reps, contact centers, email, and printed materials.[21]

A better understanding of how to orchestrate multiple channels leads to greater customer loyalty and higher levels of spending. Industry experts say that the multi-channel shopper spends 30 percent more on average. This is another opportunity.

[handwritten: Differentiation is just because medium—most products are similar.]

Furthermore, products are becoming more and more alike. As manufacturing techniques become more flexible and automated, and supply chains more integrated and efficient, product differentiation derived from the manufacture of goods has diminished. Fast cycle "reverse design" and manufacturing times have reduced first mover advantage. Six Sigma manufacturing and ISO standards have made product quality a given. Proliferation of product categories and products has created higher "noise" levels. It's more difficult now to get someone's attention based on product attributes alone. The

---

[19] Carrie A. Johnson, *The U.S. Consumer 2004: Multichannel and In-Store Technology*, 2004.
[20] John Gaffney, "Finding the Right Fit," *Inside 1to1*, March 2005.
[21] Ibid

[handwritten at bottom: Now is VALUE TIME. WHAT DOES VALUE MEAN IN YOUR CATEGORY. How can you pre-empt the value proposition.]

traditional 4 Ps of marketing—product, place, price, and promotion—are now table stakes, not the source of sustainable competitive advantage.

The Search for Meaning

Customers today are looking for more than an assurance of quality from their brands; they are looking for meaning. Meaning is often defined by the relationship between the customer and the product and/or service. One way meaning is provided is by customization of the product and/or service to better meet the needs of the customer. More producers are letting the customer design the final performance and "look" of the product, down to having the customer's name on the product. Many car manufacturers offer their customers the opportunity to choose from hundreds of options online, and design their own car. Instead of mass markets, we're moving towards markets of one. In a world of parity products, those that can differentiate and define their brand via customization create value.

Technology and the rising rate of discovery enable the rapid development of new technologies and faster rates of obsolescence. Those companies, and their brands, that can rise above their physical or technology-based underpinnings, and migrate from one technology platform to another, will represent ongoing value. Those brands that can cross the chasm of changing technology will be able to generate ongoing trust and value as they extend their relationship with their customers.

Beyond the performance options and features of the product or service, the real change in the relationship between the customer and the brand is focused on the emotional meaning the brand imparts to the customer, and vice-versa. This has created a need for a whole new way to look at the leadership and management of the company producing the brand, and how its customer-facing employees and channel partners engage and service the customer.

Showing one face to the customer is critical if the relationship is to be extended into the future. However, many companies are structured as "silos," and more time is spent on internal departmental agendas than on the customers' agenda. Given today's demanding and fickle customer, that is a prescription for failure.

Of course, the way many companies keep score via their standard cost accounting systems and organizational structures, encourages a silo-driven, inside-out view of the customer. Sub-optimization of the customer relationship is often the end-result, with customer churn being the inevitable outcome. This destroys value. As an example, in many companies the sales department is often compensated for adding customers and volume with little regard for the ability of the organization to properly fulfill the promises made to those customers. That's because the overall focus of the firm is on share growth. Every customer is a good customer—or so it appears. That's old economy thinking, based on old metrics.

There is a need for new measurement systems that look at each customer as a unique opportunity. Share of customer (or share of wallet along with customer longevity) must receive at least equal emphasis with share of market. Share of market, blindly pursued, can actually reduce profitability. Each customer must be valued individually in terms of their fit with the company providing products and services to them. The focus switches to customer profitability, customer longevity, and the creation of greater brand asset value. This focus creates extraordinary value.

Thus, the search for meaning has implications for today's companies in terms of focus, organizational structure, pricing policy, hiring and recruitment practices, offerings, channels, and brands. For the CEO and other C-level executives, the meaning is clear, they must become knowledgeable about their company brand, product brands, and service brands, and have a vision for how their organization can create value for their served markets in a manner that is sustainable, understandable, and actionable. Each CEO must view themselves as the Chief Brand Officer, or they need to hire someone to fill that role that reports directly to them.

Convergence

Another aspect of change can be summed up by convergence. For public companies, your customer and employee may also be your shareholder. With the rise of the affluent middle class, and the accumulation of trillions of dollars by the baby boomer generation, we are witnessing the first generation of truly widespread workers/owners. For the first time in the United States, over half the households (56.9 million) owns stock, either directly or through a mutual fund.[22] A company's employees and customers may also be the owners, either directly through ownership of the company's stock in a tax-advantaged 401K or other qualified retirement plan or in a taxable account, or indirectly though participation in a mutual fund that owns shares in the company, and is housed in a similar plan. The same stakeholder effect also is at work in debt-based instruments like corporate grade bond issues and funds.

---

[22] Investment Company Institue (ICI) and Securities Industry Association (SIA) Survey, "Equity Ownership in America—2005," Federal Reserve Board, Survey of Consumer Finances and U.S. Census Bureau.

We Truly are Becoming an Ownership Society

As the boundaries between employees, shareholders, and customers blur, the implications for the company and their stakeholders are profound. With this change to an ownership society, our expectations of the companies in our lives have changed and risen. We now hold corporations to a higher standard; they are personalities within our lives. As such, we hold them responsible for their actions and the effects of those actions on local, national, and international communities.

This promises to accelerate, or at the very least support, a movement towards companies re-examining their relationship with their communities. There is a need for new thinking in the area of corporate social responsibility that will positively impact value creation. This is another opportunity, and the implications for leaders, managers, and corporate brands are many.

What Determines Winners and Losers?

To answer this question, we must ask several more questions:

- What changing role must the CEO play in helping his or her firm be among the winners—and how can he or she survive long enough to have a positive impact?
- What changed role must marketing, advertising, IT, HR, and other departments play to support the CEO and help the firm prosper?
- How can this be accomplished in a way that provides financial types the transparent intangible asset value information they need?
- Will that buy the CEO and the rest of the management team the support and time to see initiatives bear fruit?
- How can individual investors spot the winners?
- What are the implications for the people that work for the firm? For strategic partners, channels, and other stakeholders? For their communities?

Most of all, is there an overarching principle and approach that can

1. Synthesize all the pressures on CEOs, their companies, and service providers
2. Provide them with a way to rationalize what is happening
3. Arm them with insight to put this into a context that is understandable, provides motivation, can be executed throughout the organization—and be measured?

Our solution addresses and satisfies each of these questions.

We know that the focus on short-term results often creates programs and behaviors that weaken the opportunity for long-term value creation. A strong case needs to be established for patience in the boardroom and on Wall Street, based on a better understanding of what will build value over time. A lack of knowledge about brand practice and measurement as a tool for leadership and management; and about other value creation tools like innovation in products, processes, strategic partnering, licensing, and so on lead many to confuse frantic activity with progress.

Our solution separates the important from the not so important, and provides the framework and discipline necessary for leadership and management teams to focus on the truly important.

A New Way to Look at Value Creation

In summary, there is a need for a new approach due to

1. The move towards flatter, less hierarchal organizations where it's not possible to look over everyone's shoulder
2. The rise of the largely self-directed knowledge worker
3. The role of intangible assets as the major source of value creation and investment allocation
4. The move from being constrained by capital to being constrained by having the right people
5. The shift from share of market to share of customer
6. The transformation from mass markets to mass customization
7. The ubiquity of information via the Internet, and the rise of transparency
8. The change from an inward silo's focus to an external focus on one face to the customer
9. The convergence of customers, employees, and shareholders
10. The emergence of the corporation as a responsible member of society

These ten developments have created an opportunity for a new type of leader and manager—a leader and manager who operates not by command and control in the traditional sense, but by creating a "pull" force field throughout the organization that resonates with employees, customers, suppliers, investors, boards of directors and other stakeholders of the firm. Leaders and managers who understand how to create an invisible hand that guides the actions and decisions of all stakeholders so as to create and maximize value over the long term while motivating all players to operate with enlightened self-interest.

We will offer ideas upon which a consciously competent foundation for effective and efficient leadership and management can be built. These ideas create a more unified view of leadership and management, and make the brand value of the enterprise the centerpiece of value creation and measurement. It offers CEOs and their management teams new thinking about the mission-critical role of brand in their company, and how enlightened brand strategy conserves and creates value and reduces risk in a sustainable manner in an increasingly competitive environment. It also serves as a warning to those who don't understand, ignore, or act in violation of the basic values inherent in their corporate, product, and service brands.

These ideas can be used by those executives whose companies are doing well, and want to do even better. Executives who welcome a way to challenge their organization and to enjoy their success even more. They're open to a big idea that can help them fill in a blank sheet of paper that describes the future as they'd like it to be.

These ideas are useful for companies that are treading water, getting results that are OK, but not making much progress in terms of generating more business or value. It gives people throughout the organization ideas they can apply to raise the company to the next level of performance.

These ideas may be most useful for companies and management teams that are in real trouble, getting ready to "prepare three envelopes." Companies at risk may be ideally positioned to benefit the most from this book, since there is a direct correlation between how much trouble a company is in, and the willingness of its employees to embrace change and try new solutions. We'll give the management team a prescription for what to do to reverse negative performance with a breakthrough concept.

These ideas are also intended to provide insight for service companies like ad agencies, PR firms, and other trusted advisors who need to redefine their role in order to be once again viewed as trusted advisors, rather than hawkers of media. Current trends towards ubiquity of information, customization of products and services, fast cycle times, and "niches of one" serve to redefine the relationship of their clients' customers to the clients' companies. Ad agencies and other service companies who can provide an objective, outside-in view of how these trends will impact the client firm; the implications for future innovation, brand and related marketing initiatives, and value creation and measurement based on the ideas in this book will have a competitive advantage. This insight is key to turning the tide of client defections and program cancellations. It also opens up the possibility of linking enhanced brand building and value measurement techniques into agency performance-based compensation structures.

For brand practitioners within companies, creating a better understanding of the contribution of the company's brand(s) and brand practices to the company's future value will help practitioners be successful in protecting and garnering budgets and programs needed for success. This understanding will also position the brand practitioner as a vital part of the executive team.

Financial types within the company can get great insight into how the current metrics are inadequate to the task at hand. They'll gain a greater understanding of the role and challenges faced by marketing, and the ability of the organization to create and destroy value. This insight and understanding will lead them to develop new measures, and new ways of keeping score.

Financial types outside the company can use this book to develop a deeper appreciation of the value of intangibles, and how to better understand the unrealized potential, and challenges, that merged or acquired companies may represent. Investors can use the ideas so as to better perceive the hidden value in the firm, and the prospects of the firm over the coming months and years. Everyone will have a tool with which to better evaluate performance, long-term risks, and use this to arrive at more rational stock prices—within the overall context of the economy and market.

An expanding part of our economy is represented by so-called non-profit firms. The non-profit/not-for-profit sector in the United States consists of 1.4 million organizations with reported combined 2004 annual revenues of $1,400 billion, and $1,300 billion in assets. Eight out of ten non-profits make a profit; they call it a surplus.

One in 12 Americans work for a non-profit either full or part-time.[23] According to the MetLife Foundation's 2001 survey report, *Giving and Volunteering in the United States*, 83.9 million American adults representing the equivalent of 9 million full-time employees gave time valued at $239 billion. We believe that for-profit firms can learn a lot from the way leading non-profits leverage principles-centered brand leadership to create value. There are many non-profits that can learn and apply these lessons as well.

Much of what we write about is also applicable to individuals. Look at the ideas in this book through the lens of how they apply to your company, as

---

[23] IndependentSector.org., "The Nonprofit Almanac in Brief," *Independent Sector,* 2001 and 2007.

well as through the lens of how they personally apply to your life and future career choices. We'll give you tools with which to evaluate your company's corporate brand, its product and service brands, and how your own personal brand fits in. Similarly, company human resource professionals can use our concepts to improve their recruitment, training, recognition, compensation, and retention practices.

Our framework describes a way to continuously transform the enterprise while creating greater value—a way to create your own good luck; a way to create meaning in all you do. It's a journey that need never end.

CHAPTER 2

WHAT'S THE SOLUTION?

"The best-performing companies are managed by those who walk the talk. Here at Key these values drive everything we do. Ethics are not just words on pieces of paper. Values aren't merely posted on a door. The shadow cast by leadership is the starting point for how our values cascade down from the top so that they permeate the culture and can be felt by everyone we touch."

—Henry Meyer III, Chairman and CEO, KeyCorp

"Prepare three envelopes?" Jack Eli considered, then rejected that step. He hadn't spent the last year working up to 80-hour weeks only to give up simply because this had turned out to be a greater challenge than he'd expected.

He had built his career on being persistent. Yet, every initiative he'd tried in this situation hadn't worked—at least not yet. Is it possible that he was looking in the wrong places and applying the wrong tactics? If he admitted to that possibility—and based on the results to date, that was a strong possibility—what were the implications?

Well, the first implication he considered was that he had screwed up and wasted 12 months. The second implication was that he was running out of time, and the board would be very unhappy to hear this news—if they didn't already hold that opinion. The third implication was that he did not have any answers, or at least the right answers. Not a happy picture. Jack knew he needed a breakthrough. But what?

What were the options? He could call more meetings and gather more advice from his direct reports, but he'd already done that. Apparently, they did not have insight into the situation that would create a breakthrough solution. Besides, much of the "advice" he received was designed to strengthen the role of that person's department, often at the expense of another's.

He could call a special meeting of the board, and could point out the obvious, that all remedies tried to date had not produced the desired results—and the company was still struggling. This was probably not a bad idea, but with no proposals for a new strategy or approach, what was the point?

Could he get "outside of the box," and try to receive some outside-in counsel?

That had a lot of appeal. If he could find a group of knowledgeable, business-savvy, wise strangers who cared about his company and his future, perhaps he could at least get some objective counsel on whether he was fighting a losing battle. And, if he wasn't fighting a losing battle, maybe he could get some fresh thinking on how to turn the situation around, and get his company back on track.

Given the current situation, he didn't have much to lose. And, time was running out.

Trying Something New

He called a friend, JB, who was CEO at another company, and whom he vaguely recalled had mentioned being a member of an organization that served him as a sort of *Ex Officio* board of directors. On condition of confidentiality, he described the situation to JB.

After listening, and asking a few questions, JB confirmed that this course of action had merit—and gave examples of how his group had helped him though some very sticky business problems. JB added that part of the power of the group's recommendations came from the fact that each member of the group belonged to a non-competitive company from a variety of industries, and brought a lifetime of different experiences to each discussion.

At each meeting one of the members would present a key issue for the group's consideration and advice.

JB then gave him the names of several organizations that might meet his needs, including the name of the organization that he belonged to—Vistage.

Jack decided to call the chair of the organization to which JB belonged, and see what happened. Jack called Frank Reasoner and explained his pressing needs and the urgency of the situation. Frank set up a day and time to meet with Jack later that week, and, after the meeting, promised to get back to him the next day.

Jack got a call from Frank. "Jack, your interview went fine. My biggest concern, however, is the short-term need that's driving you to join this organization. We are not a drive-through business counseling service. You've assured me your commitment extends beyond your current issue, and that you will attend at least 10 out of the 12 meetings each year, and I accept that. Welcome aboard!"

On the ride home that evening, Jack felt better about the day's progress. At last he was going to get some outside-in thinking and perspective from business professionals who did not have a personal agenda. So Jack expected he'd be receiving some straight talk and advice. That night he slept soundly for the first time in weeks.

The First Meeting

A few days later Jack found himself at his first Vistage meeting.

Before the meeting formally started, Jack had the opportunity to meet the other members, all of whom came up to him and introduced themselves while welcoming him to the group.

Frank Reasoner called the meeting to order, with Jack seated to his right, and the other twelve of the group's fifteen members taking seats at a large oblong conference table.

Frank briefly introduced Jack to the other members. After reviewing the meeting's agenda, Frank invited each member to report on their past month's business, personal activities, and developments.

Jack had some difficulty following much of what was said, since he did not know the genesis of many of the comments and remarks. He knew that as time went by he would become familiar with each fellow member's situation. What he did observe was each member's keen interest in each report, and their playful and insightful banter. It was obvious to Jack that this group operated in an atmosphere of respect and trust mixed with fun.

Frank beckoned Jack to the front of the room as he addressed the group.

"Jack F. Eli is here as our newest member, and he has an urgent issue that he will share with you. Jack . . . "

Jack looked around the table. To his left was Frank, the Vistage chair, a longtime consultant who enjoyed the role of chair and trusted advisor. Around the table were nine men and three women, all CEOs or managing partners. They represented many different types of business including law, HVAC service and distribution, benefits consultants, HR services, non-profit, venture capital, insurance, public relations, construction, manufacturing, banking, and retail.

"I'd like to start out by thanking each of you for inviting me to be part of your group. I also appreciate that you've allowed me to share a key issue with you during my first meeting.

"As part of my introduction, I'll share with you a bit of background information about me: I have a chemical engineering degree from Purdue, and an MBA from Northwestern. The challenge I face most in my job is how to run a process more efficiently, and how to squeeze out greater productivity from operations.

"My strengths are strong analytical skills, planning, negotiating, finance, and networking. Areas where I need to improve include humility (everyone laughs), listening better, and saying 'No' more often.

"Things I value and care about deeply include my family, faith, community, and fellow employees. Things that upset me are when people aren't treated with respect, and not keeping commitments.

"I'm married to the former Kathy Benson, and we have two grown children, both of whom are attending college.

"I've come up the ranks through operations, and before becoming president and CEO of TasteRite, I was COO of a small baking company in Chicago. While there, I helped them renegotiate their union contract, modernize their production lines, and improve their productivity and profitability.

"In the next three to five years, I'd like to see my current company grow 50 percent, and dramatically increase its stock price. With my current options, that would enable me, as well as others at my company, to be secure financially. The obstacle or challenge to that happening is the current difficulty I'm having with my company's profitability, or lack of it . . . "

The Key Issue

"OK, that gives you a bit of an introduction and some background about me. Now, here's the key issue . . . starting with a description of my company . . . "

All of the Vistage members leaned slightly forward, their eyes on Jack.

"My company's name is TasteRite, and we provide spice and seasoning mixes and sauces nationally to the food service and food processor markets, and, regionally, to the retail food market. Customers pay us to develop bulk spice and flavor formulations to meet their specifications, to provide packaging that meets their operational needs, and to operate so that the right product gets to the right location at the right time at a competitive cost. We make money by 'buying right,' operating efficiently, and keeping costs as low as possible. We sell our products through a direct sales force as well as a network of brokers and distributors. We also have a key account program aimed at major food service operators and food processors. Finally, we offer a product line of single-use, pre-mixed seasoning formulations for sale at retail.

"I've been in the position of CEO for about a year, and the company has about four hundred employees, with annual sales of about 150 million dollars. The company started in business 45 years ago, underwent a modernization of production capabilities about four years ago—after which I was brought in to accelerate the company's growth and profitability. The company is public, traded O-T-C, with a controlling interest held by the family of the founders. With one minor exception, none of the family is employed within the company. Employees can elect to receive up to 50 percent of their bonus in the form of company shares. The bonus plan is tied into the company's overall revenue growth and profitability. Plus we also provide a 401K plan, with matching contributions based on performance against a profit plan. And finally, as I mentioned previously, key members of the executive team have stock options that vest under certain conditions.

"My issue is this: After a year on the job, I have failed to achieve our aggressive sales growth goals, and the company's profitability has been flat to slightly down. The investment in the new plant modernization is not generating the expected profits. When I took the job I felt that the fix was in improving the operational efficiency of the company. I feel that we have accomplished much in this area, but the results in terms of sales and profit growth don't yet bear out the progress I think we've made. Competition does not explain the situation either: The market has been fairly stable with the usual downward pressure being exerted on prices, while demands for ever better service continue. Raw material prices have been stable.

"This issue is significant for obvious reasons: My welfare and the welfare of many others depends on this working. We need to start showing double-digit sales growth if we're to have any hope of achieving the profit goals that the plant modernization investment was predicated on.

"My ideal outcome would be to understand what the barriers are to achieving our objectives. I'm frustrated in that what I've already tried has not yet worked. Morale is down. New product development is bogged down. There are channel conflicts. Service costs are up, as are RGAs (Returned Goods Authorizations). I've been working 75–80-hour weeks trying to engage the business unit heads on increasing service levels and customer satisfaction, communicating with analysts, flying the flag at industry events. We're also trying to manage diligently on the cost side of the equation, trying to cut costs while trying new initiatives like our most recent ad campaign to the food service and food processor markets, and a sales promotion to the channel.

"My options are to keep on trying what I've been trying, or seek a new solution. That's why I'm here—to see if I can get some new thinking that will shed some light on what's going on, and why what I've been doing hasn't generated the desired results.

"So, what I'd like from you are suggestions on the following: 'What options am I missing?'; 'What would you do differently and why?'; and 'What should I expect as a result?'

"Thanks for listening . . . "

Clarifying Questions

Mel Douglas, the rotund 60-something CEO of an HVAC sales and distribution company started things off by observing, "You know Jack, it takes some real courage to get up in front of a group you've just met and throw open your kimono—figuratively speaking, of course." The group laughs. "My question to you is, in your efforts to drive sales revenues, what additional market segments have you pursued?"

"Mel, that's a good question. We've been pursuing large national account chain business in an effort to add some significant volume and thereby leverage our increased operational efficiency."

"And how's it working?"

"Well, not as good as we'd like. We've added some significant volume, but we've not seen the impact on the bottom line—and, in fact, we've seen decreases in sales from our other non-chain business."

"Why do you think that's happening?" Mel asked.

"Well, perhaps some of our distributors are feeling a bit threatened by our emphasis on chain business. They worry that it will take away from our ability to service their business. We've assured them that it won't. It may take time to demonstrate that to them . . . "

"OK," Mel added, "please tell me, Jack, at what level of capacity are you utilizing your plant?"

"We're operating 52 weeks with two shifts currently, averaging about 78 percent of full capacity. We have plenty of unused capacity, and we can always add a third shift. We cross train our plant employees, so that we have terrific flexibility, and don't have to shut the plant down for maintenance."

Next around the table: Nina Cortez, in her early 40s and the owner and CEO of a fast-growing firm that provides HR consulting and counsel on an outplacement basis. "Jack, please tell me what your company's values are? Do you have a mission statement, and what is that?"

"That's another good question," Jack said as he searched for the right words. "Our mission is 'Provide seasoning blends and sauces with flavor profiles that meet or exceed our customers' expectations while earning a fair return for our stakeholders.' I'm not sure that we've ever formally listed our values. But I would venture to believe that some would include 'treat each other with respect,' 'operate efficiently,' 'have fun,' 'be fair,' and 'integrity in all we do.'"

"I also have another question. What is the outlook for your industry in terms of growth?"

"The industry is pretty mature, but there are some trends in place that indicate moderate growth in the foreseeable future. Those trends include population growth, a continuation of consumers seeking convenience and time saving via eating out and meal replacements or take-home foods, and consumers' continued interest in finding varied flavor experiences in the at-home and away-from-home dining categories. This industry is huge, and our overall share of it is relatively small."

Nina nodded, and looked to her left. Sitting next to her was Mary Dyer, CEO of a compensation and benefits consulting firm. "Jack, tell us about the family that owns much of TasteRite. What is their role in terms of day-to-day operations?"

"They are pretty much hands off. They don't get involved in the day-to-day. They made the investment in the new operations, set out the results they expected, and have been pretty much hands off—with the exception of changing out the former CEO when the operations did not pay off as expected. But, they showed some patience—they waited almost three years for results. I'm not sure they're willing to wait another three years . . . "

"That's interesting, Jack. What makes you say that? Have you talked to them about the current situation and the lack of results?"

"No, I haven't—at least not directly. The facts are pretty obvious to anyone who reads the weekly management reports. But I guess I'll have to reconsider that . . . "

Sitting to the left of Mary was Bruce Fleming, the head of a local bank.

"Jack, I've looked over the information you sent to us prior to the meeting in order to get a good feel for the financials that you're working with. It looks like most of your debt is to the family; they own most of the bonds used for the plant modernization, as well as stock in the company . . . is that right?"

"Yes, that's correct."

"And it looks as if the debt is a reasonable amount, given the overall cash flow of the business—so your company is not overly leveraged. Would you agree?"

"Yes."

"Well, that's very good news—you're not trying to dig yourself out of a deep hole."

"That's a good observation Bruce. We are in pretty good financial shape—the company has been a slow growth 'cash cow' over the years, and much of the plant modernization was paid for through internally generated cash, as well as the bond debt. But, since the family owns a large equity position, they, and the investment firms that recommend our stock to their clients, are looking for above-average, risk-adjusted returns."

"So," Bruce added, "this is not a short-term survival issue; it's a long-term opportunity realization issue."

"That's correct," said Jack. "But I may not really know how 'long-term' long-term is."

Bruce nodded in silent agreement.

Next around the table was Larry Labovitz, a lawyer in a local prestigious law firm that specializes in corporate law. "Jack, do you have an employment contract with TasteRite?"

Jack answered, "Yes, I do."

"Does your contract contain specific performance criteria, or is it general in nature?"

"It's general in nature. My bonus and stock option plans are specific in terms of performance criteria that trigger vesting and qualify me for varying bonus levels."

"And if things don't work out," Larry continued, "what are the transition elements for you?"

"I don't want to dwell on that," Jack replied. "Right now I'm keeping a can-do attitude. But to answer your question, there's a 12-month separation payment given in partial consideration for a non-compete clause, plus the use of an outplacement firm for counseling, temporary office space and support, help with finding a new position, etc. It's not exactly a golden parachute, but then again, this isn't a Fortune 500 company, either. My biggest worry is making sure that we're in compliance with SOX.[1] Violating SOX would be a game-breaker—and that's specifically stated in my contract."

---

[1] SOX is the acronym for Sarbanes-Oxley legislation and its compliance and reporting requirements.

Wrong Assumptions

Next was David Solomon, CEO of a non-profit that specializes in providing camping experiences for kids with special medical needs. In his early 40s and with an air of authority about him, David commented, "Jack, you've described morale within your company as being low, and you've told us that you believe it's low because the firm's performance is not meeting financial expectations, correct?"

"That's right."

"Is it just possible that this assumption is wrong, that the real reason for low morale may have nothing to do with overall financial performance?"

"Yes, I guess it's possible," Jack allowed, "but we've all been so focused on operational improvements and the expected financial benefits, that I'd find it hard to believe that it's something else . . . but, yes, it's possible . . . "

Don Rogers turn was next, and Don, in his late 50s and president of a venture capital firm, said, "Dave, that's an interesting observation, let me follow-up on that. Jack, have you ever had an outside third party gather information about what your employees are really thinking, or have you based your opinion on the reason for their low morale on what they tell you, and on what you hear through your direct reports?"

Jack replied, "No, Don, I've never had any third parties interview the employees."

Don nodded and turned towards the person sitting to his left. Bill Petrie, a dignified looking man with silver hair said, "Jack, thanks for sharing this information with us. My clarifying question is: If you don't start making plan, what do you think the outcome will be in terms of key employee turnover?"

"Well, we've not made plan since the plant modernization was completed. That's been four years. We've lost a couple of key people, and if you take what they said as their reasons for leaving at face value, they're leaving for reasons that are not directly related to the company's performance. People seem to like working here, and they are frustrated with our apparent inability to grow the business and reap the benefits of our operational improvements. But, there are limited opportunities in our part of the country in food manufacturing, and people like the community."

"So Jack, what you're saying is if your employees had alternatives you might be experiencing higher turnover?"

Jack looked a bit startled. "Well, yes, I suppose that's possible," he replied.

Laura Regal, the PR person was next. In her late 30s, Laura had a "we can take on the world" kind of attitude. She said, "Jack, you mentioned that you did an ad campaign. What kind of results did you get?"

"We generated a lot of inquiries, and I think we improved TasteRite's brand awareness in our category, and seem to have favorable share of mind among top food service executives—we just haven't converted that into enough sales."

"Have you gotten any feedback from the sales organization?"

"Yes, they seem to have liked the campaign, but there seems to be a lack of conversion of the interest that was initially created compared to the sales that resulted. It always seems that the first big order from the customers who inquired is 'just down the road'. We did get some business from a couple of large chain operations, but the margins on that business is very low and it's a highly competitive segment."

"What was the main point of the ad campaign?" Laura asked.

"The campaign was aimed at large operators and chains, and talked about our capability to deliver high volumes to spec, and at a competitive price. We used testimonials from some of our current customers to get the point across, and to create credibility."

Laura then asked, "Is TasteRite the only brand that you have?"

"No," Jack answered, "we have several brands for the food service market, depending on the segment.

"In the non-commercial or captive segment we offer our DietRite brand line of low sodium and other specially formulated seasoning and sauce mixes that are designed to meet dietary requirements, or flavor requirements, for different types of patients. And, separately, for visitors' food service applications, we offer our Deli brand line of seasoning mixes and sauces.

"In the commercial segment we offer our SteamTable brand line of seasonings for hot dishes, Buffet brand line of seasonings for cold dishes, and Deli brand line of seasonings for fast food and sandwich shop applications.

"For food processors, we offer our EasyFlow brand line of seasonings, packaged to be easy to use within their operations.

"And, finally, for retail supermarket and grocery store channel sales in the Southeast U.S., we offer, via brokers, our South Coast brand line of packaged spices for quick meals—just add the ingredients and cook as instructed."

"Well," Laura said, "I was going to ask you to describe your served market segments, but you've just taken care of that."

Chris Kalapolos, an energetic guy in his late 40s, who operates a string of franchised stores, was next. "Jack, when you think of your customers, what experience do you think they have with your company, and how does that experience line up with what they expect from your company?"

"Good question, Chris. We've been doing customer satisfaction surveys, and we get consistently high marks from our customers. However, we have experienced some turnover among our customer base, and the reason we're given is that we're not price competitive. I find that hard to believe, as we've been working very hard to get our operations sharp, and cut our costs in order to improve our ability to price aggressively. And since we monitor our competitions' pricing, we know that we're in the ballpark. So, there's more to learn here."

"Thanks Jack. Can you also tell me if you're tracking your brand awareness and image among both customers and potential customers?"

"No, Chris, we aren't, at least not on an organized basis. Every now and then, one of the trade magazines will do a tracking study and will cover parts of our served market, but that's about it . . . "

Sitting to Chris's left was Del Westin, owner of a large commercial construction company. A small, neat looking man, Del turned to Jack and said, "I really don't have any clarifying questions that haven't already been asked. But I would like to know one thing. Are you having any fun?"

Jack laughed. "Not lately. I have to admit, I'm frustrated at my inability to get the company's performance to match our expectations. If I can show some progress towards our goals, I'd be able to enjoy life a lot more . . . "

The last member was Stan May, a 60-something executive who owns a contract manufacturing business. "I hate to say this Jack, but my experience has shown me that I always tend to view the world through my own rose-colored glasses. And if I want to really understand what's going on, I have to get outside of my way of looking at the world. So what I suggest . . . "

Frank interrupted Stan by saying "Stan, let's please hold our recommendations or proposed next steps until we're done with the clarifying questions. Do you have a clarifying question to ask that would help you and the group better understand Jack's key issue?"

"Thanks Frank—I'm always a bit impatient and charging down the road. Yes, I do have a clarifying question. How does your company's performance compare to your competitors'?"

"Well," Jack answered, "I don't want to seem evasive, but that is a really difficult question to answer.

"The answer depends on how you define who our competitors are, the markets they serve, and then try to get an apples-to-apples comparison. And then there is the question of which metrics to use: sales, revenue growth, margins, number of employees, etc.

"Based on available information, and with lots of best-guess estimating, we believe that we are among the top five companies in the industry, but by no means are we the largest. Depending on the measure used, we're either third, fourth, or fifth largest.

"Does that give you what you need?" Jack asked.

"Yes, it does, thanks . . . " Stan replied.

Frank then stepped to the front of the table, saying, "Are there any other clarifying questions that any member would like to add?" David Solomon raised his hand, and Frank gestured for him to continue. David said "Jack, please describe what your customers would say the TasteRite brand image is, what the brand stands for, and why they do business with TasteRite."

"Our slogan is 'Get the great flavor you deserve.' Our customers expect us to provide seasonings and sauces with flavor profiles that meet their requirements, are packaged and delivered to meet their needs, and are priced fairly. You know, the basics—on time, good quality, and great price. People do business with us because our products help them increase their sales."

Don Rogers raised his hand and said: "I have another clarifying question, unless David has a follow-on . . . "

"I'll wait until after you ask your question," replied David.

Don asked, "What is your rate of customer churn? Or, expressed another way, what is the lifetime value of a customer? And how does that compare to your competitors?"

"Wow," Jack mused, "that's a tough question. We turn over about ten to fifteen percent of our customer base per year. But that doesn't factor in the importance of the customers involved, in terms of size or profitability. I don't know what the lifetime value of one of our customers is, since we have so many different types of customers, with varying requirements. And I don't know how our customer churn rate compares to competitors. Unlike the auto industry, our industry does not have a company like J.D. Powers & Associates coming in to measure customer satisfaction, loyalty, and renewal rates."

"Do you have a CRM system installed and operating," Don asked, "and does it gather the kind of information from which you can estimate answers to my questions?"

WHAT IS YOUR BRAND PROMISE? ARE YOU DELIVERING IT TO YOUR CUSTOMERS?

"Yes, we do have a CRM system, but I'm not sure if we've extracted the answers to your questions," Jack answered, "but I'll find out . . .

Frank walked over to the flip chart and wrote down under Next Steps:

Jack to find out if CRM system has customer lifetime value information by . . .

"Jack, when will you report back to the group on this step?"

"At our next meeting," Jack replied.

"Good," Frank said as he added *by 11/10 meeting.* Then as he was returning to his seat he asked Don, "Do you have any other follow-on questions?"

"Nope," Don answered.

"Dave, would you like to ask your follow-on clarifying question now?"

"Thanks . . . Jack, what is your brand promise, how does it compare to your customers' brand experience, and how does that either create or destroy value within your firm?"

"Well, our brand promise, if I understand your question is 'Great Flavor'; and our brand experience is very different for different customers.

"For some of our customers it's 'Here's our specs, fill to order at the best price, and deliver to our plant when we need it.' For these folks, as long as we meet their specs and deliver on time and budget, we never hear from them. For others it's 'We need your help in developing new ideas for our customers.' When we can deliver on that need, we are operating in a true partnering mode with those customers. They want to be engaged with us, and they value our insight, creativity, and innovation. We lose these customers when we fail to engage and challenge them.

"And for our retail customers, it's 'Here are single-use packaged seasoning and sauce mixes that generate good returns per square foot of shelf space.'"

"And how, in each case, do you create or destroy value?"

"Well, in the first case the emphasis is on operating with excellence— getting the specs, fulfillment, logistics, billing, etc. correct every time. So, when we drop the ball and miss a detail, or ship late, or ship incomplete, there's very little forgiveness, and we usually either find our next order reduced or skipped or we've lost a customer."

"And in the second case?"

"Those types of customers are much more forgiving. Then again, we're giving them more time and attention in terms of working with them to develop product solutions for their menu and new product needs. I mean, they don't like it if and when we drop the ball, but they don't react nearly as sternly as the other group of customers. They're used to working with us in a partnering mode—where things are more fluid and subject to last-minute changes as we work together and develop new thinking. As long as we challenge these customers, and work with them to invent the future, as we call it, things are fine."

"And in the third case?"

"Our retail accounts look to us to keep them in stock on a timely basis, and to offer pricing that creates good margins for them. We're usually competing against national companies, so our South Coast brand product line must offer niche flavorings that appeal to consumers in the Southeast U.S., especially the Carolina coastal region, where cooks use our product to flavor dishes that are local and regional in nature."

"How would you typify the type of relationship you have with the customers in each group?" Dave wondered aloud.

"I'd say the first group was transactional in nature, the second group is more of a partnering approach, and the last group is transactional in nature, as well," Jack answered.

"So," Dave added, "what are the implications of that in terms of each groups' profitability?"

Jack thought a minute, his brow furrowed. "That's not an easy question to answer. The first group tends to place larger orders that improve our operational efficiency. The second group requires much more handholding and R&D input. The third group is pretty stable, and we use that business to fill in slow times between production runs for the other groups. So it is difficult to say . . . "

"Well, let's add another 'next step' to the list. I'd like to know more about each group's profitability, and more about how your organization views each group. Can you help us with this insight?"

"Sure," Jack replied.

Frank added another entry onto the Next Steps chart: *Jack to find out more about each groups (transactional/partnering) profitability . . .*

"Jack, when can you report back to the group on this point?"

"I'll commit to having that information for you, to the best of our ability to ascertain it, by our next meeting, in 30 days."

"Great," said Frank, and as he added *by 11/10* to the chart and returned to his seat, he said, "Dave, do you have any more clarifying questions for Jack?"

"Just one more . . . Jack do you know how various parts of your organization think or feel about each type of group you've just described? You know, the transactional type versus the partnering type."

"No, Jack said, "I don't. But that's an interesting question . . . "

Frank stepped up to the flip chart and added: *Jack to report on employees' feelings/thinking regarding transaction-type vs. partnering type customers.*

HOW DO YOUR EMPLOYEES FEEL ABOUT YOUR BRAND?
WHAT DO YOUR CUSTOMERS SAY ABOUT YOUR BRAND?

Jack didn't wait for him to ask, he just said, "I'll have that by 11/10 as well."

Frank added *by 11/10* to the last entry on the flip chart page.

Proposed Solutions, Suggestions and Next Steps

Then he said, "We've had a chance to ask Jack clarifying questions, and now we can propose suggestions, solutions, and next steps to him. Who wants to be first? OK, let's start with Mel. And let me remind everyone that this isn't a dialogue, just give your thoughts, and Jack, you just listen, but don't comment. You'll have a chance to comment when you report back on your follow-up next month. OK, Mel . . . "

"Jack, you have some important assignments to follow up on, and I'd certainly like to have the benefit of that information. However, we can't wait 30 days, so I'll make my recommendations today on the basis that you evaluate it based on what you find out when you follow up on the flip chart entries."

"Fair enough," said Jack.

"My first observation is that you need to dig a little deeper into what's really going on in the minds of your distributors. Every bone in my body says that something is out of whack. Every manufacturer has a love/hate relationship with his channels, and vice versa. Each party is jockeying for advantage, even though they're also supposed to be 'partners' in building the business. Since I assume you're paying your distributors drayage for any direct business to chains in their markets . . . "

Jack nods in the affirmative.

" . . . I can't understand their reaction at your efforts to build your chain and volume business. There may well be another reason at work here for the fall off in your non-chain business. So, my suggestion is that you dig into what's going on with your brokers and distributors a little bit deeper, and don't accept the premise that it is solely their reaction to your chain business initiative. If you find out your assumption is not correct, then you can address the real issue—which is why your distribution channel isn't delivering more growth."

"OK," Frank asked, "who wants to go next—Nina?"

"I'll pass for now," Nina responded.

"Mary?"

"Jack, my thinking centers on the idea that you're feeling pressure to perform in the short term when that pressure, in fact, may not be there in the way that you imagine. My experience tells me that it's always a good idea to get the key investor stakeholders involved in your vision for the future, and the barriers to getting there, so they understand even when the revenue growth isn't there in the short term, that you're making progress to overcome the barriers. Often that progress is not very visible until you reach some sort of tipping point. And even if their expectations are unrealistic given the barriers, it's better for everyone to have all their cards on the table. At least then you know what you're up against, and the time you have to get it fixed. Sure beats guessing . . . and having the family and other major investors understand the situation and the game plan helps take pressure off of them, as well.

"I also expect, as a result of some of the things you may hear today, that you'll have an engaging story to share with them."

Frank next looked at Bruce.

"Having been through my share of work-outs, I can certainly second what Mary just said. Personally, if I know what's going on, and the customer keeps me informed along the way, I'm much more likely to hang in there. Your company is in good shape financially, you just need to meet everyone's expectations, including your own, in terms of revenue and profit growth.

"My recommendation to you is to open yourself up to new ideas—maybe the reason has little to do with getting better operationally, but has to do with something else. You've already agreed to dig into employees' feelings about transactional versus partnering initiatives. You say you have good listening skills, now is the time to put them to good use. You just never know what you may learn . . . "

"Thanks Bruce. Are you ready, Larry?"

"Yes. Yes, I am. I recommend that you consider having your contract changed. But only after you fully understand, as a result of some of the group's recommendations, what is going on. Once you understand what the real barriers are to revenue and profit growth, and you believe that they can be overcome, I'd recommend that you propose a new contract. But you have to put some skin in the game—so be willing to defer—not forego, but defer—some current income, and trade that for a bigger payoff when you meet downstream objectives. This will put real credibility into your statements on what it will take to achieve the company's goals, and demonstrate your willingness to not only share in the risk, but your confidence in the outcome. Whether the board actually approves your proposal is moot; the payoff is in making the proposal."

"Thanks Larry. David are you ready with your comments?"

"Sure. Jack I listened with great interest as you described why morale was low. I've learned in the non-profit business, where, by the way, we don't even pay the bulk of our 'employees', that when morale is low, and I take my best educated guess as to why, I'm invariably wrong.

"I've learned the hard way that the only way to really understand what's going on with our employees and volunteers is to sit down with them and have a conversation. And nine times out of ten, the reason boils down to some issue having to do with the organization's failure to fully serve its constituents for one reason or another. Our people are committed to achieving our goals by serving our constituents, so this really frustrates them. Good people want to do great things. Invariably, it's the organization that stands in the way. Or there's something that's out of alignment with what's been promised, and the ability of the employees to deliver as promised.

"It's my job to ferret out those misalignments and then help the organization, through revised roles, rules, regulations or budgets, to overcome them. In rare cases we find out that we have the wrong people in place, and need to adjust personnel.

"My advice to you is to look at any gap between your brand promise, and your customers' and, just as important, if not more important, your employees' view of the brand experience—and try to understand the importance of the gap, its implications, and how to close it.

"The more insight you gain into why each gap exists, the more insight you'll have on how value is being created and destroyed by your operations.

"I also agree with the advice you've been given to use outside folks to do the digging. In the future, I'll keep this in mind as well, especially for use with our paid employees."

"Thanks David. Don, you're next . . . "

"Well, we've already agreed that you're going to do third-party interviews of employees. I think this will reveal some interesting points of view that will open up new thinking.

"Combine that with the feedback you're going to get about the different performance of customers in terms of profitability, share of wallet, and lifetime customer value, and you should see some interesting patterns develop.

"My tip to you is to pay special attention to customer dissatisfaction—especially lost customers and why they left. Listen for what they were looking for when they first started to do business with you, and why they were disappointed, or what eventually disappointed them ... then relate what they've said to your brand promise. As David said, this should pinpoint areas for focused effort in terms of where value is being created, and where value is being destroyed."

"Bill, you're up."

"Thanks, Frank. My business experience has taught me about the relationship between a company's values, its brand promise, its employees' values and performance, and how all of that works together to give customers an experience that meets or exceeds their expectations, or not.

"Companies that promise a lot, and deliver, prosper. Companies that promise a lot and don't deliver, wither away. And companies that don't promise much, but deliver a lot, grow, but grow slowly because folks just don't know about them—that is, until enough folks find out so that sometimes a buzz is created, accelerating their growth. And, finally, companies that don't promise much and don't deliver much just float along, mainly because of customers' reluctance to change due to barriers to leaving, like having to fill out forms, or learn a new system.

"Finally, there are companies that make a promise that isn't quite right for the market they choose to serve. In this case, the company has difficulty getting good trial and repeat sales.

"So, my recommendation to you is to find out which of these scenarios describes your company. Is there a brand promise to customer experience gap? Or is there a problem with the brand promise you're making in relationship to the market you've chosen to serve? Or perhaps, both.

"If you can come up with an answer to these questions, you'll have gone a long way to figuring out what's going on and how to fix it.

"The real challenge, however, is in being able to 'monetarize' the answers to these questions so you can make rational decisions on what will build your company's value over time.

"In other words, look at what some of my colleagues have said in terms of customer value and compare that to what I've just said about brand value.

"In the short term, you'll want to look at measurements that tell you what your real return is on your marketing initiatives. In the long term, you'll want to look at how to measure the value of the TasteRite brand—at the corporate brand level, and at the individual product and service brand levels—and how your brand value impacts your firm's overall value in the eyes of various stakeholders, including your investors.

"Once you can get your employees, channels, investors, and other key stakeholders talking the language of brand value creation, you'll have gone a long way towards getting beyond the short-term and often counter-productive thinking associated with traditional P&Ls and balance sheets.

"OK, Laura, you ready to go?"

"Thanks, Frank, yes I'm ready. Jack, I was very interested to hear you describe that the ad campaign you ran created some good leads, but the leads were not converted to sales. My recommendation is that you talk with your sales personnel about their thoughts as to why the conversion was so low. Try to create shared understanding, in other words, when they tell you something of interest, even if you think you understand it, say to them 'I want to make sure that I've understood what you're saying, is what you mean that . . . '; then repeat your understanding of what they've said back to them. They'll tell you if you've gotten the full meaning. That's shared understanding. It eliminates all assumptions.

"I'd also suggest that you focus in on their understanding of the intent of the ad campaign, and compare that to how they conduct their sales calls. During the follow-up to the campaign, did they sell from a prearranged script, assuming that because the prospect inquired that they were mainly interested in the offer, or did they do a situation-and-needs analysis?

"I'd then compare those answers to the answer to this question: 'What are your organization's core competences? What gets your personnel fired up about coming to work each day? And how does that relate to your customers' opinions on how your company creates value for them?'"

"Thanks, Laura. Del, you ready to go?"

"I'm ready to go, Frank. Jack, I've heard your description of your different brands. You're in an industry with a large number of competitors; there's a lot of noise out there in the food industry in general, and in your part of the industry in particular. And, there are lots of people competing for distributors' shelf space, as well as share of mind and wallet of food service operators. I question whether using multiple brands is the best way to make your mark. It complicates things, and puts added pressure on marketing and sales to communicate all of those stories. You may want to consider consolidating and focus how you deploy your brand at the corporate, segment, and product levels."

"OK, Chris, what are your comments?"

"We've heard some really interesting ideas so far. My recommendation has to do with what you've said Jack, about your satisfaction scores, and turnover. I think you lack insight as to why your satisfaction scores appear to be so high, yet you have 10–15 percent turnover in customers. There appears to be a disconnect. And since each point of customer churn is worth, on average, about 1.5 million dollars, this is an important point. Especially since you've already paid to acquire them, get them into your system, learn their business, and so forth. What they are worth in terms of lost sales isn't the whole story. You're losing your acquisition investment in them, as well as what they would have been worth had they been a customer for years—and that's even more significant.

"So, you either have a problem here, or, as the young boy said when he walked into the barn and saw a pile of manure: 'There has to be a pony around here somewhere.' I'd rather look at this disconnect as a potential opportunity.

"Your company's 10–15 percent turnover means that you need double-digit growth in new customers just to stay even. Many of the other members' remarks address aspects of this. My focus is on the need for more in-depth understanding and insight into your brand awareness and image attributes. I believe there's something out of whack here with your brand promise—and that doesn't take into account the problems with having a complex brand offering.

"Thanks Chris, and last but not least is Stan May. Stan . . . "

"Jack, one of the penalties of being last is that many of my ideas have already been expressed.

"My fundamental thought though, is that you have to do a top-notch job of interrogating reality. And to do that, you need to get rid of the filters that normally distort feedback. One of those filters is connected with who is doing the interrogating—if it's you, you'll usually get feedback that's politically correct, or at least what the person thinks is politically correct. Or it may be motivated by that person's perception of what may be in their best interest, from the point-of-view of their department.

"The other issue with feedback is that each of us tends to view the world through our own rose-colored lenses. In other words, if I'm an expert on operations, all problems look like they stem from operations issues. And all opportunities look as though they can be realized through improved operations. Neither assumption may be correct.

"I also urge you to use outside third parties to help you with your interrogation of reality. When people's responses are held confidential, they are much more likely to open up and are less afraid of hurting someone's feelings, real or imagined. Outside consultants are also trained to couch questions so that the answers are organizationally or departmentally neutral. You'll get much better feedback that way.

"Use that feedback to understand how your company's values and brand promise impact each department. Part of the secret of achieving a fully functional company in terms of your brand promise, is to understand how each department looks at your brand, and how they translate that into action coordinated with the other departments so as to deliver a brand experience that meets customers' expectations. Getting everyone focused on delivering the brand promise, rather than inward on each of their silos, is fundamental to achieving your goals."

Frank looked around the room to see if there were any other comments. Nina stood up. "Oh yes, Nina, do you have something to add?"

"Yes I do. My colleagues have recommended many ideas that have already given you much to consider. As you continue to gather information internally, you'll learn more. I'd like to tell you about five ideas that I use with my clients that have proven to be of great value in helping them organize and apply information. One or more of them may be of value to you.

"The first idea adapts the hierarchy of effects model. This involves creating a funnel with each of the stages that your customers must move through for your advertising to convert prospects into loyal customers. You're looking for the stages that separate brand ignorance from brand advocacy. By plotting how many customers you lose at each stage, and why, you can see where the weaknesses are and where remedial action and investments are justified. This is a great tool for understanding your sales conversion ratio, as well as customer loyalty. This also makes for great graphics that you can show to others within the organization to help them understand why they may need to change.

"The second idea puts the reality of service delivery in graphic form.[2] You map each step of your service process in a horizontal sequence; however, some steps are separated vertically by a 'line of visibility.' Above the line, activities are visible to your customers; those below the line are not. The map provides a graphic look at potential failure points. Some are vulnerable to delivery issues, some are complex loops with lots of steps that warn of log jams, and too many steps below the 'line of visibility' indicates a lack of perception on the part of your customers. An accurate service map can help you more easily streamline and improve your service delivery. It helps you better understand why margins are thin and customers are frustrated. Again, this is also a terrific teaching tool.

---

[2] Service Mapping designed by Professor James L. Heskett, Harvard University (1980).

"The third idea is called a change equation.[3] Once you've properly diagnosed your needs, and formulated your treatment plan, you'll need to get the employees up to speed and committed to the treatment plan. The change equation tool is a simple formula that measures the likelihood of effecting changes in organizational behavior. $D \times V \times F > R$, where D = dissatisfaction with the way things are; V = a clear vision of how things could be; F = achievable first steps that could be taken. If any of these is zero or close to zero, the product will be too, and will be insufficient to overcome R = resistance. You'll want to use this tool with each department leader in order to drive change down through the organization as will be necessary.

"The fourth recommendation is a balanced scorecard to link measurement to action.[4] It calls for a battery of measurements arranged in a grid that reflects four broad business perspectives: financial, customer, internal and innovation. The balanced scorecard framework is designed to force you to specify actions for each measurement score. For example, in the customer area, you may want to measure how customers rate attributes for your company and for the key competitors in a consideration set. The key here is to look at the gap between your ratings and your key competitors'. The importance of the attribute to creating customer perceptions of value, and the size of the gap will help to determine where you focus. This also is a handy way to encourage the creation of appropriate measurements throughout the organization.

"And finally, the fifth recommendation makes use of five criteria for segmentation.[5] Use these criteria and you'll make sure that the segments you serve make sense in the real world. The five criteria are effective, identifiable, profitable, accessible, and accountable. First, effective: Are the needs of the people within the segment homogenous but different from the needs of people outside of the segment? Identifiable: Can customers in the segment actually be isolated and measured? Profitable: Is the segment large enough to still achieve economies of scale? Accessible: Can the segment be reached in media without too much overlap? Actionable: Does the business have the resources to segment its offer in the first place?" Nina smiled, and sat down.

segmentation

---

[3] Change Equation designed by Richard Beckhard, adjunct professor at MIT Sloan School of Management, based on work by David Gleicher of Arthur D. Little (1987).

[4] Balanced Scorecard designed by Professor Robert S. Kaplan and David P. Norton, Harvard (1992).

[5] Segmentation Criteria developed by Professor Peter Doyle, Warwick University (1994).

Jack responded, "Nina, could I hire you for the next 30 days? Thanks, Nina."

"Jack, I'd like you to summarize what you've heard, and what you will do to follow-up."

Summary and Follow-Up

Jack slowly stood up and looked around the room. "First, my thanks to each of you for your thinking and recommendations. I'm amazed that this group could generate this type of thinking after knowing about my issues a very short time. That simply reflects the kind of business acumen and experience that's in this room.

What I've heard is that many, if not all of my basic assumptions about how to turn this company around may be flawed. That itself has been of value in helping to open up my eyes, and take a 'zero budget' approach from here on out.

"As each of you talked, I made up a list of actions that I will commit to as a result of your comments. In no particular order of importance, here they are:

"When I was asked what I thought the companies values were, I answered 'respect, operational efficiency, fun, fair play, integrity.' When I was asked what were key drivers of customer value in different segments, I used values like insight, innovation, creativity, engage, challenge and partner. I need to understand how those two sets of answers really relate to each other.

"To do that, I'm going to hire a third-party firm to help interrogate reality, especially among employees, and I'll also depend on their outside-in point of view to interpret the data.

"I need to learn more about our channels, our various served customer segments, and our employees—especially what their morale level really is, and why. And I need to do that for each department within the company, but especially the departments that interact with our customers and channel partners. I'll also be looking specifically at what those employees think about our transactional versus our partnering customers. And, with sales, I'll look at why our sales conversion rates are low. I have a hunch we're all going to learn some new things.

"As an extension of that, I'll be trying to better understand how the organization views its core competences, what gets our employees excited about working at TasteRite, and how that relates to what creates value for our customers, and, when it doesn't create value, how that contributes to customer churn.

"I will be working with my executive committee on these topics, and will engage them in getting answers to what our CRM system can tell us about our customers, segments, and customer lifetime value. I'll be working with my CFO and top marketing executive to better understand the trade-offs between what we've discussed today, and the potential impact on top-line revenues versus bottom-line profits.

"I'll also be engaging my marketing department in a discussion of our brands, and how they're deployed to serve our markets.

"I'll also employ some or all of the five tools that Nina mentioned, as we work our way though this to develop and then execute our action plan.

"Finally, I'll be updating the family on these initiatives—and when the treatment plan is in place, on the plan and on what we expect to accomplish. I'll bring other investors up to speed after the treatment plan is in place. I hope to do this with the benefit of many insights, and a better understanding of how to shape expectations for performance on the part of all stakeholders in TasteRite.

"Thank you for your help. I deeply appreciate your thinking and effort."

Frank stepped to the front of the table, and said, "Jack, we're looking forward to your report next month on the progress you've made, and the feedback you can provide to us.

"Now, our next agenda item is . . . "

The rest of the meeting flew by, and Jack was in his car, headed home. His head was filled with all the questions for which he needed answers. Fortunately, he had a meeting with his executive committee already scheduled for that week. He called his secretary, and gave her his revised agenda for the meeting, along with a list of questions to distribute to each member of the committee and instructions that they be prepared to discuss answers to each question based on currently available information.

Jack worked hard over the next 31 days to respond to the commitments he made during the Vistage meeting. His family noticed his newfound enthusiasm.

Soon, it was time for the next Vistage meeting.

Stand and Deliver

"The next item on our agenda this afternoon," Frank announced "is the follow-up from Jack in response to the key issue he shared with us last month, and the actions he committed to as a result.

"Jack, please stand up and let us know what's happened in the last 31 days."

"My thanks to each of you, once again, for your insight and advice," Jack began.

"My first order of business was to call a meeting of my executive committee, and discuss my Vistage meeting with them. I shared with them, while protecting your identities, many of your comments, observations, and recommendations. I also asked them for their help in answering the questions you raised about customer lifetime value and churn, market segment profitability, and employees' feelings about transactional versus partnering customers.

"After much discussion, we all agreed that we did not really understand the answers to those questions. We had lots of opinions, but there was no rigorous standard against which to judge each opinion. So we agreed that we would create a standard for performance.

"After our meeting I posted a request on the 'Vistage Members Need Help' Web site service, and received several replies recommending outside consultants who could help me 'interrogate reality' regarding the brand-related issues that we discussed.

"I interviewed two of the recommended firms. I hired the one who has done work for other Vistage members, and this is what they will be doing for us over the next several months:

"They will measure the value of our product/service brands in each of the market segments in which we currently enjoy sales. They will also give us an estimate of brand value for our corporate brand and how much that contributes to the purchase decision. As part of their program, they will be conducting qualitative interviews with our employees, selected customers and prospects, lost customers, and channel members for insights on how our brands create value for each of them, and how they define the categories in which we compete. They will also look at the potential value of our brands in segments that we either currently don't serve, or under serve.

"Using their 'Brand Value Model' approach, they will disaggregate the value of our brands to show us how much was driven by tangible performance attributes, and how much was driven by product/service intangible attributes. As they explained to me, tangible attributes have to do with the actual physical performance features of our products. Intangible attributes have to do with the emotional and image aspects of our products and service offerings.

"They will further disaggregate those values into individual product performance issues, individual channel performance issues, individual intangible 'positioning' issues, and individual intangible 'alignment' issues. This will give us the information we need to address the issues that we discussed at the last meeting.

"We'll take this information and insight, and use it to leverage our firm's performance to positively impact the following areas (Jack puts up a flip chart and walks the audience through a series of areas to be addressed):

- How we make our branding investments, including advertising and sales promotions as well as our intranet and extranet Web sites, and what we should reasonably expect as a result.
- Where we should focus our quality improvement investments, and what aspects of our products and services are most important to our customers from a quality control perspective and why.
- How we should manage our pricing so as to achieve an optimum balance between growing our volume and maximizing our margins.
- How to best manage and support our channels.
- The impact of our activities on our CRM program and customer loyalty.
- Leadership and process alignment activities—so we understand which levers to press, at what time, and what to expect as a result.
- Insight into our employees belief systems and values, and how that relates to our core competences, and to how we create value for our served markets. That insight will also be used to refine our compensation and recognition practices.
- Insight into our served markets, if they are defined as they should be, and how that relates to their profit potential—this should give us much better focus.
- Finally, the impact we can reasonably expect from our action plan on our profit and loss statement in the short run, and on our balance sheet and stock value in the longer run.

"I've met with my executive committee and filled them in on my meeting last month, and the direction to which we are now committed. I have groups working on addressing our CRM system and its ability to provide lifetime customer value data, as well as customer churn rates, and I have a separate memo that summarizes their findings, for anyone who would like to review it.

"By the way, I have found out that our understanding of what employees think about transactional versus partnering customer types is poor. I have also investigated the profitability of each of our served market segments, and have concluded that we do not have the insight into this that we really need. I suspect that how we define our segments, and how we measure profitability, will undergo major revisions as a result of some of the work now going on.

"I have a meeting set up with the family at which time I will inform them how disappointed I am with my performance to date, and what we are doing about it—including the emerging outline of our treatment plan. Any questions?"

Frank walked over to Jack's side, and smiled as he said: "Jack, thanks for the follow-up from last month's meeting. I hope that you'll keep us updated on your progress monthly as the treatment plan develops and is put into action."

"I sure will," Jack replied. "And again, thanks to each of you for your help and support. I've learned much in the last thirty days. And I have a hunch that this is just the beginning. Thanks."

★ ★ ★

So, what has Jack discovered? What are some of the lessons that Jack learned from his meeting? We've listed these lessons, along with the part or parts of this book that offer further insight into each lesson, and how that lesson may be applied to the benefit of Jack's company and stakeholders. Jack's lessons learned include the following:

1. How we view the world is severely influenced by what we know based on our past experiences. Getting outside of our customary frame of reference is eye-opening.

2. The values of various stakeholders within and outside of TasteRite are not well known or understood, and are not in alignment (see Chapter 3).

3. This misalignment is creating lots of organizational distortion, mischief and disconnects, destroying value via customer and supplier churn, and creating lots of heretofore undetected opportunity costs (see Chapters 4, 5, and 7).

4. Stakeholders' key value-driving attributes, by extension, are not optimized. Jack needs to have a detailed understanding of those attributes (including trust and image attributes associated with values) for all aspects of the Value Model (see Chapter 7), and will be well-served to go outside of TasteRite for this insight and information.

5. Combining the preceding insight with data from TasteRite's CRM system on customer lifetime loyalty, by served market segment, may reveal surprises about which customers are profitable, and which customers aren't (see Chapter 8).

6. This can impact segmentation strategy (see Chapter 11), new product development programs (see Chapter 9), product offerings and service offerings, pricing, terms and conditions, hiring practices (see Chapters 11 and 14), compensation practices (see Chapter 14), recognition and reward programs (see Chapter 14), and communications (see Chapters 9 and 14).

7. The information and insight may also have implications for the corporate, product, and service promises being made by TasteRite (see Chapter 8, 11, and 14).

8. That, in turn, will impact what is measured, how often it's measured (set of brand value measures that have equal status with the accounting numbers in the corporate suite and in the boardroom) (see Chapters 12 and 14).

"I've outlined what I need to do. Now I need to learn more about each step."
—Jack F. Eli, CEO, TasteRite

CHAPTER 3

WHAT IS A BRAND? WHAT ISN'T?

*"During the early days of Starbucks, we were determined to create a company with
a heart and a conscience—one that would continually deliver shareholder value
while touching people's lives and enriching the human spirit. . . . The phenomenal
success Starbucks has achieved confirms my belief that a company can do good
and do well at the same time. . . . Our ongoing success will be measured by how well
we balance our fiscal responsibility with our goal to enhance the lives of those
whom we serve and who serve us."*

—Howard Schultz, Chairman, Starbucks

*"What does our company stand for? How are we currently viewed by our customers,
employees, suppliers, investors, and other stakeholders? What's our vision of how
we would like to be viewed? What are the implications for how we must perform?
How might those answers energize the entire organization?"*

—Jack F. Eli, CEO, TasteRite

The Basics

Brands are assets (or liabilities) that convey values, value, and meaning.

For providers, brands can create a sustainable, competitive advantage. For users, brands are a way to choose among offerings. For employees brands provide identity, community, and opportunity. For investors, brands shape expectations of future returns. For channel partners, brands can create a shared bond of cooperation and understanding. For top management, brands act as a leadership and motivational tool.

Brands started out as tangible marks craftsmen put onto their goods to tell everyone the identity of the maker. Prospective buyers would know to look for the mark of the artisan whose level of craftsmanship or breadth of offering they knew from prior experience, or by word of mouth.

The "trade" mark functioned as a quality assurance device.[1] Most quality gurus define quality as "performance to a standard." Craftspeople strived to either

---

[1] Our thanks to Dr. Shelby Hunt for his suggestion of brand as a quality assurance device.

meet the needs of their customers (an outside-in, market-driven standard) and/or to achieve their vision of an esthetic goal expressed as the design/finish of their product (an inside-out, producer-driven standard). As the market-driven standard was met, the mark became a symbol for the quality of the product, the values the brand stood for, and the value users derived from that product.

Value was created when the product worked (benefits) as good as or better than the buyer's expectations (beliefs) when compared to the purchase price.

Of course, in the time of craftsmen and handcrafted goods, most goods were grown, made, and traded in or near the place where the people lived. The local village or town had a market or markets, and goods and services were available locally, mostly from other townspeople, or from nearby towns.

So, in addition to, or instead of, the maker's mark, buyers often depended on the place of origin—the village, town, or region, as an indication of the quality of the goods being offered and the terms and conditions associated with a purchase. The town name often meant that the specialty of the town could be depended on: Limoges for its fine porcelain china, Toledo for its finely wrought silver goods, Strasbourg for quality smoked meats, and so on. The values of the place modified the values associated with the maker. Or, put another way, the place of origin became a major attribute of the maker's mark.

In a time (prior to the eighteenth century) when most people lived their entire lives in close geographical proximity, people shared fates when they shared place, especially at a time when feudal chiefs, lords, and landowners controlled much of village life, and invaders or plagues destroyed entire villages or towns. The values of the town or village often said much about the maker's mark, and vice versa. *The merchants of Toledo are honorable, and replace any item found to be wanting.* This implied warranty accompanied each product sourced from that place of origin.

Place of origin and its associated attributes became part of the maker's mark; in some cases, it was the mark. So, too, in this sense, place of origin either as a brand attribute, or as the brand, functioned as a quality control or assurance device.

Marks, usually the name or mark of the maker, and/or the place of origin, eventually developed into trade names and trademarks, with some of the legal rights of property—like ownership and the ability to be registered.

The Plot Thickens . . .

The advent of the printing press and more recent forms of electronic media led to the further development of trademarks into what people today call logos (customized typography used for the name, also called logotypes), logo symbols, icons, emblems, avatars (animated symbols), used in varying combinations along with category descriptors and tag lines. These combine to form elements of a brand applications system—which is used to guide how the elements are consistently applied and used by the owner or licensee in their efforts to create a consistent identity. While all of this describes elements of a brand, none of these are the brand.

Further, the brand isn't the maker, product, service, company, trade name, founder, spokesperson, logo, factory, place of origin, or ad—although each of these may contribute in important ways to building and promoting the brand. It can be any and all of these, but brand is much, much more.

That's because brand, which started out as a tangible, physical mark on a product, has taken on many other attributes, many of which are intangible (not physical, you can't hold it or see it) in nature. This has happened, in part, because people have gradually become removed from place. The village or town that used to form the lifelong core of existence, and did much to determine shared fates and values[2] from cradle to grave, as well as a shared perception of value,[3] plays a reduced role in today's world—especially among those living in developed countries.

Beyond friends and family, we have lost place as a center of gravity joining values with value.[4] Producers and sellers of goods don't mingle with buyers and consumers of goods in the markets, town halls, and communities of towns and villages. People today enjoy mobility among many places, instant worldwide communications, easy access to information, global trade, worldwide logistics, higher levels of education, widespread literacy, increased aspirations, and greater ability to buy amid a proliferation of product categories featuring a mind-boggling array of products and services. We meet on eBay®, Yahoo!®, Priceline.com®, and at the mall, and we do business with strangers. This change has happened quickly—over the last several generations.

Over the last 200 years, as place and personal contact have been supplanted, media has been substituted. Newspapers, catalogs, flyers, posters, brochures, trade and consumer magazines, radio commercials, television advertorials and commercials, and Internet Web sites and search engines are examples of media being substituted for face-to-face contact. As we've lost

---

[2] 'Values' as used herein, refers to beliefs, ideals and principles: social values, family values, political values, etc. Morals are values that deal with concepts of 'right' and 'wrong' based on societal standards. All morals are values, not all values are morals. Ethics deals with acting in a way that is consistent with one's morals.

[3] 'Value' as used herein refers to perceptions of worth: economic value, financial value, investment value, market value, etc. Value describes an estimation of current or anticipated worth expressed in monetary terms.

[4] Douglas K. Smith, *On Value and Values*, Prentice Hall, 2004.

our personal contact with the producer, we've substituted brand—but in a way that the originators of makers' marks never imagined.

We've gone from a world of scarcity, where handcrafted goods were expensive, and often beyond the reach of the masses; to where mass-produced goods were more readily available; to today, where goods are custom produced to meet the needs of individuals yet are readily available. We've become a world of abundant choice and supply.

> *"i don't know what's wrong with the youth of today*
> *wandering lost, it's true what they say*
> *and who is to blame? tv and magazines*
> *they'd have you believe that everyday is Halloween"*
> —Lyrics by Buck 65 from the song "463"
> off the album *Talkin' Honky Blues*[5]

The people that buy these goods have also undergone a metamorphosis. From a world of place based on towns and villages, to a world of purpose based on where we actually live our lives: in organizations, networks, markets, and among friends and family.[6] We live in these constructs as consumers, employees, investors, networkers, family members, and friends, yet we often feel alienated, alone in a crowd. We are rushed to get everything done. There is never enough time. Somehow, after we traded in the village, town, or shtetl for the big city, and accumulated more things of value than we had ever dreamed of, we feel increasingly empty and unfulfilled. We've discovered that you can't buy happiness—although you can buy distractions. This is the angst of modern life.

We long for the places of yesterday, yet those places have changed, as have their values, as have we. The loss of place created a vacuum in our lives.

Value and Values Diverged[7]

We venerate democracy, yet many eligible voters don't vote—perhaps because we find it unconscionable that lobbyists can buy favorable treatment and "game" the system. Where's the fair play?

We know the importance of education, yet we watch as learning deteriorates due to budget cuts and turf battles. Where's the belief that education builds the future?

---

[5] Richard Terfry, Buck 65 Music Inc.
[6] Douglas K. Smith, *On Value and Values*, Prentice Hall, 2004.
[7] Ibid.

We understand the importance of the environment, yet we see environmental damage too often unaccounted for by corporations, governments, and markets around the world. Where's the wisdom?

We value freedom, yet fear that our materialistic culture may not offer a sufficient promise to people seeking alternatives from fundamentalism, terrorism, and tyranny. Where's the willpower?

We want meaning in our lives, but spend too little time at work, home, and with friends building relationships. Where's the respect?

We understand that financial gain entails risk taking, but recoil at the greed, self-dealing and gamesmanship among company top executives, auditors, sell-side analysts, accountants, and lawyers who bend the rules to enrich themselves. Where's the honesty?

The Role of Brands

In the future, we will be reconnecting value and values in our roles as leaders and employees in organizations, consumers and investors in markets, and as networkers in networks.[8] This has already begun, and is well underway.

Brands and organizations are the new place. Brands help us to merge value and values.

This happens for two reasons. One, people are looking for meaning in their lives. Two, organizations and brands conspire to provide that meaning in an appropriate way. They do so in order to exercise their enlightened self-interest, constrained so as to balance the interests of employees, customers, investors, suppliers, channels, and other stakeholders. When properly done, this creates a sustained, differentiated, competitive advantage for the firm. Value and values are each considered, and both are maximized for all concerned stakeholders, as much as is humanly possible.

Brands are deployed to accomplish this in several ways.

Corporate Brands

Corporate brands have attributes that reflect the needs and values of their various stakeholders. Examples of attributes include personality, location, advisor, friend, haven, protector, status, safety, danger, maverick, inspirer, heroic, environmentalist, ecologist, health, self, discoverer, nostalgia, innovator, narcissist, genuine, energetic, aspiration, and so forth.

---

[8] Ibid.

First and foremost, brand reflects the values held dear by their customers, investors, and other key stakeholders. If their customers' values embrace the environment, worker safety, respect for others, honesty, and so on, for the company, and its products and services, then the corporate and product/ service brand attributes had best do the same. And those values must be consistently demonstrated in everything the company says and does. If not, the corporation will need to seek out new customers to serve who do share the corporate values and the corporate brands' attributes.

This is simply performing to an outside-in, customer-centric standard— using the brand as a quality assurance device that reflects the values and needs of its customers. But now, in addition to tangible performance or physical attributes, having intangible attributes that reflect customers' values is what mainly creates or destroys value. When a company acts in a manner consistent with its brands' intangible attributes/values, and its customers increase their share of business with them, and continue to be loyal customers, everything else being equal (that is, the costs of serving those customers do not rise), revenues will rise in the short term and/or relationships will be strengthened, and enterprise value will be created over the long run, as well.

In some cases, acting in a manner consistent with the brands' attributes and the customers' values, everything else will not be equal—the cost of acting in a manner consistent with the company's brand attributes may raise expenses dramatically in the short run.

A well-documented example of this was the Johnson & Johnson Tylenol® poisoning case, where the company immediately announced a nationwide product recall, and introduced tamper-evident packaging. Although, according to some reports, this cost Johnson & Johnson upwards of $100 million in the short term, by quickly acting in a manner consistent with their corporate values (the Johnson & Johnson credo) and the Tylenol brand's attributes (in this example, customer safety), they demonstrated their genuine concern for their customers' health and safety.

Had Johnson & Johnson not acted forthrightly, their customers may have altered their perception of their brand, negatively impacting their brand's image (how a stakeholder group currently views the brand).

However, customers found the company's actions and performance consistent with their values and their expectations for the company's performance based on those values. So the company retained their customers' business, and found that revenues more than recovered over the mid-term, and value was created over the long term, even given the expenses incurred.

From a brand perspective, the company's brand image was endangered by the crisis. Brand image is arrived at based on the company's brand promise and its performance in delivering on that promise over time. Brand identity is the brand image the company would like the brand to have at some point in the future. Differences between the brand image and the desired brand identity are reconciled by the company's brand strategy—or the company's performance in delivering on their brand promise.

In this case, customers' expectations based on their perceptions of the corporate and product brand images were successfully met by the company's actions: The brand promise was consonant with the customers' expectations and experience.

The point, though, is that the company's leaders did not know precisely what would happen when they made their values-driven decision to recall the product and restock with tamper-evident packaging. They had to make decisions in the heat of a crisis. However, given their company's values, their corporate and product brands' attributes and their customers' values, it was simply the right thing to do. It was a values-driven decision.

The fact that it ultimately led to a recovery in and expansion of the firm's business demonstrates the positive link between making values-based decisions that align with the brand attributes and customers' values. Johnson & Johnson successfully merged value and values.

The key to being able to do this is to have a clear understanding of the firms' values, the brand attributes, and the served markets' or customers' values, and the relationships between each. This understanding becomes a benchmark for action, a standard for performance.

Conversely, if the company violates one or more of its values and their customers respond by cutting their orders, that sends a powerful message. Or if their investors respond by selling their shares, that sends a powerful message. Value is reduced or destroyed. It's important to note the similar roles values play in competing for customers and competing for investors or capital.

The Johnson & Johnson case is a good example of how to protect your brand's image in a crisis situation. Most brand strategies, however, are executed under less dramatic circumstances. Every company, product, and service has a brand image, whether it's created on purpose or by default. Companies often gather data from served markets on how to make their brand more compelling and, based on this information, they develop a desired brand identity. Their brand strategy is the various programs and stratagems that will bridge the gap between their current brand image and their desired brand identity. Brand strategy should be viewed as a merging of value and values within a defined category for the benefit of all stakeholders.

We look at how this works for employees, investors, suppliers, and other stakeholders in greater detail in Chapters 4 and 5 for corporate and for product and service brands.

Because tangible performance attributes (those associated with product physical features and performance) are easily copied, and therefore, often do not create a sustainable, differentiated advantage—intangible attributes, especially ones based on customer-centric values, are where value will be created or destroyed in the future. And the ability of the firm's employees to deliver on those values—to meet or exceed stakeholder expectations—creates a differentiated, hard-to-copy competence.

Part of this competence may be based on knowledge assets—for example, an understanding or insight on the part of the organization's employees of the complex relationships among the stakeholders, or about the network of which they are a part. Knowledge assets, like brands, are a form of intellectual property—an intangible asset. Knowledge assets and skills created to support or realize the full potential of corporate values and brand attributes, either by forming cross-silo cooperation, supplier support, channel cooperation, and so on, are a form of innovation creating additional resources and competences to be used for competitive advantage.[9]

And like any asset, financial or otherwise, this asset has value because it represents future profit potential. For example, after the Johnson & Johnson Tylenol brand pain reliever scare, the public saw Johnson & Johnson as having experience handling this type of emergency, and developed greater confidence in their ability to handle this type of situation compared to other drug companies should it happen again in the future. And, that perceived improvement in competence likely transferred to other performance areas in the minds of customers and consumers. As a result of the Tylenol scare, Johnson & Johnson may have developed response systems (based on innovative procedures developed during the crisis) to quickly and effectively handle other crises in the future. Their customers and newly aware prospective customers noticed that they behaved in a manner consistent with their corporate values and brand attributes. Customers may then have assigned greater value to those brand attributes (now that they were dramatically proven under fire.) And/or, customers may

---

ENGAGE VALUE w/ VALUES

have created new or enhanced intangible attribute(s) for Johnson & Johnson's corporate brand: *honesty, courage under fire*, and *crisis experience*.

Johnson & Johnson's logistics and distribution chain was well served by Johnson & Johnson's forthright actions. Their distributors and retailers had to be impressed by the swift action taken by Johnson & Johnson to protect them and their customers.

Note that brand attributes are often assigned or created by the various stakeholders in a market in a manner often not envisioned by the company who ostensibly owns the brand. Poor company performance, competitors' actions, government regulators' actions, media, word-of-mouth, activists' actions, rumors, and other sources can often be very powerful in creating brand attributes, and, therefore, brand images other than those chosen or desired by the company.

Since brands exist in the minds of stakeholders like customers and employees, these stakeholders have the power to easily define brand image based on their own sources of information and experience. This puts added emphasis on the importance of brand value and values being aligned—serving as a counterweight to "rogue" brand attributes being accepted, and/or serving as an endorsement of brand attributes created "in the wild" that are in alignment with the brand's values.

Corporate Social Responsibility

Another aspect of corporate brand attributes aligning with stakeholder values is demonstrated by Corporate Social Responsibility (CSR) initiatives. The United Nations Global Compact/Sustainability statement defines corporate social responsibility as ". . . business that embodies transparency and ethical behavior, respect for stakeholder groups, and a commitment to add economic, social and environmental value."

These are programs whereby the corporation understands the values of its various stakeholders, and based on how those values and the values of the company intersect, decides to create programs that can create value for various stakeholder communities. These brand-building strategies provide examples of proactively engaging value with values.

A brief example of this is Starbucks Coffee®'s environmental efforts all along its supply chain.

- Starbucks worked with Conservation International to develop guidelines that pay premium prices to coffee producers when they meet agreed-to labor, quality, and environmental standards.

- The Starbucks Coffee Agronomy Company helps farmers to improve their farming methods so they grow quality, sustainable coffee.
- Starbucks has an alliance with TransFair USA to certify Fair Trade coffee, and help farmers get fair and stable prices for their coffee. Starbucks offers Fair Trade Certified coffee in its stores.
- At the end of the supply chain, Starbucks offers used coffee grounds to its customers for free to use as compost in their planters and gardens, thus taking millions of pounds of waste out of the solid waste stream to the benefit of the community.[10]

Because many of Starbucks' customers (and non-customers) are environmentally aware and concerned, these initiatives resonate with their values while strengthening their perceptions of the Starbucks brand. And the coffee grounds are good for their plants.

Another of Starbucks' corporate values is creating a great work environment based on the values of respect and dignity. Accordingly, they started one program that offers eligible part-time partners (employees) the same comprehensive healthcare benefits that full-time partners receive, despite overall increases in healthcare costs.[11] This positively impacts employee tenure, attitude, and performance. In turn, this provides their customers with superior service. *FORTUNE Magazine* named Starbucks one of the "100 Best Companies to Work For" in 2006, the eighth time they've been so honored. As a result of programs like this, Starbucks enjoys a level of employee turnover that is much lower than average for retail establishments in the United States. This competence in employee retention directly creates a competitive advantage for Starbucks, and economic value for many stakeholders associated with the Starbucks brand.

The central challenge for Starbucks over the next decade will be to maintain the formula of *valuable brand + values = value creation*, while Starbucks continues to grow in terms of size, global reach, and relationships.[12]

This lesson may have been well summarized by the United Nations Global Compact Learning Forum in Berlin at which the following was observed: "With the fast spreading commitment to CSR a case can be made that a fundamental new business model—one that respects stakeholder and shareholder values simultaneously is evolving."

---

[10] Starbucks Coffee Company pamphlet, *Starbucks Commitment of Social Responsibility–Striking a Balance*, Starbucks Coffee Company, 2005.

[11] Ibid.

[12] Ira A. Jackson and Jane Nelson, *Profits with Principles: Seven Strategies for Delivering Value with Values*, Currency Doubleday, 2004.

Business Week asked, "Can business meet new social, environmental and financial expectations and still win?" The question was answered in the affirmative when the Social Investment Forum awarded the 2004 Moskowitz Prize for outstanding research to a study entitled "Corporate Social and Financial Performance: A Meta-Analysis." The meta analysis of fifty-two studies published between 1972 and 1997, containing a total of 33,878 observations, found that there is a "virtuous cycle" between corporate social and financial performance; that strong corporate social performance leads to strong corporate financial performance, but also that strong corporate financial performance allows companies to spend on social responsibility measures, which can lead to increases in corporate social performance, and so on.[13]

The study goes on to state ". . . market forces generally do not penalize companies that are high in corporate social performance; thus managers can afford to be socially responsible. As findings about the positive relationships between [corporate social performance and corporate financial performance] become more widely known, managers may be more likely to pursue [corporate social performance] as part of their strategy for attaining high [corporate financial performance]."[14]

The relationship between the company and its customers, and other stakeholders, based on shared values and reflected in the corporate brands' intangible attributes, becomes a basis for communication via exchanges of meaning ("They're my type of company"; "That's my type of product") accompanied by a rise or fall in exchanges of money. The brand serves as a powerful diagnostic device.

Brand As a Diagnostic Device

At the corporate level, any misalignment of corporate values, corporate brand attributes, and stakeholder values and expectations will lead to friction. In the case of customers, that friction will evidence itself as higher levels of complaints, reduced levels and/or frequency of purchases, and customer churn. For investors and analysts, it may evidence itself in negative e-mails to management, "hold" or "sell" recommendations, derogatory Web sites that focus on the company's failings, contentious shareholder meetings, stock churn and a falling stock price. For employees, it may evidence itself

---

[13] Marc Orlitzky, Frank Schmidt, Sara Rynes, *Corporate Social Performance: A Meta-Analysis*, http://www.socialfunds.com/news/article.cgi/1555.html, 1999.

[14] Ibid.

as higher rates of absenteeism, shrinkage, accidents, turnover, and in extreme cases, outright sabotage.

Ultimately, company values and the corporate brand and its attributes are often about what the employees of the company do, the totality of their performance.

When friction becomes apparent, it is important to identify the values that are being compromised, their relationship to the stakeholders' behavior, and if this has created a key constraint. This becomes a powerful tool for diagnosing the problem, and beginning to understand, plan, and execute the solution. When the solution is effective, value and values are integrated and the friction and related constraint[15] is minimized or eliminated.

The other value of brand as a diagnostic tool is that, by definition, it is context specific. When executives groomed in one corporate environment leave to take the CEO's job in another company, they often try to apply the practices that were so successful at their former company in the new environment. A good example of this is all the executives groomed at GE under Jack Welch. Many of these executives, after a successor to Welch was named, left to head up other companies. Several of them have had limited success, at least in the short term, when they tried to apply the same practices that had worked so well at GE, elsewhere. Those practices were specific to the context of GE, and not necessarily applicable to the different contexts of the new companies.

What makes up context? Founding values (beliefs, ideals, principles), myths, former and current practices, procedures, processes, personnel, rules, regulations, history, type of industry, served market mix, product/service mix, organization (decentralized/centralized), country of location, to name just a few, conspire to create a unique context. When we view the corporate brand and its attributes as a shared belief system, that system must be custom built to fit the context of each company. When it fits, it's an effective diagnostic tool.

One of the benefits of using brand as a diagnostic tool is that it then becomes a basis for learning, both formally and informally within the company. Properly used, it becomes a powerful tool for adaptation, helping the organization cope with changes (representing threats and opportunities) in technology, markets, economy, and so on. The key is never to take the brand and its relationship with key stakeholders for granted.

The gold standard to determine when a corporate brand is fully alive and engaged within the company is when the employees, standing around

---

[15] Eli Goldratt, *The Goal*, North River Press, 1992.

the water cooler, talk about brand-related issues and lessons learned with as much animation and passion as they have for sports or gossip. Your front-line, customer-facing employees are the ones who can do the most to help keep the organization's brand(s) aligned with its various stakeholders.

When that is achieved, we'll have come full circle, with organizations, markets, and networks along with their values-driven brands being modern-day equivalents of the places of yesteryear, only with a purpose. The purpose? The successful creation of value via the use of brand values designed and applied to serve multiple stakeholders for their mutual benefit.

Today, the brand is the business. The brand is the strategy.

Brand Architecture

Product and service brands are different from corporate brands. They exist under the corporate umbrella, and depending on the brand architecture, may be closely allied to the corporate brand, or may bear little or no resemblance to the corporate brand.

For example, Toyota Motor Car Co. Ltd. is an umbrella over an extensive line of product-related brands. Toyota Camry, Toyota Tundra, and other Toyota product offerings are all closely allied to the corporate brand. General Motors Corporation on the other hand, holds its products at arm's length, with their product brands organized by car groups, such as Buick, Pontiac, Chevrolet, and Cadillac. Specific automobile product offerings are associated with each car group, rather than with the corporate brand.

In some markets, where customers cluster around different sets of attributes, it may make sense for a company to offer brands that appeal to each attribute set. For example, in many product/service categories there are upscale, high-income, "status" buyers; middle-of-the-market quality buyers; and middle-of-the-market transactional buyers. Each group seeks different sets of values or attributes for a variety of reasons having to do with their own needs, values, and economic circumstances.

The decision as to how to align the product/service brand with the corporate brand is usually based on the legacy of the corporate brand. For example, if the corporate brand's heritage is as a low-end price brand, then very often the brand architecture strategy is to develop new brands with little or no connection to the parent. If the parent or corporate brand started out or achieved a high-end acceptance, then it is more likely that the new niche or segment brands will be more closely aligned with the parent brand. But, there are potential dangers in each strategic choice if the relationship between values and value is not clearly understood.

NICE EXAMPLE!
Segmentation

Very often brand architecture is influenced by acquisitions—when they are made, what is bought, and how the purchased brand aligns with the parent and other brands.

Examples of brand architecture are:

Marriott International, Inc. The Marriott brand started out as a chain of food service businesses under the Hot Shoppes, Inc. name. Soon the company also branched out into hotels, changing its corporate name to Marriott Corporation in 1967, and eventually sold the food service businesses in order to focus on the hospitality category. They have developed and acquired a large stable of hospitality brands, to serve many segments of the hospitality market.

The Marriott Hotels & Resorts brand consists of quality-tier, full-service hotels and resorts that "provides consistent, dependable and genuinely caring experiences to guests on their terms." There are 482 Marriott Hotels & Resorts worldwide.

JW Marriott Hotels and Resorts is the most elegant and luxurious Marriott brand. It "provides business and leisure travelers a deluxe level of comfort and personal service on their terms." There are twenty JW Marriott Hotels worldwide.

Renaissance Hotels & Resorts are a quality-tier, full-service brand "providing guests with the ambience of a boutique, with a 'street' restaurant and savvy service." There are 130 Renaissance Hotels, Resorts and Suites worldwide. This brand was acquired in 1997.

Courtyard by Marriott is the moderately priced lodging brand "designed by business travelers for business travelers." The brand has recently increased its number of downtown locations, often through conversions of historical buildings. There are 638 Courtyard by Marriott locations worldwide.

Residence Inn by Marriott is designed as a "home away from home" for travelers staying five or more nights. It features a residential atmosphere with spacious accommodations. There are 454 Residence Inn by Marriott locations worldwide. The Residence Inn Company was acquired in 1987.

Fairfield Inn by Marriott offers "consistent, quality lodging at an affordable price." There are 530 Fairfield Inn by Marriott locations worldwide, mostly in the United States.

TownePlace Suites by Marriott is the mid-priced, extended-stay brand that "provides all the conveniences of home in a residential atmosphere." There are 112 TownePlace Suites by Marriott locations in the United States.

SpringHill Suites by Marriott is their moderately priced, all-suite lodging brand, and offers "guest suites that are up to 25 percent larger than standard hotel rooms." There are 116 SpringHill Suites by Marriott worldwide, mostly in the United States.

The Ritz-Carlton Hotel Company, LLC is the "worldwide symbol for the finest in accommodations, dining, and service," and offers signature service amenities. There are fifty-seven Ritz-Carlton hotels and resorts worldwide.[16]

Since Marriott was not in the luxury end of the hotel business, it would have been difficult to stretch the corporate brand name up into a market where attributes of selectivity, fine service, expense, and excellence were the norm. A move in that up-market direction may also have had adverse effects on Marriott's other brands, giving them the undesirable attribute of not being deemed affordable.

Marriott solved the problem by buying a brand already established and accepted in the luxury category. Marriott acquired 98 percent of the Ritz-Carlton Hotel Company, LLC in 1995.

Marriott also wanted to attract more customers looking for other attributes not offered by a mid- to high-end hotel, since the size and growth of those segments was much higher than the premium and luxury segments in which Marriott was now already well established. And, there would be scale and scope advantages to doing so.

It made sense to use the Marriott brand, and extend it into other segments of the hotel market—but in a way that differentiated the newer brands from the mainstream Marriott brand. They did this by introducing several new brands, among which were: Fairfield Inn by Marriott introduced in 1987, and Courtyard by Marriott opened in 1983.

Courtyard by Marriott was a specialty brand designed for the needs of business travelers, with limited dining facilities and convenient to local businesses and office parks. Fairfield Inn by Marriott was designed to meet the needs of families on a budget, and was in suburban areas easily accessible to major highways.

There are always potential trade-offs when applying an established brand to a new market. The values of that market (economy/convenient/fast) may tarnish the values of the established brand—although in this case each of the Marriott brands is quite different in terms of some of their brand values, and

---

[16] http://www.marriott.com/corporateinfo/culture/heritagetimeline, 2005.

most of their amenities and locations. Some of the values that are similar—consistency, friendliness, cleanliness—work for all of the brands. Plus, the association with Marriott may be limited to the Marriott corporate organization's brand, rather than the Marriott Hotels brand. On the other hand, having the endorsement of the Marriott name made it much easier for the developers, owners, operators, and potential customers of the new Courtyard, Fairfield, and other brands to have confidence in these operations.[17]

Brand architecture specifies brand roles, the nature of relationships between brands, and each brand's relationship to served markets. Poor brand architecture confounds different brands, where stakeholders are confused about the brands' values and how those values serve the various stakeholders. Competent brand architecture manages multiple brands so as to create clear alignments with each brand and its served markets, limiting cross-brand confusion.

An understanding of brand architecture is particularly important when evaluating mergers and acquisitions. How will the values of the firms mesh? How will the various brands' attributes fit in with the new corporate parent? What are the implications for each product/service brand, and its future with its served markets? What are the implications for channels, and investors, from a brand perspective? Good brand architecture preserves value while creating potential for even greater value creation for all stakeholders in the future.

A good example of this can be found in co-branding. Co-branding occurs when brands from different organizations combine to create a new offering. A research study by Kodak showed that for a fictional entertainment device, 20 percent of prospects said they would buy the product under the Kodak name and 20 percent would buy it under the Sony name, but 80 percent would buy it if it carried both names. Apparently, prospective buyers thought the combination of names could represent an advance that could not be credibly claimed by either brand alone.[18] The innovative use of the two names in combination is an example of brand architecture strategy used to create competitive advantage.

Similar lessons apply to licensing brands to or from other companies. Carefully considering all the ramifications in terms of corporate values, brand attributes, and other stakeholder values and needs, and their potential impact on the current brand image and desired brand identity, is central to understanding the risks and opportunities involved.

---

[17] David A. Aacher and Erich Joachimsthaler, *Brand Leadership*, The Free Press, 2000.
[18] Ibid.

The Four Levels of Brand

Brands exist on several levels, in a manner similar to a Russian doll, nested one inside the other.

- Authority Brands—These are broad-based brands that represent the ultimate producer—3M, General Motors, Ford Motor Company, Toyota, Marriott, Brown Forman. They put the authority of the manufacturer and its values behind all the products associated with it.
- Strategic Brands—These are the brands that fit a particular category or a set of closely related categories—Scotch, Chevrolet, Lincoln, Camry, Courtyard, Jack Daniels. They may or may not be closely aligned with the Authority Brand—Scotch Tape by 3M, GM Chevrolet, Lincoln by Ford Motor Company, Toyota Camry, Courtyard by Marriott. Jack Daniels is not aligned with Brown Forman, on purpose.
- Operating Brands—These are brands for a specific product or service—Scotch Painters Tape, Chevy Impala, Lincoln Continental, Toyota Camry LX, Jack Daniels Small Batch. Operating brands can be synonymous with the Strategic Brand in cases where there are no significant variations in the operating brand, such as Courtyard by Marriott. These may also be viewed as sub-brands.
- Personal Brands—These are brands that describe individuals. Henry Ford, Bill Clinton, Ghandi, Madonna, Picasso, Mother Theresa, and Jack Welch, are each a nano brand. A synonym for "personal brand" is reputation. Personal brands are important when it comes to defining how the individual in an organization relates to the organization's mission and values, and how they perform to fulfill the Authority Brand, Strategic Brand, and/or Operating Brand promise. The individual is responsible for managing their personal brand within an organizational setting so as to advance their career, or outside of the organizational setting, to create a good life as they see it.

This brand architecture classification system is imperfect and fuzzy at best. There are many shades of gray between and among these classifications. Most brand practitioners have their own version of a classification system, which further adds to confusion surrounding the topic of brands. There is a need for a generally accepted set of standards to help to define brand architecture.

Brand Vision

A statement of where you'd like your brand to be in the future is your desired brand identity. In order for your brand vision to be realized, your various stakeholders must view your brand as authentic, genuine and relevant. If you are the leader of the company, they must also view you as authentic, genuine, and relevant.

Authenticity is achieved when value and values are aligned and are kept in alignment as time passes and conditions change. Genuine is achieved when people act in accordance with agreed-to values. Relevance is achieved when people accept that change has misaligned value and values, and they undergo the personal changes in outlook, attitude, behavior, and expectations often required to achieve realignment.

Resistance to change is a major barrier among most stakeholder groups to the sustainability of brands. The reluctance of people to embrace change is well documented. Change is painful. It requires that we endure the pain of learning new ways of thinking, being, and doing,[19] while we mourn what we leave behind.

Leaders, to be effective, must be adept at convincing people of the urgent need for change. The change can be evolutionary or revolutionary as circumstances dictate. Effective leaders dramatize for people, in a way they can't ignore, the misalignments between values and value, and tie that in to a call to action. Better yet, they engage employees in the discovery of the misalignments between various stakeholders' value and values, the risks and missed opportunities, the changes necessary for realignment, and the performance and results to be expected. This creates a powerful pull force throughout the organization.

"I realized that my key assets weren't plant, equipment, inventory, and other tangible assets—but were far more difficult to understand intangible assets, the most critical being brand. And I would have to learn to deal with and measure the nature and performance of these intangible assets in a way that is quite different from the way that I'm used to dealing with and measuring the performance of tangible assets. Only when I change can I expect my company to undertake change."

—Jack F. Eli, CEO, TasteRite

In the next chapter, we explore brands as financial assets—in the sense that they are owned by the firm and its shareholders; and the implications for accounting practices and for measurements of return on marketing, and other types of investments.

---

[19] Lee Thayer, *LEADERSHIP: Thinking, Being, Doing,* Xlibris Corporation, 2004.

CHAPTER 4

BRANDS AS FINANCIAL ASSETS

"If all Coca-Cola's assets were destroyed overnight, whoever owned the Coca-Cola name could walk into a bank the next morning and get a loan to rebuild everything."

—Carlton Curtis, VP of Industry Affairs, Coca-Cola North America Foodservice & Hospitality Division

"If this business were split up, I would give you the land and bricks and mortar, and I would take the brands and trademarks, and I would fare better than you."

—John Stewart, Former CEO, Quaker

"What do our brands stand for, and how does that translate into hard financial value?"

—Jack Eli, CEO, TasteRite

Part and parcel of understanding value creation within a corporate setting is to understand how values and value converge—and the role of brand in facilitating that convergence. The previous chapter defined what a brand is in terms of its qualities—that is, the values and attributes that make up a brand, how brands operate to create meaning, and how that creates value for participating stakeholders.

This chapter looks at brands as financial assets. It examines how the value that brands help to create is viewed from a financial perspective.

This is important to CEOs and their management teams simply because stagnant or falling stock prices often signal that a change in CEO will—sooner rather than later—take place.

The Oracle of Omaha

Several years ago, Warren Buffett addressed a group of graduate students at Emory University's Guizueta School of Business. Why should we care about what Warren Buffett had to say? Simply because he is acknowledged to be the most successful allocator of capital that ever lived. His insights into brands as financial assets, and their role in creating shareholder value, are illuminating and instructive.

His ability to invest in companies that handsomely reward his confidence over the long term is legendary. How does he see value where others haven't?

After all, for every buyer of a stock, there has to be a seller. So when Buffett buys a stock he's making a bet that the stock will out-perform the market and competitors in its industry. The seller is making a bet that the stock has run its course, and will under-perform.

Buffett is invariably right. This ability to see value where others haven't has made him the third richest man in the world (behind Bill Gates and Carlos Slim Herue). His 38 percent stake in Berkshire Hathaway, the holding company for his investments, with a market cap of $137.83 billion,[1] was worth $50+ billion early in 2006. He is one of the few people who created such wealth primarily through stock market investments. When he talks, the rest of us should listen—closely.

During his talk at Emory, Buffett recounted the basics that have made him a successful investor, many of those basics coming from Benjamin Graham's thinking on "value" investing:

- Invest in companies you understand.
- Look for a track record of high returns on equity.
- Look for reasonably low levels of debt.
- Look for companies with management that's passionate about the company.
- Look for a margin of safety—pay 25 percent less than the company's intrinsic value.

Then one of the students asked him to describe the secret of the thought process he goes through to identify companies that make *great* investments—those with high intrinsic value not reflected in the company's stock price.

Buffett answered that he thinks of companies as castles surrounded by a moat. He said that the castle represents the tangible assets of the firm—buildings, equipment, patents, receivables, contracts, cash, land, and so on. The moat surrounding the castle represents the intangible assets of the firm—relationships, brands, pricing power, R&D capability, and a reputation for quality.

He then described the economic moat that surrounds the castle, and the *sustainable* competitive advantage it confers on the company, as being of far greater importance in forming his investment decisions than the castle itself. He observed that the moat surrounding the castle is the only thing that protects the castle, and provides security (of earnings) far into the future. If the moat is broached, the castle falls.

---

[1] Yahoo! Finance, January 7, 2006.

The width and depth of the moat, therefore, *reduces risk* while it creates *sustainable competitive advantage* over other companies in the industry. A wide moat also acts as a barrier against other companies wanting to enter into an industry.

Buffett talked about the companies that he has invested in. Most of them feature the equivalent of wide, deep moats, namely brands, quality reputations, and other intangible assets that make the company uniquely able to compete effectively over the long term while producing ever greater amounts of revenues, free cash flow, capital appreciation, and dividends—superior shareholder value.

It is his understanding of the role of intangible assets that gives Buffet insight into the intrinsic value of companies that other investors do not see. He sees value where others do not. He clearly recognizes the powerful role strong brands play as financial assets that have been clearly undervalued, or largely ignored, by other investors.

At the very least, Buffett expects a company he invests in to become fairly valued over the long term. He also hopes the company's assets will generate above-average returns, and will become attractive to other investors, thus bidding up the price—after he has bought the stock, of course.

In addition to Buffett's value style of investing, another style of investing is called growth investing. In this strategy, an investor seeks out stocks with good growth and potential for capital gains. In most cases a growth stock is defined as a company whose earnings are expected to grow at a rate above the average of its industry or the overall market.

Some observers of the stock market maintain that growth investing and value investing are two distinct and opposed styles. But according to Warren Buffett, a better way to view these two approaches is that "growth and value investing are joined at the hip." Peter Lynch, another famous and successful investor, pioneered a hybrid of growth and value investing called GARP (Growth At a Reasonable Price).

Regardless of the style of investing, the objective of investors is to buy a stock that will increase shareholders' total value. And the point made by Buffett and other successful investors is that the key to future success is to be found not in the tangible assets of the firm, but in the intangible assets of the firm.

Whereas the key to growth and success had previously been access to capital to fund the building of infrastructure (real property—tangible assets), the realization now is that the key to growth and success today in developed economies is more associated with intangible assets. Tangible assets may be necessary, but they are not sufficient for success in many industries. Savvy investors realize that companies that create and grow intangible assets have created an effective set of competences that serve to provide *sustainable* competitive advantages that, in turn, generate higher levels of free cash flow and above-average returns in their industry.

There is a critical difference between sustainable competitive advantage and operational efficiency, although they look similar and are hard to distinguish from each other. *Operational efficiency* means a company is better than its competitors at doing a certain thing by using the least amount of resources—but that advantage usually doesn't last very long. *Competitive advantage* means that a company is better than its competitors at doing different things or doing similar things in different ways—but competitors may be able to eventually mimic those advantages.

Sustainable competitive advantage means that a company has developed competences and attributes that are difficult to copy, often unique to the context of the company, are able to adapt those competences to changing conditions, and effectively apply those competences to achieve stated objectives. Often this is done while the company exhibits enlightened self-interest, carefully considering the impact of their initiatives on all stakeholders. These companies are expanding the breadth and depth of their moats over time in a way that competitors find difficult, if not impossible, to emulate. Brand building is a key way to do this.

So, now that we understand this we can become billionaires like Warren Buffett, right? Not exactly. The reason why that won't easily happen is clear when we look at most companies' financial statements and annual reports—and their limitations in giving investors the information they need to fully understand the intangible assets and intrinsic value, both existing and potential.

Limitations of Current Financial Reporting

An asset is defined as anything of value or usefulness that creates future benefits. If it doesn't create future benefits, it's an expense or liability.

There are many different ways of classifying assets. For our purposes, we'll refer to two types of asset classes, intangible assets and tangible assets.

As we've already stated, tangible assets consist of real property, equipment, money, buildings, and other entities. They're the building blocks of Buffett's castle. They can be current in nature (short-term assets that can be liquidated or converted to cash in less than one year), or long term in nature (long-term assets to be depreciated over time). Tangible assets that are long-term in nature appear on the balance sheet of most companies.

Asset book value is the value at which an individual asset is carried on a company's balance sheet, calculated as the cost of the asset less accumulated depreciation.

Company book value is the net asset value of a company's total assets, calculated as total assets less intangible assets (patents, goodwill) and liabilities. For example:

BV (book value) = TA (total assets) − IT (intangible assets) − L (liabilities).

Intangible assets (the moat surrounding the castle) consist of things that are not physical in nature, like patents, goodwill, intellectual property, customer relationships, brand equity, and so on. Up until 2001, intangible assets like brands did not appear on company balance sheets, making it difficult for investors and other interested parties to know the value of these assets. And even today, only acquired brands are shown on balance sheets, but not "homegrown" or internally developed brands.

And if, as some observers claim, intangible assets today account for upwards of 90 percent of firm value in some industries, how can investors make rational decisions when data about the assets most responsible for value creation is not readily available? The answer is, most of them can't—but they guess at it anyway, and the result has been greater investor uncertainty and higher levels of volatility in stock prices.

Intangible assets, other than acquired brands, don't show up on the balance sheet, but they do show up on the P&L as expenses. Expenditures for R&D, brand building, and marketing are treated as expenses by today's accounting standards. Expensing what are really investments (because they generate cash flows beyond the current fiscal accounting period) results in higher expenses in the current period, and therefore, depressed earnings. The result is "a disconnect between financial information and market values."[2]

Brands valuation is done for three reasons:

1. Accounting purposes. U.S. Financial Accounting Standards Board (FASB) requires per FAS rule 142 that goodwill in an acquisition (the excess of the purchase price over the value of the tangible assets acquired) be allocated to the intangible assets that the company

---

[2] Baruch Lev and Paul Zarowin, *The Boundaries of Financial Reporting and How to Extend Them,* Organization for Economic Co-operation and Development, 1998.

is acquiring. International Reporting Standard 3 also requires this. Further, "rules of impairment" require that excess goodwill be written off in the year of impairment. This means that brand valuation is now part of the due diligence performed before an acquisition, and required annually after an acquisition.

2. Transactions. There are generally four types of transactions:

   • Securitization involves using anticipated future revenues as security for borrowing. Basically, the value of the brand becomes collateral to secure a loan or bond issue.

   • Brand-based tax planning involves transferring ownership of a trademark and/or other intellectual property to a holding company that charges a royalty to the operating companies using these brand assets.

   • Brand licensing enables participating firm's to employ the brand for their purposes, with the brand owner recovering economic benefits via a royalty rate or licensing fee.

   • Acquisitions require that the companies understand the economic value of the brand assets involved so that a purchase price can be reached.

3. Brand leadership and management. The purpose of brand leadership is to develop metrics associated with the brand strategy and execution that are used to measure progress toward creating a desired brand identity via a positive brand experience on the part of the stakeholders.

A further disconnect is created, at least for value and growth investors, by the fixation of Wall Street on quarterly earnings numbers. This has led to an arcane set of behaviors designed to manage, massage, guide, and tickle the numbers, even if it means sacrificing the longer-term financial well-being of the company.

The consequence is a less than optimum allocation of capital among companies. "… we find the evidence clear that the usefulness of traditional financial measures such as earnings and P/E ratios has declined, and new measures for recognizing the value of intangible assets and evaluating performance on nonfinancial [*sic*] dimensions have increased in importance."[3]

---

[3] Robert Eccles et al., *The Value Reporting Revolution,* John Wiley & Sons, Inc., 2001.

The bottom line is that the relationship between *reported* earnings and stock price performance has been found to be tenuous at best. Reported earnings measure past performance, but because of pressures from sell-side analysts and momentum investors and speculators, extreme pressure has been exerted on management to manage earnings numbers for the short term—which masks and too often denigrates true long-term value creation behaviors and prospects.

One solution to measurement distortions caused by expensing items that are really assets is to capitalize them. Steve Wallman, a former commissioner of the Securities and Exchange Commission, is a vocal advocate of this.[4]

This solution has tremendous implications for investors, management, and society, and for future measurement techniques. But for the time being, it is not the way things are currently done.

Another proposed solution is to use Economic Value Added® or EVA, a measure of profitability developed by Stern Stewart, which incorporates a charge for capital. The idea is that valuation, decision making, and compensation should all be tied to EVA, defined as "operating profits less the cost of all the capital employed to produce those earnings."[5] This approach has the merit of discriminating between activities that create true economic value—and grow shareholder value, and those that do not—thus destroying shareholder value.

The Value Reporting Revolution

In response to the shortcomings of reported earnings, "The Value Reporting Revolution" has suggested four commonsense steps to hasten the rise of what they call the Value Reporting Revolution:[6]

- Step 1: Construct a business model that shows the cause-and-effect relationships among the key value drivers; then identify the most meaningful measures for them.
- Step 2: Develop new measurement methodologies if they don't already exist.
- Step 3: Validate the business model and the measures through testing and use.
- Step 4: Compare management's view with the market's view on what measures are important.

---

[4] Ibid.

[5] G. Bennett Stewart, III, *The Quest for Value: A Guide for Senior Managers*, HarperBusiness, 1999.

[6] Robert Eccles et al., *The Value Reporting Revolution*, John Wiley & Sons, Inc., 2001.

Applying these four steps would go a long ways toward providing CEOs, CFOs and heads of investor relations with outside-in information, and a new perspective on what information is really valued by investors.

According to a series of surveys conducted by accounting firm PricewaterhouseCoopers over a four-year span, one area of information that investors value highly is more and better information about brand assets—especially brand equity.

In fact, investors and analysts value information about brand equity and brand visibility much more highly than does company management. The conclusion is that the market disagrees with most managers' valuations of their companies, in part because investors and analysts lack enough information to make a proper determination.[7] The move toward greater transparency in disclosure should address this weakness.

Brand Value versus Brand Equity

You've probably seen the articles reporting on brand value in popular business magazines. Each year the magazines breathlessly report on the rise and fall of brand values for global brand icons such as Coca-Cola, Microsoft, GE, BP, and others. Each year the brand value numbers gyrate up and down, usually because they're based on an extrapolation of earnings taken from the company's profit and loss statement. Some describe brand valuations conducted this way as "brand beauty contests."

Most brand value methodologies take current financial numbers to create estimates of future operating profits, using the net present value of the profits *likely* to be generated by the brands under review. There are many problems with this approach.

First, brands don't fit the 12-month time scale of annual financial statements (not to mention quarterly earnings announcements!). This has been likened to the difference between water in a lake versus water in a stream. Short-term (12 or fewer months) earnings are akin to the water in the stream. Measuring brand valuation by extrapolating from short-term earnings flow is not a measure of true long-term value. As London Business School's Senior Fellow, Tim Ambler says, based on a two and one half year research study on marketing metrics, "net present value" is "guesswork, not science."[8]

---

[7] Robert Eccles et al., *The Value Reporting Revolution,* John Wiley & Sons, Inc., 2001.
[8] Tim Ambler, *Marketing and the Bottom Line,* 2nd Edition, FT Press, 2004.

Brand equity is a measure of the water in the lake ("a reservoir of cash flow earned but not yet released to the income statement"[9]) which is akin to long-term value. The water stored in the lake is, "What's in people's heads about the brand"; "the storehouse of future profits which result from past marketing activities."[10] Brand equity serves as an "early warning device"[11]—if it's rising it indicates that the company has been investing in future value—even when it's not reflected (when treated as an expense) in current earnings.

When it's falling, as when a company tries to pump up revenues by selling on price promotion, or by "loading" dealers' shelves by offering purchase incentives, it serves as an early warning device that the company is sacrificing future cash flows and value for short-term gains. We have clearly seen this phenomenon at work with American automotive manufacturers—and the negative impact on their brand value, brand equity, market caps, and credit ratings.

Brand equity is where values and value converge in the minds of stakeholders. As you may recall from the last chapter, brand attributes should relate to the values of each group of stakeholders inside and outside of the company or organization. When the relationship between stakeholder values and brand attributes gets out of alignment, this indicates that there is a constraint(s) either sub-optimizing brand equity (potential value) or destroying it.

This convergence of values and value (brand equity) becomes a financial asset when it's assigned a monetary value by one or more groups of stakeholders. Warren Buffett sees value where other investors do not because he understands that brands (brand equity) are reservoirs of value, and that this value will be expressed as future cash flows over time. He also apparently knows where to look "beneath the surface" for sources of brand equity. The fact that homegrown brands are not listed on the balance sheet helps to distinguish his insight into what constitutes a company's intrinsic value.

Another shortcoming of brand value "beauty contests" is that the outcome can be easily manipulated. Want to raise your return? Lower the size of your investment on your spreadsheet by accelerating or delaying recognition of expenses. Or, change your assumptions about future interest rate levels.

---

[9] Tim Ambler, *Marketing and the Bottom Line*, 2nd Edition, FT Press, 2004.

[10] The authors would extend "past marketing activities" to include all activities associated with a brand that impact the brand experience.

[11] Ibid.

Finally, it's important to understand that there are different types of brand value:

1. Trademark value. This refers to the legal protection afforded the owner of a trade name, trademark, logo, and so on.
2. Product/service brand value. This includes intellectual property rights such as product design, recipes, processes, channel rights, packaging, copyrights associated with descriptors and advertisements; and associated goodwill—specifically, confidence that the product/service will conform to expectations.
3. Corporate brand value. The legal rights above as they apply to the corporate brand plus the unique context (culture, values, people, programs) that differentiate and create value based on stakeholder confidence that the company brand will conform to expectations.

Brand equity is a subset of product/service brand value and corporate brand value. See Chapter 7 for a more detailed description of brand value and brand equity, and why they are different. Chapter 7 demonstrates that brand equity is a subset of overall brand value—and that brand equity is the part of brand value that is most powerful in creating a sustainable, differentiated advantage and, therefore, future cash flows.

Implications for Leadership and Management

One of the keys, therefore, to value creation, is to fully understand the relationship of values to value, and therefore, how the company operates to create, sub-optimize, or destroy brand equity as a financial asset.

The measures to use depend on the values in play, and their relationship to the creation of value. For example, if you're leading a high-tech or pharmaceutical company, innovation is most likely critical to your ability to create a sustainable, competitive advantage. Therefore, you need to understand the values of all stakeholders related to innovation (such as team player, creative, iconoclast, persistence, learning, and so on and the personal attributes associated with those values). You then need to make sure that the organization is hiring, training, supporting, and nurturing these values and traits and their associated performance.

Having a "map" of the relationships between values and value makes it easier to understand who needs to know what, when, and why. An explicit communications plan can be created that ensures that all participants understand their roles and attendant expectations. This goes from the boardroom to the call center.

By making the relationship between values and value explicit, you have a much better chance of discovering hidden misunderstandings, disagreements and other constraints. If your company has the proper culture and values, these should not remain hidden long.

The measures chosen will determine the way that behavior is reinforced, recognized and rewarded by the company, both internally with employees and associates; and externally with investors, analysts, customers, trade and channel partners and suppliers.

In the example of a high-tech company, outcomes may be measured in terms of patents issued, research citations, number of alpha sites, number of beta sites, and so forth, ultimately leading to some measure such as, "We want more than half of revenues (and at least 35 percent of our profits) to be derived from products that are less than five years old." Each product's brand, and their impact on the corporate brand's reputation, can combine to define that company's brand equity—and, therefore, the company's likelihood of achieving their long-term objectives.

These metrics could form a shorthand way of communicating diagnostics—a brand dashboard. Are these metrics precise, like financial metrics are, using specific dollar amounts? No, but multiple indicators of brand equity can be very valuable in measuring overall progress toward the ultimate objective. They can report on key indicators, like adding the right kind of profitable customers, loyalty behaviors, sources of competitive advantage, and pricing premiums. They can also apply a reasonable range of dollar values to the outcomes associated with these indicators. Company management would be well served to share as much of this dashboard with the market as is appropriate.

The benefits of becoming a company based on brand values are many:

- Your ability to create sustained, long-term earnings is enhanced by your brand's ability to create higher margins via premium prices, and/or higher volumes. This can fund new brand development and line extensions.
- Financial markets can operate to make the costs of borrowing lower (just like the bank at home—when they think you don't really need the money they're eager to lend it to you at low rates).
- Rising stock prices indicate to the community at large that you are an attractive place to work—thus enlarging your potential pool of qualified job applicants.

- Investors will want to be in on the action, putting further buy-side upward pressure on your stock price.
- Employees like seeing the admiring looks they get when they mention the corporate brand. That reduces employee churn, so your HR costs are contained.
- Channel and trade partners will want to benefit from the halo effect of being associated with your brand—and will negotiate deals accordingly.
- Ditto for suppliers.
- You'll find it easier to create mutually beneficial strategic partnerships with other companies.

Of course, the above effects tend to be cumulative. They work together to reduce risk, increasing the probability that you will realize the full potential of your brand equity while you continue to grow it. Brand equity truly is the gift that keeps on giving. The following sections further demonstrate this concept.

Mergers and Acquisitions

Mergers and acquisitions were the original reason for valuing brands. Now companies use brand equity metrics as an ongoing indicator of business performance.

Management (internal rates of return)

Brand equity is increasingly seen and used as a management tool in organizations to evaluate new product and market development opportunities, set business objectives, allocate budgets, help measure behaviors and performance, evaluate managers, and reward and recognize employees. Remember, however, that brand equity is a long-term measure.

Brand Architecture

Understanding the drivers of brand equity of current brands can inform proposed brand architecture strategies so that the brand portfolio is optimized.

Royalty Rates

There may be many affiliates, subsidiaries, or divisions that make use of a brand. Many companies charge royalties to their affiliated business operations for the use of these brand assets. This also has the effect of reducing tax costs.

Licensing and Franchising

When companies license or franchise their brand, brand equity valuation can be the basis for appropriate fees.

Tax Planning

Tax authorities worldwide have an interest in brands as financial assets. Global organizations plan the most cost-effective strategy on where to "house" their brands so as to minimize tax implications.

Securitized Borrowing

Banking has recognized the asset value of brands. As a result, brands are used to secure loans, especially in the United States, where some companies have borrowed significant amounts of money using their brand name as security (for example, Disney). In a twist on this practice, combined with aspects of royalty rates, Sears recently issued $1.8 billion in bonds collateralized by their Kenmore, Craftsman, and DieHard brands' value. It transferred ownership of the brands to another Sears entity, to whom it pays for the rights to use the brands. Should Sears ever decide to sell these brand bonds to outside investors, it will have succeeded in turning intangible assets—brands—into cash.

Litigation Support.

Brand value—especially the brand equity component—has been used as a basis for calculating damages in cases involving illegal use of a brand name. Brand value has also been used in bankruptcy cases to prevent the assets of the business from being undervalued.

Challenges

The challenge facing *companies* is that boards of directors "devote nine times more attention to spending and counting cash flow [related to operations, supplies and suppliers, corporate governance, financial matters, etc.] than wondering about where it comes from [the motivations of the ultimate consumer] and how it might be increased." Marketing is "about generating cash flow … if we started talking cash flow rather than marketing, then… industry would pay more attention."[12] Since brand strategy informs marketing strategy, the conversation will be even more powerful when we talk about

---

[12] Tim Ambler, *Marketing and the Bottom Line,* 2nd Edition, FT Press, 2004.

the creators of brand equity. Therefore, it may be more effective to talk about service flow rather than cash flow, since service flow, both inside the company among internal customers, and outside the company to external customers and other stakeholders, is what really delivers on the brand promise, and thus maintains and builds brand value. Service flow realizes the present value potential of the brand, and reinforces its future value. Cash flow is an expression of that value.

The challenge facing sell-side *analysts* and *institutional investors* is to not play the short-term earnings game, but to focus on true value creation.

The challenge facing *investors and companies* alike is to assure transparency and the full disclosure of brand equity metrics so that markets can efficiently allocate capital and other resources.

"I get it—this is like a self-fulfilling prophecy. Select the right vision, align the attributes and values of your company and product brands and stakeholders with the values of your chosen markets in a manner that profitably builds brand equity, and you've tilted the odds in your favor to achieve sustainable, competitive advantage in your industry—especially if your industry is in a sector favored by the investment community. Add in competent and transparent communications to the investment community and your reward should be higher P/E multiples and stock prices. Easy to say. Hard to do."
—Jack Eli, CEO, TasteRite

CHAPTER 5

VALUE CREATION/VALUE DESTRUCTION

"It's not hard to make decisions when you know what your values are."

—Roy Disney, Film Writer, Producer, Nephew of Walt Disney

"Executives will have to invest more and more on issues such as culture, values, ethos and intangibles. Instead of managers, they need to be cultivators and storytellers to capture minds."

—Leif Edvinsson, pioneer on Intellectual Capital,
in *Corporate Longitude,* 2002

"If I can hone in on what values and related activities are creating value, and what are destroying value, I can effectively figure out my company's problems and focus on what to change, and how to change it."

—Jack Eli, CEO, TasteRite

What Is Value?[1]

The very definition of what "value" is cries out to be put into better focus. For example, the *American Heritage® Dictionary* features ten different definitions of what that word means in noun form. The first three definitions deal with economic value:

1. An amount, as of goods, services, or money, considered to be a fair and suitable equivalent for something else; a fair price or return.
2. Monetary or material worth: the fluctuating value of gold and silver.
3. Worth in usefulness or importance to the possessor; utility or merit: the value of an education.[2]

The word value, ironically, has been so overused as to have lost much of its meaning, and, therefore, its value. Whenever a salesperson uses the word value in a presentation, the buyer automatically goes on "snooze control,"

---

[1] This also prompts the question "What are values?" and how do "value" and "values" differ? Where "value" generally suggests economic worth, "values" are the beliefs, ideals, and principles of individuals and organizations, formally and/or informally stated.

[2] *American Heritage® Dictionary of the English Language,* Houghton Mifflin, Fourth Edition, 2000.

making a bet to themselves about how long it will take for the phrases "value added," or "great value," and so on, to rear their overused heads.

In the early 1990s, during an economic downturn, many companies were touting "value pricing" and "value deals," which were euphemisms for "cheap." They were simply dropping their prices to encourage consumers to purchase.

Value, as used currently, has been trivialized. It represents an old way of looking at customers that dates back to the industrial age.

We need a better definition of value. Neil Rackham, in his book *Rethinking the Sales Force,* uses this definition for value:

"Value equals benefits minus cost."[3]

What's interesting about this definition is that it suggests three ways of increasing value: (1) increase the perceived benefits, (2) reduce the perceived costs, or (3) a combination of the first two. What's also of great interest about these three methods is that they can be fine-tuned to reflect ways in which customers prefer to have value created, as we discuss in considerable detail in Chapter 7.

Some customers see the product as a commodity with the world as a fixed pie—they want transaction and other costs reduced so that they enjoy a larger share of the revenues available from that pie. To them, business is largely a win-lose, zero-sum game.

Other customers see the product as just one factor among many in how value is created. They want their suppliers to work with them to help them create a stronger value chain associated with that product category so that they can derive greater benefits from their relationship with their suppliers. They see the world as a win-win game.

Still other customers view the product supplier as a source of expertise with complementary and valuable competences to be combined with their own competences creating network effects, often centered on innovation, with new opportunities emerging that benefit all parties. They see new worlds.

It's good to keep in mind that customers represent diverse ways of relating to the world around them, and that this is often *not* directly related to the size of customers' accounts. In fact, the relationship between account size, profitability, and customer profile has become increasingly murky. Large accounts can often be demanding and unprofitable, and can fall in any one of the three categories.

---

[3] Neil Rackham, John DeVincentis, *Rethinking the Sales Force*, McGraw-Hill, 1999.

The concept of *choosing your customer* is of primary strategic importance, which then begs the question, "On what basis do you make that choice?"

Customers, Employees, Value

If you are an executive in an enterprise, it must be comforting to know that as you read this book your enterprise is creating value, just as it must be discomforting to know that as you read this book your enterprise is also destroying value.

How can that be? How can two diametrically opposed actions be occurring at the same time—and depending on the size of your enterprise, happening dozens, hundreds, thousands, even millions of times per day? Here's how: Let's start with prospects and customers. Figure 5.1 shows how a typical—albeit simplified—relationship between a prospect and a company may look.

Each "smiley" face is a customer/company interaction that has gone well. In other words, the prospect or customer has had their expectations about the product and/or service experience (the "purpose" of the place) met or exceeded. So, at the bottom left side of the graph is the first smiley face. This first smiley face indicates that the prospect has decided to become a new customer, has had their first interaction with the company, and the interaction has been successful.

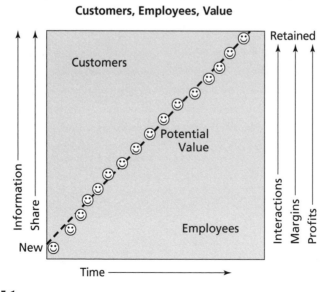

Figure 5.1

At this point the company probably doesn't know all that much about their new customer. Their share of business of that customer, especially when viewed in terms of customer lifetime revenue (CLR),[4] is just starting out. Share of CLR will grow, over time, as the customer repeats purchases of goods and services and continues to find their expectations of value met or exceeded. And, in the case of some product/service categories, the customer may also increase the volume of products and services purchased on each purchase occasion, further accelerating revenues and CLR creation.

Over time, the company will learn more about the customer's likes and dislikes, beliefs and values, how they prefer to do business, and, based on all of that, what they consider value to be. This will help the company to understand what sub-segments the customer may prefer to be placed in. Also, the customer will learn more about the company, and that may lead them to increase their purchase volume, purchase occasions, or length of time they do business with the company.

To keep this example relatively simple, let's assume that the customer continues to do business with the company on an "as is" basis, described by a relatively straight line, and doesn't become more or less demanding over time. Under this scenario, the company can expect that customer to represent ever-growing margins and profits as described by the "potential value" line. Why? Because the "sunk" costs of acquiring that customer are being absorbed over time, and the longer the customer does business with the company, the less the acquisition costs are as a percent of the customer's revenues. So higher customer loyalty results in lower costs per unit sold, over time.

In addition, by keeping that customer, the company won't have to invest as much as they otherwise may have in acquiring other customers to replace those that are lost due to "churn." Depending on the industry, buying cycle, and many other factors, the ratio of cost to *win a new customer* versus *retaining a current customer* varies from 2:1 to 20:1. Studies done by Fred Reichheld of Bain and Company and Earl Sasser of Harvard's Business School indicate that a 5 percent increase in loyalty can result in a 100 percent increase in profitability.[5]

---

[4] Customer Lifetime Revenue (CLR) is defined as the period of time that the customer will be purchasing the goods and/or services, and the amount of goods or services purchased per occasion over time. For example, if consumer 'A' buys a car in the $35K range every 2 years, and will buy cars for 50 years, the CLR will be $35K × 25 = $875,000 plus revenues from service and other ancillary sales, as well as revenues from referrals. If consumer 'A' does business with Dealer 'A' for all of those years, then dealer 'A' can be said to have 100 percent of that consumer's CLR.

[5] Frederick F. Reichheld, *The Loyalty Effect: The Hidden Force Behind Growth, Profits and Lasting Value*, Harvard Business School Press, 1996.

As mentioned previously, the other benefit of keeping a customer over time is that you learn more and more about them: Specifically, what their values are, and based on those values what they need and want, what they consider value to be, and how they prefer to buy. This insight enables you to become smarter about anticipating and meeting their needs, and crafting your brand promise so as to increase your brand's differentiation and relevance. So customer loyalty not only drives costs down; it also helps you drive revenues up through better products, services, new products, and better marketing—you enjoy a larger percentage of that customer's purchase volume at any given point in time, as well as over the "lifetime" of the customer. Customer Lifetime Value (CLV) represents CLR less the costs of acquiring and keeping that customer, expressed as CLR − Costs = CLV.

Also, the customer represented in this example was so delighted with your company's products and services that they told lots of other people. They spoke of your company's brand and its attributes in glowing terms, describing to friends, family, and associates how smart they are to do business with your brand. They expressed their commitment to your brand.

The line of smiley customer faces in Figure 5.1 describes the *potential* CLV of a well-executed customer relationship. If all your customer relationships were this well executed, your company would likely be very profitable. This graph describes an ideal situation of value creation. It describes the full potential value of a customer to your company. If you were to multiply this figure by the number of customers you have, and hope to have, this will give you a mark to put on the wall—something to strive for. Imagine if you achieved that kind of performance!

Many executives when they see this graph remark, "It's easy to have lots of smiley faces like that; just drop your price below competition." However, these examples are predicated on the assumption that the prices charged for the goods and services provided are at least comparable to the industry average. So what creates these smiley faces is not a lower price (unless of course, you're Wal-Mart, and lower prices are your brand's promise) but something else.

That something else is what we referenced in Chapter 3. To attract prospects to try the brand's products and services, the tangible and intangible attributes of the corporate, product, and service brands resonate with the values of the prospect in a way that elicits trial. During trial, the prospect finds that the experience satisfies their expectations; the brand promise is appropriate and met. Meaning is being provided. Values and value have converged. When that takes place consistently over time, loyal and committed customers, more trial, accelerated revenue growth, lowered costs, and enhanced profitability are the outcomes. Value is created.

What is it like to work for a company with loyal and committed customers? The company meets customers' expectations by creating products and services that meet or exceed customer-based performance standards. The brand promise is the performance standard, and the brand acts as a quality assurance device. All employees understand the brand promise, and the attributes—both tangible and intangible—that create and support that promise. They understand the relationship between their job performance and the ability of the company to deliver the brand promise. Their values are consonant with the company's values; they embrace them as their own. They take responsibility for the customer's experience and loyalty.

Their performance and personal improvement plans reflect their desire to become ever better at delivering on the brand promise. Employees are recognized, rewarded, and compensated for behavior that achieves loyal customers. Advancement and economic well-being in a company like this are above average when compared to other companies in their industry. They are proud to tell their family and friends where they work.

Companies with loyal customers tend to have loyal employees, and vice versa.[6,7] Lower employee turnover or "churn" has several benefits to the company. Apart from the customer-related benefits, loyal employees strengthen the culture of the firm. They represent the firm well when dealing with suppliers and partnering firms. They communicate clearly the values of the firm, and the intent of the firm's corporate, product, and service brands—which helps the supplier and partnering firms to cooperate and work more effectively to improve productivity and better deliver on the brand promise.

According to a survey of 170 human resource professionals conducted by Human Capital Institute and industry researcher Aberdeen Group, the average cost of replacing staff, measured in terms of disruptions in customer service, production, and direct HR costs, was $13,295. Employees at the executive level, according to Aberdeen, cost $80,515 to replace. So, for a 1,000-employee company, 10 percent turnover could cost $1.3 million annually—which may represent a significant reduction in profitability.[8] This is one example of the financial benefits of employee loyalty.

---

[6] Ibid.

[7] Leigh Branham, *The 7 Hidden Reasons Employees Leave*, AMACOM, 2005.

[8] Rideau Recognition Solutions, Inc., *New Research Shows Link Between Recognition and Retention*, press release, February 10, 2006.

Firms with loyal employees tend to be singled out by the media for positive recognition about their employment and company practices. This positive press further builds brand equity.

So loyal employees are good for the bottom line and for the future worth of the company. Value is created.

When investors see the enhanced free cash flow that often results from this scenario, and compare it to the performance of competitors, they tend to look at the value of the company as being in the ascension over the long term, and buy the stock in anticipation of future capital appreciation and dividend growth. They view the brand and its attributes and values as part of an invisible network that confers competitive advantage. Stock market value is created. We have described a virtuous cycle.

For many businesses, however, their reality is far different from the example in Figure 5.1. For these companies, who we may call "underachievers," their reality is shown in Figure 5.2, where things have not gone as well.

The customer/company relationship started off in good fashion—the first two interactions went fine. Then, something went wrong. Perhaps the shipping department mailed it on the "ship" date, but it did not arrive on the delivery date the customer was expecting. Or perhaps the cashier rang it up incorrectly. Or perhaps the color or model was wrong. Or perhaps

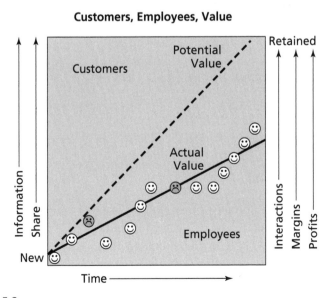

Figure 5.2

the order was incomplete. Or perhaps it was any one of the hundreds of other things that can and do go wrong in company/customer interactions. The customer's expectations were not met, hence the "sad" face.

The good news, though, is that the company's customer-facing employees really came through. The customer service person promptly followed up, found out why the customer was disappointed, and quickly remedied the situation. So, the company, rather than losing a customer and absorbing the expenses invested in initially acquiring that customer, received another chance. The customer was impressed by their problem resolution process, and by the enthusiasm and caring attitude of the customer service employee, and bought from them again, perhaps—*just to make sure things were right*—at a reduced volume.

And things went along just fine for several more purchases, and the customer eventually increased order quantities back to the previous level, until, again, something went wrong. Perhaps this time it was an invoice that was incorrect, or another "short shipment," or defective product, or poor quality control on a service call, or any one of the dozens of things that can and do go wrong. The customer's expectations were once again not met, hence another "sad" face.

But customer service again rode to the rescue. And the district sales manager spoke with the customer, and the engineering manager spoke with the customer, and after much hand-holding and expressions of regret, and sincere apologies, (and perhaps a discount or rebate) the customer continued to buy, albeit at a reduced volume.

By the end of the same period of time as shown in Figure 5.1, the customer in Figure 5.2 had created an actual value that was well below the Figure 5.1 example. The difference between the potential customer value of Figure 5.1 and the actual customer value of Figure 5.2 is a "value gap," as shown in Figure 5.3.

This value gap, or opportunity cost, may be viewed as unrealized value.

In those cases where company and employee performance has degraded over time, resulting in customer defections and lower CLV levels, value has been destroyed compared to prior performance.

What are the implications of Figure 5.3?

For customers, the implication is that the brand promise was only conditionally or sporadically met, interspersed with periods of pain and disappointment. This may have muted customers' desire to recommend the company to friends, family, and associates—thus depressing referrals and raising customer acquisition costs. This destroys value.

Customers, Employees, Value

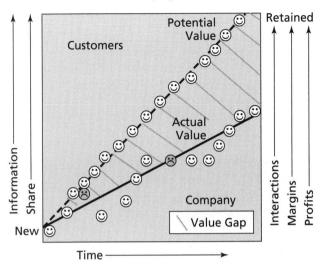

Figure 5.3

Also, each "sad" face may have led the customer to try a competitor's product or service. And that increased the risk of the customer defecting, and the company losing their business entirely. It also increased the probability of the competitor learning something of interest about an operational vulnerability of the company.

It also means that the company will have to recoup their costs of acquiring this customer over a smaller CLR base. Therefore, their margins and profits are degraded, compared to Figure 5.1. Value is destroyed.

If the customer were to defect to a competitor, then the company would have to replace that customer's business and incur the acquisition costs. They would also lose their acquired insight into the current customer, and have to start over with a new customer. This will negatively impact productivity. If their customer "churn" rate is relatively high for their industry, they will find their costs rapidly getting out of line, degrading their ability to compete—thus destroying value.

For employees, it's not much fun working in this company. The pressure to uncover mistakes and do triage with customers is wearing. Hearing customers complain because they've been disappointed or feel let down gets old fast. Because margins are tight, and profits thin, training, recognition, compensation, and opportunities for promotion via growth are not readily available.

Conversations with other employees tend to dwell on what's wrong rather than on what's right. Underlying these conversations is a feeling that the company's brand promise is hollow, and that the values espoused by the brand are false. The employees feel demotivated. Ennui and negativism take hold. Black or gallows humor increases, with management being the butt of most of the stories.

Being an employee of this company makes it tough to talk about work to family, friends, and associates. As an employee, you wouldn't recommend this company to anyone else as a place to work. The company's recruitment costs rise. Their conversion rate of qualified resumes to hired employees degrades. They don't know why. More value is destroyed as HR costs rise.

Absenteeism, sick days, shrinkage and in extreme cases, outright sabotage, increases. Employees become increasingly cynical. As their jobs lose meaning, employee churn and turnover rise. Often, the best, brightest, and most employable are the first to leave. More value creation potential is destroyed.

It's expensive to replace qualified, experienced employees—especially when they have ongoing relationships in place with customers, and you lose all of their accumulated unwritten knowledge. Hiring costs, training costs, support costs, lost production, lost productivity, and administrative costs all conspire to weaken margins and profits. Research by Sibson & Company estimates that employee turnover in the high-tech field averages 25 percent annually and costs the industry $44 billion. That's a lot of value destroyed.

Suppliers and partnering organizations quickly pick up on the bad vibes. Their perception of risk increases, and they become nervous about the impact on their brand of being associated with your brand, and even about getting paid. The word spreads throughout the communities in which the company is located.

For a public company, investors see the weakening cash flow position of the company, and confidence in the company's future drops. Revenue and growth targets are routinely revised downwards. Perceptions of risk rise. They sell their shares. The company's share price falls, destroying stock market value. The cost of borrowing for the company goes up, thus further weakening their ability to compete. More value is destroyed.

For a private company, succession and exit strategies (if they formally exist) are thrown into disarray with the loss of key executives. Degradation of P&L performance seriously sets back timetables for selling the firm. Ability to borrow at the most attractive rates may be lessened due to negative "scuttlebutt" in the community. Private investors may find that their investment is in jeopardy. For a family-owned and run enterprise, this is when family-related issues of sibling rivalry, jealousy, envy, and so on often rise to the surface and reveal themselves.

For non-profits, it becomes more difficult to attract and keep donors; volunteers give less of their time; professional employees leave or are difficult to recruit—the ability of the organization to fulfill its mission becomes compromised.

We have described a negative cycle.

What are the key differences between the scenarios of Figure 5.1 and Figure 5.2? What are the factors underlying the two situations? How do we change value destroyers into value creators—or, even better, avoid value destroyers?

Keys to Employ Value Creators and Avoid Value Destroyers

To appreciate the key differences between the scenarios of Figures 5.1 and 5.2, and to avoid the value gap in Figure 5.3, let's look at what factors fundamentally set the stage for value creation and value destruction.

In their landmark book, *The Discipline of Market Leaders: Choose Your Customers, Narrow Your Focus, Dominate Your Market*, authors Michael Treacy and Fred Wiersema explore what it takes for a company to create a dominant value proposition that leads to the position of market leader. Their book asks, "Why is it that some companies endear themselves to us while others just don't seem to know how to please?"[9]

The authors conclude that the answer lies in the way that companies relate to their served markets—the most successful companies don't try to be all things to all people. The most successful companies get to understand the values that their customers value most, and hone their ability to deliver those values with excellence. These companies focus on the values and needs of the served market, on their customers' expectations, rather than predominately on the benefits of their product or service offerings. This is a market-driven approach.

As the title of the book indicates, this involves making choices. Which customers? What strategic focus? Which delivery system?

Part of the appeal of this approach is that it simplifies everything. Whether you're an entrepreneurial start-up serving one market segment or a huge multinational conglomerate, this is a template you can apply to the markets served by each business unit.

---

[9] Michael Treacy and Fred Wiersema, *The Discipline of Market Leaders: Choose Your Customers, Narrow Your Focus, Dominate Your Market*, BASIC BOOKS, a member of Perseus Books Group, 1995.

Discipline of Market Leaders Model

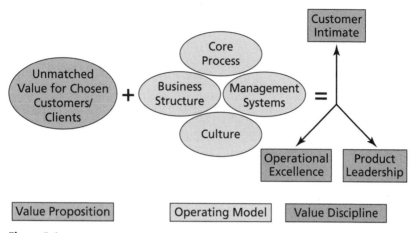

Figure 5.4
From Discipline of Market Leaders by Michael Treacy. Reprinted by permission of BASIC BOOKS, a member of Perseus Books Group.

The overall model used by Treacy and Wiersema looks like that shown in Figure 5.4.[10]

The first step is to use market research to fully understand what "unmatched value for chosen customers" really means—what the "value proposition" is based upon. This understanding and insight, which we extensively address in Chapter 7, helps the company determine the best operating model with which to deliver that value. The operating model consists of core processes, business structure, management system, and culture. This yields the appropriate value discipline for that served market.

Part of the preparation for the creation of this model is to answer the questions posed in Figure 5.5. Where is your company in terms of currently delivering on specific components of value? How does your value discipline compare to your competitors? Where are your potential customers in terms of values desired? What are the implications in terms of volume, price, and margins? And, therefore, which discipline can you most beneficially deliver on?

After examining many companies, and the reasons underlying their success, the authors concluded that having a value discipline (not trying to be all

---

[10] Ibid.

Value Discipline

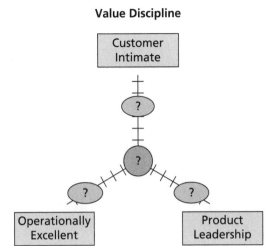

• Where are you?
• Where are your competitors?
• Where are your potential customers?

Figure 5.5[11]
From Discipline of Market Leaders by Michael Treacy. Reprinted by permission of BASIC BOOKS,
a member of Perseus Books Group.

things to all people) is a key determinant of success, and a key driver of value creation. The authors take care to point out that *every company needs threshold levels of all three disciplines,* but it is the decision as to which one will be *emphasized* that leads to the most effective value creation. Once that decision is made, then the company focuses on improving their value proposition, year after year after year, by continuously fine-tuning their value-operating model.

Each value discipline has a specific set of attributes associated with it. For example, **operational excellence** focuses on providing low prices with outstanding supply-chain management and logistics. Value is created by delivering basic performance for the category—the table stakes—at a very good price.

So, when Wal-Mart advertises "Everyday Low Prices," they mean it. And they mean to have the item in stock, in sufficient quantities to meet demand. Their strategy is to work with their suppliers to continuously improve the

---

[11] Ibid.

"OE" Attributes

The culture is based on conformance, is process focused, and is highly disciplined. The organizational structure tends toward centralized functions with high skill levels at the core of the organization. Core processes are designed to ensure dependable product availability and delivery, with a basic service offering—standardized, fixed assets are employed. Management systems tend toward command and control, with compensation schemes based on cost and quality per transaction. Information technologies would be integrated, low-cost transaction systems based on mobile and remote technologies that drive information and decision making toward the centralized functions.

performance of all players in the supply chain. The commitment to central control is so complete that the temperature of every store in the Wal-Mart system is controlled from the Arkansas headquarters.

"By focusing constantly on trying to become more operationally efficient, Wal-Mart sets itself apart from its competitors," writes Michael Bergdahl, author of *What I learned from Sam Walton: How to Compete and Thrive in a Wal-Mart World*.[12]

Now, imagine that you've read a Wal-Mart ad and go to their local store to pick up the advertised product. Now imagine that the store is out of the product. Has Wal-Mart created or destroyed value in your mind's eye? Well, if they give you a rain check on the item, and a couple of savings coupons, they might repair the damage. But, if this were to happen with any frequency, they would not be delivering on their brand promise, they would not be meeting your expectations, and they would be destroying their brand's value in your case.

Wal-Mart's three pricing policies—everyday low prices, price rollbacks, and special purchases—all clearly support Wal-Mart's operationally excellent model.

The key question is whether the Wal-Mart model is sustainable over the long term. Communities are resisting efforts to open Wal-Marts in their areas, fearing the impact on local businesses, on the local economy, and on

---

[12] Michael Bergdahl, *What I Learned From Sam Walton: How to Compete and Thrive in a Wal-Mart World*, John Wiley & Sons, Inc., 2004.

the fabric of the community. Wal-Mart's labor problems are well known. However, their price advantage due to their superior operations is without question, and they enjoy healthy margins for a discounter. Since one of their core values is honesty, they should be able to respond intelligently to their critics. If they can do that, their future looks extremely bright. If they can't, and violate their core value of honesty, they will have created a values disconnect between their values and how they create value. This brand dissonance will end up destroying value.

Product Leadership focuses on driving innovation; being your own fiercest competitor while aggressively managing the product/service lifecycle via inspired marketing.

High-tech companies are often adapters of this model. In fact, companies like Intel, Microsoft, and Cisco have raised this discipline to a fine art. One of the unique challenges of the high-tech sector is that firms operating in this sector must innovate internally to succeed. Yet, true success may also be heavily dependent on the ability of other outside firms to supply complementary innovation.

The leaders in product leadership in the high-tech sector have adapted a corollary strategy called Platform Leadership, defined as "companies that provide the technological foundation on which other products, services, and

---

"P/L" Attributes

Here individual talent and creativity is a core competence, with the culture based on conceptualization and trend spotting, the willingness to experiment, and an aggressive "winner take all" mind-set. The organizational structure is based on a more loosely constructed "team" approach, with highly skilled people found in the outlying business unit structures. Core processes are designed to support invention and commercialization; and to exploit discrete market opportunities. Management systems tend to reward individual innovation contributions, and product profitability. Information technology supports collaboration and person-to-person communications, enabling cooperation, knowledge management, and rapid market development and penetration.

systems are built. Interdependency and innovation are the hallmarks of these companies."[13]

Thus, although high-tech companies want to "own" the platform on which their technology rests, they often find out that they are highly dependent on other companies supplying technology "modules" that help create value for all the platform's players. Their future value is intimately involved in the fortunes of these other companies, or places. Successful players understand the value of cooperation, alliances, networks, sharing, skillful yet fair negotiation and compromise.

An excellent example of this value discipline at work was reflected in the October 20, 2005, meeting of 300 top managers of Intel. New CEO Paul S. Otellini challenged Intel to play a key role in several fields, including consumer electronics, wireless communications, and health care. In addition to just microprocessors, he challenged the organization to create all kinds of chips, as well as software, and meld them together to create "platforms." "This is the right thing for our company, and to some extent the industry," he added. "All of us want [technology] to be more powerful and to be simpler, to do stuff for us without us having to think about it."[14]

Otellini is making big changes in the way products are developed. In the past engineers worked on ever-faster chips and then let marketers sell them. Now, teams of people with a cross-section of skills—chip engineers, software developers, marketers, and market specialists—all work together to come up with compelling products.[15]

An example of this new approach is a doctor who practiced internal medicine for 15 years, and joined Intel to develop technologies for digital health. He works with Intel's ethnographers to figure out which technologies might help in monitoring the vital signs of the elderly or track the diets of people with Alzheimer's.[16] This is typical of the atypical new employees being hired into Intel.

Industries could be turned upside down, and be forced to rethink their business models. The ultimate goal: to provide the manufacturers of everything from laptops and entertainment PCs to cell phones and hospital gear with complete packages of chips and software—to provide the platform and to drive the platform into end-user markets.

[13] Annabelle Gawer and Michael A. Cusumano, *Platform Leadership: How Intel, Microsoft and Cisco Drive Industry Innovation*, Harvard Business School Publishing, 2002.

[14] BusinessWeek Online, *Inside Intel*, The McGraw-Hill Companies, Inc, 2002–2006.

[15] Ibid.

[16] Ibid.

"CI" Attributes

The culture is client and field driven with a "we'll make the solution fit you" approach. The organizational structure is based on highly entrepreneurial client teams that feature in-depth knowledge about the client's needs and the elements of the solutions. Application engineering is often a core competence of customer intimate firms. Core processes are client development, solutions development, and flexible and responsive systems. Management systems tend to reward client success in terms of growth in revenues/billings with exclusive client engagements the optimum situation. Client feedback is important. Information technology supports the linking of databases; often consolidated to maximize the value of knowledge built around client experiences and company expertise.

The lesson to be learned here is that all players prosper or perish as the platform on which they depend for mutual benefit flourishes or shrivels.

This is creating some dissatisfaction among some of the Intel engineers. High-level desktop PC chip design engineers, in particular, were always the "stars" of Intel. So, some engineers have defected to join rivals, like Texas Instruments. While this has destroyed some value in the short term, Intel's profits remain healthy, and the new initiatives have the potential to create tremendous value in the longer term.

If Otellini's ideas of driving the platform succeed, entire industries could be transformed.

Perhaps Andy Grove, Intel's founder, expressed it best when he said, "this program strikes me as one of the best manifestations incorporating Intel values of risk-taking, discipline, and results orientation that I have ever seen here."[17]

And that's precisely the point. Value disciplines must be grounded in the values of the company's customers, employees, and channels. It is counterproductive to select a value discipline that is not fundamentally based on the values of the key stakeholders in the company and its supply and distribution chain when there is the potential for value creation.

---

[17] Ibid.

Customer intimacy focuses on creating total solutions for customers, sharing the risk with the customer, and understanding your customers' customers.

Many engineering, architectural, systems developer, and other consulting firms are "customer intimate." More and more firms are considering a customer intimate value discipline as it becomes increasingly difficult to execute an operationally driven or product leadership strategy in a way that can sustain a differentiated competitive advantage. However, depending on a variety of factors, the decision to migrate toward a customer intimate strategy may be ill-advised.

A customer intimate value discipline is not to be entered into lightly, and it's not for everyone. The costs of maintaining a customer intimate value discipline are substantial, and require large investments in highly qualified people, ongoing training in the customers' served markets, a tracking process to continuously monitor how you're doing in the customers' minds, and the capability to "investment spend" on certain accounts before there is a commensurate return. Plus, there's high risk when you offer to share the risk with the customer, or provide service outcomes that are guaranteed.

Plus, there are certain types of customers who want a no-frills, strip-away-all-extra-costs approach. These customers would reject a customer intimate or product leadership approach. They prefer an operationally excellent value discipline based on their vendors being the lowest-cost provider.

A customer intimate approach, however, even given its potential liabilities, can often be an effective way of creating a sustained, differentiated, competitive advantage, unparalleled value, and very high customer loyalty. An example of this is a company that one of the authors worked with as a consultant.[18]

The client: an engineering company that provides plasma torch products to the steel industry. A plasma torch creates high temperatures used to maintain molten steel's flow within the tundish (the refractory where the molten steel pools prior to being poured into castings). The client was focused on designing, installing, and maintaining the best possible plasma torches. They were a product leader in their field.

Research among steel industry end-users revealed that although they valued good performance on the part of the plasma torches, what they valued most highly was a way to ensure product quality downstream to their customers.

---

[18] This reflects a market research and strategic planning process conducted for this client. Certain information has been modified to protect client confidentiality.

That led us to help the client view themselves not as a product leadership company but as a customer intimate company. Instead of stressing their product's specifications and features, they would change their approach to offer consulting services focused on quality control. Instead of selling the plasma torches to the steel companies, and having to get capital expenditures approved at the customer's board level (a time-consuming, limited "window of opportunity" process), our client offered the plasma torches as part of a service offering—and took responsibility for the operation of the torches in their customer's plant. This made the plant operations people the approval point, since they were now paying for an ongoing service—and could pay for that service out of their operating budget—a budget they controlled at the local level.

Our client also developed a database knowledge offering that gave their customers information on the relationship between the operation of the plasma torches and the quality of the steel produced in every batch. Our client also offered their customers a knowledge-driven quality control service based on contacting their downstream customers about the quality of product they received from the steel plant. This feedback was vital to continuously improve the operation of the plasma torches and, by extension, the quality of the delivered product. This, in turn, reduced product returns, and other value destroying behaviors, while increasing our client's customers' loyalty and share of customer.

The implications of the change of focus were profound. Our client's employees were no longer engineers focused on building the best plasma torches. That was necessary, but not sufficient. They were now engineering consultants focused on helping their client achieve desired levels of quality throughout their downstream customers' distribution chains.

Their steel plant customers were no longer focused on the details of the plasma torch product and installation. That was now, properly, the responsibility of our client's engineering department. Change orders and revisions became a thing of the past. Their steel plant customers were now focused on the value of the service.

Best of all, by creating a knowledge database specific to their served customers and their customer's downstream customers, our client succeeded in building a service offering with tremendous value. The first source of value was the value of the information provided and its role in supporting quality assurance levels. Second, by getting "first mover" advantage in offering this service, our client clearly differentiated themselves from all other engineering companies trying to sell plasma torches. Third, the number of data points and the value of the information in the database increases over time and use, thus creating a barrier to competition, and conferring a competitive advantage. Fourth, as our client's personnel got increasingly skilled in providing this service and applying the information in the database, they created further competence-based advantages for their company and additional barriers to competitors.

By adapting a customer intimate value discipline, our client successfully aligned their values more powerfully with the values of their customer, and their customer's customers. What were the values at work here that determined the success of this outcome?

Interviews with employees of our client revealed a high level of frustration with the sales and product installation process. The root causes of this frustration pointed to a misalignment between what our client's personnel were focused on (product design and installation) versus what their customer's personnel were focused on (creating a steel product that met or exceeded quality levels regardless of volume being produced). The key finding was that their steel plant customers were focused on quality because that was their key to profitability. Besides, many of the steel plant workers were former farmers, and took pride in producing a quality product—one that met their downstream customers' requirements.

Those same interviews with our client's employees revealed a high level of frustration with the product design and installation process. Although everyone believed in quality, no one could define what quality was once the steel was poured—until, of course, it came back as a product return. Quality was subsequently defined by a number of attributes associated with the plasma torches' ability to reduce inclusion and porosity levels in the steel while creating a more uniform microstructure. Inclusions are often a source of weakness in the finished material. Feedback from our client's customers and their downstream customers "closed the loop" on our client's customers' improved ability to deliver steel that moved ever closer to their customers' specs.

Other client-employee shared values were "integrity," "excellence," "entrepreneurial spirit" and "team player." These last two values may seem at odds with each other—but they can coexist quite nicely within most organizations. These client employees' values were reflected in the client intimate value discipline and operating model that was adopted by this company. We didn't have to create them from scratch, even if we could. They were already there, waiting to be "set free." And once they were set free, they positively impacted brand equity and enterprise value.

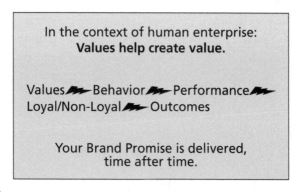

In the context of human enterprise:
Values help create value.

Values➤➤Behavior➤➤Performance➤➤
Loyal/Non-Loyal➤➤Outcomes

Your Brand Promise is delivered,
time after time.

Figure 5.6

How Do Values Work to Create Value?

Figure 5.6 is a graphic representation of looking at the role of values in creating value.

If we look at values as being ideals, principles, and beliefs, then we can see how the values we have accumulated through exposure from family, school, community, and so on shape our view of the world around us. Do we think out every behavior that we engage in? No one has the time or energy to do that. We use our accumulated store of values, almost automatically, to guide us in our decision making. *Should* we do this? *How* should we do this?

If a behavior is in alignment with our values then we don't need to give it much thought. If a behavior is not in alignment with our values, then we need to think long and hard about the implications of engaging in that behavior. When we behave in a way that is inconsistent with our values, we are said to be in conflict and in distress. Most people try to avoid distress and conflict. Unless, of course, the distress and conflict are in alignment with the engagement of one or more of their values, like freedom is in the case of soldiers.

When we behave in a way that is consistent with our values, we usually perform well. When we perform well, we feel good about ourselves and about those around us. For example, if one of my values was "perfection," and I gave a piano recital (performance) that was without error, I would probably feel rather good about myself—as well as feel good about all the time I had spent practicing (behavior). If, on the other hand, the performance was full of errors, I would feel terrible. And would not be fun to be around.

The same thing happens in an organizational setting. When people behave and perform in a manner consistent with their values, they have good morale, all things being equal. Conversely, when people are in an environment where they behave and perform in a manner that's inconsistent with their values, they often experience low morale, and other destructive behaviors and attitudes, or they totally disengage from what they are doing.[19]

The organization's mission and brand form the basis for the "fit" between the person's values and their ability to behave and perform in a manner consistent with those values. When this happens correctly, the employee feels good about their job, and satisfied with their employer. When this doesn't happen, the employee may not feel competent, suffer from low morale, and may seek employment elsewhere—creating HR churn and value destruction. Employees with low morale often provide unsatisfactory service to customers—leading to customer churn and value destruction as described earlier in this chapter.

One of the keys to the success of the plasma torch company's program was the ability of company leadership to use the new brand promise as a way to inculcate a customer intimate value discipline throughout the organization in a way that resonated with each part of the organization. This encouraged each part of the organization to define the implications of the value discipline in terms of how it would impact core processes, business structure and all the important and not-so-important roles, rules, and regulations that often govern company life—also known as "how we do things around here."

This is a critically important step because when it's properly done, it enables the company to show one unified face to the world, as shown in Figure 5.7.

Normative values are those values that society at large has generally accepted. Certainly, in most companies it is reasonable to assume that all the employees believe in the sanctity of human life.[20]

Core values are those that are reflected in the company's vision, mission, and brand. These are values that everyone throughout the company are expected to understand and embrace. However, the devil is in the details. What do these values really mean when brought down to the individual departmental or "silo" level? Here's where most corporate initiatives to establish a value discipline run into the "That's not how we do things around here" barrier, and lose momentum.[21]

The antidote is to ask the sub-organizational units to take the proposed value discipline and answer the question "How do we fit in?" so that everyone in the sub-organizational unit understands what the value discipline *means* to

---

[19] Leigh Branham, *The 7 Hidden Reasons Employees Leave*, AMACOM, 2005.

[20] James G. Bleech, Dr. David B. Mutchler, *Let's Get Results, Not Excuses: A No-Nonsense Approach to Increasing Productivity, Performance and Profit*, Lifetime Books, Inc., 1996.

[21] Ibid.

Values Hierarchy

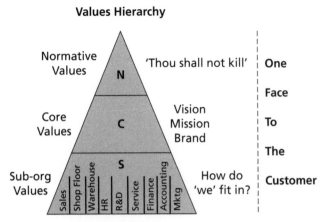

Figure 5.7
Source: Adapted from James G. Bleech, Dr. David B. Mutchler, *Let's Get Results, Not Excuses: A No-Nonsense Approach to Increasing Productivity, Performance and Profit,* Lifetime Books, Inc., 1996.

them, and how it will align values to create better outcomes. This inquiry will raise many questions about "How we do things around here." And it will result in the answer to that question being changed as the organization adapts to the new reality.[22]

In our example of the plasma torch company, the sales department had to switch gears from being focused on selling a product to their customer's board, to adapting a consultative selling approach geared to plant operations management.

The shop floor could stop worrying about building a product to customer specs, and focus on building it to meet operational requirements.

HR would have to change the profile of many positions, focusing on those people with the values and skills to support a consultative sales approach, and a field-driven mentality. Compensation, training, and recognition practices will be revised to reward the new values-based behaviors and performance.

R&D would switch focus from improving the product, to integrating the database and platform.

Service would be less concerned about being a P&L, and more concerned about providing system uptime.

Finance would switch gears from product sales financing, to the benefits of owning the product themselves and depreciating it, as well as exploring other financing possibilities—and the implications for return on assets.

Accounting and IT would be focused on the creation of the database, and how to charge for ongoing services.

---

[22] Ibid.

Marketing would look at potential customer profiles and migrate toward those that showed a proclivity for outsourcing; while switching the focus of brand building from product sales to service provision.

These changes add vitality and life to the employees' values of integrity, excellence, entrepreneurial spirit, and team orientation.

These obvious—and the many not-so-obvious—changes required at the sub-organizational level would be the real proof that the value discipline had been accepted, internalized, and was being actively supported. And only when that had been accomplished would the company actively deliver on its brand promise in a manner that creates value.

Continuous Quality Improvement and Value Creation

It's a bit ironic that our example of the plasma torch company is based on an example in which their service offering is a system to continuously monitor and improve quality. Ironic, because that is precisely what a brand is designed to do.

In order to understand how this works, let's start with what quality is. Most of the quality gurus, from Deming on, define quality as "performance to a standard." The question then becomes, "Who sets the standard?" The answer is, "Whoever the customer is."

As a way to illustrate this idea, let's consider two automobiles, a Honda Civic hybrid sedan that sells for about $20,000, and a Mercedes Benz S class sedan that sells for about $80,000 and up—with the emphasis on "up."

Which of these two is the better quality car? Most people when asked this question answer the Mercedes, because, they say, it's built better, costs more, is more powerful, drives faster, and so on. None of that may make a difference in quality.

The first question is, "Will the same consumer be the prospect for either car?" Obviously, the answer is "no." And, it's not just about the difference in price. Even though some people who drive a Honda can easily afford a Mercedes, they will never buy one. And even though most, if not all, people who drive a Mercedes can easily afford a Honda, they will never buy one—at least not for themselves. Why?

The answer lies in how each group of consumers defines quality. One group may define quality as agile, economical, small, easy to park, good trade-in value, low cost of total ownership, and friendly on the environment. They may also view themselves as concerned about the environment, a good citizen, safe, frugal, careful, and so on. Their attitude is "Waste not, want not." The Honda Civic hybrid brand resonates with their values.

The other group may define quality as power, speed, status, roominess, comfort, luxurious appointments, and so on. They may view themselves as captains of industry, hard chargers, hard workers, and achievers who deserve the fruits of success. Their attitude is "If you have it, flaunt it." The Mercedes S class brand resonates with their values.

So, the answer to the question "Which is the better quality car?" is "Both are!"—if they each meet the needs and satisfy the values and self-image of each served market reasonably well, especially when compared to other competitive offerings aimed at the same market segment.

The challenge facing most businesses is to recognize that their brand encodes their quality. In fact, their brand is their Quality Assurance Device.

As we discovered in the discussion of value disciplines, the fit between the values of the served market and the experience delivered by the brand must be in alignment. To the extent that the Brand Promise, or the unique set of expectations associated with the company and/or its products and services are not met, then value is destroyed over time. Value creation and value destruction can take place on the part of customers, employees, suppliers, strategic partners, channel partners, media, investors, legislators, special interest groups, community, and others—any one of which can support or confound the value creation chain, and all of which can comprise the various constituencies that both help to create and to refine the relationship between the company's values and definition of value.

If we look at the company as a mid-level social formation/organization that "connects" micro-entities (family, friends, and individuals) with "macro" entities (markets, networks, nations), then the organization (and its brand, brand purpose, brand promises, and so on) provides the mid-level "motives" that coalesce shared paths, roles, ideas, purposes, and fates into strong, predictable shared values operating in markets, networks, and nations. When companies stumble, it is always due to insufficient empathy, skills, strategies, and shared values—in favor of either/or pursuits that value one constituency over others, value over values, I over we.[23]

We can ask if the blend of value and values in the brand promise and brand experience of the organization's common good is good.[24]

The key is to align the right served market with the right brand promise, and then to deliver so as to meet or exceed expectations of all stakeholders associated with the brand, and to do this in a manner that is responsive to

---

[23] As adapted from: Douglas K. Smith, *On Value and Values*, Financial Times Prentice Hall, © 2004.
[24] Ibid.

changes in the market, the environment, the community, and other stake-holder groups.

Ideally, the CEO will view the customer as their alter ego, and will include the customer in all decisions. The value-creating power of the enterprise extends from its ability to understand the customer and their values, predict how they define value, share that insight internally so that resources are deployed correctly, shape customer expectations, and then execute on promises made to the customer by providing products and/or performing services that create loyal customers and new customers—and do this in a way that's consistent with the needs of the other stakeholders in the organization, especially employees. The smaller the company, the more directly involved in each step is the CEO.

Since so much of an enterprise's value is in its intangible assets—most of all its brand—it is imperative that better methods for measuring and tracking the value of brands and other intangible assets are developed. These metrics need to be useful not only for the day-to-day operations, but for the longer-term assessment of whether the firm is creating or destroying economic value.

In the next chapter, we talk about current measurement systems and their shortcomings, as well as the limitations of many current accounting practices in providing leadership and management with the type of information that would be useful in managing intangible assets.

"Now that I understand the role of values in creating and/or destroying value, how do I measure the outcomes?"
        —Jack F. Eli, CEO, TasteRite

CHAPTER 6

THE CURRENT STATE OF BRAND MEASUREMENT

"The hypothesis has been proposed that if the mind of Man is exposed to the economy of nature, as revealed in the workings of living systems, he will become sensitized to recognize the necessity of balancing values. Thus measure is established as the source of wisdom."

—Dr. Jonas Salk, The Survival of the Wisest

There are myriad approaches to brand equity measurement, ranging from purely accounting manipulations through expert opinions and simple surveys to complex statistical models. Some of the approaches attempt to translate the findings into economic values, while others do not.

Recent literature addressing brand equity shows that in the various measurement models brand equity is addressed at either the corporate level or the product/service category level and is also addressed using internal data, external (market) data, or a blend of both.

At the corporate level, various organizations have attempted to assess brand equity using internal financial data from the firm's accounting system, or by assessing comparative financial performance data from similar firms (i.e., external data). At the category level, there have been many attempts to address brand equity using unit profit margins in comparison to unit marketing costs, and/or in comparison to the costs of other products in the category. Alternatively, the most attempts have been to use consumer surveys to measure the perceived value or willingness to pay for the product/brand compared to other products/brands in a category. These alternatives are categorized in Table 6.1.

Table 6.1

	Internal	External
Corporate Level	P & L statements	Financial comparatives
	Balance sheets	Industry norms
Category Level	Unit margins	Customer surveys
	Unit profitability	Statistical models based on surveys and experiments

Generally, the use of internal financial data has not met with much success in measuring brand equity. As we have pointed out previously, current financial reporting procedures are not oriented to measuring the value of intangible assets beyond trying to parse out the difference between the selling price and the book value of a firm that is sold.

Likewise, the use of financial comparatives and industry norms has not met with any significant success in isolating the value of brands. There is always the question of which comparatives and which norms for which product/service categories are the appropriate ones for any one industry.

Tim Ambler describes the brand performance measures actually practiced by firms in the United Kingdom based on a survey of 200 top marketers and finance executives, and contrasts this list with the measures the same firms consider important enough to share with their boards.

Table 6.2   Most Commonly Used Metrics (United Kingdom)

	% Firms Using Measure	% Rated Top for Assessing Performance
Awareness	78	2
Market share (volume or value)	78	36
Relative price	70	37
Complaints (dissatisfaction level)	69	45
Consumer satisfaction	68	46
Distribution/availability	66	18
Total number of customers	65	40
Perceived quality/esteem	64	35
Loyalty/retention	64	67
Relative perceived quality	62	62

Source: Ambler, Tim. *Marketing and the Bottom Line.* London: Pearson Education Limited, 2000.

As Table 6.2 demonstrates, there is a wide variety of brand measures that are actually in use, but none of these include a specific measure of the economic value of brands or brand equity.

Ultimately, brand value boils down to what buyers are willing to pay for a given bundle of tangible and intangible attributes associated with a particular branded product or service.

Thus, one of the major considerations for developing adequate measures of brand value and brand equity is that buyer perspectives must be taken into account—something that financial accounting procedures don't do well. So in this chapter we are going to concentrate primarily on the measures in the lower right-hand box of Table 6.1—external measures of brand equity at the category level.

Even though we are narrowing our focus to this set of models, we will subsequently see that there are extreme variations in the approaches taken by different research and consulting firms, using different definitions, different underlying assumptions, and different approaches to measurement and analysis. Most of the models being offered by research firms, consultants, and advertising agencies have some proprietary elements to them. Thus, it is unlikely that they have been subjected to independent testing and review.

Before we assess these various approaches, we need to first set the criteria for what constitutes an acceptable measure of brand equity. And before we get to that, we need to make a key distinction between brand value and brand equity.

As we discuss in detail in Chapter 7, it is our view that for a buyer, brand value equals the value of the bundle of tangible performance attributes plus the value of the bundle of intangible performance and trust attributes less the cost of those bundles of attributes. The value of the bundle of intangible attributes alone is the brand's equity. Thus, the value of brand equity is a portion of the value of the total branded product or service. In some categories, that proportion of total brand value that can be attributed to brand equity can be considerable—such as in pocket personal computers, beer, or soft drinks. In other categories, it can be very small, such as for electric utilities or industrial machining equipment.

Our rationale for this definition is that a manufacturer or service provider can deliver almost any combination of tangible product attributes at a particular price, at least in the short run. The tangible product attributes are not in and of themselves unique to a brand name. Only the bundle of intangible attributes is conveyed by the brand name. Again, we greatly expand on this rationale in Chapter 7.

Two of the most widely published authors on brand equity—David Aaker and Kevin Lane Keller—do not take this same view of brand equity. Both authors tend to define brand equity in more holistic terms encompassing the total value of a brand, including price premium, satisfaction, product attributes, image attributes, public opinion, and so forth. We discuss their views in the next section.

It is our position that brand equity can best be measured by determining the price premium that buyers in the category are willing to pay for a branded product or service compared to an unbranded product or service with the same performance characteristics. This definition is dependent upon the assumption that buyers seek to optimize value in any transaction. We note that "convenience" has a value and is therefore taken into account in this optimization process.

In the following section we discuss several of the better-known brand equity measurement programs that are available to businesses.

Criteria for Measuring Brand Equity

In the following list, we set forth our thinking on the essential elements that must be considered for a measurement of brand equity to be acceptable and useful.

1. **Buyer-focused**—Focuses on purchasers and likely purchasers in the product or service category and excludes those who are unlikely to be purchasers; does not exclude likely purchasers.
2. **Valid**—The measurement of brand equity is based on a logical and supported theory or definition of brand equity. The measurement or modeling methodology is well established or has been subject to competent independent review.
3. **Reliable**—The measurement can be consistently replicated over time, settings, and circumstances.
4. **Focuses on tangible and intangible attributes**—The model can isolate the value of the bundle of intangible attributes associated with an individual brand. That is, it must go well beyond a simple beauty contest and partition brand value into tangible and intangible values. Ideally, it would further identify the principal individual tangible and intangible attributes that are driving brand value for the targeted brand.
5. **Actionable**—The metrics must provide diagnostic insight and translate the key measure of brand equity into economic or currency values for investment decisions and linkage to business goals.

In addition to these essential elements listed here, we believe that any measure of brand equity should also include the following key attributes.

1. **Diagnostic**—The measures must be able to pinpoint specific areas of brand performance that are exceptionally strong or weak.

2. **Predictive**—Given changes in marketplace dynamics, such as changes in competitor price or technologies, the measurement must be able to predict how such changes would affect the targeted brand's value. In addition, if there are changes in the targeted brand's product/service performance, then the measurement of brand equity should be able to show how those changes would impact the targeted brand's value.

3. **Targeted**—Allows the measure of brand equity to be broken out by specific markets or identified subgroups, such as socioeconomic or customer segments.

Some Comments on Currently Popular Measures of Brand Equity

In this section, we provide an overview of some of the more popular and well-known survey-based measurement techniques for assessing brand value and brand equity. In Chapter 7, we discuss our own technique for measuring brand equity.

Harris Interactive's EquiTrend®

EquiTrend fields an annual survey to approximately 20,000 consumers utilizing several brand measures: perceived quality, familiarity, purchase intent, brand expectations, and distinctiveness. Respondents use a five-point scale to rate up to 80 brands.

Brand equity is calculated as a combination of the quality, familiarity, and purchase consideration variables, calculated by weighting the familiarity measure, multiplying that by the mean for quality and a weighted mean of purchase consideration. The result is a 100-point index of brand equity. Brand relevance is calculated in a similar fashion.

In 2006, over 23,000 consumers were polled and 1,275 brands were rated. EquiTrend's top 10 brands were:

1. Reynolds Wrap Aluminum Foil
2. Ziploc Food Bags
3. Hershey's Milk Chocolate Candy Bars
4. Kleenex Facial Tissues
5. Clorox Bleach
6. WD-40 Spray Lubricant
7. Heinz Ketchup
8. Ziploc Containers

9. Windex Glass Cleaner

10. Campbell's Soups

Details on the methodology can be viewed at http://www.harrisinteractive .com/news/allnewsbydate.asp?NewsID=1063.

Our Comment: Essentially, this is a beauty contest recording peoples' familiarity with consumer brands. We note that all of the brands that are listed in the EquiTrend top ten brands are those that dominate their rather small consumer goods categories.

There is no apparent control over who rates which brands; thus, this measure fails the "buyer-focus" criteria.

Although the survey methodology likely passes muster in terms of its validity and reliability, it does not focus on the issue of willingness to pay for a branded product over an unbranded product with identical or very similar performance characteristics.

There is no distinction between tangible attribute performance and intangible attribute performance, thus the "focused on intangibles" criteria is not met.

The EquiTrend survey does provide some limited diagnostic insight in terms of the measures of familiarity, perceived quality, and purchase intent, but it does not specifically parse out the value of the intangible aspects of brand equity. Nor do the results translate into economic terms.

Young & Rubicam—BrandAsset Valuator®

Young & Rubicam Brands (Y&R), formerly Young & Rubicam Inc., is one of the advertising and media services units of UK-based WPP Group. The proprietary BrandAsset® Valuator, developed and maintained by the Corporate Research Group at Young & Rubicam, has been using consumer surveys to measure brand health since 1993 in terms of the four key constructs of (1) differentiation, (2) relevance, (3) esteem, and (4) knowledge. These constructs are calculated based on 55 individual perception measures for each brand in the survey. At last report, the survey queried approximately 350,000 respondents in 44 countries and covered 20,000 brands.

Differentiation is a construct of the brand's unique points of difference and is related to the brand's ability to generate premium margins.

Relevance is a construct of how appropriate the brand is to the target market, and represents a measure of market penetration.

Esteem is a construct of how well the brand is regarded and represents a measure of how well the brand delivers on its promise. It is considered a measure of perceived quality and popularity.

Knowledge is a measure of how well the brand's promise is understood within the target market and relates to understanding the overall customer experience and intimacy.

Y&R's basic hypothesis is that brands are built sequentially, starting with differentiation, then to relevance (to the target market), to esteem, then to (brand) knowledge—that is, what the brand stands for.

Brand strength (or *vitality*) is derived by multiplying a brand's *differentiation* score by its *relevance* score.

Brand stature is derived by multiplying a brand's *esteem* score by its *knowledge* score.

Brand value is the addition of *brand strength* and *brand stature*.

Recently the BrandAsset® Valuator data was aligned with a financial database of the Economic Value Added (EVA®) database developed and maintained by the financial consulting firm, Stern Stewart & Co.

The work by BrandEconomics, a subsidiary of Stern Stewart, purports to demonstrate that the valuation of companies can be expressed as a function of their profitability and brand health. Profitability, measured in terms of returns above the cost of capital alone, typically explains some 50 percent of the variance in the observed valuation of companies. Adding a brand health variable—measured in terms of *relevant differentiation*—typically raises the explanatory power to between 70 and 80 percent of the observed variance in valuation.

According to BrandEconomics, valuation is a function of three primary variables: profitability, growth, and risk. Investors care about the level of free cash flow of a company (profitability), the prospects for increasing cash flow (growth), and the volatility of these cash flows (risk). BrandEconomics' work implies that brand health provides a powerful proxy for investors' expectations about the growth potential and riskiness of a company.

Details on this model can be found at http://www.yrbav.com/.

Our Comment: The BrandAsset® Valuator is probably the most widely used and widely quoted measure of brand value worldwide. However, at its very base is a consumer opinion survey.

The methodology is clearly buyer-focused. However, one must question the accuracy of self-reported brand purchases, purchase volume, and purchase frequency. These measures are notoriously inaccurate in typical opinion surveys.

The underlying measurement protocol is based on a popular and logical theory of the drivers of brand value, and the measurement system (consumer surveys) is well established. However, it is unclear to us just how the 55 individual measures are translated into the four key constructs. Apparently, that is proprietary.

The measurement system appears to be reliable in that it appears to produce consistent results across markets and over time. Furthermore, there is sufficient sample size to allow the individual brand assessments to be broken out by market and key targeted segments.

Since we cannot get access to the 55 underlying questions, we cannot assess whether the model is focused sufficiently to uncover the specific tangible and intangible elements of brand value.

Y&R and their partners have developed considerable literature that purportedly demonstrates the actionable relationship between brand value and financial performance and linkages to business goals. Not having access to the underlying questions and the manner in which they are consolidated to form the four key constructs does not allow us to assess the veracity of those claims. Furthermore, given the rapidity of consumers to change their *opinions* of brands and brand performance, we question the ability of this model to be predictive beyond the short term.

We assume that the individual 55 measures would likely provide rich diagnostics, allowing one to pinpoint areas where a brand is performing well, and areas where it needs improvement. Again, not having access to those individual measures does not allow us to verify the diagnostic value of the model.

Y&R claims that the *Brand Strength* construct is a leading indicator and thus somewhat predictive. However, the model does not appear to be sufficiently predictive to allow one to observe changes in brand value based on changes in the product's performance or based on changes in competitor actions.

Having said all of this, we believe that the basic approach of the Y&R Brand Asset Valuator represents a solid conceptual approach to tracking brand performance over time and within specific markets.

Interbrand

Interbrand, a division of Omnicom, is a brand consultancy headquartered in London, England. The company has developed a quite different approach to measuring brand value and brand equity.

Here is how BusinessWeek Online describes the Interbrand approach:

"BUSINESSWEEK chose Interbrand's methodology because it evaluates brands much the way analysts value other assets: on the basis of how much they're likely to earn in the future. The projected profits are then discounted to a present value, taking into account the likelihood that those earnings will actually materialize.

The first step is figuring out what percentage of a company's revenues can be credited to a brand. (The brand may be almost the entire company, as with McDonald's Corp., or just a portion, as it is for Marlboro.) Based on reports from analysts at J.P. Morgan Chase, Citigroup, and Morgan Stanley, Interbrand projects five years of earnings and sales for the brand. It then deducts operating costs, taxes, and a charge for the capital employed to arrive at the intangible earnings. The company strips out intangibles such as patents and management strength to assess what portion of those earnings can be attributed to the brand.

Finally, the brand's strength is assessed to determine the risk profile of those earnings forecasts. Considerations include market leadership, stability, and global reach—or the ability to cross both geographic and cultural borders. That generates a discount rate, which is applied to brand earnings to get a net present value. BusinessWeek and Interbrand believe this figure comes closest to representing a brand's true economic worth."

See http://bwnt.businessweek.com/brand/2006/.

Essentially, the Interbrand methodology merges three separate analyses:

1. A financial analysis that derives economic earnings due to the brand by projecting five years of earnings and sales for the brand. It then deducts operating costs, taxes, and a charge for the capital employed to arrive at the intangible earnings.

2. A market analysis—then Interbrand deducts the value of other intangibles, such as patents and management strength, to assess what portion of those earnings can be attributed to the brand. Through their proprietary analytical framework, called "role of brand," they calculate the percentage of intangible earnings that is entirely generated by the brand. The role of brand is a percentage—thus, if it's 50 percent, they take 50 percent of the intangible earnings as Brand Earnings.

3. A brand analysis that is based on a very subjective brand strength score. According to Interbrand:

> "The assessment of brand strength is a structured way of assessing the specific risk of the brand. We compare the brand against a notional ideal and score it against common factors of brand strength. The ideal brand is virtually 'risk free' and would be discounted at a rate almost as low as government bonds or similar risk-free investment. The lower the brand strength, the further it is from the risk-free investment and so, the higher the discount rate (and therefore the lower the net present value)."

Brand strength is assessed based on seven measures, as shown in the following table.

Factor	Weight	Description
Leadership	25%	Rank among other brands in the category. Measured by market share, awareness, positioning, and competitor profile.
Stability	15%	Measured by longevity in the marketplace, coherence, consistency, brand identity, and risks.
Market	10%	In categories with growing or stable sales levels and price structures—measured by market definition, nature of market (e.g., level of volatility), size of market, market dynamics, and barriers to entry.
International	25%	Extent of global reach—measured by geographical spread, international positioning, relative market share, prestige, and ambition.
Trend	10%	Long-term trend in terms of sales and market share, sales projections, sensible brand planning, competitive pressures.
Support	10%	Received consistent and quality investment—measured by consistency of brand spending, consistency of message, strength of the brand franchise.
Protection	5%	Strength and breadth of the brands trademark protection—measured by trademark registrations and registerability, common law, litigation, and disputes.

The brand's strength score is converted into a discount rate that is applied to the economic value added to arrive at a calculated brand value as the net present value of the earnings the brand is expected to generate in the future.

The Interbrand 2005 and 2006 ratings are shown in the following table.

2006 Rank ▲	2005 Rank	Name	Country	2006 Value ($Mil)	2005 Value ($Mil)	Change in Value (%)
1	1	Coca-Cola	U.S.	67,000	67,525	−1%
2	2	Microsoft	U.S.	56,926	59,941	−5%
3	3	IBM	U.S.	56,201	53,376	5%
4	4	GE	U.S.	48,907	46,996	4%
5	5	Intel	U.S.	32,319	35,588	−9%
6	6	Nokia	Finland	30,131	26,452	14%
7	9	Toyota	Japan	27,941	24,837	12%
8	7	Disney	U.S.	27,848	26,441	5%
9	8	McDonald's	U.S.	27,501	26,014	6%
10	11	Mercedes-Benz	Germany	21,795	20,006	9%

Our Comment: We repeat the criticism of many other critics of this methodology—it's just too subjective. The financial analysis for deriving the economic value of all intangibles is quite solid. However, the "market analysis" methodology then subjectively parses out the economic values generated by non-brand intangible assets, with the remainder attributable to the economic value created by the brand. Assessing the intangible value of management strength is clearly a very subjective exercise—and is imprecise, at best. Then, the brand is subjectively assessed on the seven brand strength factors and weighted in accordance with the table shown previously. The weights in that table are applied to all categories. Our own experience in brand research indicates that this is not appropriate because the importance of the seven factors will change from category to category. Furthermore, the measures themselves are highly subjective and amount to a conglomeration of multiple measures from multiple sources.

According to Interbrand, the information used for deriving the brand strength score comes from a variety of sources:

> "Interbrand refers to a wide array of primary and secondary sources that are applicable to each brand. These include, among others, Datamonitor, ACNielsen, Gartner, Hall & Partners. Moreover, Interbrand engages its network of brand valuation experts from offices around the world to ensure that the league table considers the brands from a global perspective."

Said another way, Interbrand reviews the information from these disparate sources and comes up with a subjective estimate of each of the seven elements of brand strength.

This methodology is not buyer-focused. It relies almost entirely on the subjective opinions of brand "experts."

The underlying theory appears to have some validity—especially Interbrand's approach for deriving the economic value of all intangibles. However, that measure is dependent on the accuracy of the five-year forecasts from their sources, which in and of themselves leave a lot of room for error. But the basic focus of considering the added values generated by a firm's intangible brand assets, combined with their brands' presence in the marketplace, and the brands' strength among the set of relevant buyers has a basic appeal and captures much of the recent developments in brand research.

However, the methodology runs a high risk of confounding differentiation embedded in the tangible product performance and the brand intangibles.

To the degree that they are accurate, the measures used in the Interbrand model do appear to be actionable and translate into currency values and linkages to business goals.

The measures of brand strength provide multiple diagnostics, but it is unlikely that they are very predictive of future values when the marketplace or the associated products undergo significant change.

Prophet (David Aaker)—Managing Brand Equity

David Aaker, who is vice chairman of Prophet, and a professor of marketing strategy at the Haas School of Business, University of California at Berkeley, defines brand equity as "a set of assets (and liabilities) linked to a brand's name and symbol that adds to (or subtracts from) the value provided by a product or service to a firm and/or that firm's customers. The major asset categories are:

1. Brand name awareness
2. Brand loyalty
3. Perceived quality
4. Brand associations[1]

---

[1] Aaker, David A., *Building Strong Brands*, pp. 7–8.

We note that Aaker's definition makes no distinction between tangible assets and intangible assets, and that Aaker's definition encompasses both. That is, the intangible assets that in our view define a brand's equity are not distinguished from the tangible and sometimes unique performance characteristics of the product or service with which the brand is associated.

At Prophet, they have apparently added a fifth dimension, and crafted the elements of brand equity as:

1. Brand awareness
2. Brand loyalty
3. Perceived quality
4. Brand associations and differentiation
5. Market behaviors

At Prophet, they classify these into brand perception metrics and brand performance metrics using ten separate measures to specify five higher-level constructs.

- Loyalty
  1. Price premium (willingness to pay)
  2. Satisfaction/Loyalty
- Perceived Quality/Leadership
  3. Perceived quality
  4. Leadership/Popularity
- Associations/Differentiation
  5. Perceived value
  6. Brand personality
  7. Organizational associations
- Awareness
  8. Brand awareness
- Market Behavior
  9. Market share
  10. Market price & distribution coverage

These ten measures are quite disparate for each of the ten criteria. Judgment is used to weight the measures, depending on the product category, in order to construct a single summary measure of brand equity. Prophet does not reveal how this aggregation is accomplished.

Our comment: Somewhat in support of our more narrow definition, Aaker states, "The price premium may be the best single measure of brand equity available, because it directly captures the loyalty of customers in a most relevant way."[2] As you will see in Chapter 7, we extend this concept by using "willingness to pay" to help us discern between the product's or service's tangible performance attributes and the intangible trust and image attributes.

The Prophet measures are clearly buyer-focused and the underlying theory as described by Aaker in his two books, *Managing Brand Equity* and *Building Strong Brands,* certainly seems valid.

Based on Prophet's survey methodology, we presume that the basic measures are reliable, in that they can be consistently replicated over time, settings, and circumstances. However, we cannot determine the consistency of the judgmental weights given to each of the summary measures, which likely depreciates from that reliability.

It is doubtful that the Prophet model can discern which particular tangible or intangible product/service attributes are driving brand equity; thus this model fails the "focused on intangibles" criteria.

Furthermore, most of the underlying questions all seem to be higher-order summary measures of brand image and brand satisfaction, thus there is little "actionability" that can be discerned from the ratings. For this same reason, the diagnostic capabilities of this model are very limited.

Ultimately, this model is based on the judgments of the weights for each of the composite measures.

Research International Equity Engine™

Equity Engine™ is a proprietary, survey-based approach developed by Research International, another of the advertising and media services units of UK-based WPP Group. "The objective of such studies is to identify and understand the current value of a brand and the factors that drive that value."

The Equity Engine™ approach gathers data on the performance of each brand in a market category on the key buying factors. RI splits the key buying factors into two main categories, functional and emotional. They have developed a proprietary battery of questions to measure nine attributes in the emotional category, which they label *brand affinity.*

RI defines brand equity as the sum total of the perceived benefits of a branded proposition to an individual in the absence of price.

Research International promotes their model as follows:

- Equity Engine™ is a toolbox developed by Research International to measure (and track) the key components of brand equity to consumers.

---

[2] Aaker, David A., *Building Strong Brands*, p. 321.

- Equity Engine™ provides a "total equity view" with an understanding of brand characteristics.
- It uses universal concepts of branding, for example, the same methodology in all markets.
- Equity assessment can be reduced to core topics for tracking and monitoring.
- It provides a quantified measure of equity, together with a diagnostic understanding of the key drivers of equity.

The conceptual framework is shown in the following graphic.

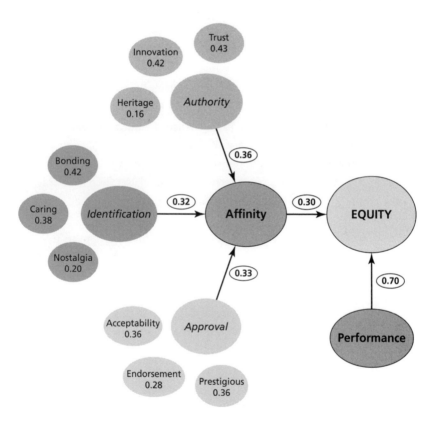

Results: The main data analysis covers the following:

- Absolute brand equity for each brand covered by the study.
- Relative brand equity for each brand compared to the norm for the category.
- Each brand's location in relation to the equity line for the category, expressing the relationship between brand equity and price.

- The values of standard attributes defining the emotional dimension for each brand, the values of combined ratings in the collective categories of brand authority, identification and approval, and also the overall assessment of the emotional dimension (affinity) for each brand.
- The combined rating for the functional dimension of each brand.
- Coefficients expressing the share each of the dimensions have and the shares of the specific elements of these dimensions in forming brand equity.
- Gauges defining assisted awareness of brands and the level of this awareness.
- Rating of customer loyalty toward brands by splitting customers into three segments by degree of loyalty.

Our Comment: The RI Equity Engine™ is yet another survey-based model. Unlike the others in this group, it does attempt to make a definitive distinction between the product/service performance attributes and emotional, or intangible attributes.

The methodology is clearly buyer-focused. However, again we must question the accuracy of self-reported brand purchases, purchase volume, and purchase frequency. These measures are notoriously inaccurate in typical opinion surveys.

The underlying measurement protocol is based on what appears to be an expansion of the Y&R measures. However, it is unclear to us just how these individual measures are translated into the four key constructs. Apparently, that is proprietary.

The measurement system appears to be reliable in that it appears to produce consistent results across markets and over time. Furthermore, there is sufficient sample size to allow the individual brand assessments to be broken out by market and key targeted segments.

Since we cannot get access to the underlying questions, we cannot assess whether the model is focused sufficiently to uncover the specific tangible and intangible elements of brand value.

RI and their partners have developed considerable literature that purportedly demonstrates the actionable relationship between brand value and financial performance and linkages to business goals. Not having access to the underlying questions and the manner in which they are consolidated to form the four key constructs does not allow us to assess the veracity of those claims. Furthermore, given the tendency of consumers to change their views of brands and brand performance, we question the ability of this model to be predictive beyond the short term.

We assume that the individual measures would likely provide diagnostics, allowing one to pinpoint areas where a brand is performing well, and areas where it needs improvement. Again, not having access to those individual measures does not allow us to verify the diagnostic value of the model.

There are many other models out in the marketplace. These models are typically promoted by research and consulting firms, and are mostly proprietary. In general, they represent rather minor variations of the models already discussed in this chapter.

The Disparity in the Definitions of Brand Equity

One of the main problems with getting a handle on brand equity is the rather extreme disparity in definitions and explanations of just what it is, as we can see in the following selected definitions.

Robert Passikoff, president of New York–based marketing firm Brand Keys:

> "Brand equity is the degree to which a brand meets or exceeds the consumer expectations for a category in which it competes."

David A. Aaker, in *Managing Brand Equity:*

> "Brand equity is a set of assets (and liabilities) linked to a brand's name and symbol that adds to (or subtracts from) the value provided by a product or service to a firm and/or that firm's customers. The major asset categories are: (1) Brand name awareness, (2) Brand loyalty (3) Perceived quality and (4) Brand associations."

Kevin Lane Keller, in the *Journal of Marketing,* Vol. 57, No. 1 (Jan. 1993), pp. 1–22 (Abstract):

> "Customer-based brand equity is defined as the differential effect of brand knowledge on consumer response to the marketing of the brand. A brand is said to have positive (negative) customer-based brand equity when consumers react more (less) favorably to an element of the marketing mix for the brand than they do to the same marketing mix element when it is attributed to a fictitiously named or unnamed version of the product or service. Brand knowledge is conceptualized according to an associative network memory model in terms of two components, brand awareness and brand image (i.e. a set of brand associations). Customer-based brand equity occurs when the consumer is familiar with the brand and holds some favorable, strong, and unique brand associations in memory."

Rory Morgan, Research International in RI presentations:

"RI defines brand equity as the sum total of the perceived benefits of a branded proposition to an individual, in the absence of price."

Interbrand:

"A mixture of tangible and intangible attributes symbolized in a trademark, which, if properly managed, creates influence and generates value".

Of course, if you really want to get confused, try a Google search on the definition for "brand equity."

Our Definition and Its Rationale

Our approach to the definition of brand value and brand equity is straightforward. We call it the Brand Value Equation. We start with the basic definition of value:

Brand Value = Benefits − Costs

Benefits can be parsed into two types of benefits—the bundles of tangible and intangible (or emotional) benefits. Thus,

Brand Value = Tangible Benefits + Intangible Benefits − Costs

Recognizing there are different sources of tangible benefits, we can further expand our Value Equation to

Brand Value = (Product Benefits + Service Benefits + Channel Benefits) + Intangible Benefits − Costs

In contrast to the tangible benefits, the "intangible benefits" of this relationship equation are less well understood because they are more complex and more difficult to measure. But, understanding this component of the Value Equation is the key to understanding how buyers make choices in the marketplace.

The intangible benefits in this equation are all communicated to the customer and the consumer by the brand name. It is the brand promise—what the customer/consumer believes the brand stands for. It has been described as an implied contract between the producer and user.

The value of that set of intangible benefits is the brand's equity. Brand equity encompasses a gestalt of intrinsic values, with associated perceptions of benefits that complement the tangible benefits delivered by a particular product or service. These intrinsic equities may include such things as the image of self imparted to the purchaser, trust, communication consistency and perceived quality, long-term reputation for reliability, customer support, social responsibility, previous experiences with the brand, and various other meanings.

In this model, Brand Equity is a subset of total brand value. Thus, our Brand Value Equation now becomes:

Brand Value = (Product Benefits + Service Benefits + Channel Benefits) + Brand Equity − Costs

This definitional relationship provides a strategic framework for understanding the asset value of brands. It clearly separates the benefits attributable to the product or service itself (for example, the tangible performance characteristics that can be replicated by competitors) from the intangible perceptual and emotional benefits associated with the brand name aligned with a particular product or service.

The key assumptions behind the Brand Value Equation are:

- Buyers' assessment of value drives choice in the marketplace.
- Buyers' seek to optimize value in a given purchase situation.

This Brand Value Equation has several benefits in terms of measurement and integration into classical business metrics. First and foremost, this model provides a bridge between the drivers of customer choice and managerial actions that can drive that choice. In other words, the model clearly shows the various levers that management can use to enhance a buyers' perception of value, thus choice and market share—product deliverables, service deliverables, channel deliverables, price, or brand equity. The model implies that there are trade-offs that can be made between the set of tangible benefits, the set of intangible benefits, and price in order to present a value proposition to the potential buyer.

In Chapter 7, we greatly expand on these levers and further decompose them into particular performance attributes.

Summary

After reviewing these five popular measures of brand value and brand equity, it's no wonder that Ambler's list of brand performance measures does not include any of them. Ambler's list is composed mostly of hard numbers and direct measures. All of these brand equity models have substantial subjective elements or are simple results of consumer surveys.

Nor do any of these models fulfill the criteria of a good, stable brand value measurement system, although each has elements of some of those criteria.

What senior corporate managers instinctively know is that valuable assets must be deployed for a profitable return, and if brands are indeed a valuable asset, then their effect must show up on the bottom line of their P&L and in the price of their stock. Thus, the "brand" assets must be deployed so that they induce potential buyers to make the purchase decision in favor of the firm's offering.

A brand is an asset only if it can create and drive purchase behavior. Changes in customer attitudes may be interesting and boost the marketer's ego, but they do not directly affect the bottom line by driving profitability. Only buyer purchasing behaviors do that.

Thus, most of the common survey-based measures used in the foregoing and similar models—awareness, familiarity, esteem, perceived quality, and the like, along with their composite measures—are not suitable as measures of brand equity because there are only very weak associations with those measures and actual marketplace choice behaviors. And marketplace choice is what drives sales and profitability.

We have provided a brief introduction to an alternative framework for understanding brand value and brand equity, using the Brand Value Equation. In the following chapter, we will present our own methodology that we feel meets most of the criteria we have set forth at the beginning of this chapter and bridges the gap between attitudes and marketplace behaviors.

"You've piqued my interest in brand value measurement, and the types of information it may provide as 'levers' for value creation. Tell me more ..."
—Jack F. Eli, CEO, TasteRite

CHAPTER 7

UNDERSTANDING BRAND VALUE AND BRAND EQUITY

"What gets measured gets managed."

—A TQM mantra generally attributed to Peter Drucker

Most people refer to brand value and brand equity as interchangeable and equal entities. They're not. In fact, the difference between brand value and brand equity goes to the core of understanding how to create value in today's world.

The Brand Value Concept

Several years ago I was helping a friend look for an automobile to purchase. He was looking for a smaller SUV with good reliability and was quite partial to Honda and Toyota. After we looked over several models, he focused in on the Honda Passport as just about the best combination of size, comfort, economy, and price he was looking for.

Hearing his description, I did a few searches of *Consumer Reports* and found that the Isuzu Rodeo was an identical vehicle and it retailed for a lot less. I told my friend to look at the Isuzu, instead. He did, but then bought the Passport—paying about $4,500 more than he would have for an exact duplicate vehicle with a different nameplate. Basically, my friend paid $4,500 for a Honda emblem on a perfectly good Isuzu Rodeo.

Why would he do such a thing?

The answer goes to the heart of understanding the concepts of brand value and brand equity.

The answer lies in what my friend perceived to be value. Value is most generally defined as a measure of worth, which is expressed as benefits less costs.

Brand Value = Benefits − Costs

The benefits part of this Value Equation is where most of the complexity lies. A branded product or service should be viewed as a bundle of tangible and intangible performance benefits. When you accept that premise, then we can expand the Value Equation to:

Brand Value = Tangible Benefits + Intangible Benefits − Costs

Back to my friend—since there was no difference between the two vehicles in terms of tangible benefits (with the possible exception of minor differences in depreciation and trade-in value) he placed high value on the intangible aspects of the Honda brand name. In fact, the value that he placed on the Honda nameplate was around $4,500.

Not only is this Value Equation essential in understanding brand value and brand equity, but it also provides the framework for valid and accurate brand value measurement.

When we are talking about tangible benefits, we are addressing the objective performance benefits delivered by the product or service to which the brand name is affixed. These tangible benefits may be delivered by the product or service itself or by the channel in which the product or service is available.

For example, for automobiles, the tangible product benefits may include vehicle type (wagon, van, sedan), the horsepower of the engine, handling characteristics, safety features, warranty, and so forth. The intangible benefits might include your trust in the brand name, perceived reliability, styling, how the image of the brand name aligns with your self-image, and so on.

The channel (dealership) may add additional performance benefits such as location convenience, selection, onsite service and maintenance, readily available parts and expendables, loaner cars, a comfortable waiting room, and so on.

Recognizing these different sources of benefits, we can once again expand our Value Equation to:

Brand Value = (Product Benefits + Channel Benefits + Intangible Benefits) − Costs

Some products, especially in B2B categories, also have a significant service component that is an integral part of the product and its value. Examples of adjunct service components include online technical support, troubleshooting services, maintenance reminders, and so on. Turning to our automobile example, the service attributes may include a free-maintenance period, roadside assistance package, and warranty service reminders.

These service attributes should be viewed as separate components of the Value Equation, thus we expand our equation one more time.

Brand Value = (Product Benefits + Service Benefits + Channel Benefits + Intangible Benefits) − Costs

And, of course, if we are talking about a primarily services category, such as banking services or real estate services, this is the appropriate value equation.

In contrast to the tangible benefits we've just been discussing, the intangible benefits of this relationship are less well understood because they are more complex and more difficult to measure. But understanding this component of the Value Equation is the key to understanding why my friend paid $4,500 more for a Honda Passport, compared to an identical Isuzu Rodeo.

In reality, the intangible benefits in the Value Equation are all communicated to the customer and the consumer by the brand name. It is the brand promise—what the customer/consumer believes the brand stands for. It has been described as an implied contract between the producer and user.

The value of that set of intangible benefits is the brand's equity. Brand equity encompasses a gestalt of intrinsic values, or benefits, that complement the tangible benefits delivered by a particular product or service. These intrinsic equities may include such things as the image imparted to the purchaser, trust, communication consistency and quality, long-term reputation for reliability, customer support, social responsibility, previous experiences with the brand, and so forth.

In this model, Brand Equity is a subset of total brand value. Thus, our Value Equation now becomes:

Brand Value = (Product Benefits + Service Benefits + Channel Benefits + Brand Equity) − Costs

In the marketplace, this concept of brand equity allows Honda to charge a price premium over Isuzu because the Honda name conveys more value to most consumers than does the Isuzu brand name. That price differential allows Honda to reinforce their brand equity through improved product quality, higher levels of customer service, investments in socially responsible programs, and more effective promotion. It also gives Honda pricing power—the power to trade off margin against share. Even at a $4,500 price premium, Honda Passport outsold the Isuzu Rodeo by more than 3 to 1 in the U.S. market in the mid-1990s.

The Elements of Brand Equity

Consumers may also see a particular brand name as a contract. A brand's name may reduce consumers' sense of uncertainty, allowing them to purchase uncertainty reduction, or trust, thus improving their sense of value. In this sense, a brand is a quality assurance device.

Our research has shown that there are two major components to brand equity. The first component is a set of beliefs about how the branded product or service will perform—how well the brand will fulfill its promise. We call these the perceived performance attributes, or *trust attributes*. For example, in automobiles, these trust attributes might include:

- Reputation for reliability
- Economy
- Safety
- Performance
- Customer support

These are distinct from, and distinctly different than, the objective, tangible attributes like warranty, gas mileage, cost of parts and repairs, number and types of airbags, braking distance, horsepower, and so forth. The trust attributes deal with consumer values (defined as beliefs, principles, and ideals) not necessarily product performance facts. They are the higher-order emotional constructs that connote a valuable benefit.

The second set of components in brand equity is the brand *image attributes*. These are the attributes that determine whether the brand's image, or public persona, aligns with the purchaser's personal self-image, and are also related to their values. Sticking with our automobile example, these image attributes may include:

- Prestigious
- Luxurious
- Utilitarian
- Sporty
- Fun to drive
- Flashy

It's not always easy to separate these two classes of brand equity attributes. For example, safety is typically a trust attribute. But a brand image of safety may also reinforce what the buyer wants to say to others about themselves—"I purchased this brand because I'm concerned about my safety and the safety of my passengers. One of my values is safety."

Economy is another confounded attribute. The buyer may perceive that the vehicle is economical to operate and maintain, but the buyer may also desire to communicate to their friends and the public at large that they are a frugal person.

The best way to keep them separate is to think of the trust attributes as dealing directly with perceived performance of the product or service and the image attributes as dealing with the desires of the purchaser or user to express and reinforce their self-image. Both trust attribute sets and image attribute sets are based on the consumer's values, either consciously and/or subconsciously.

Let's discuss the last element of the Value Equation—cost. In some product categories, especially in B2B and in consumer durables, cost may also have several elements: initial purchase price, operating costs, and maintenance costs. These should be included in the Value Equation if they apply to your product or service category.

One special case of price is financing. The importance weight of the initial price of a product may be moderated by stating the price in terms of a down payment and monthly payments over a specific period of time. Thus, instead of saying the initial price of our Honda Passport was $25,000, we may say $25,000 or a $999 down payment and $464 per month for 5 years. Or, it could be stated as a lease rate of $329 per month for 36 months. If your brand is operating in a category where price is a major factor, these options for stating price must be included.

We can graphically summarize the Value Equation in Figure 7.1.

If we look at the Brand Value Equation for an individual purchaser, we can imagine each arrow in the equation as having an importance weight. Each of those weights is a summation of a set of individual attribute weights for each element of the Brand Value Equation, as shown in the bottom part of Figure 7.1. And these individual importance weights are derived from the utility each customer/consumer places on the various levels of performance of each attribute.

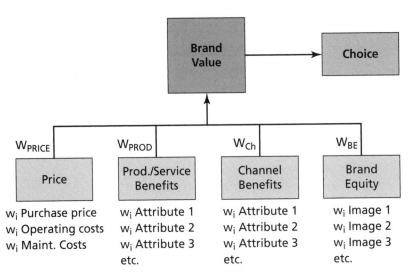

Figure 7.1 The Brand Value Equation.

This set of weights may be viewed as the individual purchaser's "value equation." It provides a *preference structure* for guiding the customer in making a choice between a competing set of offerings. That is, given a set of competing brands in a category and their performance levels and price, if we know a purchaser's value equation, we can predict with high reliability which of those brands he is likely to purchase.

The details for deriving these attribute utilities and importance weights are covered later in this chapter and more extensively in the Brand Value Model Technical Addendum in the Appendix at the end of this book.

Strategic Implications of the Brand Value Equation

At this point, let's consider the strategic implications of knowing these weights and utilities for your customers.

First, **value drives choice.** Once your brand is in the potential purchasers' consideration set, the brand with the highest overall value will typically be chosen. We will expand on this concept in Chapter 8 when we discuss customer loyalty and branding. But suffice it to say that the elements of this model, properly crafted for the product/service category in which your brand competes, completely encompasses and explains why purchasers choose, or do not choose, your brand. The Brand Value Equation can explain *why* my friend purchased the Honda Passport rather than the Isuzu Rodeo, despite the $4,500 price premium.

The next implication is that the Brand Value Equation model offers **a strategic framework for successfully competing in the marketplace.** By deriving the utility (value) of different performance levels of each individual attribute for both your customers and the customers of each competing brand in a product/service category, you can determine your strengths and weaknesses for any group of customers or prospects. This process will pinpoint where you should invest in improving perceived value for each market segment in which you compete. In the automobile example, my friend ascribed value to certain attribute performance levels for which he was willing to pay, both tangible and intangible. For example, the prestige of driving the Honda, rather than the Isuzu, was worth some portion of the $4,500 premium he paid. The Brand Value Model will help Honda management (or a competitor) better understand what that portion is worth.

Another strategic implication is that corporate management has **four separate levers that can be manipulated to improve brand value**—price, product/service performance, channel performance, and brand equity. Analysis of the importance of weights coupled with a realistic competitive assessment indicates where management will get the most increase in comparative brand value for a given investment in the brand's performance. Any change in attribute performance can be priced out, so that a rigorous cost-benefit analysis can be undertaken. In our automobile example, this gives managers of each brand insight into which tangible and intangible attributes to invest in, along with pricing strategies to achieve the best outcomes. It gives management insight into how their employees, channels, and partners are doing in satisfying the customer's expectations regarding the various tangible and intangible attributes and associated value promised by the brand.

Brand Equity Implications

Yet another implication, and perhaps the most important, is that this model allows you to better understand the **role and contribution of brand equity in determining total brand value.** If your brand competes in a category in which at least some brands enjoy high brand equity, then you can identify and better understand what specific image and trust attributes are associated with customers' underlying values and which contribute most to overall brand value. If your brand competes in a category in which there are weak brand equities, you can explore the opportunities and likely outcomes of making higher investments in brand equity. Again, for our automotive example, this means that Honda managers would better understand how to maximize margins and volumes by understanding the intangible product, service, and channel benefits that their customers most value, which ones to feature in advertising and other promotional efforts, and the importance to customer loyalty when the organization successfully delivers those attributes.

Furthermore, the **Brand Value Equation provides management with a quantitative measure of brand equity.** And that measure can be converted into a currency value at the unit level. More on this issue, later.

In today's hypercompetitive marketplace, brand equity is the only element of the Brand Value Equation that can be used for long-term competitive advantage. Competitors can beat your prices, they can usually duplicate or exceed any of your product/service performance advantages and they can normally successfully compete in your channels. Your only truly defensible asset is your brand equity. It is not easily defeated by competitor actions, only your own. Failing to keep the brand promise, engaging in questionable business practices, or engaging in socially irresponsible actions can depreciate, or even destroy brand equity, thus your key business asset.

Promotion of a brand can address price, tangible brand/channel attributes or brand equity. Brand equity is communicated using consistent visual cues and consistent messages, allowing the consumer to quickly and efficiently distinguish between brands and their intrinsic product or service attributes and underlying values. As a purchaser considers the tangible product or service features in concert with brand equity and price, they arrive at a set of products in a category that they will consider for purchase—their consideration set. Thus, a brand's equity is somewhat dependent on effective communications to the target market(s), and brand equity can often be improved with more effective communications. However, communications alone cannot overcome a reputation for poor product quality or service, social irresponsibility, or a lack of trust. And communications certainly cannot overcome the ongoing poor performance of an organization in not delivering on the brand promise by not creating the total brand experience that the customer is anticipating. Brand equity is heavily dependent on the reality of the brand experience.

A brand's equity therefore becomes part of the trade-off exercise a consumer considers as they first select their consideration set, and then decide which product to purchase from those in their consideration set. That is, purchasers actively trade off both the perceived tangible benefits and the perceived intrinsic benefits delivered by products in their consideration set, against price, to arrive at their value hierarchy, and ultimately their purchase decision.

This trade-off is not always a cognitive process. In categories in which there is low involvement and regular repurchase, such as consumer packaged goods, the purchasers will often conduct an initial evaluation of the competing brands in the category, make a selection, and stick with that brand as long as it meets their performance and image expectations. Only when something goes wrong, or their requirements change, or when a competitive offering redefines the consideration set, will they make a cognitive reevaluation of their choices.

Brands that have high perceived value are almost always included in a purchaser's consideration set. If a brand's combined tangible and intangible equities are consistently higher than any other brand in the category, that brand will have the highest market share and the highest customer loyalty in terms of purchase, repurchase, and recommendation. Competing brands can only improve their loyalty against the brand equity leader by lowering price in the short term, improving their product's performance on tangible features in the mid-term, or improving their brand's intangible benefits, or brand equity, in the long term.

However, how good a job the brand does or does not do in meeting expectations after the purchase will impact individual performance attribute weights on future purchases, and/or the purchasers' hierarchy of brands, and their next choice. Therefore, the experience with the brand after purchase will impact the attribute weightings, brand value perception, and future choice. Exceeding expectations in the areas where a purchaser places high importance (thus higher utility) reinforces brand equity. Disappointing performance will decrease brand equity.

Measuring and Modeling Brand Value

As we discussed in Chapter 6, the challenge to both marketers and marketing researchers is determining how we accurately and precisely measure total brand value and especially brand equity and how we connect that value measurement with our attempts to improve customer loyalty.

Any such measure of brand equity should meet the criteria of buyer focused, comparability, reliability, and validity, a focus on both tangible and intangible attributes, and actionability, as we discussed in Chapter 6. Surprisingly, the measurement tools have been generally available to us since the early 1990s.

By the late 1980s, it was becoming evident that a new class of survey research-based measurement tools was vastly improving our ability to predict customer preferences and choices. These were generally called trade-off experiments and were designated as two distinct classes of models—conjoint models and discrete choice models. Conjoint models generally are used to understand and model customer preferences. Discrete choice models, as their name implies, are used to understand and predict customer choices. There are hybrid models that take advantage of both approaches.

Essentially, these models allowed us to understand the value (or utility) that purchasers placed on each performance level for any particular product or service bundle in order to make a choice or express a preference.

These experiments present a set of alternative product bundles to a set of representative consumers and ask respondents to express their preference or make a choice. The construction of the alternative bundles takes a bit of work and needs to follow what statisticians call a "main effects experimental

Table 7.1

Brand	Price	Capacity	Loaf Shape
Braun	$159	1.0 lbs	round
Oster	$129	1.5 lbs	rectangular
Sears	$149	1.5 lbs	square
Acme	$149	1.0 lbs	round
Braun	$139	2.0 lbs	square
Oster	$139	1.5 lbs	square
Sears	$149	2.0 lbs	rectangular
Acme	$129	1.5 lbs	square

design," which is discussed in the Brand Value Model Technical Addendum in the Appendix. Each bundle typically includes a price, a brand name, and varying performance levels of each key product and channel attribute. As an illustration, if we were discussing automatic bread makers, some of the alternative bundles might be as shown in Table 7.1.

In this case, we have four attributes – brand, price, capacity, and loaf shape. Each attribute has a level—there are four brands, four price points, three capacity levels, and three loaf shape levels.

When respondents are presented with several subsets of these product bundles, they may be asked to rate or rank-order their preference for each bundle in the subset (for a conjoint experiment) or they may be asked to choose which product bundle in the subset they would purchase, or indicate they would not purchase any of those alternatives (choice experiment). If this experiment is properly designed, then it is possible to derive the utility (value) each respondent places on each level of each attribute. From these weights, we can further calculate how important each attribute is in driving the respondent's preferences and choices.

At SDR Consulting, we extended these models in two directions. We used conjoint (preference) modeling to drive the set up of a unique discrete choice experiment, and we expanded the procedure to encompass a further decomposition of the utility of "brand" into its key drivers.

A detailed discussion of the procedure may be found in the Brand Value Model Technical Addendum in the Appendix at the end of this book. The general procedure for deriving this model is as follows:

1. Specify the target audience. That is, specify in detail the end-users and potential end-users in the product or service category in which

your brand competes. This must be a fairly definitive statement of just who you believe is the target market for your branded product or service. The target market should be defined in terms of demographics/firmographics, product/service usage, and any other criteria that defines likely purchasers in the category. This level of specification is required so that you can randomly select a sample from the target audience that is suitable for projecting the results of the trade-off experiment to the entire targeted population.

2. Specify the key cost elements, product/service performance elements, channel performance elements, and the image and trust drivers of your brand. Do the same for each major competing brand. This should not be done by simply sitting around the conference room and deciding what those individual attributes are—use market research to have end users tell you what they are. Eliminate attributes that are (1) not important in driving customer preference and choice and (2) attributes that do not differentiate between the competing brands.

3. Design the trade-off experiment to have a representative sample of purchasers and potential purchasers choose the product bundles (combinations of price, performance attributes, and brand) they most prefer and those that they would likely purchase.

4. Execute the trade-off survey.

5. Use the results of the experiment to derive the Brand Value Equation (the set of utilities) for each respondent in the trade-off experiment. This procedure usually requires the use of a special type of regression model or a logit model, depending on how the data is collected.

6. Derive the importance weight of each element of the Brand Value Model for each respondent in the trade-off experiment and average those importance weights for your customers and the customers of each competing brand and compare. This will provide tremendous insight on the specific elements of your brand that purchasers value compared to how they value the individual elements of competing brands. We expand on this analysis in Chapter 11 when we discuss values-based segmentation.

Using this information, you can build a choice simulator that allows you to vary cost elements and product performance elements for both your brand and competing brands so that you may evaluate how changes in any of those elements, alone or in combination, will affect share of choice and overall market share. This also offers you insight into how to best define served market segments so that you can optimize media and other targeting efforts.

Utilizing the Brand Value Equation

Let's return to our Brand Value Equation. We can now view each element of the Brand Value Equation as having an "importance weight." These weights are derived from the trade-off exercise administered via a trade-off survey and the statistical modeling of those responses.

Brand Value $= (W_P$ Product Benefits $+ W_S$ Service Benefits $+ W_C$ Channel Benefits $+ W_B$ Brand Equity$) - W_P$ Costs

Each of these importance weights are calculated based on the utilities of the individual attribute levels. We cover that process in detail in the Brand Value Model Technical Addendum. For example, in our breadmaker exercise, the utilities and the derived attribute importance for a single respondent may look like that shown in Table 7.2.

In this example, we see that for this customer, price is the most important attribute (35.02%), followed closely by brand name (31.40%), then capacity (26.82%), and finally loaf configuration (6.77%).

Furthermore, we can observe that a Braun breadmaker with a 1.5 pound capacity making a round loaf priced at $159 has a total utility of (27.86 + 17.52 + 5.10 − 28.11 =) 22.37. Compare that to the utility of a Sears brand with a 1 pound capacity in a square loaf at $139.00. Summing those utilities (−12.92 − 26.63 + 0.95 + 15.77) yields a value estimate of −22.83. If only these two choices were in this consumer's consideration set, the consumer would very likely select the Braun. Don't be concerned about these negative utilities; they are simply an artifact of how we calculate utility for each performance level of each attribute. (You may note that the sum of utilities for any one attribute is zero.)

Having these individual utilities available for a representative set of potential customers would allow you to build a market simulator to estimate share of choice for each brand name with a known or proposed attribute profile and a particular price. Thus, we can observe the effects on share of choice for price changes and changes in feature performance for any brand or brand combination or, for the introduction of a branded product extension. A series of simulations whereby we only vary price, holding features

Table 7.2 Rescaled Second Conjoint

Level	Brand	Utility	Capacity	Utility	Loaf	Utility	Price	Utility
1	Oster	8.89	1.0 lbs	−26.63	round	5.10	$129	29.55
2	Braun	27.86	1.5 lbs	17.52	square	0.95	$139	15.77
3	Sears	−12.92	2.0 lbs	9.10	Rect.	−6.04	$149	−17.21
4	Acme	−23.83					$159	−28.11
Abs Diff		51.69		44.15		11.14		57.66
Importance		31.40%		26.82%		6.77%		35.02%

137

constant, allows us to develop estimates of price sensitivity for any brand at the total market or for any market segment.

More importantly, this model allows you to put a specific dollar value on a brand name at the individual unit level. You do this by setting each brand in the model as having the exact same performance characteristics (the average performance across all brands). Then you vary the price of each brand so that the total brand value of each brand is equal—that is, the consumer is ambivalent as to which brand they would chose. The price differential between the brands is a precise estimate of the dollar value of brand equity at the unit level. The math for doing these calculations is explained in more detail in the Brand Value Model Technical Addendum.

It should be obvious that this modeling approach also can also be used to determine how much of a brand's equity can be initially transferred into another product or service category. You simply derive the value model for the new category, including the new brand introduction and its performance characteristics and your target price. Then derive the Value Model, set the performance characteristics for each brand as equal, then adjust prices so that purchasers would be ambivalent as to which brand they would buy. The difference between the price of the introduced brand and the brand with the lowest equity represents the dollar value of the introduced brand's equity in the new category.

Finally, we can monitor a brand's equity over time through a series of market studies. The results of experimentation with the marketing mix can be easily monitored in this manner. Furthermore, this process would allow you to track how experiences with your brand affect your brand equity. If you are meeting or exceeding your brand promise, then the value of brand equity will rise; if you are not meeting your brand promise, it will fall.

You can even form a **brand promise-to-brand experience ratio** by dividing each respondent's brand equity for your brand by the number of total purchases of all brands they have made in the category. This will provide a tracking tool that will quickly help you understand whether brand value is being created or destroyed by your organization in terms of how employee behaviors and attribute performance is delivering the expected attributes, or not.

Another brand promise-to-brand experience "model" would contrast whether the brand was a high promise/high experience; low promise/high experience; low promise/low experience; or high promise/low experience.

Table 7.3   The Relationship Between Brand Promise and Brand Experience

		Low	High
Brand Promise	**High**	Defections Declining Profits	Optimizing Brand Equity
	Low	Commodity Market	Building Brand Equity

Brand Experience

The implications of each set in terms of the impact on revenues and profits could then be examined. For example, the high promise/low experience quadrant would be expected to produce rapidly declining revenues, losses, and customer churn. You can view the relationship between your brand promise and brand experience as shown in Table 7.3.

Although we have used a very simple illustration of the Brand Value Model, these models can be designed and used in any product or service category. However, the designs can get quite complex. Users need to make every effort to keep the model focused on the key purchase drivers in the category and eliminate unimportant and redundant attributes.

Information Provided by the Brand Value Model

One huge advantage of this modeling approach is that we calculate the utilities and importance weights at the respondent level. Thus, we can break out and compare results by known user groups such as your customers versus a competitor's customers, or heavy users versus light users, or by any other classification scheme, assuming you have an adequate sample size in each group.

The Brand Value Model and its accompanying computerized market simulator provide the following detailed information.

1. An estimate of overall brand equity for each brand in the study and the average *per unit* price premium that equity is worth at the market level or within defined market segments. Given accurate volume

estimates, the per unit price premium can be projected to a total value of the brand in any particular category.

2. Brand equity, price, and product/service feature values derived for each respondent can be used to segment the marketplace into benefit groups such as price sensitive, service sensitive, brand loyal for an individual brand, brand-combination loyal, and attribute importance groups. See Chapter 11 for a detailed discussion of this process. Within each segment, the equity of each brand in the category is calculated.

3. Market simulations can be run to estimate share of choice, given each brand's equity derived from the model, coupled with a known or contemplated product feature profile and a particular price. Thus, the user can observe the effects on share of choice for price changes and changes in tangible product attribute levels for any brand or brand combination. A series of simulations whereby only price is varied allows the user to develop estimates of price elasticity and cross elasticities for a brand at the total market level or within any market segment.

4. In a similar fashion, the model can be used to test and evaluate the extension of a known brand name into a new product/service category and to evaluate the equity transfer of the brand name into the new category.

5. Longitudinally, the user can observe the effects on brand value, brand equity, and share of choice due to changes in the marketing mix or a brand repositioning for any brand or combination of brands—yours or your competitors.

6. Given additional ratings of brands on the more intrinsic features of a brand's image (such as trust attributes, brand image attributes, quality of advertising, contribution to the community, social responsibility, protecting the environment, and so on), the model can directly relate brand equity values to particular activities of the firm.

More broadly speaking, corporate financial officers can use this tool to provide a very accurate estimate of the asset value of brand names or trademarks. This may be very useful for "Management's Discussion and Analysis" in annual financial statements.

The model can also be used to assess the value of brand names and trademarks in an acquisition situation in which the true value of a firm may be understated because the value of brands and trademarks are not adequately reflected on the balance sheet.

We explore the implications further in Chapter 12 when we discuss how the financial community can apply this type of economic analysis for valuation of brands:

The advantages of the modeling approach described in this chapter, using external surveys are:

1. The model is not dependent on internal financial data, but the information from the model can be directly integrated into financial planning and risk analysis.

2. After the initial design and a baseline study, it is relatively fast and easy to replicate the process over time using these proven research methods.

3. The survey and model derivation can be executed at any time in the business cycle. That is, it is not dependent on internal cyclical accounting changes.

4. It takes into account all major relevant brands in a defined product/ service category.

5. It measures brand equity relative to other current and potential brands in the category, including unbranded or store-brand items when they exist in the category.

6. It can be used to measure the transfer of a brand's equity into another category.

7. It recognizes that value of any one brand's equity can be defeated in the marketplace by competitor pricing strategies, at least in the short run.

8. It allows calculation of *total brand value* and *brand equity* over alternative pricing scenarios and volume scenarios for total market, or within defined subsegments.

9. Results can be projected to estimate the total value of a brand name under alternative sales projections. Thus, this modeling approach can be used to evaluate the total dollar value of a brand name for purposes of evaluation and acquisition.

10. If self-explicated ratings of the components of brand equity are acquired from the same respondents, brand equity can be further decomposed into specific equity-building activities.

11. The results can be used as part of a closed-loop process to create more effective definitions of subsegments as part of an overall brand quality management and continuous improvement initiative. We will discuss this further in Chapters 11 and 12.

The Brand Value Model and FAS 142

Does this model comply with the criteria we described in Chapter 6? Do this model and the measurement of brand equity comply with the requirements of FAS 142 and meet the criteria of comparability, reliability, and validity?

The model is clearly customer-focused. The utilities and importance weights are derived on how respondents reacted to the offerings in a controlled experimental setting.

The model is clearly valid. The basic choice model approach was initially developed by marketing academics in the 1970s. Since then, it has been tested in a very large number of different product and service categories by both academics and practitioners.

Initially, the model was applied very successfully to forecasting shares of new products prior to launch. Since then, it has been used to better understand how to improve share of choice in the marketplace, and to better understand the role of brand equity in driving brand choice. It is now a standard research procedure among professional marketing researchers. However, the model is not strictly mechanical. It requires careful selection of the set of key drivers of preference and choice in the category under study, and it requires some initial decisions concerning the algorithm that is to be used for deriving the utilities.

Is the model reliable? That is, if we take multiple random samples of a given population and administer the same trade-off experiment, will the results be the same? The answer is a definite yes. At SDR Consulting we have been using trade-off models since the mid 1970s and have demonstrated repeatedly that they are reliable. Our colleagues in academia and the marketing research field report high levels of reliability.

Is the model focused on both tangible and intangible attributes? Clearly it is. Not only can we observe how respondents value each level of each performance attribute, but we also can understand the values they place on each of the key drivers of brand equity.

Are the results diagnostic and actionable? Again, clearly the answer is yes. The utilities and the calculated importance for each attribute provide diagnostic insight and translate the key measures of brand equity into economic or currency values for investment decisions and linkage to business goals. The model has high diagnostic value because it can pinpoint specific areas of brand performance that are exceptionally strong or weak.

The model is predictive. Given a change in competitor offerings, or a change in your offering, the model will accurately predict how share of choice will likely change.

A weakness with the model is that its predictive power and reliability will be degraded when there is a change in what the marketplace values. For example, as digital photography started becoming popular, the fundamental requirements for computer color printers began to change. Consumers who were into digital photography developed a different value equation—one that emphasized true color reproduction, high resolution, and fast drying inks. When these types of value changes are detected in the marketplace, the Brand Value Model must be recalibrated with a new baseline study.

Can the model be targeted to specific market subsegments? Because we derive measure of brand equity at the respondent level, the model can be used to report utilities and importance for any benefit groups that make sense for your category such as price sensitive, service sensitive, brand loyal for an individual brand, brand-combination loyal, and attribute importance groups.

Are the results comparable? That is, if we derive the value of brand equity in one category and state that in a currency (such as U.S. dollars) at the unit level, is that value comparable to the currency value, at the unit level, of another brand in another category? Again, the answer is yes. The measure—the currency—is the same, and that currency value is derived from the utility of brands estimated by the regression or logit algorithm applied to the choices made in the trade-off exercise.

Do these comparable, reliable, and valid estimates of brand equity meet the criteria for measuring and reporting the value of intangible assets as specified in FAS 142? As of this writing, that has not been settled. However, below we quote paragraph 24 of FAS 142, dealing with Fair Value Measurements, with our emphasis added. You decide.

> 24. If quoted market prices are not available, the estimate of fair value shall be based on the best information available, including prices for similar assets and liabilities and the **results of using other valuation techniques.** A present value technique is often the best available technique with which to estimate the fair value of a group of net assets (such as a reporting unit). If a present value technique is used to measure fair value, estimates of future cash flows used in that technique shall incorporate **assumptions that marketplace participants would use in their estimates of fair value.** If that information is not available without undue cost and effort, **an entity may use its own assumptions. Those cash flow estimates shall be based on reasonable and supportable assumptions and shall consider all available estimates.**

The weight given to the evidence shall be commensurate with the extent to which the evidence can be verified objectively. If a range is estimated for the amounts or timing of possible cash flows, the likelihood of possible outcomes shall be considered. Concepts Statement 7 discusses the essential elements of a present value measurement (paragraph 23), provides examples of circumstances in which an entity's cash flows might differ from market cash flows (paragraph 32), and discusses the use of present value techniques in measuring the fair value of an asset or liability (paragraphs 39–54 and 75–88). Appendix E of this statement incorporates those paragraphs of Concepts Statement 7.

"Okay, now I get it—I've been focusing on operational efficiency since I got here, and now realize that I should have also been focusing on my brand equity and my brand promise."
  —Jack F. Eli, CEO, TasteRite

Chapter 8

Brand Loyalty and Brand Performance

"In order to be irreplaceable, one must always be different."

—Coco Chanel, Founder, Chanel, Inc.

Customer loyalty has become one of the marketing issues du jour in most industries and product categories. Unlike many other management fads, loyalty has a direct and obvious impact on the bottom line. Improvements in the retention of profitable customers reduces marketing costs, reduces employee turnover, reduces manufacturing and production costs, reduces delivery/channel costs, improves market share, and usually improves the hit rate on new product development via brand and line extensions.

Frederick Riechheld, in his book *The Loyalty Effect: The Hidden Force Behind Growth, Profits, and Lasting Value,* specifically Chapter 2, "The Economics of Customer Loyalty," demonstrated how improvements in customer loyalty reduce costs and improve financial performance.

Like many issues of this type, there is a myriad set of often-conflicting concepts, processes, and procedures for addressing customer loyalty fostered by management consultants and marketing research agencies. Too many of these are based on analogy and opinion that is not backed up by strong and converging research.

One of the more disconcerting findings of research over the last several years is that the link between customer satisfaction and customer loyalty is weak to nonexistent. After the expenditure of millions of dollars, senior management is being told that they may have been measuring the wrong thing! Yet the link between customer dissatisfaction and customer defection is strong. This apparent contradiction can be explained rather easily once we further examine the loyalty concept in light of the Brand Value Model.

In this chapter, we attempt to provide a rational conceptual framework for addressing the issues of customer loyalty and brand loyalty. This framework is based on some original research by the Marketing Sciences Institute, as we have interpreted it, and several years of applied research by both SDR Consulting and a few other firms.

One of the most interesting findings of this research has been the discovery that there are different kinds of loyalty. The varying motivations for behavioral loyalty allow us to classify customers into different loyalty groups, each requiring a different marketing approach. This classification scheme, based on the different types of loyalty, allows us to develop very effective strategic marketing programs for both the defense (reducing customer churn and improving retention), and the offense (new customer acquisition and greater share of customer spending, as well as improved new product success).

Definitions and Conceptual Framework

Let's start with a most basic concept—*loyalty is a behavior!* Behavioral loyalty is the bottom-line issue. Those who repeatedly purchase your brand at the exclusion or near exclusion of other brands represent an asset to the organization that directly translates to measurable financial performance. In other words, loyalty is completely linked to purchaser choices. Attitudinal loyalty (as defined by overall satisfaction, intent to repurchase and/or intent to recommend) is useful, but unless it translates into repeat purchases or higher share of expenditures, it's of little value. Furthermore, attitudinal loyalty, like that measured in customer satisfaction surveys, is generally a poor predictor of whether a customer will remain loyal or switch to another product or service.

From a behavioral viewpoint, you may view loyalty as a *lack of switching behavior,* given a set of available competing products or services. People and institutions may be loyal to a brand or they may be loyal to a brand set from a specific producer or manufacturer. Within each one of these loyalty constructs, purchasers may have widely varying motivations for being loyal. But loyalty should be expressed as a behavior—that is, the outcome of choices in the marketplace.

When customers or consumers are considering a purchase, they clearly evaluate the performance levels of each attribute that is important to them, the channels in which the product is available and the value it adds, as well as their trust in the brand and the image that brand conveys to them. They trade those values off against price to arrive at a total value for each offering. Managers must understand that the motivation for repurchase, or defection, must consider all elements of the value equation, not just the attitudinal component. To consider only the attitudinal element can be very misleading and may point the marketer to make the wrong investments. To put it bluntly, even the highest brand equity can be defeated by a competitors' product/service performance and/or price.

Indeed, our research in many product and service categories, both B2B and B2C, clearly demonstrates that of those customers who show high behavioral loyalty, very small percentages are truly attitudinally loyal. That is, very few place such high utility on a brand name alone, that it totally dominates their choice of which product or service to buy on their next purchase occasion. Most are either optimizing the tangible benefit set or are declining to engage in repeated search and evaluation activities. We believe that it is extremely important for marketers to know all the elements that are driving repeat purchase as well as those that are barring repeat purchase. Concentrating on just the attitudinal components (the brand's equity) provides only part of the answer of what drives value and choice, as we illustrated in Chapter 7.

Having said that, it should still be obvious that any incremental improvements in brand equity provides an overall improvement in total brand value and is often the key basis for product/service differentiation and improvements in share of customer. **When there are few differences among competing brands in the marketplace in terms of product performance and price, then brand equity becomes the tie-breaker—the source for sustainable competitive advantage.** A good example is in American pilsner beers. It has been shown repeatedly that few Americans can distinguish among the more popular brands of pilsner beers in a blind taste test. However for many beer consumers there is considerable loyalty to a particular brand and its sub-brands. Given little discernable difference in product performance and price, brand equity reigns—providing the key differentiator and the main basis for behavioral loyalty.

For any particular purchaser, loyalty behavior can vary from category to category. For example, a person may be loyal to a particular manufacturer of automobiles (a Quest for the family, a PathFinder for themselves, and a Sentra for the college-bound child—all produced and marketed by Nissan). At the same time, that purchaser may be brand loyal to a particular brand of lawn mower (Cub Cadet, although Cub Cadet's manufacturer, MTD, produces several other brands of mowers), and channel loyal for their dog food and pet supplies (PetSmart). Likewise, they may be very prone to switching when it comes to frozen dinner entrees, purchasing those brands that seem like the better bargain from the closest available grocery store.

Operationally, many managers think of brand loyalty as primarily applying to consumer product markets and customer loyalty as primarily applying to services and business markets. However, this simple dichotomy can be very misleading, and requires considerable clarification if we are to adequately manage it.

From a behavioral perspective, brand loyalty is really just a more narrow definition of loyalty than is customer loyalty. In many product and some service categories, a single manufacturer will have multiple brands. That is, if brand name and producer names are synonymous in a particular category, brand loyalty is the same as customer loyalty in that category. On the other hand, if a producer has more than one brand in a category, like Nissan, customer loyalty has a somewhat different definition than does brand loyalty, encompassing all of the brands of a single producer/manufacturer.

More precisely:

Brand loyalty may be defined as the proportion of times a purchaser chooses the same brand in a specific product or service category compared to the total number of purchases made in that category over a specific time period, under the condition that other acceptable products/services are equally available.

This definition specifies the following:

- Brand loyalty is an individual behavior based on the act of choosing to purchase. It applies equally to persons (consumers) and institutions (specifiers, influencers, and buyers acting on behalf of the institution).
- The measurement of brand loyalty should be restricted to a specific category of products/services that are functionally substitutable. For example a consumer may be very loyal to the Honda brand for automobiles, but not at all loyal to the Honda brand for lawn mowers.
- There are degrees of loyalty; it may be expressed as a proportion or as a percentage ranging from zero to 100 percent.
- An accurate measurement of brand loyalty requires that purchasers be measured over a sufficient time period (for example, several purchase cycles), or under different competitive circumstances (for example, experimentally) whereby there are multiple opportunities to observe and/or record purchaser selections in the product/service category.
- Competing brands in the category must be equally available. That is, barriers to switching must be minimized, or at least measured and taken into account for assessing brand loyalty. Of course, a viable marketing strategy is to erect and maintain barriers in order to dampen customer switching. However, in the long run, such barriers to switching often build up customer resentment and are ultimately self-defeating.

The concept of *customer loyalty* may be viewed as very similar to that of brand loyalty, the difference being that the focus of the choice behavior is not necessarily on a single brand, but rather on a set of products and services offered by a single producer/distributor in a specific category. Thus, customer loyalty can be defined as follows:

> *Customer loyalty is the proportion of times a purchaser chooses products/services from the same producer, manufacturer, and/or provider in a specific category compared to the total number of purchases made in that category from all producers, manufacturers, and/or providers, over a given time frame, under the condition that other acceptable products/services are equally available.*

The definition of customer loyalty simply recognizes that some producers may have multiple brands/products/services in alternative channels for a specific category and purchasers may switch between a producer's offerings and/or channels. A good example is Black & Decker, which, in the handheld electric power tool category, has two brand names, Black & Decker and DeWalt, each of which is distributed through multiple, sometimes overlapping, channels. Yet each of those brands has different price points and is perceived as having different performance characteristics. The Black & Decker loyalist may purchase the value-priced Black & Decker reciprocal saw for occasional use around the home but pay a premium price for a DeWalt cordless drill with all the bells and whistles for more frequent and vigorous use.

A key point of these definitions and subsequent discussion is that loyalty is only relevant to a specific product or service category. A specific category is one where the product or service performance features are considered substitutable by the purchaser. We note that sometimes this definition of a category is at variance with conventional categorizations used by the advertising and publishing community. For example, from a consumer behavior point of view, "flavored fruit drinks" and "sports drinks" are often seen as interchangeable. That is, for most consumers, they are in the same consideration set. But for other consumers, they definitely are not.

Given these definitions, it should be obvious why typical customer satisfaction surveys do not measure loyalty. Satisfaction is an attitude, and questions relating to satisfaction do not measure the utility a purchaser places on "brand." Loyalty is a behavior—it's "choice." There is a 50-year stream of marketing research that demonstrates stated attitudes are very often poor predictors of future behaviors. Additionally, the measurement of attitude tends to be imprecise, highly variable, and subject to prevailing social norms and economic outlook. The measurement of behavior is much more concrete and precise—a person either chose to purchase a particular brand/product from a particular channel at a particular time, or they did not. And, when we understand what drives choice, we understand what drives loyalty.

So, under these behavioral-based definitions of brand loyalty and customer loyalty, we have a straightforward measurement, although capturing that behavioral data can be challenging in some product and service categories. That's another reason the Brand Value Model is so useful. It rather precisely allows us to predict customer choice from samples of representative customers. And once we segment the market into homogeneous groups of customers with similar values, we can better understand what is driving loyalty behavior, as we discuss in detail in Chapter 11.

The rub, however, is motivation. What motivates purchasers to be loyal or not loyal to a particular brand or producer? The short answer is their perceptions of value, or more precisely, their utilities, as we discussed in Chapter 7.

A Divergence—Customer Loyalty with Customer Satisfaction Surveys

Unfortunately, many companies believe they are already measuring customer loyalty in their customer satisfaction surveys. Typically, three questions are asked:

1. Overall, how satisfied are you with _____?
2. Would you recommend _____?
3. Do you intend to repurchase _____?

The analytical procedure is to measure each response on (usually) a five-point scale. If the respondent gave the highest value (top box) on all three measures, that respondent is designated a "secure" or "loyal" customer. Anything less, relegates the customer to "satisfied," "vulnerable," or "dissatisfied."

We believe that the three measures are redundant measures of satisfaction and are no different than asking, "How satisfied are you?" "How REALLY satisfied are you?" and "How REALLY, REALLY satisfied are you?" Said differently, the advocates of this approach are asking you to believe that a customer will treat all three questions as independent measures of how the customer considers the producer's performance. That is, the underlying assumption is that whether or not a customer is totally satisfied with the producer's performance has little to do with (or, in other words, is independent of) whether they would repurchase the brand or recommend it to others. We are very skeptical of that position and believe that the three questions are simply measuring different points on the same satisfaction continuum.

We have seen the correlations between these three measures range from 0.75 to as high as 0.95, assuming there is no measurement error or response error (which is tough to assume). That leaves very little independent variation from which to draw conclusions about the differences in response patterns. Indeed, if we perform a statistical test, called a reliability test, on the three measures, we find that the measure of redundancy is so large that any one of the questions will adequately represent any of the other two questions.

To verify that, on several occasions the data from those questions were subjected to a principal components analysis, which is a type of scaling procedure. In all cases, only one significant principal component (scale) could be found. In one typical case, the answers to the three questions correlated to that one principal component at the following levels: 0.86, 0.89, 0.92. That's about as redundant as you can get in survey data among a large sample of customers.

One of the effects of this procedure is that the number of secure (loyal) customers is considerably overstated mainly because this attitude-only model narrows the focus to three redundant measures of overall satisfaction.

In a study by SDR Consulting, we used our Brand Value Model to derive customers' preference structures and validated those with a choice experiment. We also asked the three "loyalty" questions using a 0–10 point scale. The results were strikingly different. The Brand Value Model revealed that 4 percent of customers were brand loyal. That is, their utility for brand name of the client would offset reasonable competitor advantages in price and performance levels. Calculating loyalty using the three loyalty questions showed that 35 percent of customers were brand loyal (in other words, secure)—they gave all three measures a top two-box score on a 0–10 point scale.

Loyalty and the Brand Value Concept

Loyalty to a brand or producer is expressed as a choice, and, as we demonstrated in Chapter 7, value drives choice.

Let's reconsider the Value Equation we developed in Chapter 7.

Brand Value = (W_P Product Benefits + W_S Service Benefits + W_C Channel Benefits + W_B Brand Equity) − W_P Costs

Recall that each of the importance weights in this Brand Value Equation is the summation of the importance weights of individual attributes, which are derived from the utility a purchaser places on each performance level of each attribute.

Brand Value can be viewed as the total utility a person places on each product/service available to him or her in a category. Rational buyers will purchase the product or service in a category that they perceive gives them the highest value (utility) of those available at the time of purchase.

Each product or service in a category delivers a bundle of *tangible benefits* to the purchaser. These tangible benefits are the real, physical deliverables of the product or service that are used by the purchaser to satisfy their perceived needs. Thus, individually and as a group, tangible benefits represent value to the purchaser. These are called the performance attributes of the product or service. They may be delivered by the product or service itself and/or by the channel (outlet) or person (sales force) by which the product/service is delivered.

Each product or service also delivers a bundle of *intangible benefits* to the purchaser. These intangible benefits are the trust and image drivers associated with the producer's or manufacturer's brand name (and in some cases the channel name) and are used to satisfy other perceived needs and wants of the purchaser (such as trust, reinforcement of self-image, social responsibility, risk reduction). As a bundle, these intangible benefits may be thought of as the *brand's equity*. These intangible benefits also represent value to the purchaser to some greater or lesser degree.

Purchasers trade off the value of the bundles of tangible benefits and intangible benefits against price to arrive at a total value for each product/service in their competitive set. Rational purchasers then choose the product/service that provides the best value or greatest utility. Thus, a product's or service's relative value drives customer choice, and therefore loyalty behavior.

If, over time, a particular brand or manufacturer/producer maintains a significantly higher perception of value to a purchaser than any other product/service in the category, that purchaser will consistently buy that product/service proportionately more than any other products/services in the category. Conversely, as products/services in a category become less differentiated in terms of tangible and intangible features, price becomes the more important differentiator of value, and there is less loyalty.

In some B2B categories, purchasers will secure two or more suppliers for critical supplies, components, and/or services. Their rationale is that they need to optimize reliability of supply and ensure price and service competition. Information is shared with all suppliers concerning price and service enhancements. This is a form of risk management. On the surface, this appears to be an exception to the "rational purchaser" assumption behind the Brand Value Model. However, if the model includes performance levels such as "always delivers on schedule," "willingly participates in multiple-supplier bids and negotiations," and "guarantees best-price contracts," we can understand the amount of utility each purchaser places on these performance levels.

Furthermore, in the choice simulator that is based on the Brand Value Model, you can design and program it to show proportional shares of choice instead of the first choice only. Thus, the producer can see how their current and contemplated performance levels will change their proportion of sales with any one purchaser or across groups of purchasers. We discuss this process in the Brand Value Model Technical Addendum.

Analysis and Observations

Having applied this model and its measurement system in a very large number of product and service categories, we have made some interesting observations.

The weights in the Value Model vary dramatically by product/service category. In heavily promoted and branded categories, brand/company equity will have greater relative importance. In weakly branded categories, price has a greater weight. In categories with differentiated products and services, or with competing channels, specific deliverables have greater weights. Table 8.1 shows some examples.

Table 8.1   Relative Average Importance of Value Elements*

Category	Price	Product/Channel Attributes	Brand/Co. Equity
Carbonated Soft Drinks (Heavy users of a particular type)	22%	40%	38%
A Class of Automobiles (1994 Price range $14,000 to $22,000)	24%	68%	8%
Consumer Paper Products (Purchase branded products)	48%	46%	6%
Sports Drinks (Age group that is performance-oriented)	8%	34%	58%
Canned Pet Food (For a particular animal type)	50%	43%	7%
Industrial Electronic Equipment (Particular production process)	16%	72%	12%

Note: These examples are for specific defined segments within each category.

The levels of active involvement (cognition) purchasers undertake varies from category to category. In high-involvement categories (automobiles, financial services, industrial machinery, real estate brokerage services, and so on) most purchasers tend to make a cognitive trade-off of features and benefits (both tangible and intangible) at every purchase opportunity to arrive at their best value and, therefore, choice.

In other categories, especially those where there is a short purchase cycle or low involvement, such as consumer packaged goods, a relatively large number of purchasers make a cognitive trade-off early on in their purchase history. If the purchase meets their expectations, then they tend to use the brand name or producer's name as a substitute for a cognitive reevaluation in subsequent purchase occasions—seeking to minimize the time and cost of that reevaluation.

The weights in the Value Model vary highly from purchaser to purchaser in the same category, depending on their individual preference structure or brand value equation. Some purchasers put high value on brand equity. Other purchasers in the same category put high value on one or more performance attributes. Still others are price sensitive, desiring just the basic performance characteristics of products in the category for the lowest possible price. Table 8.2 shows how several respondents varied in terms of the value they placed on selected aspects of an automobile within a certain price range.

These findings led us to the observation that there are different types of loyalty. Inspection of the weights in individual preference structures over many studies of this type led us to the conclusion that there are several

Table 8.2   Relative Importance of Selected Drivers of Value—Automobiles*

	Price Importance	MPG	ABS Brakes	Engine Size	Total Importance of All Performance Attributes	Brand Importance	Brand with Highest Utility
Resp. A	8.3%	3.1%	8.3%	2.4%	51.1%	34.6%	Camry
Resp. B	31.3%	18.5%	3.1%	11.3%	64.6%	4.1%	Civic
Resp. C	12.3%	1.3%	12.4%	21.1%	77.3%	10.4%	Altima
Resp. D	10.2%	4.3%	5.9%	7.2%	69.9%	18.9%	Saturn, Mazda626

*1994 data

different types of loyalty and disloyalty present in every product/service category.

Committed Loyalists

Committed loyalists are both behaviorally loyal and attitudinally loyal. They put high value on their preferred brand's name or producer/manufacturer's brand name. In order to get them to defect or switch brands, it takes a large increase in price utility (such as a much lower price) and/or large increases in important attribute utilities to offset the purchaser's perceived value of brand. Respondent A in Table 8.2 is a good example. She has a high preference for a specific brand name—Camry. In order to get this purchaser to switch to another automobile, a competitor would need to offer her a much better value in vehicle features and/or price. So much so that it most likely would make it economically unattractive to do so.

Alternatively, a competitor may attempt to change her preference structure so she puts more value on specific product attributes (for example, side air bags and ABS brakes) that favor the competitor.

Yet another alternative for a competitor is to convince the purchaser that their brand better aligns with the purchaser's desired self-image. And indeed, this is where a lot of automobile marketers are concentrating their advertising. Unfortunately, in our opinion, the current advertising messages are mostly missing their mark by (1) failing to provide strong alignment between the brand and the target market's shared belief system—their self image or (2) reaching too far outside their established brand image. Positioning a Chevy Impala as a luxury automobile is just too much of a stretch for most consumers.

These committed loyalists are the marketer's dream. Recall my friend in Chapter 7 who basically paid $4,500 for having the Honda nameplate on his SUV. Committed loyalists will pay a premium to get the brand name they want. That is, they place high value on the bundle of intangible benefits represented by the brand name. They are least susceptible to switching. They will continue to place high value on the brand/manufacturer name unless that supplier fails miserably to deliver on their brand promise, or does something so socially irresponsible or untrustworthy as to force the purchaser's reevaluation of brand equity. Unfortunately, for most firms their truly brand loyal customers represent a very small percentage of their total customer base.

Good examples of brands with relatively high percentages of committed loyalists are Starbucks, Honda, Harley-Davidson, BMW, IBM, Tide, Midwest Airlines, and Coca-Cola. The values these firms consistently espouse in both trust and image attributes are in alignment with their target markets' belief system and their desired self-images. This alignment of values gives these firms the ability to create lots of brand equity, and, therefore, brand value and market value.

The basic strategy for marketing to committed loyalists is to continually and consistently reinforce the brand promise and its alignment with purchaser needs and wants. That is, continually and consistently reinforce the brand promise and the manner in which the firm is fulfilling that promise in everything the firm does and says.

The execution of the Brand Value Model, and specifically the decomposition of brand equity, will provide the firm with a better understanding of which specific image attributes are most resonating with customers and potential customers, and which are not. For example, in a study of large commercial and industrial purchasers of electric supply services, we found that the following trust and image attributes were the key drivers of brand equity for the client brand.

- Honest in its dealings with customers
- Progressive and innovative
- Respects me as a customer
- Is well managed
- Efficient in coordinating the service activities of different departments
- Keeps me informed of energy matters that are important to my business
- Professional in negotiations and the regulatory environment

Shopper Loyalists

Shopper loyalists shop around for a specific set of performance attributes. Thus, they put very high utility on a specific bundle of performance attributes they feel they must have. Once found, they strongly believe one brand/company delivers that set of attributes better than any others. Brand equity is not very relevant except as an identifier for the producer of the bundle of performance attributes they desire. The benefits from these performance attributes are what these purchasers are seeking. Thus, a competitor must match or exceed these attribute performances, or alternatively, make a major increase in price utility (by lowering price) and/or brand equity to get them to defect. Respondents 2 and 3 are good examples.

Respondent B puts very high value on miles per gallon (MPG) and price, and low value on brand name. A competitor would need to match and/or exceed MPG, and/or offer a much lower price, and/or load on enough other accessories/features to overcome this purchaser's choice for the best MPG and price in the category. On the other hand, Respondent C puts high value on engine size and ABS breaks—he wants a performance car. To get this respondent to switch, a competitor would need to offer a better performance package, and/or a set of other accessories/features that would offset the value of engine size and ABS brakes and/or a much cheaper price.

Typically, marketers address shopper loyalists by promoting product/service performance features and their related benefits. The producer is very vulnerable to switching when another producer either exceeds the desired performance characteristics or matches these performance characteristics at a lower price. In which case, this group of purchasers will switch rapidly in order to maximize value. These folks are behaviorally loyal until someone comes along with a better mousetrap.

Many times marketers will attempt to identify specific groups of people who desire a very specific set of performance attributes and address those groups with brand extensions or flanker brands. Thus, we see automobile brands with a "GT" option, or Jack Daniels produce a "Single Barrel" bourbon option.

Another viable alternative strategy for addressing these shopper loyalists in some product categories is to try to change their preference structures to put more utility on the features best delivered by your product or service. Of course, if there is little actual product/service differentiation, the marketer must rely on a strong branding strategy, emphasizing the bundle of intangible benefits, or revert to pure price/channel competition.

Convenience Loyalists

Convenience loyalists typically do not want to expend the time and effort to make a cognitive evaluation of the competing alternatives at every purchase opportunity. As a matter of convenience and time saving, they tend to stick with their brand as long as that brand continues to fulfill the basic needs they seek from the category. Although one would typically not see a convenience loyalist in the automobile category (because of the typical high involvement in the purchasing process), Respondent D shows some of those tendencies. Her preference structure puts relatively high importance on two different brands, yet no one product attribute is very important, nor is price that important (although the bundle of attributes, as a whole, are very important). Survey results of her two most recent purchases reveals that these are the two brands with her highest utility. She would typically trade off price against any one of the two acceptable brand alternatives UNLESS she has a performance or service problem with one (or both) of those brands.

These convenience loyalists can be a marketer's nightmare. Although they appear to be behaviorally loyal over time (because nothing changes, so they keep purchasing what they have in the past) a single performance flaw or a single bad service encounter raises this type of customer's awareness and they will make a cognitive reevaluation of the competing alternatives, usually defecting to another supplier or producer.

The discovery of these convenience loyalists reinforces our belief that customer satisfaction is a multifaceted and discontinuous construct. Customer satisfaction does not drive choice—value does. But, *customer dissatisfaction* does drive defection because it forces a conscience reevaluation of the competing alternatives under circumstances where the current supplier is at a tremendous disadvantage.

Said differently, customer satisfaction simply keeps a brand in the customer's consideration set. But value drives choice among the brands in the consideration set. And if a brand fails to deliver on its brand promise, then it will no longer be in the purchaser's consideration set.

In many categories convenience loyalists represent the majority of repeat-purchase customers. When asked, these customers typically give high satisfaction ratings to their usual brand/supplier. Then a single negative incident—a product failure, a service failure, a publicly irresponsible act, or nonavailability—raises their awareness, triggering a cognitive evaluation of alternatives. Under these circumstances, the convenience loyalists will usually switch brands because the brand they purchased previously is no longer in their consideration set. This is why immediate, proactive service recovery is so important to the retention of customers. This is also why there is a strong relationship between dissatisfaction and defection, but only a weak relationship between higher levels of satisfaction and purchase choice.

As a matter of policy, this phenomenon is why we often recommend that most customer satisfaction research be reoriented to concentrate on understanding the drivers of *dissatisfaction*. Dissatisfaction takes you out of the consideration set, thus the probability of being chosen is zero. On the other hand, acceptable satisfaction only guarantees you will be considered, but there is no guarantee you will be chosen. That depends on how you stack up against the other brands in the consideration set in terms of perceived value. So, from that point of view, it is more important to minimize dissatisfaction among the largest possible percentage of customers than it is to maximize satisfaction among those that are already sufficiently satisfied with your performance so that you remain in their consideration set.

Once you understand this relationship between satisfaction and choice, that raises another key issue—how much satisfaction is enough? In other words, how can a firm economically justify striving for very high levels of customer satisfaction when the only economic justification for satisfaction is to keep you in the consideration set?

There are really two answers to the question of how much satisfaction is enough, depending on how your brand is performing in the categories in which you compete. And that takes us back to the Brand Value Model.

If the key drivers of value in your category lie in the tangible performance attributes, and your brand is not generally considered the top-performing brand in the category, then you will improve your loyalty (that is, your share of choice and repeat purchase) by investing in improving your performance in those tangible attributes that have the highest utility to your customers and potential customers. On the other hand, if the key drivers in your category lie in the brand equity attributes, or if you are already nearly optimizing your performance in the tangible attribute set, then you will improve loyalty by investing in improving your imagery in both the trust attributes and/or the image attributes. It just so happens that the investments you make to improve customer satisfaction usually line up with improving your performance on the trust attributes. So, in some circumstances, striving for ever higher levels of customer satisfaction is justified for some firms in some circumstances, but only if your product/service is performing at near optimal levels, or if brand equity is the key differentiator in your category.

Channel Loyalists

Channel loyalists are relevant when there are alternative channels readily available and the channel provides added value. Often the channel (or for industrial products, the sales force) will provide highly valued service benefits—warranty repair, technical knowledge, guarantees, time convenience, location convenience, and so on. A good example is personal computers. Traditional retail outlets, specialty stores, mass merchandisers, mail order, and the Internet are all viable channels for many of the same brands. Typically, channel loyalists place high value on benefits delivered by the channel, put undifferentiated values on the basic performance characteristics (product attributes) in the category, and do not put high value on any one brand name, but typically put nearly equal value on each brand in a constrained brand set. In many value models we have developed, price and channel interact because of the variations in perceived mark-up by channel.

In categories where there are several alternative channels, the marketer must understand the benefits provided by both the product/service and the channel to fully derive the Brand Value Model. Because of the complexity of channel effects in some categories and because of the interactions between channel deliverables and product deliverables, we often execute the Brand Value Model separately for each major channel.

One effective strategy for some firms has been to develop operating brands that are specific to a channel. For example, Yamaha uses different model lines for its stereo tuners—the premium RX-V series for its affiliated dealers and the HTR series for department stores, mass merchandisers, and Internet retailers. The effectiveness of this strategy is dependent on there being obvious and significant differences between the performance characteristics of the operating brands and the channels.

Price Switchers

Price-sensitive purchasers put high value (utility) on price and put very even values on the basic performance characteristics (attributes) in the category, and very low importance on both nonessential performance attributes and brand/company equity. These purchasers are simply seeking basic performance from products or services in the category and will purchase that basic set of performance characteristics at the best price, which maximizes value for them.

One of the very interesting findings from our research over the years is that buyers are not nearly as price sensitive as management believes they are. There are many reasons. In one study we conducted in the B2B arena, senior managers believed that, on average, the importance of price accounted for over 50 percent of the purchase decision. Among the twenty or so senior managers polled, price importance ranged from 30 percent to 90 percent. The Value Model revealed that, on average, price only accounted for 15 percent of importance in choosing a supplier. How could management have been so wrong?

In the B2B arena, where the sales force is dealing with purchasing agents, purchasing committees, or distributors, the main discussions often deal with pricing issues. So, pricing concerns represent the bulk of the market information received by senior management. Furthermore, sales force incentives are often geared to sales volume, not profitability. So, the sales force itself often pressures management to make price concessions in order to secure a sale. In many B2B firms there is a prevailing myth that senior management knows their customers better than anyone else possibly could, so there is little incentive for funding independent customer research, especially in the pricing arena. Finally, senior management often fails to understand the role of brand equity in the purchase decision, believing that the purchase decision is totally driven by product performance and price. And if there is little significant difference in product performance among competitors, then price becomes the key leverage point.

In consumer markets there are also many reasons why senior managers believe price is more important than it is among consumers. More often than not, marketers have trained consumers to be price sensitive. The knee-jerk reaction to declining sales or share in a category is to drop prices. That signals consumers that there are few differences in the actual performance of the brands and that brand equity doesn't matter. Then, in order to gain short-term share, marketers will offer indiscriminant discount promotions, which again tells consumers that price is the key differentiator between competing products. In essence, these marketers are cashing in their brand equity at a discount of true value for short-term gain. Once cashed in, that brand equity is very difficult to rebuild.

In consumer packaged goods, the discounting has been so prevalent and predictable, that consumers have been trained to delay purchases to await the next round of price promotions. Then they will purchase to stock up on the product, making the promotion seem a resounding success. In fact, these promotions are simply disrupting normal purchase cycles and depreciating brand equity. The marketer is again saying that there are no significant product differences and that brand equity really doesn't mean much. The major reason that store brands have been so successful is that marketers of branded consumer packaged goods have failed to address differences in product performance and have failed to communicate what their brand promise really is.

If your firm is not the lowest cost producer in the category (and even if you are), it seems that there are several strategies available to you for addressing the price sensitive purchaser.

Your first consideration may be simply to ignore them. If price-sensitive purchasers represent a manageable share of all purchasers in the category, say 20 percent or less, then it may be best to simply write off that group and let your competitors fight over them. Had AT&T done that in the early days of long-distance calling competition, they would still likely be a dominant force in the long-distance marketplace.

If there are significant differences in product performance between the set of major competitors in the category, then you should emphasize those differences and the benefits they convey to the purchaser to your advantage in your marketing communications. You want to change their preference structure by raising their awareness of, and preference for, specific performance attributes.

If there are few real differences in product performance between the set of major competitors in the category, look for sustainable opportunities to add value. This could be an innovative performance enhancement, or a service wraparound. It could also be a new channel or increased availability. The key for these initiatives is that purchasers must clearly see them as adding value and be willing to pay for the enhancements.

Alternatively, if there are few real differences in product performance, and there are only limited opportunities to improve product/service performance, then you need to concentrate on the drivers of brand equity, emphasizing your key trust and image attributes. Then try to persuade these price-sensitive purchasers that your brand has the better value, all things considered.

If your brand is not compatible with the basic benefits being sought by the price switchers, then another alternative is to create or purchase a "price" brand that can effectively compete in that segment.

The existence of these loyalty groups seems to be very consistent across all product categories we have tested.

Determining Loyalist Types and Switchers from the Value Model

Because the Value Model is derived at the individual level, we can easily determine who would purchase what, given competing product performance descriptions. That is, if we can specify the brand/company name, the performance attributes, the channel attributes (if relevant), and price for each of a set of competing products/services in the category, then we can calculate the total utility or value that each respondent places on each offering, and therefore determine their most likely choice. This allows us to determine who would stay loyal and who would switch under alternative market scenarios. More importantly, we can determine why they would switch, whether it is due to specific tangible product benefits, specific channel benefits, price, or brand/producer/channel equities.

A market response simulator, based on the individual preference structures revealed by the Brand Value Model, can be set up in an Excel-type spreadsheet, allowing the user to view the results in terms of predicted share of choice for each alternative set of product/service configurations. The Brand Value Model Technical Addendum in the Appendix provides the details of how to do this, although you likely will still need well-trained marketing researchers or a research agency to handle all of the nuts and bolts of the process.

The market response simulator also allows the marketer or product manager to maximize market share by optimizing their product's delivered benefits in conjunction with a fixed brand/company equity across alternative pricing levels.

Using Loyalty Type as a Segmentation Tool

Because we derive the Brand Value Model and can determine loyalty type at the individual level, it is a rather simple task to use this information to segment a market and determine how to best approach each segment. Chapter 11 provides the framework for this values-based market segmentation scheme.

Some drivers of Brand/Company equity are universal. Once brand/company/channel equity is determined in the aggregate, it can be further decomposed into individual intangible attributes, or imagery drivers, using some rather sophisticated analytical techniques as we discussed in Chapter 7 and in the Brand Value Model Technical Addendum.

Such analysis allows marketers to understand the imagery drivers that reinforce and build brand equity. Some of these imagery drivers are unique to the product category. But others seem almost universal.

Trust is a key intangible attribute. This construct of trust goes beyond the normal warranties and guarantees that are offered as a tangible product attribute. Trust is the perception and belief that the producer, manufacturer, or channel will deliver on the purchasers' expectations—their brand promise. Trust is the perception that the producer will fix or otherwise make good a product or service failure. Trust is a universal key driver of brand equity in every category we have researched. Essentially, it is a composite measure that has many facets. We discussed these trust attributes in Chapter 7.

Image reinforcement is another key set of intangible attributes. Individuals and many firms have an image that they constantly seek to reinforce. They often use the imagery of the products and services they purchase to enhance their self-image. The concept of "a brand I like to be seen with" or "a supplier whose products support our company's image" is a key driver of a brand's equity and is almost universal. We also provided details of these image attributes in Chapter 7.

Social responsibility is another key intangible attribute. In general, customers and consumers assume that the firms with whom they deal are socially responsible. If a firm is perceived to not be socially responsible, it universally suffers lower, and even negative, brand equity. The contract with the customer/consumer has been broken and customers will defect in droves.

The Brand Value Model can address Corporate Social Responsibility (CSR) issues in two ways—as performance attributes or as image attributes. In many cases where we address CSR issues as performance attributes, such as "green power" or "contributions to the community," the results are less than encouraging.

The problem with CSR issues that are addressed as performance attributes is that in the Brand Value Model, where purchasers are actively trading off performance issues and brand equity against price, CSR activities seldom show up as important to the vast majority. In fact, they are often decidedly unimportant. This was brought home in stark reality when we did several Brand Value Models for the utility industry, which was at that time heavily investing in and promoting "green" energy. On average, this attribute had very low utility. And, for a substantial number of purchasers it even had a negative utility—implying that they preferred the no "green energy" option over having that option. The marketplace confirmed that prediction from the Brand Value Model—green energy—initially was a total bust in terms of improving customer loyalty or improving share of market.

In another example, the Brand Value Model was used to understand the key sources of value in a particular category of beverages. The model incorporated the performance attribute of "date stamping" for the client's brand. That attribute had been touted as a new initiative in corporate social responsibility with a six-month advertising blitz by the client firm. When the model showed that its inclusion on the container did not contribute to overall brand value and consumer choice, we were greeted with hoots of disbelief. Yet, one of the senior executives of the firm told us privately, after the fact, that we were right, but the CEO had invested his time and reputation in the campaign, personally appearing in several of the advertisements, and no one had the guts to tell him it wasn't making a difference. It was a flop, costing the stockholders tens of millions of dollars in advertising that was making no contribution to improving the asset value of the firm or the loyalty of its customers.

When CSR initiatives are directly pitted against higher prices or any degradation in basic product or service performance, they are given low or negative equity. Look at the problems with gas-electric automobiles to see this phenomenon at work. To date, these vehicles have been more expensive, and do not perform as well as vehicles driven by standard fuels—gasoline and diesel. In a trade-off exercise, few participants place high utility (value) on that attribute when price is higher or performance is impaired. So, the market appeal for that initiative is very limited. Yet, the pioneers in this technology, principally Honda and Toyota, have received extremely positive press and that has reinforced their brand equity and their asset value.

When CSR initiatives are addressed in the brand ratings, we generally see that they are positively and significantly related to the brand equity of the firm that has taken the initiative, thus contributing to overall brand equity, customer loyalty, and the asset value of the firm.

A widely acclaimed study entitled *Corporate Social and Financial Performance: A Meta-Analysis*[1] shows that there is a positive association between corporate social performance (CSP) and corporate financial performance (CFP) across industries and across study contexts. In most circumstances, the Brand Value Model has confirmed that association in terms of comparative brand equity.

The lesson learned is that you cannot expect a CSR program to compete directly against price and performance issues when there are significant price and performance differences between competitors in a category. However, when brand equity becomes the key differentiator between competitors, CSR initiatives can, and often do, make a significant difference.

There is a certain amount of risk you take on when you launch a CSR initiative. What may seem like a noble idea to you and your management team can fall flat on its face if it is not in alignment with your corporate image and brand promise. The soft drink example discussed previously demonstrated that "date stamping" did not resonate well with heavy consumers in that particular beverage category. They didn't store their beverages for long periods of time anyway. In another example, committing to "Preserving the Family Farm," as one famous producer of ice cream did recently, may sound like a wonderful idea. But for those who know farming, and the efficiencies and consumer benefits of scale in that sector, most consider it a rather lame idea whose time is far passed.

When CSR programs are well executed and are in strong alignment with the brand promise, they definitely reinforce brand equity, primarily through reinforcement of general positive feelings about the producer, manufacturer, or retailer. These general positive feelings, on the part of customers

---

[1] Marc Orlitzky, Frank L. Schmidt, and Sara Rynes, *Corporate Social and Financial Performance: A Meta-Analysis*, Sage Publications © 2003.

and consumers, span across many of the specific image attributes we use to decompose brand equity to find its key drivers. For example, Starbucks' environmental efforts (sustainable agriculture, waste stream reduction, clean water initiatives, and so on) as well as their fair trade efforts (paying premium prices for coffee that's grown using sustainable agricultural practices) are focused on creating sustained, profitable growth for coffee farmers—which certainly is easily integrated into Starbucks' model for creating value and apparently resonates with the values of their customers, creating a "win-win-win" virtuous cycle.

Furthermore, CSR initiatives may not be targeted just to customers and consumers, but rather employees, channel partners, suppliers, or investors. In these cases, the improvements in brand equity is less direct for the operating brands, especially if they are not tied tightly to the corporate brand, but these initiatives are likely to have a significant impact on overall corporate brand asset value.

How Much Is a Loyal Customer Worth?

Let's go back to our breadmaker example from Chapter 7 and look at the calculated utilities for our theoretical respondent.

Level	Brand	Utility	Capacity	Utility	Loaf	Utility	Price	Utility
1	Oster	8.89	1.0 lbs	−26.63	round	5.10	$129	29.55
2	Braun	27.86	1.5 lbs	17.52	square	0.95	$139	15.77
3	Sears	−12.92	2.0 lbs	9.10	Rect.	−6.04	$149	−17.21
4	Acme	−23.83					$159	−28.11
Abs Diff		51.69		44.15		11.14		57.66
Importance		31.40%		26.82%		6.77%		35.02%

We see that brand is the second most important attribute, with price being the most important. Within the brand attribute, we see that Braun has the highest brand equity for this respondent, followed by Oster, Sears, and Acme.

We observed that this respondent valued a Braun breadmaker with a 1.5-pound capacity making a round loaf, priced at $159.00, as having a total utility of (27.86 + 17.52 + 5.10 − 28.11 =) 22.37. We compared that to the utility of a Sears brand with a 1-pound capacity in a square loaf priced at $139.00. Summing those utilities (−12.92 − 26.63 + 0.95 + 15.77) yielded a value estimate of −22.83 units of utility. If only these two choices were in this consumer's consideration set, the consumer would have selected the Braun.

What if Acme decided they wanted to match Braun's product performance by introducing a breadmaker with a 1.5-pound capacity making a round loaf and sell it at the same price as Braun—$159? The expected utility for this product offering would then be ($-23.83 + 17.52 + 5.10 - 55.65 =$) -56.86. So, this respondent would still chose the Braun, which has a total utility of $+22.37$—a difference of 79.23 "utils" in Braun's favor. However, if Acme priced their new breadmaker at $129, this respondent would likely choose the Acme, because it has a higher total utility. (At this point we are ignoring any barriers to switching.) Here are the numbers:

Brand		Capacity		Loaf		Price		
Brand	Utility	Capacity	Utility	Loaf	Utility	Price	Utility	Total
Braun	27.86	1.5 lbs	17.52	Round	5.10	$159	−28.11	22.37
Acme	−23.83	1.5 lbs	17.52	Round	5.10	$129	29.55	28.34

Now, the question is at what price would Acme need to offer this new bread maker so that our theoretical respondent would be ambivalent? That is, what price would Acme need to charge so that our respondent placed the same value (utility) on both products? That's rather easy to calculate. Acme would need to overcome the superior brand equity of Braun, and that is ($27.86 - (-23.83) =$) 51.69 units of utility. The change in utility from $159.00 to $139.00 is 43.88 utils. That leaves ($51.69 - 42.88 =$) 7.81 utils to account for in the change of utility from $139.00 to $129.00. The total utils for that price difference is 13.78. The ratio of $7.81/13.78 = 0.5627$, which represents the value of $129.00 + 0.5627*$10.00, which equals $134.63. So if Acme priced their new breadmaker at $134.63, our respondent would assign the exact same utility to both offerings.

From Braun's point of view, this respondent is worth ($159.00 - $134.63 =$) $24.37 because that is the amount she is willing to pay for the Braun name on her breadmaker, compared to the baseline Acme nameplate, when all the performance attributes are equal. Obviously, these same calculations could be made for the Sears or Oster brand names.

Note that the value of the brand is not absolute. It is relative to the other brands in the category. When we use the Brand Value Model to derive the economic value of a brand's equity, we typically include a store brand or a nonexistent brand to establish a baseline to which we can compare all of the other brands in the category.

That $24.37 represents a 19 percent premium that this purchaser is willing to pay for the Braun name compared to the base brand (Acme) in the category. We can expect that she would be willing to pay a similar premium for other kitchen electrics from Braun. If she purchases, for example, ten products in the categories in which the Braun brand competes over, say, ten years, that customer has a potential worth of approximately 19 percent of the base sales price of those products.

A key strategic question is what do the owners of the Braun brand do with that premium? They have several options:

1. Pocket the difference and reward the current stockholders in the short run.
2. Reinvest in new products under the Braun name.
3. Reinvest in product improvements of the current Braun line.
4. Reinvest in building even higher brand equity.
5. Launch a new brand in the same categories to capture different value segments.
6. Cut (or, for some segments, raise) the Braun price in an attempt to gain share.
7. Or any combination of the above.

Each of these strategies has its positives and negatives. The key to selecting the best strategy for optimizing sustainable competitive advantage is to understand how the Braun product line is delivering value in each category in which it competes, or could compete. The Brand Value Model provides that insight.

The implications of the calculation of the financial value added of a brand's equity are far reaching. We covered those at the end of Chapter 7.

In addition, this discussion on brand loyalty and brand performance reinforces the utility of the Brand Value Model. Change in the asset value of brand equity is the ultimate ROI on marketing investments. It represents a precise summary measure of the value of marketing expenditures. It captures the effects of investments in customer-facing employee training and customer service operations. It captures the ultimate payoffs in product/service innovation. And, of course, it captures the effects of changes in customer loyalty.

Summary

Customer/brand loyalty is a bottom-line issue. Improvements in the retention of profitable customers reduces marketing costs, reduces operations and manufacturing costs, reduces delivery/channel costs, improves market share, and usually improves the hit rate on new product development via product and line extensions. Marketers and product managers can better understand the drivers of loyalty, understand that the loyalty of their customers springs from different motivations, and learn how to better manage loyalty using a conceptual framework centered on the Brand Value Model.

The Brand Value Model provides a viable construct for understanding value, therefore choice, and loyalty. Furthermore, it lends itself to rather precise measurement and prediction. Results from properly estimating the weights of the Brand Value Model—preference structures—allow marketers to better understand their markets and their customers, allows them to optimize the marketing mix, manage loyalty, and improve profitability.

Ultimately, the Brand Value Model provides a precise and rational measure of the financial worth of brands within a category, and is the ultimate ROI for marketing expenditures.

"The Brand Value Model is a powerful tool that my organization can use to gain insight into our markets, and to develop 'go-to-market' strategies."
—Jack F. Eli, CEO, TasteRite

Chapter 9

What Is Branding?

"The way to gain a good reputation is to endeavor to be what you desire to appear."

—Socrates (469 BC–399 BC), Greek Philosopher

"It is not the strongest of the species that survive, nor the most intelligent that survives. It is the one that is the most adaptable to change."

—Charles Darwin (1809–1882), Naturalist, Author

Now that we understand that brand is an asset, what is the magic behind creating that asset and increasing its value?

The answer lies in the realization that brand building is a complex, recursive process, marked by a series of actions designed to achieve a sustainable, differentiated competitive advantage. What makes branding a complex process is that the actions and outcomes are somewhat unique to each part of the organization and to each separate stakeholder group. Everyone "owns" the brand; yet, in many organizations no one entity "owns" the brand or fully understands their role in, and impact on, the branding process.

How each part of the organization and its stakeholder groups view the brand may be likened to the group of people with their eyes covered trying to describe an elephant via their sense of touch. The person by the elephant's leg described it as a tree. The person by the elephant's tail described it as a long vine. The person by the elephant's trunk described it as a thick snake, whereas the person by the elephant's belly described it as a huge boulder. What each person "saw" through their sense of touch was determined by where they stood around the elephant. No one person had the full picture—and their assembled observations created a disjointed picture of something other than an elephant.

In most organizations, there is not one coherent view of the brand, there are many views of the brand, resulting in an inconsistent brand image on the part of the employees—the very people who must communicate and deliver on the brand promise.

This situation exists in many organizations. Each part of the organization defines the brand and served markets in relation to their needs, assignments, responsibilities, challenges, rewards, compensation, training, experiences, and so on as seen through the lens of their department or "silo." The result is that the clarity and coordination necessary to meet or exceed your brand promise and the market's expectations, and achieve the desired business outcomes, is often lacking and the outcomes are sub-optimized. This is a source of great frustration to many CEOs and their staffs.

Furthermore, the branding process may be viewed by top management as "something those folks in marketing do." However, as we've discovered in previous chapters, the brand and the branding process are core elements of leadership, and are crucial to the ability of internal employees to successfully do their jobs, and, therefore, to the ability of the company to meet or exceed the expectations of internal and external stakeholders. Brand and branding are too mission critical to be left to the marketing department, alone.

This point was demonstrated to one of the authors during a corporate brand campaign presentation to the CEO of U.S.-based operations of a major global engineering company. After seeing the brand promise, he asked: "What does this mean to the guy working on the plant floor?" He then went on to say that he wanted the campaign to have meaning for every employee in the company, even those who aren't "customer facing."

This CEO clearly recognized the power of the brand process to inspire, provide meaning, and resonate with employees throughout his organization. He also recognized the need for every department and silo to have a holistic view of the brand promise, in the hope that they would interpret it in terms of what they had to do to make it happen—even if that meant cross-silo co-operation! This requirement adds another layer of complexity to the branding process. However, it also provides direction on how and what to communicate to internal stakeholders so they can successfully interpret the brand promise in terms of "What does this mean to me?" "How must I act?"

The branding process is also complex because it's trying to hit a moving target against a background of change.

A Moving Target: Brand Image to Brand Identity

Every company, product, service, and individual has a brand image. It's what people think of your brand now. However, most companies are, or should be, trying to anticipate changes that will impact their markets and customers and how those changes will affect the competitive landscape, as well as create future opportunities. This is what innovation is all about and why the brand-building process is recursive—building on what has come before.

The ability to innovate and cope with change is crucial to survival. Changes in investment, technology, competition, globalization, regulation, the political climate and/or trade alignments may prove disruptive. However this type of "sea" change often tends to lift, or lower, all boats. It's only when the change primarily impacts your company negatively that it creates a competitive disadvantage. If your company is unwilling or unable to change, it often leads to disappointing results and, sometimes, failure.[1] How does a company create a sustainable, differentiated competitive advantage despite and because of these changes?

At the 2004 Fortune Innovation Forum, leading companies from a broad cross-section of industries, each with their own challenges, came to the conclusion that innovation is looking at your customers the way your competitors don't. We maintain that innovation is also looking at employees and other stakeholders in a way your competitors don't—and that this may also provide rich sources of ideas and inspiration for innovation. It also means paying a lot more attention to your "lost" customers.

Doing this gives you possible direction for new categories for product and service development and offerings. It also helps you understand how to offer your product or service in a manner that creates a difference between your offering and your competitor's offerings.

The real magic happens, however, when you understand the full range of brand attributes that are at work making a difference between brands in a competitive set or category, how those attributes impact each served segment of your market, and how those values relate to your company's core values. Remember, each brand attribute(s) should represent or encode customers' values and perceptions of value. Done correctly, you differentiate your offering *and* make a profit.

As a simple example JetBlue Airways® eliminated first class seating so that all passengers are treated equally, as one way to achieve their Brand Promise of "bringing humanity back to air travel." You can imagine the customer values that this appealed to: being treated fairly, respect, and so on. However, JetBlue quietly gives special perks to passengers who fly more than 24 times per year—offering them first crack at exit row seats and priority status. Not having first class seating is one of the attributes that helps to clearly define and differentiate the JetBlue brand. Carefully training its customer-facing staff on how to give out and deliver special perks to its most valuable customers helps to make that program work. Both programs help to define the company's brand, and the company's external and internal communications

---

[1] Jag Sheth and Rajenda Sisodia, *The Rule of Three—Surviving and Thriving in Competitive Markets,* The Free Press, 2002.

help to communicate the brand's attributes through its employees and partners while creating appropriate expectations.

From the JetBlue 2005 Annual Report

We built upon the core elements of the *JetBlue Experience* in 2005, which includes all-leather seats with personal television screens featuring 36 channels of free DIRECTTV programming, free onboard snacks and beverages, and a selection of premium FOX Inflight™ movies. We introduced the JetBlue Card from American Express in 2005, offering card members more ways to earn TrueBlue points while building an important new revenue stream for us. The JetBlue Card was an immediate success, outperforming our expectations and contributing almost one million new TrueBlue members, raising membership to close to 4 million customers. We introduced JetBlue Getaways in 2005, our one-stop shopping website that offers affordable customizable vacation packages to hotels and resorts. We also asked Joshua Wesson of Best Cellars to be our "low-fare sommelier," to offer quality wines that rival those served in first class on other airlines.

The key to the JetBlue Experience, of course, is driven most significantly by our crewmembers' ability to deliver what we believe is the best customer service in the industry. Our crew members continue to do an outstanding job taking care of our customers, as evidenced by our exceptional brand loyalty, and we cannot thank our crew members enough for their diligent efforts.

The recipient of numerous awards and accolades since their start-up in 2000, JetBlue was recently named air travelers' favorite discount airline by J.D. Powers & Associates. JetBlue is currently enjoying some of the highest operating margins in the airline industry, and until record-setting high jet fuel costs caught up to them, was profitable through 2004—a rare accomplishment in an industry where profits are scarce.

However, non–customer-facing employees at JetBlue are also crucial to delivering on the brand promise. The behind-the-scenes mechanics, schedulers, weather people, baggage handlers, and so on all make sure that the basics of safety and on-time departure and arrival are delivered. The brand promise of all passengers being treated equally only works when the basics are delivered. The non–customer-facing employees at JetBlue are necessary but not sufficient for value creation. The customer-facing employees, however, by delivering on the brand promise of "equality of service," and making the core values of safety, caring, integrity, fun, and passion real to customers at the point of service, help to differentiate the brand, and drive value creation. Or, if and when they drop the ball and don't deliver this type of service, brand value can be destroyed.

This point was driven home in 2007 when a snowstorm stranded JetBlue planes and passengers in the Northeast. Hundreds of cancelled flights, passengers marooned on planes for up to 10 hours, and extensive news coverage of angry passengers created a public relations nightmare for Jet Blue. The term 'Jet Blew it' quickly appeared in news reports and blogs that described the event.

Trust and credibility for the airline was on the line. Former JetBlue CEO David Neeleman immediately stepped up to the plate and took responsibility for the problems, and apologized to the public and the airline's customers. Interestingly, he did not lay the blame for the problems at the feet of the employees—quite the opposite; he apologized to the airline's employees for management not having provided the staffing levels, training, and procedures to avoid this type of problem.

He also described his vision for the airlines' future performance, and his willingness that his company be held accountable for that performance. Accordingly, he issued a "Customer Bill of Rights," promising passengers vouchers in case of future flight delays and cancellations. He said, "This was a big wake-up call for JetBlue. I promise to get the right resources, tools, and support for (our employees) going forward, so that they in turn can deliver the JetBlue experience you have come to expect from us."

Although the operational catastrophe could cost JetBlue up to $30 million—including about $10 million for refunded tickets on cancelled flights, $16 million for travel vouchers, and $4 million for internal processing costs such as overtime costs, Neeleman appears to understand that the real cost is the potential harm that can be caused to JetBlue's brand asset value over the longer term. His forthright steps to accept responsibility and reassure JetBlues' passengers and employees should, over time, bear fruit.

His challenge now is to employ changes that ensure future weather problems do not result in the same negative outcomes, while protecting JetBlue's operating margins. In other words, show that Jet Blue's Brand Promise and business model are mutually inclusive.

The brand image that your company desires for your changing marketplace is called your brand identity.

Getting from your current brand image to your desired brand identity requires that your company have a brand strategy, or a migration path on how to get from today's brand image to tomorrow's brand identity. When this is done with existing products and services, it keeps your brands relevant to your served markets. As conditions change in the environment, your brand adapts to these new challenges and opportunities.

The move from today's brand image to tomorrow's desired brand identity is undertaken because the company's leadership anticipates the unserved or underserved needs of the marketplace and its key stakeholders, and understands that the company's brand must help the company communicate the need for change, how to change, what to change; and must guide the actions associated with the change.

The branding process, then, is the migration path that bridges today's marketplace with tomorrow's marketplace.

The locus of value creation is shifting from product innovation based on a mass-market model, to account management and supply chain process innovation based on precision account targeting; from standardized, broad market engagement to focused, aligned, flexible market engagements; and from functional departments with periodic budgetary and planning alignment to functional integration with overlapping responsibilities and ongoing alignment.[2]

Procter and Gamble (P&G) used to be a classic mass marketer. With the rise of Wal-Mart, P&G saw the need to more fully integrate its operations with this emerging retailing giant. So P&G worked with Wal-Mart to create inter-company supply chain processes, like vendor-managed inventory, that would increase Wal-Mart's profitability on P&G products, drive P&G sales to Wal-Mart, and hugely increase P&G's own profitability. "Wal-Mart's CFO became our prime customer" said a key P&G vice president. Not coincidentally, P&G set up master distributors to service smaller accounts, declining to serve them directly. The "one size fits all" mentality was over.[3]

We discuss the implications of this shift in the locus of value creation for brand practice in Chapter 11. For now, suffice it to say that the branding process must bridge changes in the external environment. This, ironically, calls for the branding process to play a more sophisticated and demanding role in communicating to internal employees and outside "partner" organizations,

---

[2] Jonathon Byrnes, *The Age of Precision Markets,* Harvard Business School Working Knowledge, 2005.
[3] Ibid.

especially as the sales process continues to morph into either an automated service function (ATM's, Web-based sales, and so on) or a highly complex team-oriented sales situation where a high degree of integration and interaction between multiple employees in various departments in two or more organizations is required—especially those organizations trying to enhance a network effect.

A Quality-Based Process

If the brand is a Quality Assurance Device, as we've pointed out in earlier chapters, then the process of branding is a *quality-based* process. This means that brand(s) must conform to a standard of performance, and the branding process determines that standard.

As part of this process, we've previously talked about the role of values in determining the value discipline of the firm, and the value proposition for the served markets.

We've also looked at value creation and destruction within organizations, and the importance of selecting the correct value discipline.

How does all of this tie together and relate to branding as a quality-based process?

In Chapter 3, we defined brand as a promise. Branding is the process of:

1. Understanding the values of key stakeholder groups and the brand attributes that relate to those values.
2. Understanding how those values and related brand attributes, performance features, and price combine to create perceptions of value (perceived relative quality) for a company, product and/or service offering so as to drive choice (intent to purchase).
3. Defining the Brand Promise that encodes those values in a way that creates a common set of guidelines internally upon which to base decisions, day in and day out—and creates appropriate expectations (standard for performance).
4. Communicating the Brand Promise to various stakeholder groups via mass and/or 1:1 media, speeches, collateral and point-of-sale materials, stakeholder word-of mouth referrals/recommendations, and/or unplanned or spontaneous brand experiences.[4]

---

[4] Note: Most observers of marketing give planned advertising and marketing programs and materials the credit for creating brand awareness, consideration, trial and equity. However, it is not known to what extent unplanned or spontaneous brand experiences may lead to awareness, trial, etc. For example, if a friend is picking me up to drive me to work because my car broke down, and he drives a vehicle I would not normally be in, that may lead to an automotive brand experience that creates demand for that product on my part. Marketers try to leverage unplanned brand exposures via product placements in movies, consumer generated media (CGM), and so on.

5. Delivering on the Brand Promise via the brand experience so as to meet or exceed expectations.

6. Measuring and tracking the results by key stakeholder group:
   - Customers by segments: Values alignment, share of business, frequency of purchase, margins, rate of payback on investment, strategic value, referrals, recommendations, brand equity levels, and so on.
   - Employees: Values alignment, loyalty, brand integration, performance level, achievement of business and personal goals, teamwork, and so on. These results can be tracked by department: sales, customer service, logistics, etc. or by customer segment.
   - Suppliers: Values integration, strategic value, share of business, innovation, referrals, recommendations, and so on.
   - Investors: Institutional: Level of holdings, turnover rate, CSR tie-ins, growth vs. value. Large private investors: same.
   - Analysts: Continuity of coverage, type of recommendation, beta assessment, brand values of employer.
   - Media: Trade—relative competitive position, share of voice, values integration, relationships with editors, participation, reader brand equity levels, inquiry levels, sales conversion rates, new customer profiles. Mass—relative competitive position, share of voice, values integration, relationships with selected editors, participation, reader brand equity levels. 1:1 media: activity levels, participation levels (blogs, podcasts, cellcasts, search engine ads, and so on), inquiry levels, conversion rates, new customer profiles, visitors' brand equity levels.

7. Hiring, training, compensating, and rewarding employees and stakeholders for their performance in achieving desired outcomes.

8. Fine-tuning and repeating the process while building a database of results for each step, ideally building insight into the predictive power of each step.

This serves as a "dashboard" of metrics with which to guide the thinking and future actions of the company's leaders, employees, suppliers, and served market stakeholders.

We describe in detail how to put each of these steps into practice in Chapters 12 and 14.

This is a process that never ends. It's also important to appreciate that this process takes place against a backdrop of an enduring corporate vision.

The following two sections are adapted from an article by James C. Collins and Jerry I. Porras: "Building Your Company's Vision," published in HBR's *OnPoint*:

> *An enduring corporate vision has two parts: core ideology and an envisioned future. A core ideology, in turn, also has two parts:*

1. Core values are the handful of guiding principles by which a company navigates. Disney's core values of imagination and wholesomeness stem from the founder's belief that these should be nurtured for their own sake, not merely to capitalize on a business opportunity. Instead of changing its core values, a great company will change its markets—seek out different customers—in order to remain true to its core values.

2. Core purpose is an organization's most fundamental reason for being. It should not be confused with the company's current product lines or customer segments. Rather, it reflects people's idealistic motivations for doing the company's work. Disney's core purpose is to make people happy—not to build theme parks and make cartoons. JetBlue's core purpose is to "bring humanity back to air travel." A core purpose can never be completed.

> *Identifying your core ideology is a discovery process.*[5]
>
> *An envisioned future, the second component of an effective vision, has two elements:*

1. Big, Hairy, Audacious Goals (BHAGs) are ambitious plans that rev up the entire organization. They typically require 10 to 30 years to complete.

2. Vivid descriptions paint a picture of what it will be like to achieve BHAGs. They make the goals vibrant, engaging, and tangible.

> *Setting an envisioned future is a creative process.*[6]

Think of core values as the company's genetic code. There is a relationship between the core values that create the foundation for your organization's culture and the enduring vision from which corporate, product and service brands' inspiration, innovation, and attributes are often drawn. Having an

---

[5] James C. Collins and Jerry I. Porras, "Building Your Company's Vision," HBR's *OnPoint,* Harvard Business School Publishing Corporation, 2000.

[6] Ibid.

extrinsic understanding of these precepts, and having them properly aligned so as to achieve progress is too often left to chance, or not done at all. Every company must strive to be consciously competent in this area if they hope to succeed over the long term.

Once the core values and vision are in place, then the topics of market segmentation (see Chapter 11), choosing profitable customers, growth rates, and other key issues are much easier to discuss and evaluate. They now can be viewed in context—and the company can move towards enhanced customer profitability and value creation by executing a competitively dominant value proposition in the form of a Brand Promise that's appropriate for each served customer segment. And, most importantly, they can decide which customers they should do business with. Choosing your customer is the most important decision any business will make.

The benefits of a better understanding of customer profitability are many. As Larry Selden observed in his book, *Killer Customers*: "The top 20% of customers typically account for 120% of profit. Winning with the top 20% will kill your competitors. Not dealing with the bottom 20% will kill you."[7] This is especially true since the bottom 20 percent of customers in many companies studied destroyed up to 100 percent of value! So a better understanding of customer profitability directs you to invest your research dollars into understanding the values and needs of those customers who will be most profitable. This, in turn, leads to better decision making. For example, one study of U.S. banks in the early 1990s found that only 30 percent of a typical bank's customers were profitable over the long run (meaning up to 70 percent of the bank's customers destroyed value). Seeking higher market share under these conditions is probably not a winning strategy. Seeking to increase the share of business done with the 30 percent of profitable customers makes more sense, as does carefully adding more customers whose profiles match the profitable customers.

The idea of brand as a Quality Assurance Device, and of the branding process as a quality assurance process, invites us to look at quality-based practices for inspiration on how to strengthen the company's ability to use brand as a tool for market building and profitability. CQI, or Continuous Quality Improvement, is defined as the culture, strategies, and methods necessary for continual improvement in meeting and exceeding customers' expectations. For the transformation to CQI, the future state includes constancy of

---

[7] Larry Seldon and Geoffey Colvin, *Killer Customers: Tell the Good from the Bad—and Dominate Your Competitors,* Penguin Books Ltd., 2003.

purpose, leaders who model the new way, collaboration, customer mindedness, and a process focus.[8]

Several studies have shown that customer profitability is greatly enhanced among those companies that offer follow-up services to their customers. IBM's transition from a hardware-based company to a service-based company is an example of this. Companies that desire to be successful in offering services to their customers often employ quality-based tools like brand blueprinting to really ensure that they deliver the Brand Experience the customer expects.

The Brand Experience

With the advent of skilled and educated knowledge workers, and the ascendancy of information-based, non-routine work (analyses, handling ambiguity, problem solving, decision making) in the creation of value—especially through networks of interacting cooperators—it's become clear that values-based leadership and management, and the branding process that extends from them, is more important than ever before, *especially* in companies that are engaged in creating value primarily through knowledge-based tacit interactions (as contrasted with routine low-value-added transactions).[9]

Those companies that engage in an explicit company-wide branding process enjoy better operating results than companies that do not.[10]

The reason is simple: Their employees are better equipped to successfully deliver on their brand promise. And if things go wrong, as they often do, they more quickly recognize that fact, diagnose the reason, and take corrective action to get the brand experience back on track—thus minimizing value destruction. The company's vision and brand promise act like Adam Smith's "invisible hand," guiding the thinking and actions of all involved. Personal self-interest is best served, at least in the short term, by serving the brand and the values that underlie the brand's attributes.

In organizations like this, the organizational structure tends to be more team oriented, and designed to surmount departmental barriers in order to deliver on the brand promise. The brand promise often suggests that the

---

[8] M. Johnna Shamp, Ph.D., *Total Quality Management Glossary,* http://www.quality.org, 1994.

[9] Note: Tacit interactions are defined as work in which high levels of judgment are required: managers, salespeople, nurses, lawyers, judges, mediators. Transactional interactions are defined as routine work, such as clerical and accounting. Bradford C. Johnson, James M. Manyuika, and Lareina A. Yee, "The Next Revolution in Interactions," *The McKinsey Quarterly,* No. 4, 2005.

[10] Nick Wreden, *PROFITBRAND—How to Increase the Profitability, Accountability & Sustainability of Brands,* Kogan Page Ltd., 2005.

company show "one face to the customer." And if attributes of the brand promise include "easy to do business with," "convenient," "simple," and so on, then the organization's structure reflects what's needed to deliver those attributes. Furthermore, in recognition of the increased mobility of employees, when key employees leave, "corporate memory" also leaves. In light of this, many companies understand that they must formally communicate the brand promise to new employees, so that they can quickly understand their role in delivering the promise, and can ask and answer the question "Will my decision/action hurt or help the brand and, therefore, build or destroy value?"

This, in turn, means that more employees than ever have a better understanding of the relationship between their actions and the ability of the company to serve its customers as promised, and to make a profit. More and more companies are running by an "open book" model, where financial information is readily shared so that employees can make better decisions on how to support the brand promise. For example, information on customer profitability by segment helps the sales organization make the appropriate offer to the right kind of prospect—thus ensuring long-term profitability when they get the account. Or, sometimes even more important, understanding which customers *not* to pursue. In this setting, all the players in the company understand what's needed to achieve the brand promise and are able to do so without needing to go through unnecessary layers of red tape and approvals.

As we saw in the P&G/Wal-Mart example, the relationships between companies in a value chain are becoming closer and ever more complex. The complexity of the workplace is increased further as the size of the firm increases. A large company's complexity (what the economists call the "costs of excessive largeness") can overwhelm strategic and collaborative efforts. Large companies combat this in two ways: They divest businesses that don't benefit from leveraging tangible and intangible assets for competitive advantage, as well as look at ways to divest businesses that are labor and/or capital intensive. They use the opposite formula to evaluate potential acquisitions.[11] What does this mean in terms of the branding process, and the brand experience?

IBM is a good example of values working to simplify the process and enhance the brand experience within the constraint of a large, globally diverse company.

When Sam Palmisano took over as CEO of IBM in 2002 following Louis V. Gertner's successful turnaround, he knew his challenge would be

---

[11] Lowell L. Bryan and Michele Zanini, "Strategy in an Era of Global Giants," *The McKinsey Quarterly*, No. 4, 2005.

to continue the company's transformation. He felt that a strong values system was crucial to bringing together and motivating a workforce as large and diverse as IBM's. His problem was to get IBM's far-flung business units (60-70 product lines in 170 countries), each with different financial targets and incentives, working together in teams that could offer, at a single price, a comprehensive and customized solution—without showing the organization's "seams."[12]

To further add to the challenge, IBM was successful. It's much easier to effect change when the company is gripped by crisis. But the crisis had passed. So, Palmisano had to galvanize his people not through fear of failure, but through hope and aspiration. He realized that although the company was successful, there was incredible untapped potential for growth and future value creation. His response was to reinvent IBM's values.[13]

He accomplished this by utilizing the company's intranet and inviting the company's employees to debate the nature of the company and what it stood for. Over three days about 50,000 IBM employees looked at the discussion, posting nearly 10,000 comments about the proposed values. After much discussion, analyses, and surveys, a new set of corporate values was proposed:

- Dedication to every client's success
- Innovation that matters—for our company and for the world
- Trust and personal responsibility in all relationships[14]

Feedback on the values quickly revealed some barriers to effectively employing them.

For example, there were cases where employees were unable to respond quickly to customer needs because of financial control processes that required several layers of approval. So IBM allocated up to $5,000 annually to each customer-facing team to respond to extraordinary situations. There were lots of examples of teams winning deals and delighting clients with a small amount of "walk around money." Based on the success of the pilot program, IBM expanded the program to all 22,000 of its customer-facing managers. This program "walks the talk" of the values of "trust and personal responsibility in all relationships." It required that IBM's top executives trust the rest of the organization to spend many millions of dollars wisely.[15]

---

[12] Samuel J. Palmisano, "Leading Change When Business Is Good," *Harvard Business Review*, December 2004.

[13] Ibid.

[14] Ibid.

[15] Ibid.

By honoring and supporting this value, IBM gave the organization the opportunity to act with integrity. And, with rare exception, it did. The lesson: Give trust to get trustworthy behaviors.

Another example: It was very difficult to put together a client-friendly, cross-IBM solution that cut across product lines and services at a single all-inclusive price. Every operating unit had its own P&L, and each part of IBM's 100,000 cell organizational matrix would pull out their portion of the bid, and bid it as though it were a stand-alone offering—which was counter to IBM's Brand Promise of solutions via innovation and integration. When the CFO tried to put together a deal for a key account he had responsibility for, he was told he couldn't price it as an integrated solution![16]

That quickly led to a way to set a single price for each integrated offering! The values initiative forced IBM to confront the issue, and gave them the impetus to make the change. IBM found their values to be a great inertia-busting vehicle.

Palmisano summed up the role of values as, "… I think values inject balance in the company's culture and management system: balance between the short-term transaction and the long-term relationships, balance between the interests of shareholders, employees, and clients. In every case you have to make a call. Values help you make those decisions, not on an ad hoc basis, but in a way that is consistent with your culture and brand, with who you are as a company."[17]

"In the long term, I think, whether or not you have a values-driven culture is what makes you a winner or a loser."[18]

The CEO's Role in the Brand Process

CEOs who realize the power of branding often employ storytelling as a way to dramatically communicate the core values of the brand, its meaning to the organization, how this is relevant to the market and differentiates the company/product/service. These stories often contain evidence of how the appropriate values and behavior have created a loyal customer, solved a problem, drove innovation, delivered on brand attributes, and so on. CEOs who are accomplished at this type of storytelling understand that conflict is necessary to create interest and attention, so they build conflict into their stories—usually in the form of a problem or unresolved issue that relates to a

---

[16] Ibid.
[17] Ibid.
[18] Ibid.

core value central to the brand promise. They then show how key stakeholders, inspired by the brand's core values and attributes, and their own beliefs, engage in behavior appropriate to support the brand's promise and solve the problem by delivering on the Brand Experience. The outcome of the story is usually happy customers and employees, ways to save money, and a demonstration of how to create loyalty.

In-person storytelling at face-to-face meetings is one way to "model" the brand and support the branding process. Another way is formal communications via internal newsletters, intranets, videos, CDs, and numerous other tools. Brand storytelling is a powerful way to use the legends and myths that are part of most established companies to underline the core values central to the brand promise and brand experience, show how they can be employed to overcome operational and organizational barriers and contribute to the company's success.

However, a note of caution is due at this point. We have observed that in many companies there are myths concerning customer needs and values that are not always fact-based, or have been superseded over time. When these "out-of-touch"'myths drive strategy, they can destroy brand value. For example, for a power utility we found that the prevailing myth was that one very large class of customers was extremely price sensitive and would negotiate furiously for special rate considerations. So the prevailing strategy within the firm was to openly offer to negotiate rates in order to keep these very important customers. Upon taking a representative sample of these customers through the Brand Value Model trade-off exercise, we discovered two important things:

1. The vast majority would trade off rates for higher levels of service, and
2. "Price" was of much lower importance than power reliability and service response times.

When presented with these results, the CEO and Strategic Planning Committee were literally dumbstruck, and several openly questioned the research. Yet, in a matter of weeks, a special team formed by the CEO to discuss these issues in detail with those customers confirmed that the research was correct. The company had been literally destroying value because of a false myth that prevailed within the firm.

Earlier in this chapter we discussed the eight steps in the Branding process. Skipping the first couple of steps will often result in malpractice. The lesson learned: Question long-held customer assumptions before employing them. The knowledge gained will be a rich source of insight into customer values and needs, and, therefore, ways for the firm to innovate and create more value.

Although support from top management is critical to a successful branding process, other parts of the organization play a crucial role as well. Marketing can enhance its effectiveness if it establishes clear guidelines for the rest of the organization and its outside partners on how to use the brand "dress'"—the logo, colors, and so on in presentations and materials. Many companies create a password-protected extranet/intranet site for use by employees and outside stakeholders, which contains logo designs, guidelines for use, presentation materials, examples of presentations, templates, and so on.

Through the use of mission and vision, evidence-based storytelling, and by establishing clear guidelines on how to use the brand "dress" and materials, the entire organization gains a clear view of what the brand is, the standard for performance, and clearly communicates the essence of the brand and its cultural connections to outside stakeholders as well. In the "shared place" of the organization, these stories are very important in setting expectations for performance and behavior.

Consistency in how the Brand Promise is communicated is very important to success. Companies that show the brand one way in their advertising, another way on their Web site, and don't "connect the dots" when they deliver on the Brand Experience often create confusion on the part of their employees, and the need for "firefighting." At the very least, they don't earn the brand equity they may be capable of earning.

By consistently delivering on the brand promise and creating a brand experience that creates referrals, positive word of mouth, and brand advocates among its customers and other stakeholders, the company will apply the brand process effectively and efficiently to create brands that function as Quality Assurance Devices, which successfully creates brand equity and the potential for future cash flows.

The truth is, there is no magic behind the branding process—just lots of outside-the-box thinking and hard work.

In the next chapter, we look at case history examples of companies that have employed values-based branding successfully.

"There's an old saying: 'The fish stinks from the head down.' Since I'm the CEO, that saying indicates that I'm the one who has to take charge of the brand and the brand process, making sure it's fresh, relevant, and alive."
        —Jack F. Eli, CEO, TasteRite

CHAPTER 10

BRAND SUCCESS PROFILES

"Success is not an entitlement. It must be earned every day."

—Howard Schultz, Chairman, Starbucks

"Know thyself."

—Ancient Greek saying

We have selected several companies that use brand integrity to create greater value for their stakeholders. By definition, brand integrity yields value by creating a sustainable, competitive advantage for a company in a consideration set. It often does this by deploying primarily intangible resources—values and corresponding emotion-based brand attributes in ways that engage stakeholders, provide meaning, and create perceptions of worth (brand equity) and loyalty behaviors.

We use companies' Web sites as a way to gain insight into their "soul," or corporate culture and brand practices. Our hypothesis is that a company's Web site is a fair representation of how they present their corporate and product/ service brands to their various stakeholders. To the extent that this is true, then these companies' Web sites give us examples of how they deploy their intangible attributes. The meanings associated with these attributes often are of critical importance to stakeholders like employees, in terms of how they view their roles within the company, how they perform their roles, how they're compensated/ recognized/rewarded/trained, and how they feel and talk about the company.

Some companies also provide key performance indicators on their Web sites that they believe are important to value creation. These KPIs provide valuable cues to various stakeholders on how they can best function as part of the company.

For "reviewed" companies whose stock is traded on public stock exchanges, we can look to the stock market to see how their value creation has fared—at least in the opinion of investors and analysts.

In a time when "network effects" comprised of supply chain partners, innovation partners, community partners, and so on are vital to continued success, it is important to clearly communicate the firm's values to all stakeholders as a way to allow each stakeholder to assess how they can best fit into the network, and deploy their values to create value.

So, one of the first things we look for when evaluating a company's brand practice, is how the company communicates its values via its Web site. If it is not possible to find a company's values on its Web site, then it's highly likely that the company does an equally poor job in communicating its values in other venues. If it is not possible for stakeholders to find a company's values, then it is difficult for stakeholders to understand how their values fit with the company's values. That makes it much more likely that there are communications problems within and outside the company between various stakeholders. Poor communications has a depressing effect on value creation, and often leads to value destruction.

Kellogg Company

Kellogg Company recently celebrated its 100th anniversary in 2006. The "About Us" page[1] on Kellogg Company's Web site recounts founder W.K. Kellogg's vision of and commitment to nutrition, health, and quality. The company started with 44 employees in Battle Creek, Michigan in 1906. In 2007 the company employed more than 26,000 people, had manufacturing facilities in 17 countries, sold their products in more than 180 countries, and enjoyed sales of more than $11 billion. With a market cap of more than $21 billion, that's wonderful long-term value creation.

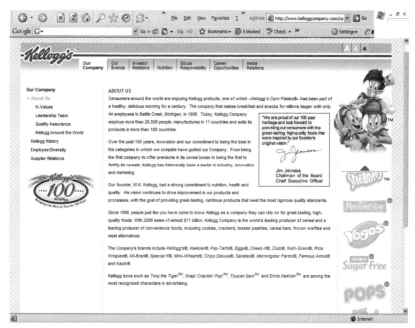

---

[1] Kellogg Company Web site page images used with the permission of Kellogg Company.

When we go to Kellogg Company's Web page (http://www. kellogg company.com/company.aspx?id=35) that deals with their values (*K-Values*™) we see:

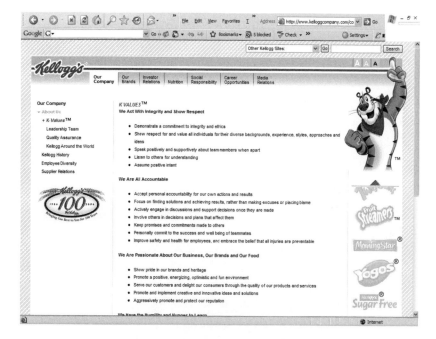

Scrolling down the page reveals the rest of the *K-Values*™:

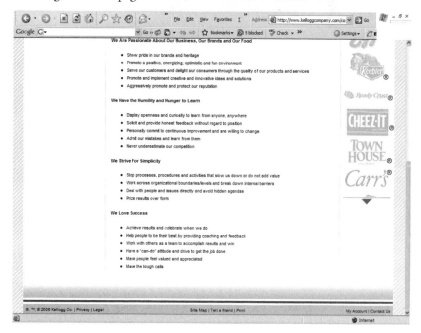

Kellogg Company's six core values (*K-Values*™) are:

- We Act With Integrity and Show Respect
- We Are All Accountable
- We Are Passionate About Our Business, Our Brands and Our Food
- We Have the Humility and Hunger to Learn
- We Strive For Simplicity
- We Love Success

Each of the six *K-Values*™ has additional underlying statements that further define and explain what it means to put each value "in action" within Kellogg Company. These principles, ideals, and beliefs guide everyone within Kellogg Company as they make decisions daily.

To see these values in action, we can look at Kellogg Company's Corporate Social Responsibility (CSR) Web page. Corporate Social Responsibility is an application of the *K-Value*™ of "We Are All Accountable," and includes elements of other *K-Values*™ as well.

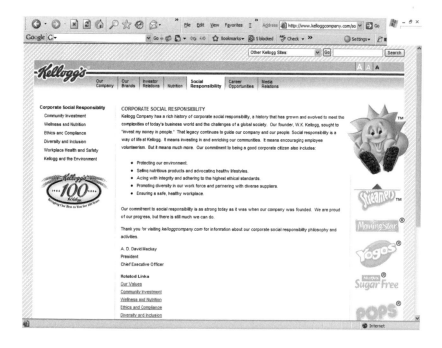

At the bottom of the CSR Web page under "Related Links," Kellogg Company lists CSR-related initiatives, and when you click on those initiatives, you're taken to pages like the following:

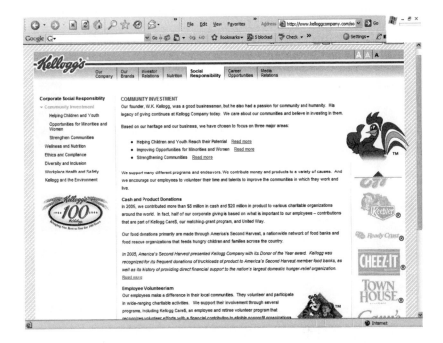

This Web page reflects the ongoing commitment of Kellogg Company to the vision of the company's founder. The company highlights several initiatives on the CSR Web pages. In addition, various contributions and community investments are highlighted, such as helping children, opportunities for minorities and women, and strengthening communities. For instance, Kellogg Company was honored for its accountability as Donor of the Year in 2005 for America's Second Harvest. However, the authors believe that Kellogg Company could increase the impact and credibility into its CSR program if it were to describe standards for performance (expectations) for their various CSR initiatives on the Web page, and report on their progress in the form of an annual CSR report, along with a direct listing of key performance indicators (KPIs), as do some of the other companies we talk about later in this chapter.

The first *K-Value*™, "We Act With Integrity and Show Respect," is highlighted on the Web site via a downloaded booklet. James Jenness, Kellogg Company Chairman, reinforces the importance of this value:

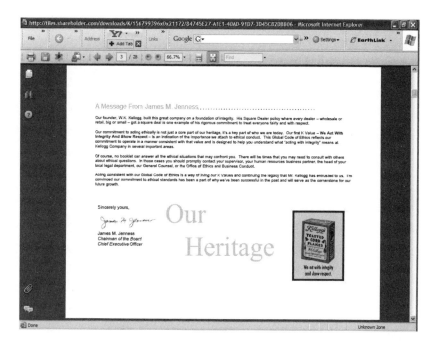

He says, "Our founder, W.K. Kellogg built this great company on a foundation of integrity. His Square Dealer policy where every dealer—wholesale or retail, big or small—got a square deal is one example of his rigorous commitment to treat everyone fairly and with respect.

"Our commitment to acting ethically is not just a core part of our heritage, it's a key part of who we are today. Our first *K-Value*™—We Act With Integrity And Show Respect—is an indication of the importance we attach to ethical conduct. This Global Code of Ethics reflects our commitment to operate in a manner consistent with that value, and is designed to help you understand what 'acting with integrity' means at Kellogg Company in several important areas."

By doing this, Jenness reinforces a key attribute of the *Kellogg's*® brand that is aligned with one of its core values, and exhibits leadership within the foodservice industry for all stakeholders to see. This sends a clear and powerful message about the way that Kellogg Company will conduct its business. Another key part of W.K. Kellogg's vision for his company was his belief in wellness. This Web page below, shows how that vision is alive and well today, including enhancements that the company is making to strengthen this tradition.

Let's look at Kellogg Company's performance through the lens of the BVM:

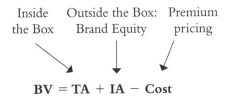

$$BV = TA + IA - Cost$$

Kellogg Company's ability to drive volume and superior pricing is based on its ability to support and deliver on its founders' vision and values. Inside every box of *Kellogg's*® cereals are ingredients that any other cereal manufacturer could duplicate, should they so choose. Outside the box, through the use of brand personalities and characters that add meaning and resonate with the parents and children who buy and consume the product, perceptions of value are created. Outside the box, through the use of values and founder's vision, meaning is created for employees, channels, investors, and other stakeholders, so that perceptions of value are created.

This combination of company ethos and product brands creates a wide moat. This is a strong indication that Kellogg Company is well positioned to create strong free cash flows, and stakeholder value, well into the foreseeable future.

Starbucks® Coffee

Starbucks mission is stated as: "Establish Starbucks as the premier purveyor of the finest coffee in the world while maintaining our uncompromising principles while we grow." They then state the six guiding principles that will "help us measure the appropriateness of our decisions. . . ." (http://www. starbucks.com/aboutus/environment.asp)

- "Provide a great work environment and treat each other with respect and dignity."
- "Embrace diversity as an essential component in the way we do business."
- "Apply the highest standards of excellence to the purchasing, roasting and fresh delivery of our coffee."
- "Develop enthusiastically satisfied customers all of the time."
- "Contribute positively to our communities and our environment."
- "Recognize that profitability is essential to our future success."

These six guiding principles are their core values, the values that they would like every stakeholder, especially employees, to be aware of and to understand their meaning when making business-operating decisions on a daily basis. The six guiding principles or values are Starbucks "standard for performance"—it is how they help everyone understand what quality is, and the best way to achieve it.

Let's take a look at four of Starbucks' six guiding principles and how Starbucks' Web site communicates and "fleshes out" the meaning for each one. To some extent, each of the six guiding principles impacts and is involved with the others; we'll look at four, and not all six, in the interest of brevity.

Starbucks first guiding principle is: **"Provide a great work environment and treat each other with respect and dignity."** Proof that this is actually being accomplished is provided on the Web site, where Starbucks proudly displays their recognition as a "*Fortune*® 100 Best Companies to Work For, 2007."

Their career center Web page (http://www.starbucks.com/aboutus/ jobcenter.asp) presents specific information to Starbucks employees and prospective employees. The second paragraph says "At Starbucks, you'll find a commitment to excellence among our partners; and emphasis on respect in how we treat our customers and each other; and a dedication to social responsibility." Their first guiding principle is reaffirmed here and emphasized for prospective employees.

The next paragraph says: "We look for people who are adaptable, self-motivated, passionate, creative team players." Note how Starbucks describes "nano" level values that are desired in new employees. They continue, "If that sounds like you, why not bring your talents and skills to Starbucks? We are growing in dynamic new ways and we recognize that the right people offering their ideas and expertise, will enable us to continue our success." Are these nice sounding, but "empty" words? Let's see . . .

Under the statement "A strong workplace environment," the copy at the top of this Web page reads: "We are devoted to investing in, supporting and engaging our partners in the constant reinvention of Starbucks. In fact, the first guiding principle in our Mission Statement is to 'provide a great work environment and treat each other with respect and dignity.' Imagine working for a company that constantly aspires to realize this principle. Chances are, it's like no place you've ever worked."

One of the authors has personal knowledge of how Starbucks principle No. 1 works to the partners', the company's, and customers' mutual benefit.

The author and his wife frequently shop at a Starbucks in their midtown Atlanta neighborhood. They were impressed that soon after they became regular customers, the partners called them by name, remembered their favorite drinks, and were very personable and engaging. Out of curiosity as to how Starbucks attracted such high-caliber employees, they asked some of the partners why they like working at Starbucks. They were told that many of the employees were actors who lived in that part of town, and needed an employer who was flexible in scheduling their hours. As actors, they also needed benefits. Starbucks "Your Special Blend" program enables part-time employees who work at least 20 hours a week to participate in a variety of programs that meet their unique needs, including healthcare benefits, retirement savings plans, and an income protection plan (with life and disability coverage). It was a "win-win" for both Starbucks and the partners. And it created a terrific shopping experience for the author and his wife at their favorite Starbucks store.

Now let's take a look at how Starbucks brings other values, such as their second guiding principle, to life on their Web site: **"Embrace diversity as an essential component of the way we do business."** For one, it's the first thing mentioned on "the Starbucks experience" Web page for prospective employees. Part of the section states: "We believe that building understanding, respect, and appreciation for different people contributes to our growth and to the growth of our partners."

Not only does this Web page clearly define the meaning of diversity as Starbucks uses it, but the page is explicit about what it means when "Putting diversity into practice." Furthermore, the company's Corporate Social Responsibility Annual Report for 2005, in the Workplace section, reports on the following KPIs for workplace diversity:

Workplace diversity	Test a companywide diversity and inclusion scorecard that will help us develop metrics and establish long-term goals	Finished developing the scorecard, but it didn't launch in fiscal 2005. It's currently scheduled for roll out in 2006.	◓	Page 67
Workplace diversity	Make diversity training an integrated element of our overall executive development process.	Launched Executive Diversity Learning Services with an initial web seminar titled "Do You Hear What I Hear?" and a Diversity Communication Guide to help strengthen our executives' diversity and leadership competencies. Approximately 30 percent of vice presidents and above have voluntarily participated so far.	◓	Page 67
Workplace diversity	Focus some of our diversity training so that partners can better understand multicultural customers and customers with disabilities.	Specific content that focused on disability etiquette and deaf culture was added to existing training modules for our baristas and field managers.	◓	Page 67

Health and safety	Install anti-slip mats in our U.S. company-operated stores.	Installed new anti-slip mats in our California stores and tested for effectiveness before complete rollout. Results were good so installation of anti-slip mats will continue and old mats will be recycled.	◖	Page 71

Key: ● ACHIEVED   ◖ MAKING PROGRESS   ○ DID NOT ACHIEVE

As you can see, workplace diversity at Starbucks is not an empty platitude on a wall somewhere, but is actually a working principle, ideal, and belief that's tracked, measured, and shared with all stakeholders. These KPIs are elements in Starbucks' version of an Action Plan, and brings their values (guiding principles) to life within the organization—with specific people responsible for achievement.

You might think that diversity is so basic a value that all companies automatically have it as one of their core values in deed as well as in word—especially companies that do business internationally. If you do think this, you are wrong. For example, no less an iconic company than Coca-Cola was sued in 1999 for discrimination in pay, promotions, and performance evaluations. In addition to the negative publicity, the incident cost the company over $190 million in settlement costs. Talk about value destruction!

Coke now sees diversity as one of their core values and as being good business. Since Coke does business in over 200 countries, this makes eminent good sense.

It also makes good sense for a company doing business locally. "Starbucks has made a business out of human connections, community involvement and the celebration of cultures. And so, it's only natural that as a guiding principle, diversity is integral to everything we do." Another example of putting words into action is Starbucks' partnering with Earvin "Magic" Johnson's company Johnson Development Corporation (JDC) in a joint 50/50 venture known as Urban Coffee Opportunities (UCO), where Starbucks locations are developed in ethnically diverse urban and suburban minority neighborhoods, creating construction and employment opportunities.[2]

---

[2] Starbucks opened its 100th Urban Coffee Opportunities (UCO) location in 2006.

The third of Starbucks guiding principles is **"Apply the highest standards of excellence to the purchasing, roasting and fresh delivery of our coffee."** As part of this guiding principle, Starbucks has committed itself to "balance business needs with social and environmental responsibilities in our coffee producing communities."

Another guiding principle of Starbucks is **"Contribute positively to our communities and to our environment."** A page on their Web site entitled, "Corporate Social Responsibility" lays out all the ways in which the company takes action to satisfy this guiding principle.

Broadly, Starbucks makes community investments in three areas: literacy, environment, and coffee origin communities. In addition, a large portion of Starbucks' giving supports local organizations that Starbucks' partners care personally about.

Starbucks Corporate Social Responsibility 2005 Annual Report, available on their Web site, provides added information about their various programs, as well as their key performance indicators, and also provides a way for their Internet site visitors to provide feedback on how well they think Starbucks is doing.

The other lesson that can be gleaned from their Web site, and its demonstration of Starbucks' values and how they "operationalize" their values, is to appreciate that Starbucks is learning as they go along. The following statement from Howard Schultz, chairman, and Jim Donald, president and CEO, in their letter to stakeholders is illustrative of this type of thinking:

> *Finally, we recognize that Starbucks exists and operates within the global society. Through the process of producing an annual CSR Report for the past five years, we have gained a better understanding of our global impacts and the importance of increased transparency. We remain committed to this type of open communication. We also will continue to engage our key stakeholders on issues material to our business, as well as participate in the United Nations Global Compact, which is a means to work collaboratively across sectors on 10 universal environmental and social principles.*
>
> *We think you will find this report worthy of your time and interest. As always, your feedback is very important to us and we encourage you to refer to the back page for information on how you can submit your remarks. In doing so, please accept our deepest appreciation.*

Their CSR report presents a summary of some of their key performance indicators for 2005:

STARBUCKS CORPORATE SOCIAL RESPONSIBILITY
Key Performance Indicators
Summary and Highlights for Fiscal 2005

	Indicator	2004	2005	2006 Target
Coffee				
Coffee and Farmer Equity (C.A.F.E.) Practices	Pounds of coffee purchased from C.A.F.E. Practices approved suppliers	43.5 million pounds (goal: 30 million pounds)	76.8 million pounds (goal: 75 million pounds)	150 million pounds
	Percentage of total coffee purchases	14.5%	24.6%	
Fair Trade Certified™ Coffee	Pounds of coffee purchased from Fair Trade Certified™ cooperatives	4.8 million pounds	11.5 million pounds (goal: 10 million pounds)	12 million pounds
	Percentage of total coffee purchases	1.6%	3.7%	
Community				
Charitable contributions	Total cash and in-kind contributions	$14.6 million	$30.3 million	Do not currently set targets for future charitable contributions.
	Percentage of pre-tax earnings	2.3%	3.8%	
Volunteerism (Make Your Mark)	Number of hours volunteered by partners and customers in the U.S. and Canada	214,000	299,000	375,000

	Indicator	2004	2005	2006 Target
Environment				
Greenhouse gas emissions	Metric tons of CO_2 equivalents	Conducted a baseline climate inventory of our 2003 emissions which totaled 376,000[1] metric tons of CO_2 equivalents.	Did not schedule a climate inventory for 2005	Purchase renewable energy certificates for 20 percent of the energy for our U.S. and Canada company-operated stores.
Electricity	Kilowatt hours per square feet of retail space	6.21[1]	6.40	Target has not been established.
Water	Gallons per square foot of retail space	23[1]	24	Target has not been established.
Paper	Percentage of post-consumer fiber (not including hot cups)	46.5%	49.5% (goal: 48%)	50%
	Percentage of unbleached fiber (not including hot cups)	86.3%	85.9% (goal: 90%)	86.5%
Workplace				
Partner satisfaction	Percentage of satisfied or very satisfied partners	82%[1]	87%	Our goal is to maintain or improve our scores on these survey metrics.
Partner engagement	Percentage of engaged partners	73%[1]	73%	
Health and safety	Injury rate per 200,000 hours worked–retail	7.85[2]	6.68	6.5

	Indicator	2004	2005	2006 Target
Diversity				
Women	U.S. executives (vice presidents and above)	31%	34%	While Starbucks values diversity and inclusion, we do not currently set targets for representation by race and gender.
	U.S. workforce	63%	65%	
People of color	U.S. executives (vice presidents and above)	15%[1]	14%	
	U.S. workforce	30%[1]	30%	
Suppliers	Amount spent with certified minority- and women-owned businesses in U.S.	$114 million	$166 million (goal: $140 million)	$206 million

[1] Information has been adjusted to reflect new data
[2] Results from Starbucks fiscal 2003 Partner Views Survey. No survey was conducted in fiscal 2004

Starbucks reports on their performance in the areas of their coffee supply chain, community, environment, workplace, and diversity programs.

This clearly is a company that appreciates that acting with integrity means you say what you will do, and then you do it. Starbucks, through their promises, actions, and willingness to be held accountable, is a company of high integrity, and integrity is clearly one of their unstated, yet core values. They understand that this value is not one that you necessarily talk about; it's one that you live every day in how you act and perform.

Furthermore, this is not a "set it and forget it" type of strategy. It takes hard work to look into the future, to anticipate change, and to understand the implications for your brand's promise and for your various stakeholders' brand experience—and then, often before a threat or opportunity is apparent, to act on the trends. The following statement from the CSR report's section on sustainable agricultural practices in the area of cocoa used to make chocolate for use in Starbucks cakes and drinks, illustrates what we mean:

"Over the past year, Starbucks Emerging Issues Council determined that
we needed to address the lack of transparency related to our cocoa purchasing.
Reports of human rights violations in some African cocoa-producing regions

further highlighted a critical need for information and expertise in this area. As a result, Starbucks engaged external stakeholders to expand our knowledge of cocoa-related issues and to get feedback on our future direction. Several significant steps were subsequently taken to develop our Socially Responsible Cocoa Sourcing Program."

We selected Starbucks as an example of a company with Brand Integrity because the main category in which they compete—their consideration set—would broadly be defined as the coffee category. If you think only a few decades back, many Americans viewed coffee as a low-interest, low-expectations category. It was, in the worst sense of the word, a commodity, and suffering declining consumption in the United States. Most coffee served in restaurants and at home was of uncertain quality and did not promise anything special. Sure, there were some coffee artisans and coffee aficionados in the Pacific Northwest who knew premium coffee could be a transcendent experience, but they did not represent mainstream America. In most of Manhattan, Chock full o'Nuts was the most visible coffee brand.

Back then if anyone had told the average American that one day there would be a premium retail coffee brand with more than 12,000 locations selling coffee and espresso drinks for up to several dollars per cup, they would have been laughed at. Today, it's a reality. What accounts for this astounding success story?

To put this story into perspective, a bit of history is in order. One of Starbucks' founders, Zev Siegl, recently told us the story of the company's beginnings. In 1971 three young partners[3] opened the first Starbucks Coffee, Tea and Spice coffeehouse in Seattle's Pike Place Market. In their early years, a gentleman by the name of Alfred Peet served as their mentor. Mr. Peet had a deep and abiding love for dark-roasted gourmet coffee, an uncompromising vision of the best way to roast coffee beans and brew coffee, and a passion for teaching. He instilled in Starbucks' founders a deep respect for the quality of the product in the cup, and how to pass along that appreciation to employees and customers. This was Starbucks' first core value. As Zev put it, "We were creating a way to connect with people so that they would upgrade their coffee."

Starbucks grew during the '70s until it was a leading gourmet coffee shop chain in the Seattle area, with four stores in 1982. Howard Schultz joined the company late that year as director of retail operations and marketing. In 1983 Schultz traveled to Italy and was impressed by the popularity of espresso

---

[3] The three founding partners were Gerald Baldwin, Gordon Bowker and Zev Siegl. Siegl left the company to pursue the development of corporate sales of coffee in the early 80s.

bars[4], and the role they played in Italian culture and life, serving as a meeting place and part of the community. Schultz had a revelation; he realized that the espresso bars were an *experience*, a place to meet and visit. It wasn't just about the coffee in the cup; it was *also* about the experience outside of the cup.

In 1984 Starbucks tested the coffeehouse concept and served the first Starbucks caffe latte. Based on this success, Schultz founded IL Giornale, offering brewed coffee and espresso beverages made from Starbucks coffee beans. The Il Giornale stores were very successful.

In 1987 the remaining Starbucks partners decided to sell the Starbucks operations in Seattle, including the nine retail stores. Schultz successfully raised the needed capital and bought the brand and operations, merging Il Giornale into Starbucks. After buying Starbucks, Schultz called the staff together and told them that his vision was for Starbucks to become a national company with values and guiding principles that employees could be proud of. He indicated that he wanted to include people in the decision-making process and that he would be open and honest with them.

Schultz said he believed it was essential for a company to respect its people, to inspire them, and to share its success with those who contributed to its long-term value. His aspiration was for Starbucks to become the most respected brand name in coffee and for the company to be admired for its corporate responsibility.

He wanted his people to think outside of the cup, while remaining committed to providing the best cup of coffee or espresso drink possible.

The innovation and creativity exhibited by Starbucks is impressive. For example, their message to investors is: "The Company is committed to offering its customers the highest quality coffee and human connection through the Starbucks Experience, while striving to improve the social, environmental and economic well being of its partners, coffee farmers, countries of coffee origin, and the communities which it serves."

By thinking outside of the cup, and remaining true to their mission and principles, they've built a powerhouse company that is positively impacting the world. Many of the principles-based initiatives that the company engages in resonate with their employees, customers, suppliers, and other stakeholders, forging relationships that are deep and abiding, and that create an enriched purpose and meaning for all involved.

---

[4] At the time of Schultz's visit, there were about 200,000 espresso bars in Italy and about 1,500 in Milan.

One way to look at the Starbucks story is from the perspective of the Brand Value Model (BVM):

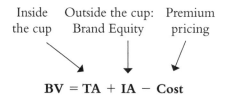

Inside the cup represents the tangible performance attributes of taste, aroma, flavor, and other beneficial aspects of the physical product. This is similar to the role that tangible assets play in the market value of the firm.

Outside the cup represents the intangible emotional attributes (brand equity) captured by the corporate social responsibility agenda and other programs based on the guiding principles of Starbucks, and their impact on all of Starbucks' stakeholders. Starbucks' values and the resultant mission and guiding principles reflect the "soul" of the organization, and when properly executed and delivered, these intangible brand attributes comprise a resource that creates a sustainable, competitive advantage. Cost represents the premium price Starbucks pays to growers, as well as the premium pricing power (and superior value proposition) they enjoy with their customers. How well has it worked?

This is demonstrated by Starbucks' performance.

At the end of 2006, Starbucks had grown to 12,440 locations worldwide[5] with 145,800 employees, a 22 percent YTY sales increase to $7.8 billion, and a market value of about $27 billion. Starbucks' relatively high market capitalization reflects investors' belief that Starbucks can maintain growth and margins into the future. Since the majority of market value is reflected in the intangible assets of an enterprise, this is also a belief in the ability of Starbucks to maintain their brand integrity.

That's impressive value creation for a business that Schultz bought for $3.8 million in 1987!

Mayo Clinic

One of the first things you notice about Mayo Clinic's original location is where it is. More than 126 years ago, William and Charles Mayo built their

---

[5] Operating in all 50 states plus the District of Columbia, and in 36 countries outside the United States.

clinic in an out-of-the-way little Minnesota town located in the middle of some cornfields. They built their clinic the old-fashioned way, one patient at a time, with delighted patients going back to their home towns telling all who'd listen remarkable tales of healing and service.

The growth and renown of Mayo Clinic becomes even more impressive when you realize, unlike "metro" hospitals, Mayo Clinic does not have a large local population to draw from. Its patients come from all over the country and the world. They have to leave family and friends, and they have to pay for travel and lodging while they're at Mayo Clinic.

Mayo Clinic now has several locations: Rochester, MN, Jacksonville, FL, and Scottsdale, AZ. They served more than 500,000 individual patients and generated over $4.8 billion in revenue in 2005, and have amassed total assets worth over $7 billion. What accounts for their remarkable success? Let's look at their Web site for clues.[6]

Their "splash" page gives us a clue; it prominently features a patient's story. It features a patient-friendly alphabetical search engine, allowing patients to easily search by disease, treatment, and service. When we click on "About" we go to . . .

---

[6] Mayo Clinic Web site pages used with the permission of Mayo Foundation for Medical Education and Research.

Here we learn that Mayo Clinic's logo represents "the three underpinnings that continue our reputation as a pioneer and innovator in medicine—patient care, medical research and academic education." And that "Mayo Clinic staff members work together to meet your needs. You will see as many doctors, specialists and other health care professionals as needed to provide comprehensive diagnosis, understandable answers and effective treatment."

When we click on "more about Mayo Clinic" we go to this page:

Here we read a message from Mayo Clinic's CEO: "The trust and hope patients place in Mayo Clinic says a lot . . . about the expectations we need to live up to each time a patient comes through our doors." Wow, that sounds like a very customer-centric point of view. When we click on "Mayo's Mission," we go to:

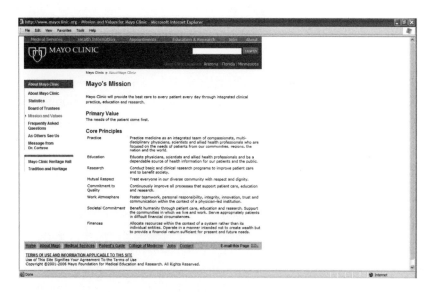

We learn that Mayo's Mission is to ". . . provide the best care to every patient every day through integrated clinical practice, education and research." Mayo Clinic's primary value tells us what "pulls" their behavior and decision making: **"The needs of the patient come first."** In support of the primary value are eight principles. It's obvious from looking at Mayo Clinic's Web site that they have built their brand on strong values, and that they reflect those values in what they say and do. However, we wanted more insight into how this works at Mayo Clinic day in and day out to build Mayo Clinic's brand integrity and, therefore, brand value.

We interviewed Kent Seltman, director of marketing and brand team leader for Mayo Clinic, to learn more about Mayo Clinic's ethos, and how its values have led to its emergence and long-term success as a world-class healthcare institution.

Kent shared the interesting observation that "if the Mayo brothers had built the clinic in a large city, it may never have developed into what it is today." Barriers of distance, being away from family, the added costs for travel and lodging "put an added burden on Mayo Clinic to deliver a superior service. Since time was of the essence, they built systems to deliver a definitive diagnosis within the week. Their systems enable next day consultations. It was necessary for Mayo Clinic to deliver complex services within a constrained time period, and they rose to the challenge."

Kent confirmed that William Mayo, in 1910 in a commencement address at Rush Medical College in Chicago said, "The best interest of the patient is the only interest to be considered." That statement defined Mayo Clinic's core value and is what the organization lives by. Kent added, "We have a popularized version of Mayo's statement that sits in everyone's calendars and says: 'The needs of the patient come first.' And that very simply is the primary value of the institution. This is a phrase that virtually everyone at Mayo Clinic knows. There's no test on it, I'm sure it's covered in orientation—but it's part of the culture, and that is what we really live by as an organization."

According to Kent, there is "a fundamental tension in healthcare between the needs of the patient and the needs of the healthcare givers. Mayo's values ensure the emphasis is placed on the needs of the patient. Therefore, systems are patient focused versus being provider focused." This alone differentiates Mayo Clinic's offering and brand from many others in their consideration set.

Kent went on to say: "Mayo Clinic has had a division called 'systems and procedures,' with about 100 individuals working in that service now, and essentially these are industrial engineers that build our systems. And some of the people who work in there now really are IS (Information Systems) specialists who deal with such things as the appointment system, and electronic medical records. They're not the programmers who create them, but they work with the systems specifications that we need to have. They also have done a lot of time and motion studies, and worked on various efficient ways to move patients through this system. They developed formulas to suggest that if there were 'X' number of people who began the appointments on a given day, then those would generate 'X' numbers of X-rays, 'X' number of lab tests, 'X' number of consults of various types, and then they were able to build access systems that were able to accommodate those needs of the patients.

"Despite our best efforts, our systems aren't perfect, but we're able to deliver good service with flawed systems because our people live and understand the 'patient first' value. They'll work on something until they figure out a way to get it done to the patient's benefit. They'll show initiative beyond that required by their job description in order to put the patient first and deliver superb service, despite limitations of the system in which they work."

To support this "patient first" value, Kent added "everyone at Mayo Clinic has their paycheck written from the same bank account, and is paid a flat amount for their job." When you read the core principles, for example,

"Work Atmosphere: Foster teamwork . . . ," you quickly understand that this principle is consonant with having salaried physicians. Therefore, "everyone at Mayo Clinic sees themselves as members of a team to meet the needs of individual patients."

Kent adds, "If you want to be a star, you are not going to be comfortable at Mayo Clinic. If you're really up front about your values, it's really not hard to recruit. If someone has worked at Mayo for 3 years, their odds of staying a long time are excellent. The Rochester, MN location has about 5% turnover."

Kent shared insight from an employee focus group that underscores this point. A nurse said, "I am a better nurse at Mayo Clinic than any other place I have worked. This is the only place where I've been able to practice nursing in the way that I learned in school that nursing should be practiced."

Or as an admittance desk clerk said, "Mayo Clinic is very famous and I can't let it down."

The positive impact this has on lowering Mayo's recruitment and training costs is huge. Plus, the lack of turnover means that more experienced, knowledgeable, dedicated personnel are available to meet patients' needs—thus supporting the core value and Mayo Clinic's brand integrity.

"Patients at Mayo get more 'face time' with physicians, 30 to 60 minutes or more, depending on the patient and their needs."

Another source of tremendous value creation for Mayo Clinic's brand is word of mouth. According to Kent, "word of mouth is what has built Mayo Clinic into what it is today. Mayo Clinic enjoys 18% top of mind *preference*. 37% of people surveyed know someone who's been treated at Mayo."

How effectively is that preference being sustained?

Kent relates that, "96% of our patients tell us they voluntarily say good things about our service. The average number of people they tell is 45 to 50. 86% advise, on average, 17 persons to go there. Each of our word-of-mouth advocates claims to average seven new patients over the years. Multiply these numbers by the over 500,000 patients seen annually, and you will see why word of mouth supplemented with strong media relations is about all the promotion we need." Now, that's service worth talking about!

Other interesting feedback Kent shared with us is that, "the Mayo Clinic brand brings meaning to people who've not yet experienced the service. 60+% of survey respondents find value and comfort in knowing Mayo Clinic exits, that *it is there if they ever need it*."

Kent ends by saying: "The Mayo Clinic brand 5 to 10 years from now will be based on every interaction, with every patient, clinician and employee today. Values are absolutely integral to a service brand."

Mayo Clinic is an excellent example of a brand in a high-interest (especially when it's really, really needed) category that understands its stakeholders' values, and has incorporated and aligned those values with its own values and operating principles. When a patient feels they are running out of time, and have one chance to get it right, they often choose Mayo Clinic.

One way to look at the Mayo Clinic story is from the perspective of the Brand Value Model (BVM):

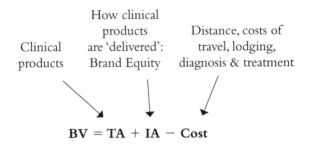

The BVM, when viewed from Mayo Clinic's patients' perspective, provides clinical products with tangible performance attributes, plus intangible services and associated emotional attributes, less the cost of these services, as well as the costs associated with traveling to the clinic, lodging, and associated costs. Based on Mayo Clinic's word-of-mouth and referrals, patients seem to highly value Mayo Clinic's brand experience and brand integrity.

The following two Web pages contain the 2005 statistics that Mayo Clinic shares with its stakeholders on its Web site:

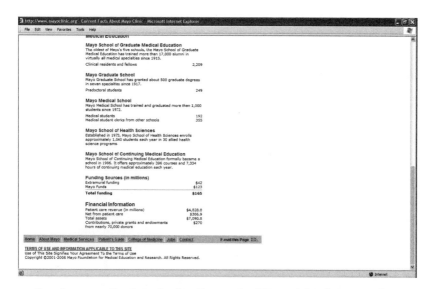

One last note: Look at the last line under "Financial Information." Mayo Clinic received $270 million from nearly 70,000 donors. Values create value.

Cascade Engineering Company, Inc.

At first glance, there's nothing about the Cascade Engineering's Web site[7] that suggests there's anything special about this company. Based on its splash page and its "about cascade" pages (below) it appears to be just another mid-sized B2B company, making engineered plastics systems and components.

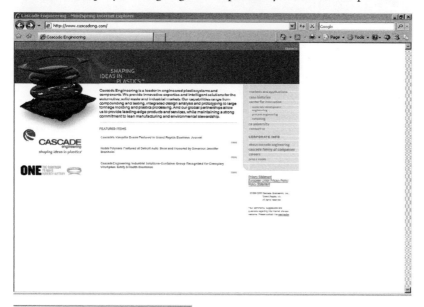

[7] Cascade Engineering's Web site "page grabs" used with the permission of Cascade Engineering Company, Inc.

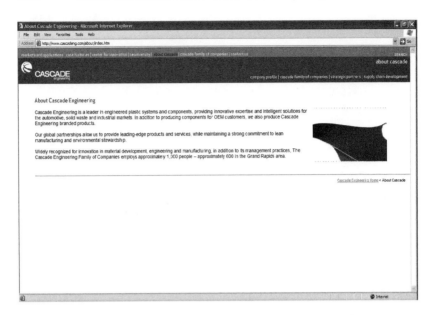

Digging a bit deeper, we click on "company profile" and are directed to this page. Here's the first sign that this company has any distinguishing characteristics. We click on "Sustainability" and are taken to . . .

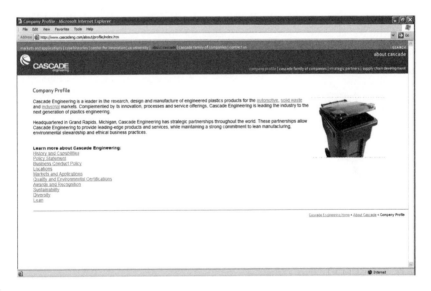

. . . this page. And it's here that we see that this company is different, when we read, "Cascade Engineering was founded in 1973 with the belief that a business could be profitable and socially and environmentally responsible. Over the years this philosophy of business has been transformed into a commitment to achieve a sustainable enterprise with specific financial, social and environmental goals. We realize that our actions today impact the world of tomorrow, and—uniquely—as a private company, we have a special opportunity to demonstrate this commitment in our daily work." We then see the statement, "Triple Bottom Line Report." Clicking on that brings us to . . .

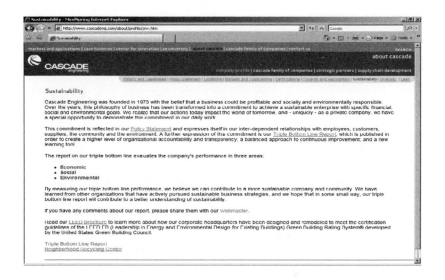

Four pages down into the Web site, we arrive at the page, shown below, that truly distinguishes this company: their triple-bottom line report. As the front cover of the report tells us: "Publishing a Triple Bottom Line (TBL) Report reflects our company's strategy to become a sustainable enterprise with specific economic, social and environmental goals. It (sustainability) has become a part of our culture and common language. Each member of our organization is responsible for finding and eliminating waste, not only in our production systems, but in our use of energy resources. We hope to maximize our interaction with the community and with each other. A new focus this year for us is that *the concept of driving sustainability actually drives innovation in the company.* (Emphasis added.)

"Sustainability is already integrated into our brand; it is one of our brand assets. The TBL Report acts as a guide and reporting mechanism for all sustainability efforts throughout our organization, signifying Cascade as a leader in these efforts and strengthening our brand while providing a clear strategy for future innovations and growth."

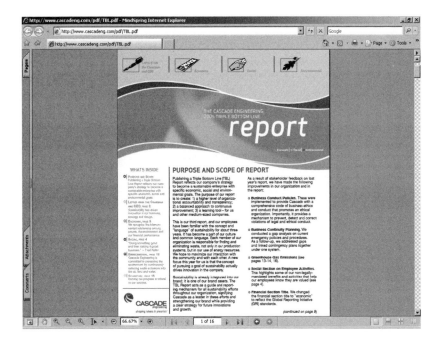

When we read the "Letter from the Chairman and CEO" we learn more about the role of "sustainability" as the core value of Cascade Engineering.

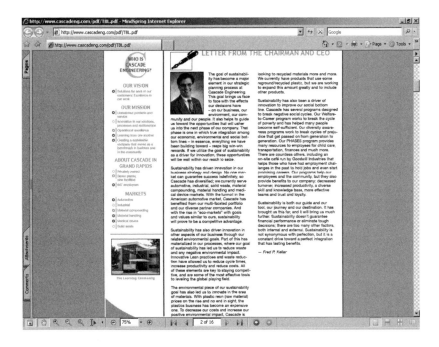

Key phrases from the letter stand out:

"The goal of sustainability has become a major element in our strategic planning process . . . it helps to guide us toward the opportunities that will usher us into the next phase of our company. . . .one in which true integration among our economic, environmental and social bottom lines . . . reaps big win-win rewards. If we utilize the goal of sustainability as the driver for innovation, these opportunities will be well within our reach to seize.

"Cascade has benefited from our multi-faceted portfolio and our diverse partner companies. And with the rise of 'eco-markets' with goals and values similar to ours, sustainability will prove to be a competitive advantage.

". . . our goal of sustainability has led us to reduce waste and any negative environmental impact. Innovative Lean practices and waste reduction have allowed us to reduce cycle times, increase productivity and reduce costs. All of these elements are key to staying competitive, and are some of the most effective tools to leveling the global playing field.

"To decrease our costs and increase our positive environmental impact, Cascade is looking to recycled materials more and more. We currently have products that use some reground/recycled plastic, but we are working to expand this amount greatly . . .

"Sustainability has also been a driver of innovation to improve our social bottom line. . . . Our programs help our employees and the community, but they also provide benefits to our company: decreased turnover, increased productivity, a diverse skill and knowledge base, more effective teams and trust and loyalty.

"Sustainability is both our guide and our tool, our journey and our destination. . . . Sustainability doesn't guarantee financial performance or eliminate tough decisions; there are too many other factors both internal and external. Sustainability is not synonymous with perfection, but it is a constant drive toward a perfect integration that has lasting benefits."

Cascade Engineering's TBL Report is filled with examples of programs and initiatives that tell the story of sustainability; how it's being adopted at Cascade; and its impact on employees, customers, suppliers, strategic partners, and communities. The TBL Report also contains a scorecard that tracks KPIs.

Since Cascade Engineering is a privately held firm, financial information on the overall value of the firm, and how it's changed over the last several years, is not available. However, the following quote by Fred Keller, chairman and CEO of Cascade Engineering, from the 2003 TBL Report, seems to sum up his view of the value of a values-based approach to the Cascade Engineering brand and business:

"As we build the social capital in Cascade Engineering to strengthen our culture to withstand the severe pressures of the market, and as we build products that are needed in an increasingly scarce resource world, we will build a business that is not only survivable, it will be sustainable and self-renewing!"

Scorecard

	2002	2003	2004	2005
Economic				
Sales Growth	10.9%	10.1%	14.3%	6.2%
Total Assets (in millions)	$103.3	$116.0	$127.4	$136.5
Taxes Paid (in millions)	$5.5	$6.2	$4.8	$6.5
Social				
Contributions	$232,000	$208,000	$215,000	$258,000
Welfare-to-Career Retention (monthly)	96.2%	97.5%	97.8%	96.2%
Average Hours of Training per Employee	36	25	26	15
Diversity/Human Rights Training (in hours)	2,521	1,936	2,548	2,190
Employee Volunteer Hours[1]	*	*	*	1,807
Environmental and Safety				
Incident Rate	13.6	7.6	5.7	5.7
Lost/Restricted Workday Rate	7.1	4.2	2.5	2.6
Citations/Fines	0/$0	0/$0	2/$500	0/$0
Water Consumption (cubic feet in millions)	1.9	2.6	2.5	2.4
Sales Dollars per Kilowatt Hours	*	$2.98	$3.26	$3.26

[1] Cascade Engineering began tracking employee volunteer hours in 2005. These volunteer hours count toward the company's goal if they meet one of the three following criteria: (1) Cascade Engineering sponsors the project/event; (2) Cascade gives the employee work time to volunteer; or (3) Cascade contributes financial support to the organization.

[2] Value is expressed in units of "metric tons of carbon dioxide equivalents" (MTCO$_2$E). Cascade Engineering conducted a facility-wide greenhouse gas (GHG) audit of its Grand Rapids "Campus" in strict accordance with the Greenhouse Gas Inventory Protocol of the U.S. EPA Climate Leaders program. The reported GHG emissions total is the sum of CO_2, CH_4 and N_2O quantities emitted from direct and indirect sources consolidated within pre-defined organizational and operational boundaries (see page 16). Appropriate emissions coefficients and conversion factors were either specific to local utilities (e.g., Consumers Energy and DTE Energy) or the default values recommended by the U.S. EPA Climate Leader program. An explanation of calculations and assumptions employed in the audit process can be provided upon request.

	2002	2003	2004	2005
Environmental and Safety				
Impact of Spills on Environment	0	0	0	0
Greenhouse Gas Emissions[2] (metric tons of carbon dioxide equivalent in thousands)	*	*	*	57.4%
Landfill Reduction	*	*	38%	38%
Use of Post-Consumer and Industrial Recycled Material (pounds in millions)	6.0	7.5	9.3	7.9

The three companies we've looked at realize it's not sufficient to "know thyself," and understand what your values are and why they're important to value creation, but to *put those values to work in all you do.* To "bake" the values into the strategies, programs, and relationships that define your firm's brand—so that your brand differentiates your company and gives added meaning to your relationships. Then you must work hard every day to make sure that what you promise is what your stakeholders experience.

Take a look at your company's Web site. Are any values evident? Are they the right values in terms of what gets your employees engaged in your business, and creates a higher value offering for your clients and customers, channels, strategic partners, and other stakeholders. Are your company's values expressed in strategies and programs and measurements, or are they just words? Are they attributes of your brand, and does the desire to deliver on your brand's promise "pull" commitment and behavior throughout your organization? If you can't say "yes" to all these questions, you'll find valuable information to help you in the chapters ahead.

"These questions are very relevant to my company's situation. Especially after hearing my fellow Vistage members' observations and recommendations. I hope the next chapters tell me how to get answers to these questions, and how to put that information to work."
—Jack F. Eli, CEO, TasteRite

CHAPTER 11

VALUES-BASED MARKET SEGMENTATION

"Values give us the stars by which we navigate ourselves through life."

—Dr. Sydney B. Simon, Author

"As commonly birds of a feather will flye together."

—Proverb recorded by Philemon Holland in a
16th-century translation of Livy's *Romaine Historie*

For most business firms, locating and specifically targeting unique market segments are essential in today's hyper-competitive market place. In developed countries, the assumptions of the mass market no longer hold true for most businesses and product categories. Indeed, in a recent article in *Marketing Management,* marketing guru Fred Webster questioned whether a sustainable mass market ever existed in North America.[1]

It has been demonstrated repeatedly that firms that develop and implement an effective market segmentation strategy enjoy higher levels of profitability compared to those that operate under a mass market strategy or those that implement an ineffective or simply convenient segmentation strategy.

Why does an effective market segmentation strategy produce higher profits? Primarily it focuses the resources of the firm on specific groups of similar customers. By doing so, it limits competitive pressure by reducing competitive impact from competitors that are addressing other segments. And, it allows the firm to develop a deep marketing-mix experience with, and core knowledge of, those targeted segments.

Creative market segmentation strategies often afford the business organization a strategic advantage over their competition. If a firm can address its markets by way of a creative vision of how that market is structured and operates and can uncover the values and needs of the segments therein, then it has the opportunity to act on that vision to enhance its own profitability, often at the expense of the competition. It is no secret that many offshore firms have entered the domestic U.S. market by segmenting the market,

---

[1] Webster, Frederick E., Jr., "Defining the New Marketing Concept," *Marketing Management* Vol. II, No. 4, p. 22 (October, 1993).

uncovering an underserved niche, and then concentrating their marketing and financial resources into that niche. Once established, and often dominating in that niche, those market invaders use their dominant position in the niche as a base of operations to expand into and penetrate other segments. One has to only look at what has happened to the North American automobile market over the last 30 years to see the evidence. Price was not the major issue. Performance, reliability, safety, economy, style, and eventually brand image dominated the preference for foreign automobiles in the U.S. marketplace. In other words, for many U.S. consumers the foreign manufacturers offered a better value proposition that was more in line with their preference structure.

What Is Market Segmentation?

In their book *Research for Marketing Decisions,*[2] Paul Green and Donald Tull provide the following, straightforward definition of market segmentation:

> *"Briefly stated, market segmentation is concerned with individual or intergroup differences in response to market-mix variables. The managerial presumption is that if these response differences exist, can be identified, are reasonably stable over time, and the segments can be efficiently reached, the firm may increase its sales and profits beyond those obtained by assuming market homogeneity."*

In this definition, Green and Tull make two fundamental points about market segmentation.

First, to be true market segments, purchasers in each segment must respond differentially to variations in the marketing mix compared to those in other segments. That is, members of each segment will respond differently to variations in product/service attributes, price, promotion/positioning, and/or variations in place/channel. This implies that for any classification scheme to qualify as market segmentation, the segments must exhibit these behavioral response differences.

Second, Green and Tull point out the four basic criteria for segmenting a market:

- The segments must *exist* in the environment (and not be a figment of the marketer's imagination).
- The segments must be *identifiable* (repeatedly and consistently).

---

[2] Green, Paul and Tull, Donald, *Research for Marketing Decisions,* 4th ed. Prentice Hall, 1978: p. 540.

- The segments must be reasonably *stable over time.*
- One must be able to *efficiently reach* segments (through specifically targeted distribution and communications initiatives).

Peter Doyle, in *Value-Based Marketing* (Wiley 2004), published a similar checklist to address the criteria for a successful segmentation:

1. *Effective:* Are the needs of the people within the segment homogenous but different from the needs of the people outside of the segment?
2. *Identifiable:* Can customers in the segment actually be isolated and measured?
3. *Profitable:* Is the segment large enough to still achieve economies of scale?
4. *Accessible:* Can the segment be reached in media without too much overlap?
5. *Actionable:* Does the business have the resources to segment its offer in the first place?

In the contemporary marketplace, just about every product and service category can be segmented. The major task is to identify the basis that should be used such that the segments demonstrate significant and differential responses to variations in the marketing mix.

Furthermore, once it is determined that various segments do exist, and can be precisely identified, the question of whether those segments are stable, in terms of time, place, and usage occasion, must be assessed. A market segmentation strategy can be very costly if put in place to address segments that are in rapid transition.

Then there is the question of reachability. Although the segments may exist, and are identifiable, and even stable, all of that is useless if those segments cannot be efficiently reached by the distribution and communications systems available to the firm.

Values-Based Market Segmentation

The Value Equation is an ideal basis for segmenting a market. It meets all of the requirements set out by Green and Tull.

Recall that in Chapter 7 we demonstrated that you can derive the value equation for each respondent in a representative sample of customers and/or prospective customers. The form of the value equation is:

$$\text{Brand Value} = (W_P \text{ Product Benefits} + W_S \text{ Service Benefits} + W_C \text{ Channel Benefits} + W_B \text{ Brand Equity}) - W_P \text{ Costs}$$

Each product benefit, each service benefit, each channel benefit, each brand, and each cost element in that equation has an importance weight for each respondent. In addition, each performance level of each tangible performance attribute has a utility. Together, they define the preference structure a customer/prospect uses to make a choice among the competing set of brands in their consideration set.

Consider the impact of defining market segments as groups of people who have similar preference structures. In any one segment, customers/prospects would similarly value the key performance attributes in the product category that was addressed in the trade-off exercise. The people in any one segment would be distinctly different from those in any other segment in terms of values and in the manner they would react to variations in the marketing mix. Thus the key criterion set out by Green and Tull is met.

There is a class of statistical procedures called "cluster analysis" that allows a well-schooled marketing research methodologist to form these segments. Keep in mind that some cluster analysis programs will produce different segments than other programs, so you need to be sure that the research methodologist is well trained in clustering techniques. Forming these segment clusters is not a mechanical process. It takes some serious statistical work, repeated trials, and artful thinking to do it right.

Assuming that the trade-off experiment was designed correctly and included the key drivers of purchase choice, then you can be assured that these values segments do exist in the marketplace. The manner in which you gathered the information to derive the importance weights guarantees that. It has been demonstrated repeatedly that well-designed trade-off experiments deeply engage respondents and rather precisely reveal the manner in which they place value on different performance attributes.

For the same reason, the segments can be consistently and repeatedly identified by repeating the trade-off exercise. In addition, the researcher who forms the segments can craft a series of simple questions that will allow the marketer to query additional customers or prospects and classify them into the proper segments with a high degree of reliability. See the Brand Value Model Technical Addendum in the Appendix for a detailed discussion of how that is done.

Will the segments be stable? Normally they will be. In general, consumers are slow to change their preference structures. However, they do change.

There are some situations we have observed that are likely to trigger rapid changes in consumer preference structures.

1. Rapid technological changes in the product or service category. Think of the impact that constantly improved processor and disk capacities had on the computer industry during the 1990s.
2. Rapid proliferation of fads and fashions. Consider how the Atkins Diet and its variations caused a rapid change in food purchases and restaurant offerings.
3. Major changes in the economy. Consider how rapid increases in housing prices changed preferences for mortgage products.
4. Regulatory and legal changes. Consider the impact of recent privacy laws on the availability of consumer information.

Reaching Out to Those Values Segments

This brings us to the final criterion set out by Green and Tull—how do you reach these values-based segments?

In order to take advantage of the values-based segmentation and target your offerings to the correct audiences in the correct manner, you must be able to communicate your brand promise and offer an effective selling proposition in a manner that aligns with the most important attributes for each segment that you are targeting. You need to be able to reach out and touch customers in any one segment with unique communications, while minimizing the number of customers outside that segment that receive that communication.

This is usually where a lot of segmentation strategies fail. Most firms do not have sufficient information about their customers and prospects to develop a meaningful way to target each segment with specific communications. Thus, you often see the ridiculous situation where companies use "mass media" to target tightly defined market segments. Not only is this very inefficient, but it produces confusing messages that depreciate brand equity. In any fall weekend, we can see a fast-food company advertising their adult-oriented fare during a football game, and then touting their give-away action toys on the following family program.

The first step in assuring that you can take full advantage of the values-based segmentation strategy is to have a marketing-oriented database of customers and prospects. This goes well beyond the typical company transactional database of contact information, purchases, and usage information. If possible, the database should also include channel usage information, other brands purchased, price sensitivity information, and any demographics or firmographics available.

Once such a database is in place, the next step is to figure out how you can classify each customer in that database into their proper values segment.

For B2B firms that have a small customer base, it may be possible to survey most or all of your customers and prospects, using the classification questions discussed previously. However, for most other firms, large B2B and consumer-oriented organizations, the cost would be prohibitive.

So, the question remains, how do you assign each customer and prospect in your database to their proper values segment?

One approach is to build a predictive model whereby you use the information gathered in the trade-off survey, line that up with the information you have in your current database for each surveyed customer, and attempt to find a statistical relationship between the two. If there is a strong relationship, then you can predict the likely segment membership of all those in the database that you did not survey. This can get very complicated very quickly and may require the use of some very complex statistical procedures that fall in the category of agent-based algorithms and artificial neural networks.

Those companies that build a predictive segmentation model based on existing data in their customer database often sacrifice a lot of accuracy in assigning segment membership since the information that they have about their customers and prospects is not as rich as the primary data collected in the trade-off survey. So even though the segmentation is based on very specific values, it is constrained by the accuracy and relevancy of information contained in customer and prospect databases that can be statistically linked to customer values and value segment membership.

A quicker, less complex, and often more accurate method for classifying customers/prospects into values-segments was developed by David Feldman at SDR Consulting.

Essentially, Feldman's procedure involves making the database of customers/prospects richer by taking advantage of existing segmentation schemes that are commercially available, such as those developed by PRIZM (Claritas), Personix (Acxiom), or P$YCLE (financial data by Claritas). In a consumer database, every consumer can be assigned to one of these clusters based simply on their residential address.

For example, PRIZM developed socioeconomic groups and specific clusters based on two easily identifiable dimensions—affluence and urbanization.

In the U.S. market, PRIZM has identified 15 socioeconomic groups breaking down into 62 clusters. Each PRIZM cluster contains rich information on demographics, life style and life stage, media usage, product preferences, and purchasing behaviors for each household.

So, if your customer database also has PRIZM cluster information appended to it, then when you do our trade-off survey to get information for developing the Value Equation, you also capture the respondents' address and therefore their PRIZM information. Then you can use standard cross-tabulation techniques and some rather straightforward statistical models to determine which data elements in your enhanced customer/prospect database best predict values-based segment membership.

When new customers or prospects are added to the database, we can easily predict their segment membership using the same predictive model.

A significant number of information firms in the United States provides additional household-level data based on PRIZM and Personix clusters. It is important that the data fields that you purchase to enrich your customer/prospect database are strongly related to the product or service category of your brand(s).

If your customers are other businesses, then the procedure is the same, but the enriching data comes from other sources, such as Acxiom or Dun & Bradstreet or some other specialized third-party provider. In this case, knowing the customer's DUNS number allows you to enrich your customer database with relevant information about the customer, and their product purchasing.

Due to the difficulties with implementing these values-based segmentations, many companies develop segmentations built around easily obtained customer and prospect information like product purchases, or product usage (such as heavy user, average user, light user, nonuser). The problem with these bases for forming segments is that more frequently than not, the benefits sought really do not vary by segment. That is, the segments do not react differently to variations in the marketing mix. This significantly limits the understanding of target customers and prospects and the unique performance attributes they are willing to pay for.

Many firms marketing in the B2B arena use SIC codes or NAICS codes as a basis for segmenting their marketplace, or as a basis for attributing purchasing needs to particular customers and prospects. It has been our experience that firms within any one SIC or NAICS have vastly different value equations. That is, what they value—thus how they make the purchase decision—varies tremendously.

The final step in this values-based segmentation process is to describe the segments in detail. The segments will have distinctly different values (importance weights), so describe those major differences first. Next, look for any descriptive information that differentiates the segments, such as demographics/ firmographics, usage information, purchase frequency, media usage, and so forth.

It is good practice to name the segments in some memorable fashion— one that will build an instant picture of the people or firms in that segment. This will help you to build and proliferate the segmentation scheme throughout your organization. Examples could include names like "Bargain Hunters" who are those that put high importance on price, low importance on brand name, low importance on service support, and that value just the basic performance attributes in the product class.

In values-based segmentations it is typical (but not always obvious) that the following segments will often emerge:

1. One or two segments where price dominates their value equation. These folks will place very high importance on price, very low importance on brand, and low importance on any performance attribute that is not basic to the product or service category.

2. One segment that places high importance on a single brand or a pair of brands. These are folks who are brand loyal. It's important to further compare those who are loyal to different brands. Those that are loyal to your brand may exhibit quite different importance weights in some areas than those that are loyal to competing brands. That is important to know. Those who are loyal to competing brands will be the most difficult to convert to your brand. Also, note that the number of people who are loyal to any one brand is going to be much lower than you expected. This is because the number of people who are truly loyal to a brand, and are willing to make brand a preeminent consideration in a trade-off exercise, is much lower than that reported in most CRM and customer satisfaction programs. More on this later.

3. There will be several segments that will give very high importance to different bundles of performance attributes. For example, in automobiles you may see the following:
   a. Safety segment
   b. Economy segment (for example, low operational cost such as fuel economy, extended warranties, and low service costs)

c. Performance segment—maybe more than one

d. Reliability segment

When this task is completed, you will likely end up with somewhere between four and ten distinct values segments for any particular product category. Within each segment, purchasers will have very similar preference structures. And those preference structures will be distinctly different on one or more key drivers of choice than purchasers in any other segment. If you average the utilities and importance weights of each segment, you will have the value equation and preference structure for that segment, and can therefore observe the key drivers of choice for all those purchasers in that segment and how they differ from other segments.

Leveraging Values-Based Segmentation

Assuming you have (1) formed the values-based segments for your product/ service category, (2) described them in detail and noted the major differences between groups, (3) named the segments, and (4) scored your customer/ prospect database such that each customer and prospect is assigned to a values segment, the question is: How do you implement the segmentation strategy?

Market Opportunity Analysis—The Brand Value SWOT Analysis

First and foremost, you need to conduct a Brand Value SWOT analysis. Your goal is to discover areas for sustainable competitive advantage within segments. Here you make a detailed examination of your brand and its strengths, weaknesses, opportunities, and threats in terms of how it aligns with the values of each segment compared to how competing brands line up.

Examine total unit purchases by brand for each segment and compare your current share and each competitor share by segment. This is data that would have been collected during the initial trade-off survey (don't rely on what your customer database tells you because that is likely biased information). Are your sales concentrated in just one or two of those segments, or do you have approximately the same sales penetration across many segments? If the latter, that is a strong indication that your offering is not well differentiated—it is not in alignment with what different segments value.

On the other hand, if your sales are concentrated in one or two segments, determine exactly why. Is it because your product attributes are in alignment? Possibly it is because of your primary channels and the channel support provided—they line up with the channel preferences for those in the high-penetration segments. Or is it because of your pricing? Maybe it's because of the intangible attributes that purchasers in those segments value. Perform this same analysis for each of your major competing brands. This analysis will initially identify your strengths and weaknesses and the strengths and weaknesses of your competitors, and the threats they pose on a segment-by-segment basis.

Another insightful analysis is to calculate the total value of your offering for each segment. That is, add up the average utilities of the individual performance levels of your offering(s) within each segment. (We demonstrated this with the breadmaker example in Chapter 7—Braun vs. Sears.) Do the same for each competing brand. Compare your total utility (and your competitors') to the total utility of the top bundle of performance attributes in each segment. The top bundle is found by summing the segment utilities of the highest performance level of any brand on each tangible performance, and channel attribute. How big of a gap exists between the total utility (or value) that your brand is offering and the best bundle in each segment? Ask where you can realistically close the gaps.

In order to uncover strengths and weaknesses in your brand's intangible attributes, we go back to the trade-off survey. Recall that we had respondents rate the performance of each brand on a set of intangible attributes in order to find the key drivers of each brand's equity. You can use that same data to develop perceptual maps of your brand and competing brands in each segment. Most well-trained marketing research professionals can construct these maps using one of several available computer programs. Figure 11.1 shows an illustrative perceptual map.

In this illustration, brands are boxed and shaded. The ovals show the image attributes that differentiate between the brands. The further from the center, the more it differentiates between the brands. Thus, we see in this segment, the major differentiating attributes are "economical." and "reliable." The bigger the oval, the more important that attribute is. The closer a brand is to an attribute, the more of the attribute is perceived to be aligned with that brand. The "Best Brand" is an artificial brand that is created by finding the best performance of any brand on each attribute. It may be viewed as the "ideal" brand location for this market segment.

We can see from this map that for Altima to become more like the Best Brand in this segment, it needs to improve its perception of being more reliable and improve its perception of being more for the "young and

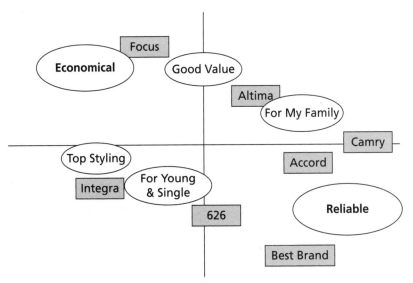

Figure 11.1   Illustration of a Perceptual Map

single"; whereas Focus would need to greatly improve its perception of being "reliable for the young and single." Also, in this segment, Focus and the 626 have little chance of competing well because their brand perceptions are so much different from what people in this segment are seeking. Integra would also have a difficult time moving to the space occupied by the Best Brand.

Furthermore, note that in this illustration, Accord and Camry are very close to each other. This indicates that this segment does not see them as being much different in terms of brand image.

These perceptual maps allow you to see in a picture just where your brand image stands within a segment—your strengths, your weaknesses, what you need to do to improve your brand position, and ultimately, whether you can compete at all in that segment with your current brand name.

There are many other analyses you can undertake to identify your strengths, weaknesses, opportunities, and threats among both your tangible performance attributes and your brand image drivers. When this analysis is completed, you and your marketing team should have a deep understanding of where you stand in each values segment. You should have a better understanding of where you are creating value and where additional opportunities to create value can be realized. You should also better understand where changes in your brand performance or your brand image may significantly reduce value.

Target Market Selection

As a result of the Brand SWOT, you should have a good feel for those segments in which you are well aligned with the segment's values and where you are not well aligned. You should be able to identify the source of any misalignments—is it product performance, price, channel performance, or some elements of your brand equity? You should have evaluated each segment in terms of perceived strengths and weaknesses of your product/service offering and your brand image compared to your competitors'. Your next step is to select those segments that offer the best prospects for your long-term growth and profitability.

First, you should select segments where you are the No. 1 brand and make two decisions:

1. Is this a segment I really want to be in? Is it growing? Is it profitable?
2. Given the affirmative to question 1, what do I need to do to defend my position and improve my value to customers/consumers in this segment? That is, how can I continue to grow and dominate this segment?

Next, select segments where you are the No. 2 or No. 3 brand and ask these questions:

1. Is this a segment I want to be in? Is it growing? Is it profitable?
2. Given the affirmative to question 1, what do I need to do to improve my value to customers/consumers in this segment to the point where I can overcome the value proposition of the leading brands?
3. Is that feasible, given my firm's capabilities and my brand promise?
4. If I make these product/channel/brand changes, will it conflict with any changes I plan for defending my position in the segment(s) where I am the No. 1 brand?

Finally, identify any remaining segments that represent high growth or high profit potential and look for ways you could successfully enter those segments. The marketplace has already told you that your current brand offering and/or its value proposition is not compatible with strong improvements in these remaining segments. Therefore, you must explore other possibilities for penetrating and rapidly gaining share:

- If your current product/service performance is not viewed as having high value in these targeted high-growth segments, but your brand image is compatible, then new product introductions or brand extensions under your current brand name will be the most likely road to successful penetration.

- On the other hand, if your product/service performance is not viewed as having high value in these targeted high-growth segments, AND your brand image is not compatible, then your best alternative for successful penetration will likely be to build a totally new brand platform or the acquisition of a leading competitor in that market segment.

- If your current product/service performance is viewed as having high value in these targeted high-growth segments, and your brand image is compatible, but your penetration of that segment is low, then your target audience is probably not getting the proper messages about your offerings or your brand promise and you likely have either a brand communication problem or a channel problem.

- Finally, if your product service performance is viewed as having high value in these targeted high-growth segments, but your brand image is not compatible, then again, a new brand platform is called for.

Marketing Mix Optimization

Now that you have picked your target market segments, it's time to take action.

For each targeted market segment, determine specifically the actions you must take to optimize your brand value, now and in the future:

- *Plan the product/service attribute performance levels you will change* for each segment in order to increase your brand value and to fulfill your brand promise. As you go through this exercise, you must be realistic, keeping in mind your firm's capabilities and core knowledge. Also, as part of the exercise you should be estimating the costs of each new initiative in changing the performance level of your offering. We will be using those costs later as we set investment priorities.

- *Plan the product/service attribute performance levels you will emphasize in your marketing communications* to each segment in order to support those performance initiatives and reinforce your brand equity. The key here is to make sure your product/service communications align with the values of customers in each targeted segment. Also, make sure that your planned communications strategy to one segment does not conflict with the communications with another segment.

- *Plan your channel/delivery strategy* to make sure that the right products get to the right target markets and avoid channel conflict. Remember, that your channels contribute to your brand equity and there can be a synergistic effect (or a dissonance effect) between the brand equity of the channels you use and your own brand equity. For example, consider the synergy between the Coach brand of leather products sold through Neiman Marcus and the dissonance caused if they were sold through Wal-Mart.

- *Plan your pricing strategy.* One of the great surprises from using the brand value model in various industries over the last 15 years is that invariably senior managers believe that price carries more importance in the purchase decision than do their customers/consumers. Typically, in a values-based segmentation, customers/prospects who are very price sensitive cluster together in one or two segments. You can chose to address that price-sensitive segment, or not, depending on your cost structure and your brand promise. Regardless, the brand value equation will provide you with rather precise price sensitivity information and price elasticity curves for each segment. In addition, the choice simulator will allow you to trade off price changes against product/service performance changes and observe how those changes, working in concert, affect share of choice.

- *Develop contingency plans for likely competitor counter-attacks.* As you successfully ramp up the value of your offering and start taking share from competitors, they will react. The typical first-line competitive response is to drop price in order to maintain share. Probably the worst thing you can do is to also drop your price. In many product categories, price is an indicator of quality. By dropping their prices, competitors are signaling to consumers that their quality may be less than expected. Meanwhile you should be signaling that you are improving your product performance and your price is worth the value received.

Each one of your initiatives in this targeting process will have a cost. Your job now is to balance the costs with the likely payoff of each of the initiatives you have uncovered in this process. Once this is accomplished, it's time to prioritize your investments such that you get the most improvement in sales and profits for a given amount of investment. Again, this is where the choice simulator will help.

The choice simulator allows you to test an infinite number of "what if" scenarios and observe changes in you share of choice. You can change your prices, your product/service performance level, or expand/change your channels and observe how your share of choice changes as a result of those actions. By estimating the costs of each new initiative, and observing the payoff in terms of improvements in share of choice, it is rather straightforward to calculate your return on investment for each initiative.

Details of the choice simulator are addressed in the Brand Value Model Technical Addendum in the Appendix.

Another caution is in order at this point. Producers often will take an undifferentiated product and wrap around a service to add value and differentiate the product from competitors, hopefully adding value to their offering. Such a strategy is limited by the perceived value of the add-on service. For example, consider two gasoline outlets on opposite corners of a busy intersection, one a full-service center and one a discount convenience outlet. For some unleaded gasoline purchaser segments, a minor price differential, say 1 or 2 cents per gallon, is sufficient to select the discounter. For other segments, a greater differential is needed to induce them to the discounter. But at some point, there can be a sufficient price differential to induce the majority of the purchaser segments to the discounter. With no differences in product attributes, pricing can often defeat a segmentation strategy, especially if the service wrap-around is marginal in value.

Take a Break

You're probably thinking about where you can get the biggest bang for the buck by cherry-picking those initiatives that will have the best short term payoff.

If you are, we strongly suggest that you stop and consider two key issues.

First, in the process of looking at each values segment individually, you may develop some initiatives for improving brand value in a particular segment that is incompatible with your position in another segment. For example, you cannot be the low-cost brand in one segment and the high-quality product in another segment. Such incompatibilities need to be resolved. This is the point where you stand back and review these initiatives in light of your brand promise to make sure your initiatives are in concert. It is essential that your planned initiatives for improving your value proposition are integrated and contribute to improving the overall asset value of your brand equity.

Second, if you believe, as we do, that the major asset of your company is its brand(s) equity, then your focus should be on how you can build that asset value, not how you can maximize short term sales and/or profitability.

When you conducted your Brand SWOT and went through the exercise of finding your best target markets, you probably found some target markets where your brand image was not where it should have been. It's now time for you to determine just what the sources of those shortcomings are, and develop long-term plans to fix them. Possibilities include:

- Failure to deliver on your brand promise—what you say you are delivering and what you are really delivering are not in concert.
- Misalignment between your brand promise and the product and/or service you are delivering.
- Inconsistent or ineffective communications of your brand promise.
- Long-term product or service performance issues, especially in the areas of reliability, durability, and service response.
- Diffused (not targeted) brand image or a brand image that is not fully compatible with some of your product offerings.

There are myriad fixes available to you and they are too numerous to address in this book. However, the main thing you need to keep in mind is that improvements in the asset value of your brand equity trumps short-term improvements in sales and profits derived from new initiatives in product/service performance. Ideally, when possible, you'd like to achieve both.

Marketing Systems Development—Tracking and Monitoring

Your final step in implementing the values-based segmentation strategy is to put in place systems for measuring and reporting performance by each values segment.

The essential ingredient to accomplish this is to make sure your customer information database maintains segment membership for each customer and that you can quickly determine the segment membership of new customers. The scoring models discussed in Chapter 7 and previously in this chapter will handle that mechanically. You will need to survey each new customer in order to ask the questions necessary for the scoring model. In most cases this can be easily done with a "new account" survey linked to an incentive for responding.

You should consider using the following metrics for each market segment you have targeted:

- New customer acquisitions
- Customer defections
- Sales—both in dollars and units, by brand purchased
- Brand sales by channel (if appropriate)

- Customer inquiries, categorized by:
  - Complaints, broken out by type of complaint
  - Information inquiries, broken out by type of inquiry
  - Compliments
  - Other types of inquiries

In addition to the above, your finance department should be reporting variable costs and profits by customer segment.

In this chapter, we have showed you how to leverage the Brand Value Model to develop a values-based segmentation strategy. And we have given you an operational framework for developing and implementing that strategy. Obviously, you will need to tailor your strategy to your particular product or service categories and fine tune it in the details.

It has been our experience that customer values are the most effective basis available for segmenting any product or service market.

"The success stories in the previous chapter have shown me what's possible. This chapter shows me the tools available with which to better understand our segments, and how to create value propositions for them that create value potential for us. I hope that the next chapters show me how to put this information to work and how to measure success."

—Jack F. Eli, CEO, TasteRite

CHAPTER 12

LEVERAGING THE BRAND VALUE MODEL AND BRAND PERFORMANCE

"Give me a lever and a place to stand, and I will move the world."

—Archimedes, Greek Philosopher, 30 B.C.

At this point you should be familiar with the Brand Value Model (BVM) and Values-Based Segmentation, and understand how to perform a baseline study to uncover the drivers of brand value and brand equity for your brands, and how to use the BVM to develop a values-based segmentation strategy.

In this chapter we stand back and explore the implications of the BVM and consider how we can use the information provided by that model, coupled with market tracking measures, to continuously track performance leading to improved financial results over the long term. We discuss practical ways to apply the measures of brand value to audiences above and beyond the operational brand manager—senior corporate leaders, chief financial officers, group brand managers, the sales force, and employees. We tie the metrics from the BVM to share of choice, pricing premium, share of served segments, and EVA.

As we have discussed, the BVM provides very rich diagnostics for deeply understanding how value is created in a particular product/service category, and, if brand equity is a significant source of that value (which it almost always is), then how to further understand the key trust and image attributes that are responsible for building the equity of the brand.

It should also be clear that the BVM gives you four distinct levers for improving the value of your brands—product/service performance features, channel performance features, intangible brand attributes, and price. Which levers to pull and how much they are pulled depends on your current performance with (1) your targeted segments, (2) the market situation in the categories in which you operate, and (3) your business cycle.

You can measure the effects of the investments you make in those areas—either as a change in the number of customers who chose your brand over the competition's, or in monetary terms due to changes in total brand value, as measured by changes in total utility (value) in each targeted segment. Strong brand equities give you a fundamental choice of trading off share of choice against profit margin.

237

Furthermore, as we discussed in Chapter 7, you can experiment with a market simulator based on the BVM that allows you to make preliminary estimates of the payoff from investments in any of these four value drivers.

The challenge at this point is how to take all of this information and set up both a financial performance reporting system oriented to brand asset values and a brand value monitoring system so that each major functional area within the firm can monitor performance over time.

New Products

For many companies and in many product/service categories, the main engine for growth is new products. We are constantly developing and testing variations of current offerings—approximately 25,000 each year—in order to gain sales and improve financial performance. Yet, we have all heard of the problems in new product development and brand extensions—90 percent (or 95 percent or 85 percent—take your pick) have failed. These failures represent a huge direct cost in terms of wasted production, distribution, and marketing expenditures. Perhaps more importantly, new product failures represent a considerable depreciation in the asset value of the brand associated with the failed new product launch.

There are many reasons that new products fail in the marketplace. The most cited ones include:

1. Inadequate or misinformed assessment of marketplace needs and values.
2. Targeting the wrong market segment(s).
3. The product launched was not the product tested.
4. Failure to build adequate channel support.
5. Inappropriate pricing strategy.
6. Insufficient communications support to generate awareness and trial.
7. Failure to build adequate channel support.
8. New products overtly cannibalizing existing product(s).

A forest full of paper has been generated to discuss and analyze these issues. Yet, these are almost exclusively the failure of marketing tactics. When a new product fails, few managers bother to examine the basic strategy that was behind that new product idea and how it would enhance the producer's brand portfolio. That is, there is usually a fundamental failure to understand how the proposed new product aligns with the brand's current portfolio and its image and position in the marketplace.

It is our belief that aside from actual product performance failures, the key cause of new product failures is the misalignment between the brand image and promoted product performance. The bone yards of failed products attest to these misalignments. Does an inexpensive entry-level Mercedes Benz for the U.S. market really make sense? What about BenGay aspirin? Or gourmet sandwiches at McDonald's?

Developing, launching, and supporting a new product eats up corporate assets. The rationale for making these asset investments is that they will pay off with higher returns on the investment than if they were deployed elsewhere, and hopefully build the long-term asset value of the firm beyond their cost.

The vast majority of new product launches are extensions of established brand names. The rationale for this is obvious. The cost of launching and supporting the new product is lowered because of the lower cost for developing brand familiarity and extending the brand promise to cover the new product. Yet the risk to the asset value to the established brand is high, but unknown, and much too often not even considered. That risk has two dimensions. If the product fails, the asset value of brand name is depreciated. Even if the product is successful, there is the risk of diffusing the brand name and what it stands for, thus reducing its asset value.

In other words, the short-term gain from launching a new product under an established brand name imposes a seldom-recognized risk on the asset value of that brand name, and of course the brand's owners. Yet, this risk is seldom assessed prior to launching the new product. Current marketing ROI formulas typically do not assess this risk.

On the other hand, if a new product is launched under a new brand name, the risk to the established brands is isolated and more importantly, there is an opportunity to build another major asset if the launch is successful. Think about the asset values of Lexus and Acura rather than if they were just line extensions and model badges for the mother brands of Toyota and Honda. The cost of launching those new brands was considerable, and considerably higher than if they were launched as mere brand extensions of the familiar Toyota and Honda brands. But the payoff has been huge in terms of asset values.

Much of the decision process of whether a new product should be launched under an existing brand name or a new brand name can be resolved using the BVM, coupled with some other basic research.

Primarily, this involves executing the BVM in two contrasting ways with the relevant target market—one including the established brand name associated with the new product and the other with the new (or unspecified) brand name associated with the new product.

The resulting difference between brand values and share of choice will reveal just how much of the established brand's equity can be transferred to the new product, and the resulting change in share of choice.

This procedure should be coupled with research-based perceptual mapping procedures, which will allow you to determine whether the contemplated new product is in alignment with the established image and trust attributes of the brand.

These results can then be subjected to a classic risk-reward or a risk-adjusted ROI analysis. Part of that risk-reward analysis needs to take into consideration the effect of a possible new product failure on the established brand's name, and the consequential drop in utility (and price premium) for the products already associated with that brand.

Furthermore, that risk-reward or risk-adjusted ROI analysis needs to consider the future value of the new brand name if the launch is successful.

We discuss the calculation for risk-adjusted marketing ROI in the Brand Value Technical Addendum. However, the authors have come to the conclusion that even risk-adjusted ROI analyses leave a lot to be desired in comparing alternative investment strategies. We discuss this in more detail later in this chapter.

This process works regardless of whether you are simply doing a product extension into an established category where your brand has already established a presence or entering a whole new category or new market with your brand.

A word of caution is in order at this point. The results of the BVM represent the end state—the point where the relevant target market is completely aware of and sufficiently knowledgeable about your brand and its associated products to have formed a judgment about its perceived performance and relative perceived value. Getting from launch to the end-point where category buyers are aware and familiar with the new brand and its brand promise can take considerable time and money.

When we use the BVM model to estimate the share of choice for a new product or line extension, we often subject the share of choice estimates to a Bass Diffusion Model or similar model.[1] The application of the diffusion model allows us to estimate the share of choice over time and under different promotional and advertising investment levels. That is, depending on the money spent for building awareness and product knowledge, the share of choice will be different at different points in time.

---

[1] Mahajan, V., Muller, E., and Bass, F. M. New Product Diffusion Models in Marketing: A Review and Directions for Research. *Journal of Marketing* 54, 1 (January 1990), 1–26.

A typical Bass curve may look like this:

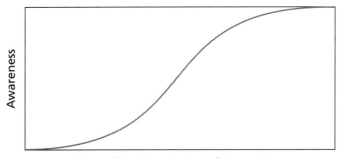

Time after Introduction of Innovation

The standard Bass curve for the diffusion of innovations over time.

The end-point of this curve is represented by the results from the BVM. The length and the inflexion points of the curve are primarily influenced by the levels of awareness and influence at any point in time. Thus, the implications are that more investments in promotion and more effective promotion will shorten the time from launch date to end state, and share of choice can be estimated based on those levels of investment at any point in time.

Tracking Brand Performance

We can monitor a brand's value over time through a series of market studies, typically called *brand performance tracking surveys*. The results of experimentation with the marketing mix from the baseline BVM and its accompanying choice simulator can be easily monitored in this manner. Furthermore, this process will allow you to track how buyer experiences with your brand shape your brand equity over time. If you are meeting or exceeding your brand promise, then the value of brand equity will rise and if you are not meeting that brand promise, it will fall.

Your brand performance tracking system should be customized to each product category in which you operate. You start with a detailed examination of the results from the baseline BVM study to identify the key product performance, channel performance, price, and brand equity drivers that have a significant impact on driving share of choice for your brand and for other major brands in the category. This is typically accomplished by deriving the importance of each attribute in driving share of choice as shown in Chapters 7 and 11.

In the baseline BVM study, each attribute was assigned several performance levels. Recall our breadmaker example in Chapter 7. The performance levels for the attribute "capacity" were 1.0 pounds, 1.5 pounds, and 2.0 pounds. This was shown to be one of the more important attributes, thus it would be included in the *brand performance tracking system*. Typically, in our brand performance tracking systems we ask respondents to rank or rate all of the performance attributes from most important to least important. Then, for those attributes that do not have an obvious order (such as brand, loaf shape, and capacity in the breadmaker example), we ask them to rank their desirability of each level. With a little bit of math, these results can be directly compared to the results from both the baseline BVM and previous results from the tracking system to determine whether there are changes in importance and desirability, and thus share of choice for each brand.

The second part of the brand performance tracking system should include the identified drivers of brand equity—both the important trust attributes and image attributes. Here we typically ask respondents who purchase in the category to rate the performance of each of the brands they are familiar with on a 0- to 10-point scale (or whatever scale was used in the baseline BVM study), from very poor performance to outstanding performance. Again, these ratings can be directly compared to the results from the baseline BVM study and previous results from the tracking system.

Typically, other basic brand measures are included in the tracking system including unaided and aided awareness, purchase and usage frequency, channel usage, and so forth. We provide a list of detailed measures later in this chapter.

Financial Interfaces

Resource Allocation

As we demonstrated in Chapters 7 and 8, the fundamental output of the BVM and its accompanying simulator is share of choice within a product or service category, given a set of performance levels attributed to each major brand/product combination in the category. The simulator can be used to vary any of the measured levels of product/service performance, channel performance, and price to estimate the change in share of choice for the relevant target market. Given that you know the margins that flow back to your firm based on each incremental sale, then changes in share of choice can be easily converted to a net return in dollars.

By making these variations in the simulator, we can easily observe the effect of those performance changes in share of choice and the economic value of any one brand/product combination. If we know the cost or cost savings from changing a particular performance level, then we can observe the estimated change in share of choice when that performance level is changed in the marketplace. It then becomes a simple matter to calculate whether such a change is economically justified. In fact, given good estimates of the marginal costs of each performance level of each product attribute, the BVM share of choice simulator can be translated into a profitability simulator. It is a rather simple matter of stating performance levels in terms of costs, and share of choice in terms of net profit per sale.

One of the interesting outcomes from changing the share of choice simulator to a profit simulator is that you will almost always see that share optimization does not equal profit optimization. The obvious reason is that the price point to optimize share is not the same price point to optimize profit. But that is not the only reason. Some product performance enhancements are quite expensive, and although share of choice may increase with the performance improvement, overall profitability may decline. The opposite also holds true. In an effort to boost profitability, performance levels may be degraded but the drop in share of choice more than wipes out the cost savings from the product performance degradation. It is this second situation that most often signals a downward spiral in brand values, thus depreciating the asset value of the brand.

What so often happens is that a board of directors installs a new management team to engineer a turnaround, or improve profitability. The management team immediately announces that it will restore growth and profitability by instituting across-the-board cost reductions. Typically, the new management team is not cognizant of the key drivers of brand value and brand equity within the firm. In fact, in most cases, consumers or buyers—those who ultimately define brand value—are not even considered part of the operating efficiency equation. So, in the cost-cutting spree, key product performance drivers are depreciated, channel support is cut, customer service is squeezed, and awareness and positioning advertising is cut. Market momentum sustains sales in the short term, but over the long term, sales decline, and more importantly, the asset value of the brand starts falling. Once on a downward slide, brand equity is very difficult to recover. Negative word-of-mouth communications quickly overcomes the weakened advertising and promotion.

So, after the excesses of indiscriminant cost-cutting becomes evident to the board of directors, usually in the form of falling stock prices, out goes the new management team, and in comes another. All the while, brand equity continues its downward spiral.

A management team that does understand the key drivers of brand value can discriminate on where they cut costs, supporting and even enhancing the key drivers of value, while selectively cutting costs elsewhere. The BVM simulator can be a powerful tool for pre-testing contemplated changes in price, performance, and service for any branded product. Furthermore, it becomes a powerful tool for guiding resource allocation.

Strategic Financial Analysis

As has been pointed out by several sources, including us, current FASB accounting methods, on average, account for less than 25 percent of the value that willing buyers and sellers—the market, place on public firms. One only needs to compare a public firm's book value to its market capitalization to understand just how much of the firm's asset value is unaccounted for in their financial statements. Being blunt about it, current financial accounting methods do not measure the majority of a firm's real value—what people are willing to pay for its ownership. Warren Buffet and other savvy investors understand this disparity and use all kinds of tools to try to find and unlock this "hidden" value.

What are these unmeasured and mostly intangible assets?

- Brand equity
- Management expertise
- Relationships with customers
- Relationships with suppliers
- Relationships with channels
- Relationships with employees
- Relationships with the public
- Core knowledge and experience
- Patents and trade secrets

However, one could, and should, make the case that almost all of these sources of unaccounted value are mostly personified by and embedded in the brands' equity—the values that investors, customers, channels, and suppliers attribute to the owner of the brands.

- Management expertise is reflected in the brands' growth volume and ability to command a premium price, or sustained growth over the long term—that is, the brand's alignment with the market's needs and desires. A well-managed brand is a well-respected brand.

- Relationships with suppliers are reflected in the focus to produce a quality product in a consistent manner that supports the brand's promise and public persona. When suppliers understand the brand's strategy they will normally align their operations to support that strategy in order to assure continued and expanding sales.

- Relationships with channels are reflected in the brand's demand, margins, availability, turnover, and the value-added support the brand is given by the producer.

- Relationships with employees are reflected in the brand's support from front-line employees and the resulting drivers of trust and image.

- Relationships with the public are reflected in the brand's reputation for quality, its alignment with purchaser self-image, and its esteem within the broader audience.

- Core knowledge and experience is reflected in the brand's perceived performance and in the trust elements of brand equity.

- Patents and trade secrets often provide the key differentiators necessary for the brand to be successful in the marketplace and contribute to the prevention of commoditization.

If we accept that the majority of a firm's unaccounted-for asset value (the difference between market capitalization and book value) is represented by its brands, then it seems most appropriate for the firm's financial management to closely monitor and report current values of those assets to the firm's owners.

More important than just reporting the current state of brand asset values and changes over time, it's essential for financial managers to understand why those changes took place and how investments in brand equity are building, or can build those asset values.

The Brand Value Model, coupled with a continuous brand performance tracking system can do that.

However, currently popular ROI techniques, using Net Present Value (NPV) calculations, applied to marketing investments do not seem to meet that need. We provide a more detailed discussion in the Brand Value Technical Addendum.

The BVM can also be useful in a merger and acquisition situation. The acquiring organization develops a better understanding of the value creation process and where their expertise and capabilities can be leveraged to increase the value of the acquisition. The selling organization gets a better understanding of the true value of the assets it is selling and can demand a fair price.

Bringing It All Together

Obviously the BVM provides a lot of information, and after reading Chapters 7, 8, and 11 you are probably thinking maybe too much information, especially for senior managers. Yet, we are talking about perhaps the most important assets that the organization owns.

One of the best ways to monitor the brand health of the organization is through a systems approach. In fact two reporting systems are needed—*one for financial management* and *one for marketing management.* Both of these monitoring systems are linked through the BVM estimates of brand value and brand equity, and are dependent on continuously monitoring the marketplace through the use of public information, internal information systems, and market surveys.

The Corporate Asset Value Monitoring System

At the corporate level we recommend a corporate asset value monitoring system. Following are the measures, we believe, are most relevant and should be considered for inclusion in the system. Whether these are updated weekly, monthly, or over some other time period is dependent upon the business cycles normal for your firm and business sector. That is, select the time period that is most appropriate for measuring change in your business sector.

Furthermore, we strongly advocate going beyond a typical dashboard effort, and lay out the elements of your corporate asset monitoring system in a series of time-dependent charts to allow the user to easily and quickly detect change over time.

In addition to the normal financial reporting data, such as weekly stock price, free cash flow, P/E ratio, and so forth, we recommend that the following key elements of financial performance be reported on a regular basis. Of course, these can and should be customized to your industry and the predilections of senior management.

- Total market capitalization by week (total value of all outstanding stock)
- Intangible asset value (market capitalization less book value)
- Intangible assets attributable to brands (as a percentage of total intangible assets)
- Estimated brand equity for each major brand (intangible assets attributable to brands, proportioned by sales by brand, times average margin per brand—adds to total value of intangible assets attributable to brands)

- Total net sales
- Share of sales by category or major merchandise line (as appropriate) broken out by brand within category
- Share of preference by category or major merchandise line (as appropriate) broken out by brand within category
- Price premium by brand within category (average price of brand minus price leader in category)
- Product/service complaints, by brand

Following are some examples of a few of these newer measures we are recommending and some of the graphics that could be used to illustrate those measures with some explanations.

The first three items on our list can be shown in one graph as depicted in Figure 12.1.

In Figure 12.1 we simply show the values of total market capitalization, contrasted to total intangible assets value (total capitalization minus book value) and total intangible assets attributable to brands for the trailing 26 weeks. This last item, the total asset values attributable to brands, can be calculated in several ways, depending on the company's specific circumstances. Alternatives are as follows:

1. Use the BVM described in Chapter 7 and the accompanying Brand Value Technical Addendum to calculate the dollar value of each brand at the unit level in terms of the price premium that brand can command in the marketplace. Multiply that by an estimate of the units sold over the appropriated time period, and then discount that value to present value. Sum across all brands to arrive at a total estimate of intangible brand assets. The difference between this figure and total intangible values (calculated by subtracting book value from total market capitalization) represents the firm's intangible assets that are not attributable to brands.

2. Subtract identifiable intangible or unaccounted for assets (such as the market values of patents, licensing contracts and other arrangements, and so on) from total intangible assets, attributing the remainder to brands.

3. Use expert opinions from professional services firms and other outside experts to arrive at a percentage of intangible assets attributable to brands.

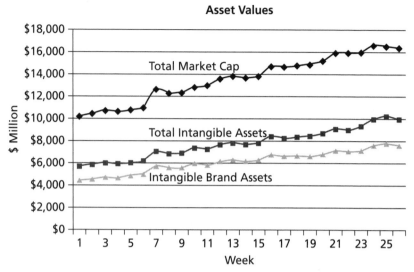

Figure 12.1

Of course, these proportions or percentages need to be periodically up-dated on a scheduled basis.

Once the chart in Figure 12.1 is developed, a companion chart should be developed to break out those results by brand—the fourth item in our list. Figure 12.2 provides an example.

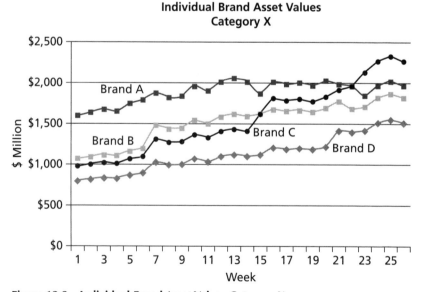

Figure 12.2   Individual Brand Asset Values Category X

This chart allows the user to better understand how each brand is contributing to the intangible assets of the firm, as well as the growth and decline of those brands over time. In this example, we see that the real growth in intangible assets is being driven principally by brand C and to a lesser extent by brands D and B, while brand A has leveled off and is likely to go into decline unless additional investments are made.

Including these additional reporting elements in the financial performance of the firm has a major impact on the firm's organizational structure. If you are going to report financial results and assets by brand, then the key implication is that the firm should be organized along a brand management structure. This type of structure allows management to focus on the individual brands or brand families, provides a rationalization for brand and line extensions, and provides a strict focus on managing brand asset values. In this type of structure, a key role of senior management is to prevent serious encroachments of one brand into another brand's category or position.

A good example where such encroachment was not prevented can be found among the American automobile manufacturers. In the automotive industry you see multiple examples of one brand encroaching on a sister brand's performance promise and positioning. Think in terms of a Chevrolet Suburban versus a GMC Yukon, or a Ford Expedition versus a Lincoln Navigator. The performance characteristics of these automotive twins are nearly identical, the positioning is nearly identical, and the trust elements are nearly identical. The only differentiation is attributable to minor brand image elements. Within a brand group (such as Chevrolet), there seems to be a complete rationalization of the brand mix. Yet across brands, you see a tremendous amount of overlap, inefficiency, and consumer confusion. Management at both GM and Ford has allowed this brand proliferation and overlap to their own detriment. Compare that to how Toyota has rationalized their brands with very distinct positioning and differentiation for each nameplate and each brand. Is there any wonder why Toyota is about to become the world's largest manufacturer of automobiles?

In another approach to bridging the finance-marketing gap, Victor J. Cook Jr., in *Competing for Customers and Capital*, has developed new thinking on the role of marketing and finance in value creation. He has developed links between the cost of enterprise-level marketing and the creation of shareholder value. His model directly links enterprise marketing expenses to shareholder value through the profit-maximizing behavior of each firm in a strategic group. He does this by calculating from financial accounting data the incremental cost of market share, and compares it with the incremental profit of market share for competitors within an industry.

This approach makes good sense because companies are competing for customers and capital. Cook employs a Competitive Enterprise Matrix to show where dollars come and go for a set of competitors (labeled Able, Baker, Charlie, and Delta in the following chart.) It looks like this:

Competitor		Sales Revenues		Cost of Goods Sold		Gross Profit		SG&A Expense		EBITDA		Share-Holder Value
Able		$100	−	$85	=	$15	−	$12	=	$3	▶	$150
		+		+		+		+		+		+
Baker		$200	−	$160	=	$40	−	$30	=	$10	▶	$500
		+		+		+		+		+		+
Charlie		$300	−	$200	=	$100	−	$80	=	$20	▶	$200
		+		+		+		+		+		+
Delta		$400	−	$300	=	$100	−	$75	=	$25	▶	$150
		=		=		=		=		=		=
Sum		$1,000	−	$745	=	$255	−	$197	=	$58		$1,000

"The Cost of Goods Sold (COGS) is primarily the domain of operations." In manufacturing companies it's the cost of operating the plant, equipment, and buying raw materials. In retailing it's the cost of products bought for resale. In restaurants it's the cost of food and beverages. In banks, it's the cost of money.

Domains of Executive Action[2]

COGS = Operations Management	SG&A = Enterprise Marketing	EBITDA = Corporate Finance

Figure 12.3
Sales Revenue − COGS = Gross Profit − SG&A Expenses = EBITDA drives Shareholder Value. There are three "domains of executive action": COGS is Operations Management; SG&A is Enterprise Marketing; and EBITDA is Corporate Finance.

---

[2] Charts adapted from Victor J. Cook Jr., *Competing for Customers and Capital,* Thomson South-Western, 2006.

SG&A: Cook describes "the soul of enterprise marketing" as a cross-functional perspective where "every member of your sales force, every customer service rep, every e-mail, every invoice, every voice mail, every interaction with every customer at any time" is a part of enterprise marketing.

"Looking at these expenses as a whole across the entire enterprise helps to break down the 'silo' mentality, and opens up the analysis to how the company should operate so as to maximize earnings."

SG&A expenses include R&D, sales, advertising and promotion, employee compensation, and legal expenses. "Each of these expenses impacts the way customers and investors feel, think, and act towards your company."

Under Cook's model, "operating expenses which include the people that play a vital role in shaping customers' perceptions must be moved into the category of enterprise marketing expenses." Tying this back to the BVM, SG&A is where the drivers of brand value are managed, both the tangible set of product performance attributes, and the intangible attributes, and the pricing of those offerings.

Cook adds, " . . . the main reason financial managers overlook the potential of enterprise marketing for creating shareholder value is their focus on earnings. Earnings before interest, taxes, depreciation and amortization (EBITDA) is what's left over after operations management and enterprise marketing expenses are subtracted from sales revenues. Management of EBITDA is the domain of corporate finance, but financial managers need to look further back up the income stream for new opportunities for creating shareholder value." That is, financial managers need to fully understand where the leverage points are and what levers to pull in the BVM in order to optimize EBITDA in the long run.

The plus, minus, and equal signs in Cook's chart identify "the financial accounting relationships among the rows and columns." Add up the sales revenues of all four competitors and you've defined the total sales space. Add up the SG&A column and you've defined the enterprise marketing expenses for your competitive set. "These are the *critical resources* that contribute to (or detract from) competitive advantages among the players."

Cook's theory is that "These resources are evaluated by investors relative to those of other firms in a strategic group. The results of their evaluations imply the **future** shareholder value of each firm" as shown in the right column of the table.

Cook points out, "performance in a strategic group is relative," just as the estimated brand values from the BVM are relative to all the other brands in the category.

Using measures and ratios he describes in his book, Cook developed a measure of a company's relative productivity, where the company's actual earnings performance can be compared to its maximum potential earnings. Investors, in recognition of this outstanding performance, will bid the company's stock price up to an outsized percentage of the competitive set's total shareholder value. Its P/E ratio will be higher than its competitors. Trending this type of information over several periods will reveal insight into the future competitive posture of each company in the competitive set. In other words, "enterprise marketing and corporate finance can become partners in creating shareholder value."

Cook concludes, "Earnings cannot be maximized by financial management alone. Since corporate finance operates at the enterprise level, so must marketing—if the two disciplines are to become partners. The link is that selling, general, and administrative expenses capture all the costs of the people involved in creating and managing the enterprise marketing resources that create intangible shareholder value. Forging this link probably requires the creation of a new C-level executive position: the Chief Enterprise Marketing Officer (CEMO)."[3]

We highly recommend *Competing for Capital and Customers*, by Victor J. Cook, Jr. as a companion to this book for those who are charged with integrating the strategic marketing and finance operations within the enterprise.

By combining the insights gained from the BVM with Cook's metrics, you gain added insight into what is creating value for various stakeholders, and how to improve performance in the future. Using this information to forge a bond with finance can work to the benefit of both finance and marketing. Using these principles, finance can develop a far better understanding of brand equity and how effective investments in brand equity translate into higher asset values and higher stock prices.

This broader view of marketing at the enterprise level has implications for the role of the marketer within the enterprise. It asks that in addition to being accountable, that marketers play a more proactive role in helping other departments in the firm understand brand as a quality-based "pull" process, and the implications to them and their performance on the corporate, as well as the product/service brand promises being made to various stakeholders. This will demand a high level of formal and informal communications within the company—internal marketing, if you will.

---

[3] Victor J. Cook Jr., *Competing for Customers and Capital,* Thomson South-Western, 2006.

A good example of this is when one of the author's clients wanted to increase the utilization of some of their training programs—in this case on product knowledge and applications, as a way to improve conversions of leads into sales. Internal marketing in cooperation with the outside ad agency developed an internal communications program designed to feature the engineering employees who were delivering the training. A series of direct mailers and e-mails was employed to deliver the message to internal employees and to outside channel partners who could benefit from the training. One of the direct mailers featured a picture of one of the engineers who conducted some of the training courses. Since this engineer wore a crew cut and was a former U.S. Marine drill sergeant, the mailer's headline read: "It takes a tough man to make service easy." The copy in the mailer talked about the qualifications of the employee, the type of training, the benefits of taking the training, and the value to the company's served customers. Registration in the training courses increased dramatically, thus helping the company to get more value out of their training investment, while creating more value for other stakeholders.

Marketing must play a strong role in helping the various parts of the organization understand their impact on value creation, as well as the measurements and frequency of measurement that will help them perform as needed.

Marketing is ideally positioned as an effective agent for the CEO in helping the enterprise realize its value-creating potential. Fulfilling this expanded role and responsibility will take a new mindset on the part of marketers. They will have to expand roles from simply overseeing the functional areas of advertising, public relations, and marketing research to being the Jedi knights of the brand—helping the organization understand the full force of the brand, and how best to deliver on the "pull" power of the brand promise. Viewing themselves as internal consultants can help them be of more value to other parts of the enterprise.

If marketing truly wants a seat at the strategic decision-making table (watch what you wish for), this is their opportunity to have it.

The Brand Performance Monitoring System

Complementing the corporate asset value monitoring system is a brand performance monitoring system. In this system we need to track more of the activities that build brand value and align those with the brand's positioning and brand promise. Again, whether these are updated weekly, monthly, or over some other time period is dependent upon the business cycles normal for your firm and business sector.

We recommend that the following measures be included in that system.

Elements of the Brand Performance Monitoring System— One System for Each Brand

- Brand Awareness (unaided and aided), total and within major categories or merchandise lines as appropriate
- Total Brand Value (the brand's relative perceived value)
  - The brand's perceived performance level for each significant product attribute
  - The brand's perceived performance level for each significant service attribute
  - The brand's perceived performance level for each significant channel attribute
- Brand Equity
  - Brand rating on each significant trust attribute
  - Brand rating on each significant image attribute
- Brand Preference
- Brand Availability
- Proportion of all purchases in the category in last 3 months
- Brand Share of sales by category
- Brand Share of sales by channel
- Brand Share of demand by category
- Brand Share of demand by channel
- Brand Product/service complaints
  - Quality related (tangible product attributes)
  - Service related
  - Channel related (Availability, channel support, and so on)
  - Brand equity related (performance expectations not met, trust issues not met, social responsibility issues)

For many product and service categories, all of these measures can be gleaned from a single brand health tracking survey. For other categories, a tracking survey should be complemented with data from transaction databases, scanner services, and other accurate external sources. For service companies, the last measurement items—brand product/service complaints—are often gathered in a separate transaction satisfaction survey or from follow-ups to in-bound call centers.

Measuring *brand value, brand equity,* and *brand preference* in a tracking survey may pose some challenges for many product and service categories. The problem is that the baseline BVM can be rather complex, and it would be very costly to replicate in a tracking study.

As we described earlier in this chapter, we can use an abbreviated self-explicated trade-off model to get to that information. In this approach we typically ask respondents to rank all of the performance attributes from most important to least important. Then, for those attributes that do not have an obvious order (such as brand, loaf shape, and capacity in the breadmaker example), we ask them to rank their desirability of each level. With a little bit of math, these results can be put directly into the baseline BVM to calculate total brand value for each brand and determine whether there are changes in importance and desirability, and thus share of choice for each brand.

The second part of the brand performance tracking system should include the identified drivers of brand equity—both the important trust attributes and image attributes. Here we ask respondents who purchase in the category to rate the performance of each of the brands they are familiar with on a 0 to 10 point scale (or whatever scale was used in the baseline BVM study), from very poor performance to outstanding performance. Again, these ratings can be directly compared to the results from the baseline BVM study and previous results from the tracking system. These procedures were described in detail in Chapters 7 and 8 and in the Brand Value Modeling Addendum.

Brand preference can be derived from the BVM populated with the survey data as just described, or can be asked directly—given no difference in performance or price—which is your most preferred brand?

Results from the Brand Asset Value Monitoring System provide a continuous picture of a brand's health and can identify any changes in the brand's performance or in the marketplace that are affecting perceived brand value or brand equity. The top line results are fed into the Corporate Asset Value Monitoring system.

Summarizing the Framework

In this chapter we have attempted to give you a framework for leveraging the Brand Value Model and develop a system for continuously tracking brand performance. The key idea here is to develop that framework that works for you and your firm. We have suggested an approach, but ultimately you must develop the system that works for you and your organization.

We hope you take away the following key concepts.

1. Brands are usually the most important assets of the organization.
2. Those brand assets can be wisely leveraged to boost sales and profits if you thoroughly understand the drivers of brand value and brand equity in the categories in which you operate.
3. New products are the growth engine of most firms. However, new product introductions and brand extensions can represent a major threat to established brand equities that is usually not accounted for. On the other hand, brand extensions that are successful may mask the opportunity to build new brands and their consequent asset value to the organization and its owners.
4. Brand equity is subject to the same risks and impairments as any tangible asset, and must be closely managed to preserve and build its value.
5. Current FASB accounting methods do not provide sufficient information for managing those key brand assets.
6. Consequently, your organization should develop a financial management and brand performance monitoring system to closely track brand value and brand equity for each of your brands.
7. That monitoring system must be fully integrated with the organization's financial accounting system if it is to be taken seriously by the owners and their representatives on the board of directors.
8. Ultimately, owners must be led to understand the nuts and bolts of brand assets as well as they typically understand the other tangible assets of the organization.

The next chapter is aimed at your service partners and contains information designed to help them become more valued and trusted advisors.

"I have to drive this insight down into the organization, so that every department head understands how their performance impacts the new measures; how they create meaning and feedback for our stakeholders, and build brand equity and the firm's value."

—Jack F. Eli, CEO, TasteRite

CHAPTER 13

SALIENT LESSONS FOR MARKETING SERVICE PROVIDERS

"The definition of insanity is doing the same thing over and over and expecting different results."

—Benjamin Franklin, *American Statesman*

Marketing service providers (mainly ad agencies, research, and public relations firms and their suppliers) share a common experience. They've "turned to" and performed a miracle in order to pull a marketing communications and/or marketing program together under a tight deadline and budget. They proudly watch the program create marketplace buzz, generate lots of sales leads, and win awards. Then, with growing dismay, they watch as their innovative program has little or no long-term impact on sales and value creation. In fact, in many cases, the impact is negative.

Why is this?

If we assume that due diligence was done and the right audience (for example: high-margin users) and right product/service appeal (one that differentiates the client's products/services and is relevant to their customers' needs) were matched, then the likely culprit is that the brand promise made by the campaign was not delivered. That is, the client's offerings and organization did not perform in a manner that met customers' expectations for the brand. Either the brand over-promised or the organization under-delivered, or both.

So, even if initial interest and leads were turned into trial, the client did not enjoy repeat sales. Worse still, disappointed first-time customers may have generated negative word of mouth, thus destroying value.

Is this an isolated example? Sadly, no. It's all too common as 70–80 percent new-product failure rates and many failed branding efforts attest.

The net outcome of this cycle of value destruction or, at the very least, no positive value generation, is that the service provider is often held responsible for the lack of results and is replaced by another service provider. And the cycle mindlessly continues.

Another richly ironic outcome is that clients are now asking via RFP's (request for proposals), that service providers explain in detail how they track results and report on ROI—as if a robust measurement approach were the solution. It can be part of the solution, but it's not the solution.

The solution does not lie with the outside service provider alone. However, if the outside service provider wants to be more than a transactional "revolving door" resource, the outside service provider can play a vital role in the provision of a more effective solution. This calls for an approach unlike the traditional service provider transactional approach being employed today.

The Challenge of Change

Despite what they say, most people in their business lives and in their personal lives don't like change. Change is painful. It requires that we take our comfortable ways of thinking, being, and doing and exchange them for unknown ways with unknown consequences. Change forces us to give up some of what makes us, us.

So, when we are faced with change we go through a process somewhat akin to mourning. First, we may deny that change is necessary. Then, when faced with the unavoidable facts, we get angry. We resent that we have to change. Why us? Why not others? Then we engage in bargaining, seeing if we can exchange something less painful for the behaviors that must change. We try to limit the amount of change. When we can't do that, we become sad and depressed at our inability to avoid change—understanding at some level that we are "losing" the person who we were. Finally, after working through some form of these feelings, we begrudgingly accept the inevitable, and sometimes see opportunity.

Then, when we're well on the road to change and metamorphosis, we wonder "Why didn't we do this much sooner? What in the world were we waiting for?"

Marketing programs that ask the client organization to change the way they do business as a way to differentiate their offering or increase their relevance to current and prospective customers are asking an awful lot of them. This is demonstrated by many clients' proclivity to "put lipstick on a pig"—making cosmetic change rather than engage in meaningful change that's reflected in performance that meets customers' expectations. The client organization's ingrained resistance to change is the most difficult barrier to surmount if you want to see your innovative and creative programs truly make an impact on outcomes.

Increasing your program success batting average will require you look at your role in a new way. **Many market service providers (even those**

within the client organization) have historically looked at themselves as not having any control or impact on the success of a
program beyond the launch of the program. They say: "That's the
business unit's problem now." Or, "It's in the hands of sales." Market service
providers may now, out of dire necessity, see a larger opportunity in playing a
more dynamic role in the adoption and proper execution of brand integrity
programs in client organizations. They'll do so in order to assure the experience their client's customers have with the program matches or exceeds
their client's customers' expectations—and, that customers' expectations are
properly shaped. It's a form of self-preservation.

Salient Lessons

Therefore, before you can expect to change your client's behavior, or your
client's customers' behavior, examine your own. Fortunately, as we've pointed
out in the pages of this book, the practice of building brands with integrity
will provide the basis for many of the new initiatives that you may choose
to provide.

Also fortunate is the continued perception of value on the part of many
savvy clients for the "outside-in" apolitical, objective perspective that
only a respected professional service firm can provide. Furthermore, service provider firms often have personnel that are skilled at understanding
the emotive, intangible, attribute-based aspects of customers' interactions
with their clients—and at identifying what the most important interactions are—the "moments of truth." This perspective, however, needs to be
provided in a more rigorous context and manner, one that helps the client
organization change and adapt to the new realities of today's highly competitive markets.

The following affirmation statements can be used to examine your
behavior, and diagnose how much your organization must change in order to effectively serve as a change agent and catalyst for your client's
organization. These statements describe your agency or firm as it *should be*
viewed:

- Our company has a Mission and Vision that is focused on creating
  better outcomes for our clients and their downstream customers. (We
  begin with the end in mind. We ask: "What is success from our client's
  perspective?") If we're answering that question with any language that
  includes measures of media billings, revenues, or our margins, we're
  on the wrong track. That will come later.

- Outcomes are expressed in terms of our client's external and internal customers' values, and how those values create perceptions of desired brand attributes and value. (We've interrogated reality on behalf of our client via the BVM. We understand the sources of "pull" for each consideration set and brand at the macro [corporate], micro [product/service] and nano [individual stakeholder] level.)
- Our client is willing to partner with us and make us part of their team as evidenced by:
  1. We facilitate brand integrity "learning journeys" at business unit and departmental levels (and/or train/assist internal marketing department staff to do so) in order that the brand promise action plan be understood, internalized, and executed by the organization.
     - We understand the requirements of each consideration set, and the potential advantages of carefully defining high-value customers, and critical brand touchpoints.
     - We are media neutral until after we understand brand "pull." Then, we employ traditional and non-traditional media to best effect, including consumer-generated media, SEO, and paid media search.
     - We, and the client, understand the potential for economic value creation when we achieve brand integrity for each consideration set over time.
  2. Our personnel serve on and advise client cross-silo committees on how to achieve brand integrity for each served consideration set.
     - The client has created cross-silo intranets and extranets to coordinate action plan program initiatives, and has given us password-protected access.
     - We design and coordinate test program initiatives to demonstrate concepts, reduce risk, and establish measurements.
     - We work hard to "armor" the process, and keep programs on time, in budget, and on target.
  3. We understand "triple bottom-line reporting" and the implications of CSR initiatives to the client's various stakeholders and their brand integrity—and include that in our recommendations.
  4. We work with the client organization to help their other outside service providers understand the brand integrity concept and how to be more effective in achieving client goals.

5. We consult with management on metrics and implications for organization recognition, reward, and compensation practices.

6. (If client is a public company) We work with investor relations so they understand the potential impacts of achieving brand integrity on the investment community (large private investors, institutions, analysts, media, and so on).

7. We work with internal marketing, the business units and finance to develop appropriate metrics for marketing productivity (leads generated, sales conversion rates, and so on), customer equity (share of customer, longevity, and so on) and longer-term brand equity measurement.

8. When a program is presented to the client's CEO, CFO, or other decision maker for approval and funding, he or she asks, "How will this impact our brand integrity and metrics?" And, the CEO fully understands the implications and approves or disapproves of programs accordingly. This quickly makes the concept of brand integrity—both practice and measurement—very real and powerful throughout the client's organization.

- We enjoy performance-based compensation for our services (here's where we consider billings, revenues, and margins).
- Our client considers us their "trusted advisor."
- We strive every day in all we do to retain that high regard. To do so, we constantly measure our performance against client expectations, so as to preserve and grow our margins while we enrich the integrity of our company's brand and our client's brand.

More Lessons Learned

After reading this list you may wonder if this will work with all of your current clients. You worry that some constantly reject work that meets the criteria of the Creative Work Plan or Creative Brief and dispute invoices and time expenditures. In addition, their internal marketing department often competes with you for who will do an assignment; and/or the internal marketing communications department gives to other firms work that you believe you're qualified to handle. On the other hand, people inside these client organizations say that they feel that you don't really understand their business, are often late on delivering work, are often over budget, and are mainly interested in winning creative awards. Who's right? Answer: Whoever pays the bills.

The only solution to this situation is to take the high road. If you can make a values-based brand initiative work with your toughest clients, you can certainly make it work with clients with whom you have a good relationship—assuming, of course, that they are open to more than a transactional-type relationship with your firm. The very process of making it work for a client will eliminate some of their criticisms of your service offering and performance.

However, make sure that you can get there from here. Not every client is a candidate for this approach, especially the problematic ones.

Answer these seven questions:

- Are the client's values consonant with ours?
- Are they honest in their dealings with us (and vice versa)?
- Do they respect us (and vice versa)?
- Do our people feel good about working on their account and helping them succeed?
- Does the client offer long-term growth potential in a high interest category?
- Are they willing to engage in a consultative relationship based on brand integrity?
- Do we have access to the CEO or to a highly regarded senior executive who will act as the "brand integrity" advocate?

If the answer to *all* the above questions is an unqualified "yes," then you should proceed with this client. If the answer to any of the questions is "no," then you need to carefully evaluate if the client is a match for your agency's brand. After all, "you're known by the company you keep" and your relationship with this client may be sending the wrong signal to prospective clients and employees, the press, and the community. Alternatively, you may need to get your own house in order before you proceed.

As you build your desirable client relationships, you want to consider exit strategies for clients that are not a good fit. The first step is to consider how to engage the client in a dialogue that addresses each of the issues you identified in answering the previous seven questions. If, despite your differences, both parties value the relationship, a fierce conversation or series of fierce conversations can create the opportunity to move towards a mutually beneficial values-based relationship—one where your and your client's brand integrity are mutually enhanced.

Alternatively, if the issues are insurmountable, you will be better off to sever the relationship. In the short term this is a very difficult decision to make—especially if the revenues involved are considerable. Often, however, difficult clients are so expensive to service that they actually create losses, not profits. Spend the time you would have devoted to that client on business development and on your other clients' brand integrity programs. Fundamentally, let your company's brand integrity be your guide.

The greatest value-creating potential will be with those clients that meet the criteria suggested by the seven questions. By moving your relationship with them from a vendor or transactional-based relationship towards a "trusted advisor" or customer-intimate relationship, you will distinguish your offering while you align your brand values with theirs, and create a much stronger, respectful, and longer lasting relationship. This will have benefits in terms of less employee and client turnover, easier recruiting (both new employees and clients), higher revenues and margins, and a more satisfying sense of purpose from the time and effort you expend at work.

The good news is that this type of trusted-advisor work is highly valued by clients. They are willing to pay consulting fees to achieve brand integrity. This goes way beyond creating ads (as important as that is), or designing research, or writing press releases—it goes to the core of creating value within the client's organization by dint of your intellectual firepower and objectivity. So, if you are addicted to media commissions and are unable to give them up, then this chapter is most likely not going to hold lessons of value to you. If, on the other hand, you are willing to be compensated for creating value in a manner that is consistent with that role from the perspective of clients, via consulting fees, and engagement in a customer intimate relationship, then this chapter provides information of value in fulfilling that role.

In summary, changing your business model from a media model to a consulting model will require change. Most of all, it will require that you change how you view your company's role, and the role of many of your people.

You will go from an alignment with the media services—with their commissions compensating you and aligning you with their interests (bigger media budgets)—to an alignment with your client's best interests, with you being compensated for creating value for your client's company. You will find yourself looking at your client's operations in terms of service processes and flows—and the role of the various parts of the client organization and personnel on delivering an experience that meets or exceeds the brand promise so as to create a sustainable, differentiated, competitive position.

You and your organization can play a proactive role in helping the client see their performance with outside-in perspective, and helping them see where they can improve their service flow and performance. Service mapping is a tool that you can employ to help the client visualize their current flow, and their desired flow (see the discussion of service mapping in Chapter 14), and to help them understand more fully how their service is seen by their customers, and how it creates perceptions of value.

You can employ mystery-shopper research to identify weak links in the service chain, as well as provide recommendations for improvement. Or, you can do lost-customer surveys to gather information on where your client's competitors are performing better and enjoying success with high-value prospects. You can provide the sales department with invaluable insight into how they can improve their prospect identification, recruiting, presentation, proposal, and contract writing techniques. Imagine what a 1 percent improvement in any of these areas is worth to your client in terms of added revenues and avoided costs!

You can use this information and insight to improve interfaces between departments, improving the outcomes and performance of all. You can also help them see the future competitive landscape and opportunities via trends analysis, and continuously scanning the horizon. And, of course, you can use this information in the traditional sense, to improve messaging and media programs.

In essence, you become part of your client's continuous quality improvement and business development efforts by helping your client to align values and value, brand attributes, and promise with the customer experience so as to create a sustainable competitive advantage. Your organization becomes a critically important part of the client's learning organization and learning process, and yields understanding and perspective worth far more than your compensation.

A New Relationship

Figure 13.1 shows how this new brand learning relationship looks, with each set of arrows signifying where the service provider's outside-in insight can assist the client's learning process across silos while enriching the service provider's understanding of the client's markets, successful service flow, and source of competitive advantage.

You now represent a real source of value to your client. That, in turn, leads to clients who are very, very loyal. After all, would they want your insight and experience available to their competitors?

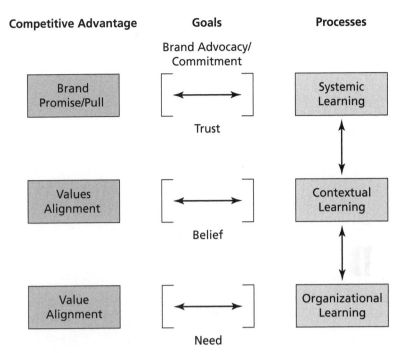

Competitive Advantage	Goals	Processes

Figure 13.1[1]

"Connect with all the passions people have and they'll follow you to the ends of the earth to support your business. They'll spread Goodwill, work hard for you—buy your products, your services and your stock with pride. You'll attract the best people, form highly motivated teams, sell the strongest brands with greatest purpose and highest values, promising all a better future."
—Dr. Patrick Dixon
Futurist, Chairman of Global Change Ltd.

---

[1] Adapted from Tim Kitchin, "Brand Sustainability: It's About Life . . . or Death," a chapter in *Beyond Branding*, edited by Nicholas Ind, Kogan Page, London, 2003.

CHAPTER 14

THE VALUE CREATION PROCESS

"We have met the enemy and he is us."

—Pogo, famous cartoon character[1]

"Any CEO who cannot fully articulate the intangible assets of his brand and understand its connection to customers is in trouble."

—Charlotte Beers, former U.S. Undersecretary of State

The branding process is a value creation process. The desired result is the creation of asset values and profits for a company via products and services it provides to sets of customers and other stakeholders. It's an exchange that creates a "win-win" for both producer and purchaser as long as the benefits to each are greater than the actual and perceived costs of obtaining those benefits. This process is shown in Figure 14.1.

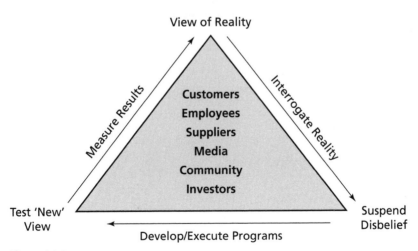

The Value Creation Process

View of Reality

Measure Results

Interrogate Reality

Customers
Employees
Suppliers
Media
Community
Investors

Test 'New' View

Suspend Disbelief

Develop/Execute Programs

Figure 14.1

---

[1] Walt Kelly, Poster, 1970.

Overall, the process shown in Figure 14.1 is designed to continuously question reality, create new views and adapt the organization's behavior to the market based on those views, and measure results in order to create feedback and response.

The late Peter Drucker powerfully stated the importance of the customer's point of view: "It is the customer who determines what a business is. It is the customer alone whose willingness to pay for a good or for a service converts economic resources into wealth, things into goods. What the business thinks it produces is not of first importance—especially not to the future of the business and to its success. . . . What the customer thinks he is buying, what he considers value, is decisive—it determines what a business is, what it produces, and whether it will prosper. And what the customer buys and considers value is never a product. It is always utility, that is, what a product does for him. *And what is value for the customer . . . is anything but obvious."*[2] (Emphasis added.)

Implementing the branding process requires that the desired result or value be understood, at least hypothetically, up front, although in practice much learning is done by trial and error. Since most products and services are sold in a competitive market, there is always a downward pressure on price. This puts pressure on the producers of products and services to extract benefits (monies, referrals, information, and favorable contract terms received from buyers) that outweigh the costs of supplying those goods and services. Competitive and other market pressures force producers to create additional sources of value. In addition to tangible performance-based attributes, these intangible attributes provide the buyer with benefits that are difficult to copy and emotional in nature—and, due to their ability to support premium pricing and/or higher volumes, while restraining or reducing the costs of so doing, are the true source of sustainable competitive advantage and value creation.

Since the competition for sustainable, competitive advantage takes place in a dynamic, ever-changing marketplace, there is a constant need on the part of producers to continuously re-examine their current view of reality, that is, their view of what is creating a perception of benefits that outweigh costs for their products and services in the minds of their customers. This is an ongoing process of learning. For customers in a product/service category, if this perception is favorable when comparing competitors' products and services, then the potential for added value has been created. So, the branding process creates perceptions of added value. But these perceptions are subject to change due to changes in the environment, actions of competitors, or

---

[2] Peter F. Drucker, *Management: Tasks, Responsibilities, Practices,* Harper & Row, Publishers, Inc. 1973, 1974.

failure on the part of the producer to maintain standards of performance—as when the experience customers undergo in using the product/service does not live up the brand promise—when the expectations of customers are not met, when learning has lagged behind reality. This effect is often seen when producers engage in "economy engineering" and other performance-weakening activities or socially irresponsible activities.

Therefore, the implementation of the brand process depends heavily on the willingness and ability of the producer to continuously interrogate reality. That is, to apply research techniques so as to learn more about the current and potential markets of its products and services. To a large part, learning more about the values of the market and how the brand's attributes may create perceptions of value requires insight into the constantly changing "mind of the customer." To do this successfully requires that the company "suspend belief," that its leaders and employees step out of their comfort zone to embrace risk in order to test assumptions about new ways to create value via brand innovation. When properly done,[3] this process creates brand integrity: The stakeholders' experience with the brand meets or exceeds the brand promise.

Companies that are successful at any point in time often find it difficult to find the will to continue to interrogate reality, embrace risk, and undertake change. Success, much like familiarity, does too often breed contempt, or, more subtlety, too much comfort. When this happens, a trigger event, such as the loss of key customers and an ensuing shortfall in revenues and/or a falling stock price, awakens the company to the need for change. The company may also lose its leadership position in a certain technology or competence or key employees may depart.

Much of the brand literature focuses on the role of research to uncover brand attributes of importance to the served market. However, it's becoming increasingly important to understand the relationship between the brand attributes and the organization's values, and how that relationship impacts the organization internally, especially the ability of employees to productively deliver as promised by the brand and as expected by its customers; to maintain the brand's integrity. In addition to employees and customers, there are also other stakeholders—media, legislators, community, suppliers, and so on—who may be impacted by the corporate, product, or service brand as its attributes change. These stakeholders, in turn, can impact the future of the brand. Think about New Coke.

---

[3] "Properly done" is defined as doing this process in a way that is productive (assets deployed are used efficiently and effectively) when compared to the actions of competitors in the same consideration set. When used in this sense, "productivity" and "sustainable, competitive advantage" are synonymous.

Corporate leaders tend to think of "market" as the market for their company's goods and services. Market tends to be synonymous with consumer, customer, or buyer. However, many stakeholders in diverse markets influence a company's fortunes. In addition to the consumer market for their goods and services, there is also a labor market, from which they get (and to which they lose) their employees, and, a stock market from which they attract their shareholders. And now, with the advent of trading in clean air and carbon options, there is also an environmental market. Corporate leadership and company management must assess the risks in each of these markets over time, although the vast majority of effort has traditionally been focused on the consumer market.

One way to minimize risk is to develop new programs and use very well-designed choice models in a simulated test market environment or execute the program in actual test markets, as a controlled experiment, or both. This is an effective way to close the loop between the assumptions made based on the research and the results from actual customers. Results can then be extrapolated onto the entire market with lessons learned baked into the launch of the new programs. There's a potential danger, though; competitors may learn of the test, and may attempt to insert short-term tactics into the test market(s) that confound the test. Being alert to this possibility and adjusting research results to account for competitor disruptions is the best defense.

Use of test markets and carefully measuring changes and trade-offs is essential to create new, more accurate views of customer needs and therefore, of reality. Measurement can be done at the corporate brand, product/service brand, and personal brand levels. At the corporate level, measurement focuses on those corporate brand attributes that are most responsible for changes in brand equity and economic value added in that company's served markets, with the industry defined as the consideration set. At the product/service level, measurement focuses on those product/service brand attributes most responsible for changes in brand equity in the product category or consideration set. And at the personal brand level, changes in brand attributes and respective levels of brand equity are reflected in performance ratings, rewards, recognition, level of compensation, and career tracks.

Another way to reduce risk is to employ game playing and what-if simulations to evaluate alternative courses of action, and to better understand which alternative has the least risk and offers the greatest opportunity to create stakeholder value. Using inputs from the BVM, and other financial information about your firm will enable you to develop alternative scenarios and simulations, and look at possible stakeholder value outcomes.

What are some of the key lessons that companies must learn to successfully put the brand process into practice in the organization and realize the attendant value creation?

Keys to Putting the Branding Process into Practice

The first key to the value creation process is to understand where you are standing, and, therefore, what you see. Your position in a competitive set or industry or product/service category often will determine how you see the world, what you believe your best options are, and how you will realize those options during day-to-day operations.

For example, if you enjoy the #1 position in a category, one key to success is the realization that *if* your platform is not burning, *if* your business is not in trouble, you ought to *pretend it is* in terms of learning how to cope in case negative scenarios become reality. Success, and its associated smugness, hubris, and arrogance often sow the seeds of future discontent and poor performance, even if changes in the environment don't. The best antidote to this is to understand the often fleeting nature of competitive advantage and the difficulty in maintaining it if you are not proactive. A little paranoia and humility can be very healthy and can lead to a trim attitude on the part of the entire organization, as well as active support for the values, behaviors, and performance that made you successful in the first place.

More importantly, it is absolutely necessary to understand how consumers and customers view your position in the marketplace and how they see the world. There is often a wide divergence between how consumers and buyers see your products and services and what corporate managers believe consumers and buyers see.

Employing market research to continuously scan the environment and spot changes that will impact the integrity of your brand is key to combating resistance to change. Communicating this information, and the potential opportunities and threats it may contain throughout the organization will help employees, suppliers, and network partners develop coping strategies to keep your brands relevant at the macro level (industry, corporate), micro level (product/service) and nano level (personal).

Since a brand is a Quality Assurance Device, and quality is "performance to customer requirements," another key to success is in creating a deep understanding of the values and attributes that connect your customers, employees, and other stakeholders in a value creation chain. This creates an integrity benchmark—a standard for performance—against which future efforts and changes may be measured. It also forms the basis for a balanced scorecard and provides measures of value creation productivity compared to competitors in the category.

Many methods can be used to gather this information and insight. A particularly valuable method called the Voice of the Customer is a qualitative approach that engages various stakeholders in discussions concerning the decision-making process of various players in a consideration set at the corporate brand level, and, for product/service brands, the values that are valued most in products and/or services in a consideration set. This is very useful in learning about perceptions of strengths and weaknesses, changes, trends, threats, opportunities, tangible attributes, intangible attributes, and related values that customers engage when they look at different vendors in the category, and how they form perceptions of value.

Since not all stakeholders are equal, it's often productive to look at market sub-segments of "heavy users," "early adapters" or other highly desirable psychographic and demographic segments in order to gain added insight into your customers' values and brand attributes within a consideration set. This gives you valuable information useful in deciding how to "choose" your prospects and customers.

Stakeholders other than customers can be included, such as supply and distribution chain partners and key media whose perspectives and opinions are often of great value in gaining insight into the dynamics of a consideration set.

In addition, it's always a good idea to encourage employees to learn more about their served market by spending time with customers. Many firms encourage their employees to work in retail outlets, attend customer meetings, and so on, so that employees can develop a better understanding of the market.

This learning is applied when the quantitative Brand Value Model (BVM) discussed in Chapter 7 is employed. Assuming that the BVM had yielded an earlier version as a benchmark, the results from the most recent BVM can then be compared to the benchmark, and the differences and changes in how brand value and equity are created would be noted. Then, the implications of these changes in terms of pricing strategy, product/service performance features, brand equity attributes, brand communications strategy and tactics, channel benefits, and so on would be discussed, and action plans to put the findings into effect would be agreed to and executed. If an earlier benchmark did not exist, the findings of the BVM would still be useful based on comparisons among competitor's scores in a consideration set. This comparison yields valuable insight into the sources of sustainable competitive advantage, and would be used to create an initial benchmark, especially among those customer segments deemed most valuable.

Since the BVM reports utilities and importance weights at the individual respondent level, the wealth of information derived from the model over time can be used to dynamically anticipate change in served markets, and respond in ways that provide time-to-market and agility advantages. What happens in most product and service categories is that success in the performance attributes breeds replication from competitors; thus, over time there is a convergence and lessening of differentiation in the performance attributes among competitors. Then, one of two things starts to happen. The product category becomes commoditized, where price becomes the only differentiator. Or, differentiation starts transitioning from performance-based attributes to the intangible trust and image attributes. Using the BVM over time allows you to observe and track this convergence in perceived performance and allows you to observe and exploit emerging differentiation in the intangible attributes.

Another insightful way to use the BVM is to ask managers to go through the BVM trade-off exercise as if they were buyers of the offered product or service. Then derive the utilities and importance weights for the management group. By contrasting that set of importance values and utilities with customers' importance values and utilities, you can fully understand the gaps that exist between management's view and the customer's view of what drives purchase decisions in the category. Be warned that this exercise can be quite embarrassing to the management group. In the few times we have been allowed to do this, we have yet to see the management group be anywhere close to alignment with their own customers. Managers tend to overestimate the importance of price and some performance attributes, and underestimate the importance of other performance attributes and especially the intangible, emotional attributes that create brand equity.

By applying the BVM to employees, and getting their utilities and importance weights for the corporate brand's attributes, you develop insights into the relationship between the employees' espoused values and their perceptions of value for the corporate brand. This provides valuable diagnostic and prescriptive information for use in recruitment and other HR practices. Use this insight to recruit employees with the appropriate values. Also use it to help those people who, after receiving appropriate training, and who still don't exhibit the desired values and or performance, to understand that their careers would best be pursued at some other company. Offer outplacement support.

More Keys to Success

Knowing what drives value in your categories, your competitive posture and advantages, and future moves is one thing. Doing something with this insight is another. Effecting change in organizations is notoriously difficult because people feel threatened by change, try to do everything at once, and don't prioritize or coordinate.[4] So it's important that the action plans that are derived from the BVM insight be executed properly and the results measured.

In order to execute the plans, the various silos in the organization have put some "skin" in the game. Each department asks

- What does this action plan mean to us?
- How does this action plan support our values and value-creating role within the organization?
- What change will be required for us to be effective in executing this action plan?
- What is our timetable for doing so?
- How will our actions be coordinated with other departments?
- How will our efforts and contributions to the success of the overall effort be measured?

Each department within the organization needs to understand the potential impact of the action plan on their operations, and their role in achieving the desired outcomes. This is often agreed to at the executive committee level, with coordination and communications coming through cross-silo and interdivisional teams.

One of the most important keys to the effective execution of action plans is the behavior of the leaders of the company. They use the information available from the research to create a new context for action. They create a sense of importance and urgency for the action plan, constantly reinforcing the values of the company that the plan supports, and explicitly explaining the relationship between the values and the action plan, and the expected

---

[4] Lawrence G. Hrebiniak, *Making Strategy Work: Leading Effective Execution and Change,* Wharton School Publishing, University of Pennsylvania, 2005.

benefits. This communication must take place so that the message is "pulled" throughout the organization, for example, in a manufacturing environment, down to the person on the shop floor right on up to the customer service people.

Many leaders are frustrated that action plans they endorse, and that are launched with much fanfare, often wind up like water into sand. To avoid this outcome, organizations must face three realities at once, and engage in three fierce conversations:

1. What values do we stand for, and are there gaps between these values and how we actually behave?
2. What are the skills and talents of our company and are there gaps between those resources and what the market demands?
3. What opportunities does the future hold, and are there gaps between those opportunities and our ability to capitalize on them?[5]

Discuss the feedback from the BVM in the context of these three questions with your direct reports. This conversation should help the organization deeply understand the need for the action plan, and its level of integrity and authenticity. The commitments made during this conversation will be deep and meaningful, especially when follow-up steps and measurements are committed and agreed to in front of a group of peers. You, as the leader, model the desired behavior by holding your direct reports accountable for their follow-up. Only you can replace the tyranny of the urgent with the long-term value creation of the important. Each exception, each "get out of jail free" card that you hand out, is a bullet to the heart and integrity of the plan. Take no excuses.

Encourage your direct reports to repeat the type of meeting you had with them, with their direct reports. Support the action plan and its adoption throughout the organization. Make the responsibility for adoption and execution everyone's business—and do so in a way that seems natural and logical to all.

Pull Thinking®

A useful way to look at what we've described is through the lens of Pull Thinking®.[6] The premise is simple: It's easier to pull than to push. Think of a rope; try to move it by pushing it—you wind up with a pile of rope. Now try

---

[5] Susan Scott, *Fierce Conversations: Achieving Success at Work & in Life, One Conversation at a Time,* Viking Penguin, 2002.

[6] Kenneth E. Meyer, *Pull Thinking®,* Alignment at Work, LLC, Publishing Division, © 2002–2005.

Figure 14.2 The Push Approach (From the Point of View of the Employee/ Manager)
© 2002–2005, Alignment at Work, LLC. Used with permission.

Figure 14.3 The Pull Approach (From the Point of View of the Customer)
© 2002–2005, Alignment at Work, LLC. Adapted with permission.

pulling one end of the rope—that works much better, doesn't it? Figures 14.2 and 14.3 sum up the two diametrically opposed approaches.

Pull Thinking® is predicated on four questions (called the Four Pull Questions.)

1. What is the purpose?
2. What are the Measures of Success?
3. What is actually being measured?
4. What is the frequency with which the measurements are being taken.[7]

Values-based branding is a way to create a powerful and coordinated system of pull throughout the organization.

The brand promise, aligned with what drives value in your categories, becomes the higher-level purpose. The brand promise is the expression of the expectations each stakeholder group or served market segment has about the experience they will have with your brand, whether it's your company, product, or service brand. These expectations are based on stakeholders' values as they relate to your brand.

---

[7] Ibid.

The Measures of Success are those stakeholder values-related elements that are crucial or most responsible for the delivery of a brand experience that satisfies the brand promise. In much of the branding literature these critical values-related elements are called the *brand pillars,* since they support the brand promise. These brand pillars may focus on a wide variety of topics, depending on what values underlie the brand promise. The brand pillars, properly executed, are critical to achieving high levels of productivity necessary to create brand equity.

For example, Microsoft's brand promise is: "Microsoft is the visionary technology leader that creates innovative software to help individuals and organizations realize their full potential." The four brand pillars that support this brand promise are:

- Responsible Technology Leadership
- Empowers People
- Supports Industry Standards
- Customer Focused

Microsoft's employees are expected to understand what is required of them in order to deliver on the overall brand promise by successfully executing on each brand pillar. For example, "Customer Focused" means, in part, that Microsoft expects its employees to understand what drives value and work with customers in a collaborative manner, adapting customers' ideas and suggestions so as to increase the value of Microsoft's products for the benefit of all. All employees are expected to have the core value of a "passion for technology." Microsoft, in turn, may offer training to its employees so that they understand how to work collaboratively. This will positively impact productivity.

The right things need to be measured. Sometimes what is actually being measured may not really reflect the values that most relate to the brand promise and experience. It's important that employees in the sub-organization elements or silos understand what really is at work to create valued offerings and customer loyalty.

For example, many organizations agree that showing "one face" to the customer is important, since it saves the customers' time and effort, and often provides better solutions. Yet, many organizations cannot achieve that harmonizing effect, due to organizational politics and constraints—each of which, if they stand in the way of achieving the brand promise, are weakening productivity and destroying value, and are simply excuses that should not be tolerated.

Therefore, even though the brand promise is the attractant force pulling understanding, learning, and behavior throughout the organization, other values are needed to support the brand. These include

1. A desire to work together to achieve common goals, usually via teams.
2. A respect for the other members of the team, and for other teams and their role in the effort.
3. A sense of responsibility for follow-through and keeping commitments.
4. Proactively sharing information that other members of the team may benefit from knowing, and sharing information with other teams.
5. Acting in the expectation that everyone shares the above four values, normally expressed as "trust in others."[8]

How often measurements are taken impacts the organization in several ways. If the measurement is not taken often enough, employees won't have the information they need to maintain the system in alignment, and to justify actions and tactics necessary to support the brand pillar (values) and, therefore, satisfy the brand promise. Those actions and tactics may include not more resources, but current resources better deployed to create alignment, and higher levels of productivity.

By creating a pull throughout the organization, where everyone understands the answers to these four Pull Thinking® questions, each department, function, and employee will then understand their role in delivering an experience that satisfies the customer's expectations, thus creating value. They will have the direct authority that's commensurate with their accountability. They'll also understand how they will be evaluated, compensated, recognized, and promoted, as well as what their personal development plans need to be based on so they are properly prepared to play their role in ensuring brand integrity.

The answers to the four Pull Thinking® questions become critical elements of all action plan elements designed to achieve the corporate and/or product/service brand promise.

So now, instead of running around the organization continuously trying to spin every department's plates to make sure that action plan initiatives don't wind down, the CEO can focus on the Brand Promise and how it creates purpose, coherence, and performance, as well as appropriate measures of success with optimum frequency to support the organization delivering on

---

[8] Gary F. Gebhardt, et al. "Creating a Market Orientation: A Longitudinal, Multifirm, Grounded Analysis of Cultural Transformation," *Journal of Marketing*, Vol. 70 No. 4 (October 2006).

their brand promise. The CEO doesn't have to look over everyone's shoulder, inspecting to see if they're doing their job correctly. Everyone understands the purpose, the measurements, the frequency, and what "service with integrity" means.[9] The organization becomes a self-adjusting, self-healing, closed-loop system for creating brand integrity. Life for the CEO and everyone else in the organization becomes relatively easier and simpler.

A useful tool for intra-industry learning and for organizing action plans designed to improve a process, is the American Productivity and Quality Center (APQC) Process Classification Framework (PCF), updated in 2004. *Each process should be carefully evaluated in terms of each of the four Pull Thinking® questions.*

Here is a description of the Process Classification Framework, taken from the APQC Web site:

"APQC's Process Classification Framework[SM] (PCF) is a taxonomy of cross-functional business processes intended to allow objective comparison of organizational performance within and among organizations.

APQC's PCF was developed in the early 1990s by APQC and a group of members from a number of industries and countries throughout the world. Originally envisioned as a tool to aid in performance improvement projects, the framework evolved into the broad taxonomy that it is today. With more than 10 years of use, the PCF has continued to evolve to meet the needs of organizations throughout the world.

The PCF now forms the foundation of the Open Standards Benchmarking Collaborative (OSBC). Organizations can participate in complimentary research projects to determine their performance against other organizations in terms of the processes described in the PCF. Furthermore, the PCF enables organizations to understand their inner workings from a horizontal process viewpoint rather than a vertical functional viewpoint. The PCF does not list all processes within a specific organization, and every process listed in the framework is not present in every organization.

(continued)

---

[9] Note: in "Pull Thinking" terminology, service with integrity is called Ultimate Service. Used with permission.

The PCF is used by many organizations of varying sizes. Smaller organizations can easily leverage the breadth of the PCF to determine which processes need additional review or development. Larger organizations leverage the deep research that is organized along PCF guidelines to objectively aid in comparing performance to that of peers or against baselines during process improvement efforts. All organizations can benefit from the abundance of key performance indicators available in terms of the processes and process categories defined in the PCF.

The PCF is organized into 12 distinct categories of business processes: five categories of operating processes and seven of support processes. Each category contains groups of processes and activities that, when considered as a whole, represent the operations of a high-performing organization."

You can find this tool available as a free download at www.apqc.org.

The Role of HR, IT, and Finance

HR can often play a useful role in supporting company-wide action plans aimed at strengthening the corporate or product/service brands. For example, one global technology firm held a contest designed to create a deeper appreciation of a new brand that was being developed. HR and marketing teamed up to develop trading cards that had questions about how people would react if they were the brand. Once five questions were correctly answered, the card was traded for another. The first people to collect all six cards won a prize. This effort created an international network of internal communications and "buzz" based on the values and ideals of the brand.[10] The end result was an effective internal communications program that helped support the Action Plan to create a new brand and deliver on the brand promise.

Another company used video from Voice of the Customer interviews showing customers talking about how they view the company, their values, and expectations. When this is shown to new employees it is combined with information about how the company's action plans are designed to

[10] Jeff Smith and Kristiane Blomqvist, "Strange Bedfellows: Could HR Be Marketing's Best Friend?" *MM*, Jan/Feb 2005.

deliver on those expectations and to satisfy the brand promise. This creates a powerful pull story, telling new employees how to view the customer and business, and creates an understanding of what is expected in terms of behaviors and how to deliver on the promises being made to customers. HR, marketing, and other departments' roles are interweaved in the story, and the result is new employees who are effective in delivering on the company's brand promise while encouraging inter-silo cooperation.

Compensation practices are key to the successful creation of value. The emergence of process-based, network organizations and knowledge workers has spawned a new way of thinking about the role of reward systems in complex organizations. These new pay and reward systems go beyond rewarding the number of products, services, or sales revenues and profits. It puts monetary rewards on customer loyalty, customer service, leadership, employee satisfaction, cycle time, quality, teams, skills, and competencies. These pay systems are predicated on the belief that you get what you reinforce. Make the reinforcement positive, immediate, graphic, and specific.[11]

Another key is to ensure that the IT department is not buying the latest, greatest, feature-laden software, but really understands the brand promise action plan, and how the CRM (Customer Relationship Management) system should provide information that is useful in executing the action plan. The CRM system must be integrated into the overall effort, not pasted on, or the information it provides will be the wrong information delivered with the wrong frequency, and will not be useful in guiding and integrating the behaviors of the organization.

Another key is to have the financial department's buy-in to the economic value creation potential of the Action Plan. This requires bridging the gap between marketing's focus on applying innovation and creativity to build competitive advantage, and the financial department's focus on efficiency and reducing waste. Discussions between the two departments that examine the relationship between the creation of customer benefits and brand value creation to the costs associated with action plans and the associated cost of capital will yield, hopefully, an in-depth, shared understanding on the importance of these programs to the future of the firm. Decisions can be rationally made based on the impact of the investment on the satisfaction of the brand promise, and the result in terms of changes in sales,

---

[11] Fred Luthans and Alexander K. Stajkovic, *"Reinforce for Performance: The Need To Go Beyond Pay and Even Rewards,"* Academy of Management Executive, Vol. 13, No. 2, 1999.

margins, brand equity, and stock price. We discussed this in more detail in Chapter 12.

The Marketing Department and the Brand

Tim Ambler, the erudite and prescient Senior Fellow at London Business School tells us, "There are only two kinds of people in business: marketers and cave dwellers." He goes on to describe marketers as the ones "who primarily empathise with consumers and fight to maximize the firm's relationships with them." He adds that marketers "may be part of the marketing department or they may be in other functions, but they are the ones who experience the market."

He also observes that many marketing departments have more than their share of cave dwellers. These are marketing wannabes who would love to meet with customers "but the meetings, planning and reports make that difficult."

Ambler goes on to say that "cave dwellers see marketing as slippery, unaccountable and constantly moving the goal posts. They believe that marketers complicate things and should be judged by a single financial number . . ."

He concludes that: "the radiance from this 'silver metric' held aloft may show what is happening in the cave but it tells us nothing about where the money is coming from, or why."[12]

Professor Ambler's insight is painfully humorous and all too true. He has touched upon why many in business, and especially marketers, feel they are in a Dilbertian nightmare: needing to justify the use of current account expenses to secure the firm's future via brand-building activities that deliver returns to the company and its stakeholders in future years. Or, when the economy softens and the company is under pressure to make quarterly or year-end figures to satisfy Wall Street's expectations, the pressure is turned on to push product out the door via thinly disguised price promotions that erode brand equity for a quick hit of revenue. Of course, when the economy softens, marketing and advertising budgets are also often the first ones to be cut.

Marketing and marketers today are under intense scrutiny and pressure. Everyone is demanding that marketing departments justify their existence by providing a measure of their ROI. How come no one asks the accounting department to provide a measure of their ROI? Or, as Zero Mostel's character in the original movie production "The Producers" asks Gene Wilder, playing an accountant: "You're an accountant, account for yourself!!"

---

[12] Tim Ambler, *"Don't Give in to Cave Dwellers,"* Marketing Management, September/October, 2006.

Fortunately, new tools are being developed, as we discussed in Chapter 12, that will enable marketers to not only justify their existence, but to reassert their place at the strategic decision-making table. Since both marketing and finance are focused on maximizing returns, they must shake hands and cooperate at the enterprise level if they are to function in a productive manner. They are linked at the hip because finance reports on SGA—selling, general, and administrative expenses. These expenses are mostly related to the people within the company who are responsible for creating and managing intangible asset value. Since intangible assets have an outsized impact on the firm stock market value, one would think that marketing and finance would be fast friends.

Since finance already has a seat at the strategic table in most enterprises, the message to marketers is clear, they need to understand and speak a language that finance and the CEO can relate to. Furthermore, it falls on the marketer to help educate finance on what drives customer perceptions of value and how the organization is delivering that value.

The Sales Department and the Brand

The sales department is usually a very special case for the successful execution of many action plans designed to increase brand value via brand integrity. Because brand value is a longer-term strategy and is dependent, in part, on longer-term customer relationships for value creation, sales quota and commission systems that are focused on meeting quarterly quotas often don't drive the kind of behavior that produces brand-building results. The focus on quarterly sales volume is counterproductive because some sales personnel will over-promise and compromise the integrity of the brand in order to meet quarterly sales quotas—which significantly depreciates the asset value of the brands and destroys stockholder wealth.

In trying to align sales force behaviors with the organization, many companies are compensating their sales force on a mix of metrics that capture many of the attributes of the brand, and encompass the values of the company and its key stakeholders. For example, customer loyalty (repeat purchases, longevity, share of customer) and customer profitability are becoming more important measures. Key customer feedback, often from CRM and sales force automation systems, is increasingly being used to reinforce and motivate sales behaviors that are in the best interests of the company over the longer term. These behaviors include responsiveness, communications ability, understanding of the customers' business needs and requirements, ability to orchestrate a coherent solution to those needs, and ability to ease the purchasing, contract, approvals, and logistics processes.

These measures can be customized to the individual profiles and needs of each trading area or sales territory.

Under this model, salespeople are trained and rewarded for reducing customer churn while increasing share of customer and profitability. Sales personnel play a key role in creating customer expectations in the first place, in part through careful qualification of prospective customers, and then in shaping and/or meeting those prospective customers' expectations. In other words, making an appropriate brand promise and managing customer expectations so that the customers' experience and the promise are in alignment. When properly rewarded, these sales people play a proactive role in helping other departments within the company understand how to satisfy customers' expectations. Everyone benefits.

Some companies post scores from these new metrics for the entire sales force to see. This is called "making performance visible" and it is highly motivating to sales people who tend to be competitive. Companies schedule coaching sessions with the sales staff to improve those scores, and to continuously reinforce the connection between the company's brand vision, mission, core values, brand attributes, brand pillars, customer values and needs, the new sales behaviors, and the value thereby created. Sales people come to understand how their score is tied into not only their compensation, but how the scores relate to the company's overall success in building its brand and creating a sustainable, competitive advantage.

Sales people are viewing their jobs as less transactional and more customer-focused, to be viewed as trusted advisors—and are willing to do what it takes inside the company to make customers loyal. The change in sales compensation is an acknowledgement that sales people want more than traditional sales quotas. They also want to develop their skills, both personally and professionally. This is competence-based and performance-based remuneration.

A good example of this type of thinking in action is when a company gives their sales force some investment flexibility. We've cited examples in previous chapters of how IBM, for example, gave its sales force discretionary dollars to spend on targets of opportunity, and how that investment has paid off handsomely.

In fact, that's true of many other areas within the company. More employees are looking for personal development plans that help them grow and increase their value. It also helps them to increase the value of their "nano," or personal brand.

Customer Service

This is especially true of "customer facing" employees, or those employees whose actions and behaviors directly or indirectly shape the customer's brand experience. These employees play a pivotal role in creating brand value and brand equity due to their impact on the brand experience, and on subsequent customer loyalty behaviors. So, employees in customer service, reception, call centers, and so on can have an outsized impact on the customer's perception of the brand experience.

Sometimes, the employees who can have an outsized and pivotally important role in creating a positive brand experience are not who you may think they are. Disney, for example, has found the street sweepers in their parks play a key role, since they are readily available to the park's guests, and are often asked directions and questions. Disney found that investing in training these employees so that they were better able to answer questions paid big dividends in their customers' perceptions of their experience at Disney's parks.

Service blueprints are a good way of making these relationships visual and can be used as an effective tool with which to identify pivotal employees, as well as the role of behind-the-scenes employees who are critical to support the performance of customer-facing or pivotal employees.

Service blueprinting was originally developed for use in service quality improvement. It creates a roadmap of current processes and outcomes. Using your vision and values (brand pillars), and what you'd like the brand experience to be, you design the desired processes and outcomes. You contrast the desired processes and outcomes (brand experience) to the current ones. You then map and address the gaps, create ideal processes to bridge the gaps, and prioritize according to how much impact it will have on satisfying the underlying core values and creating the ideal brand experience.

Figure 14.4 shows an example of a generic service blueprint.[13]

Customer actions could be things like the customer picking up the phone or using the Web to inquire about a product or a service. The "Line of

---

[13] Lynn G. Shostack, *"Designing Services that Deliver,"* Harvard Business Review, January/February, 1984.

Brand Blueprinting Maps the Customer Experience—From All Perspectives

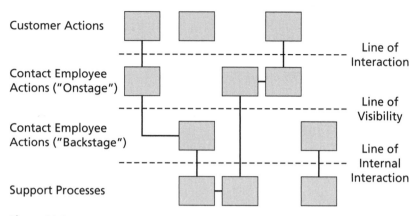

Customer Actions

Line of Interaction

Contact Employee Actions ("Onstage")

Line of Visibility

Contact Employee Actions ("Backstage")

Line of Internal Interaction

Support Processes

Figure 14.4

Interaction" is between the customer and the contact employee ("onstage" via a retail setting, during a sales call, or in a call center).

As a simple example, let's say that the business is a restaurant, and the customer has just asked the waiter if they have a certain type of entrée available. The "onstage" waiter, if they don't know the answer, will cross the "Line of Visibility," go back into the kitchen out of sight of the customer, will ask the chef if the dish is available, and will then appear in front of the customer to answer their question. The chef, in turn, may ask his helpers (Support Processes) if the materials to make that dish are in stock. This internal discussion takes place over the "Line of Internal Interaction."

Each of the top boxes in the Customer Actions area may identify the major types of actions that most customers take during their contact with the company. In addition to the ambience of the restaurant (décor, design, setting, and so on) these actions help define the Brand Experience. In the simple restaurant example, the top box actions may include:

- Choosing the restaurant
- Making a reservation
- Getting directions and finding the restaurant
- Parking
- Being welcomed and being seated
- Introduction of the wait staff
- Gathering information about the availability of "special" dishes

- Gathering information about drinks and wines
- Disclosing special health and dietary needs (no shellfish)
- Disclosing information about any time constraints
- Ordering
- Being served the meal
- Consuming the meal
- Settling the bill
- Leaving a tip
- Filling out a comments card
- Retrieving the car from valet parking

Each of those top box actions may or may not trigger a series of process flows to satisfy the action or need. In any event, how each of these process flows is handled is contingent on the restaurant's Brand Promise, and what it takes for the Brand Experience to meet or exceed the Brand Promise in the mind of the customer and the company's employees, balance the needs of other stakeholders in the process, and do so profitably. Complex company/ customer interactions can lead to multiple and/or detailed service blueprints.

The Brand Value model when combined with service blueprinting provides prescriptive and diagnostic information that guides how employees focus their efforts, increase their competence, and help the company make their brand promise a self-fulfilling prophecy.

A Brand Process Implementation Example: Medical Equipment

Assumptions:

1. We've interrogated reality, and have a brand promise in place.
2. All employees understand the brand promise that their company is making to our highest value customers (or the company's purpose as described in their vision/mission statement) and the underlying values (brand pillars).
3. They understand that this brand promise and its supporting brand pillars are pulling whatever behaviors are necessary throughout the organization so as to meet or exceed stakeholders' expectations of the brand promise.
4. They understand their role in delivering on the promise (and can visualize their role via a service blueprint).
5. They work diligently with other parts of the organization, so that internal customers are served in order that the overall organization delivers as promised.

6. The critical activities and brand attributes that actually contribute the most to success are identified and measured (based on the BVM and the alignment of value drivers with core stakeholder, company, and brand values).

7. Measurements are gathered and reported with the correct frequency so that all players can properly evaluate the effectiveness and efficiency of their actions.

8. Based on this feedback, tactics and programs are created and/or adjusted as needed, and are part of each employees performance-based personal development plan and ongoing recognition, rewards, and compensation structure.

The process can be visualized as shown in Figure 14.5.

In the above example, a medical diagnostic equipment company used research to interrogate reality and learned that "capped" costs in health care were changing how hospitals evaluated their diagnostic equipment and processes. The company's research revealed that the role of the administrators within the hospital was being expanded, and they were going to have a much more powerful impact on the future purchases of diagnostic equipment. The values that admin held centered around reducing costs, improving care, staying advanced and saving their personnel, specialists, and referring physicians time. This was a huge change from the time when the

**Values Focus Brand Behavior and Measurement
(for a medical equipment manufacturer)**

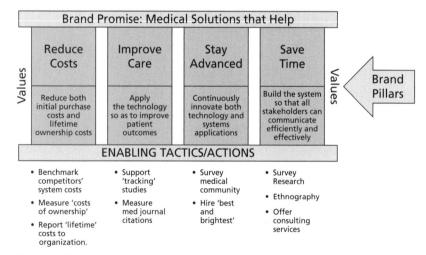

Figure 14.5

radiology department heads called the tune, and they were heavily focused on "staying advanced." They wanted the latest and greatest technology, and cost was not the primary concern.

The actions that would realize the attainment and performance of these "brand pillars" are shown under each pillar. In this simplified example, these tactics and actions are elements of an action plan designed to deliver on the brand promise in a manner that meets or exceeds stakeholders' expectations, and, therefore, creates brand integrity. It is up to all employees within the equipment maker's company to best organize themselves to productively support the brand pillars.

This medical equipment company engaged in on-going customer loyalty, lost order, and other research designed to measure the company's performance against the brand pillars. This provided feedback to the employees with appropriate frequency on how their tactics and actions were impacting customers and other stakeholders.

These enabling tactics and actions are varied for each served market segment, depending on their specific requirements. In the case of the medical diagnostic equipment company, the overall results were outstanding—the company dramatically increased their sales, share, and brand equity among their most valued target market customers. They did this by creating total solutions, helping hospital administrators understand the true cost of lifetime ownership, and how to use their other service-based offerings to maximize value and outcomes for all stakeholders.

Example: Marriott International Lodging Development: Asia-Pacific

Companies that compete based on brand integrity are using a pull model. Pull systems deal with uncertainty by helping people come together using a wide range of internal and external resources to develop ways to satisfy the brand promise despite rapidly changing customer expectations. Pull systems such as those based on brand promise use their stakeholders' passion for the mission, commitment to the brand promise, desire to do a good job, and desire to learn to create organizations and communities that quickly innovate and improvise.

Marriott International helps prospective owners and franchisees understand Marriott's different brands by presenting information about their brands on their Web site. In the fast growing Asian-Pacific region, this provides to potential franchisees and investors some of the information they need to make an informed decision.

The two Marriott brands serve different markets, each with its own pull. Marriott's brand strategies and their underlying brand pillars serve to define the pull and how the employees and other stakeholders will act to achieve levels of service that creates a lodging experience to satisfy the brand promise. Each pillar has specific behaviors that are required, as well as measurements,

	Renaissance® Hotels and Resorts	Marriott Hotels and Resorts
Brand Strategy:	Like our guests, we are ambitious, with aggressive growth goals. We target the Enjoyment Guest–guests who cherish the life well lived. These savvy guests combine business and pleasure in pursuit of adventures and life less ordinary. To forge relationships with these guests, Renaissance hotels are entertaining, stimulating, and developed around the brand pillars of Expressive Destinations, Delightful Luxuries, and Savvy Service.	Our brand has become synonymous with exceptional quality, service and value, with consistent growth throughout the Asian-Pacific region. The strategy to achieve an even greater brand preference is centered on the brand positioning of Inspired Performance. The goal is to win over Achievement Guests (individuals who are driven to perform, who thrive in excellence, whether it's for their company, family, or their own sense of accomplishment) with experiences that reflect and respond to their priorities. By combining this experiential strategy with the brand's unwavering commitment to operational excellence, we will continue to solidify our leadership position as an industry innovator.
Brand Pillars:	**Expressive Destinations:** This pillar is the foundation for the hotel design story and business positioning from distinctive, stylish, expressive design with a touch of whimsy to relevant street restaurants and bars that attract both hotel and non-hotel clientele.	**Achieve:** The professional, performance-driven side of our guests and hotels, for example, large, well-lit ergonomic work desks that pivot to enable the guest to create a conducive environment in their rooms.

	Renaissance® Hotels and Resorts	Marriott Hotels and Resorts
	Delightful Luxury: For the discerning guest who lives life to the fullest, the Renaissance hotel indulges the Enjoyment Guests' lifestyle with memorable, irreverent touches and special amenities, such as unique artwork or passes to local yoga studios. **Savvy Service:** The language and behaviors of the hotel associates set the mood of the hotel. At a Renaissance hotel, the associates 'serve with a style all our own.' They delight guests with random acts of kindness and service signatures.	**Revive:** Purposeful luxury and more personal elements of the guest's stay, for example, aromatherapy bath products, connectivity panels on a high-definition TV to enable guests to connect their personal entertainment devices such as iPods, and 300-thread count sheets. **Culture:** Warm, friendly, sincere service built on our Spirit to Serve and providing a refreshingly human touch in today's hectic world.

Adapted from http://marriott.com/development/asia-pacific/default.mi

so that those providing the service have a way to see how well they are executing the brand strategy.

Many Companies Today Are Hybrids

Today, it is difficult to find "pure play" pull companies—that is, companies that solely use pull systems. We are, however, rapidly moving from a culture of "command and control" or push, to a culture of brand promise, or pull.

John Seely Brown and John Hagel III, in an article in The McKinsey Quarterly, describe the difference between push systems and pull systems as:[14]

Push Systems	Pull Systems
Demand can be anticipated	Demand is highly uncertain
Top-down design	Emergent design
Centralized control	Decentralized initiative
Procedural	Modular
	(continued)

[14] John Seely Brown and John Hagel III, *"From Push to Pull – The Next Frontier of Innovation,"* The McKinsey Quarterly, No. 3, 2005.

Push Systems	Pull Systems
Tightly coupled	Loosely coupled
Resource centric	People centric
Participation restricted	Participation open
(few participants)	(many diverse participants)
Focus on efficiency	Focus on innovation
Limited number of major	Rapid, incremental innovation
reengineering efforts	
Zero-sum rewards	Positive-sum rewards
(dominated by extrinsic rewards)	(dominated by intrinsic rewards)

Pull systems, especially those based on use of brand as an organizing principle for leadership and competitive advantage, are emerging as the enterprise model for the new century. We are now in the early stage of adoption, with many traditional enterprises slowly moving towards pull systems and still hybrid in nature, with many elements of push still present in their model. Global competitive pressures combined with technological platforms that enable real-time collaboration among diverse stakeholders in a distributed network will serve to accelerate the transition to companies that understand the imperative for pull.

What's the message for the people in your organization today? Find people who are fulfilling and executing their elements of the brand promise. Recognize, publicize, reward, and celebrate their progress. During the successful execution of the brand promise action plan, at various stages of progress, report on the results versus expectations from the point of view of various stakeholders. The successful execution and attainment of a brand promise can become the stuff of myth, legend, and storytelling for use in the future, and a powerful, memorable way to reinforce values and desired behaviors with new and current employees—thus hastening the transition to a brand-based pull system.

Understand that the brand implementation process is a journey, not a destination. Take the time to celebrate all the small, as well as big, victories along the way. By doing this, you will imbue your workplace and company with meaning and job satisfaction that engenders greater productivity and loyalty.

We can employ Figure 14.6 to summarize the overall value creation process. It starts in the 'Soul' sector, where culture and values are to be found. Here, we have the elements that make up the "soul" of the organization

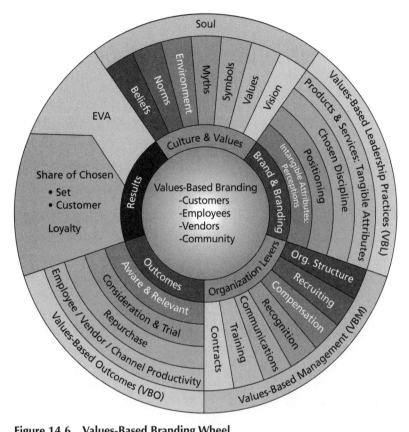

Figure 14.6   Values-Based Branding Wheel

and the served market. This is where the power potential or pull begins, revolving around the hub of key stakeholders: customers, employees, vendors, community, and so on.

The Values-Based Leadership Practices (VBL) section is where company leadership matches culture and value to market opportunity by aligning customer and other stakeholder values in a way that creates value for all. This is where values and value begin to merge.

Values-based leadership practices contained in this sector include (1) deciding which tangible performance-based attributes products and services will be featured; (2) the chosen discipline the organization will use to relate to its served markets based on the values of that market; (3) how the company will position its corporate and product/service brands so as to make them different and relevant to the needs of the market; and (4) most important of all, the intangible corporate and product/service brand attributes that will be employed to accomplish this differentiation and relevance.

The Values-Based Management (VBM) section identifies where values-based management will employ organizational levers to support the brand promise and help the organization deliver the proper brand experience. HR hiring practices, for example, will be optimized so as to find qualified candidates who exhibit values that are appropriate for success within the context of the firm's Vision, Mission, and Brand Promise.

The Values-Based Outcomes (VBO) section describes values-based outcomes or measurements that can be used to ascertain how the firm is performing in achieving higher levels of productivity, defined as improved conversion levels and retention levels as prospects become loyal customers. This is where Triple Bottom Line reporting may be employed.

The Results section reflects measures of customer loyalty and share of customer, as well as other metrics having to do with employee loyalty and productivity, vendor and channel support, and so on.

The results of these outcomes are reflected as measures of brand value, brand equity, and other measures (EVA) of long-term value creation.

"What we decide to measure and the frequency of measurement will impact our company's culture (and vice-versa) and our ability to change, adapt, and differentiate. We'll know if we have the right market-driven values and if they're in alignment. This really is a closed-loop, continuous improvement process—instead of dealing just with the tangible operating factors I'm used to, it's dealing with intangibles. I can do this!"
—Jack F. Eli, CEO, TasteRite

Chapter 15

The Solution

"It is impossible to create a sustainable competitive advantage from doing the conventional."

—Dr. Lee Thayer, The Leader's Compass

"If you want the rainbow, you gotta put up with the rain."

—Steven Wright, Comic Philosopher

Jack lightly tapped his pencil on the desk as he looked at his fellow Vistage group members sitting around the conference room table, finishing up their lunches and conversations. Had it really been almost two years since their first meeting? Incredible. Just goes to prove that time does fly by when you're having fun. Jack was hosting today's meeting at TasteRite's offices, and as the host, he would deliver a "state of the business" address. The timing was perfect. He would use today's meeting as an opportunity to summarize all of the major activities undertaken in the last two years, lessons learned, results to date, and trends.

Frank Reasoner, the group's chair, brought the meeting to order, announcing that Jack, as the host, would have up to 90 minutes to present some updated information on his company's performance to date. Frank asked everyone to hold questions and comments until the Q&A at the end of Jack's update. He reminded everyone that there would be a tour of TasteRite's facility later that afternoon. He motioned Jack to the front of the conference table...

"Good afternoon. On behalf of TasteRite, I'm pleased to be able to host today's meeting, and to report on what's been happening since my first meeting with you, almost two years ago. Before I go any further, I'd like to invite some members of my staff to join our meeting."

On cue, the door to the conference room opened, and several people took seats near the wall, on one side of the conference room.

"Why don't you introduce yourselves, telling the group your name, position, and time with the company? Let's start at this end, with Pam Hill."

A petite brunette, in her mid-40s, dressed in a tailored suit stood up. "Hi, I'm Pam Hill, and I'm the CFO of TasteRite. I've been with the company nine years."

In the next chair was a tall athletic looking young man wearing glasses. He stood up and said, "Good afternoon. My name is Bob Humphries. I'm the CMO, and I've been with the company five years."

Next was a grandfatherly looking gent in his 50s, who said, "Hello folks. My name is Barry Phillips. I've been with TasteRite for six years and I'm VP of manufacturing. Good to be here…"

Matthew Gomez was the next to stand. "Hello. I'm Matthew Gomez, vice president, sales. I've been at TasteRite for five years. It's a pleasure to meet you…"

Next to Matthew sat a medium-sized but strong looking man in his 50s with graying hair. He stood and said, "Hello to you all. My name is Abdul Saadiq, and I'm the VP of distribution and logistics. I've been with the company three years."

Next to Abdul sat Christopher Russell, a friendly looking chap in his 40s. He stood and said, "Hi. My name is Christopher Russell and I head up human resources. I've been with the company just over a year."

Last to stand was Jonathan Jessep, a youthful energetic type, with intense dark brown eyes and a quick smile. He stood, saying, "Glad to be here. I'm Jonathan Jessep and I'm VP of information technology. I celebrate my two-year anniversary in one month."

Jack smiled at his team, "I'd like to thank my executive team for attending today's meeting. As I share with you my update report on the state of our business as I see it, I will also call on some of them from time to time to fill in elements of the program that they were vitally involved with.

"Now, for the information of my staff, I'd like each member of my Vistage group to briefly identify themselves by name and company affiliation." Each member then proceeded to introduce themselves.

"My thanks to each of you for being here today. Oh, I'd also like to acknowledge one member of my team who could not be with us today. Russ Hamblin is VP of R&D, and he's been with the company for seven years. Russ is meeting with a key client as we speak.

"When I first appeared before this group with my 'issue,' I had no real expectations about what was going to happen as a result of that first meeting. I was hoping for some fresh thinking to help me view the situation in a new way. As I said to you then, I was really impressed by the caliber of thinking that I received, and by the nature of the questions and recommendations that you made. It certainly opened up my mind to new possibilities in how we could approach the issue of flat profits.

"One of the first things that you helped me see was that I had been looking at the situation through the lens of my own background and experience. As a chemical engineer trained in process manufacturing, I was really focused on the operational aspects of the company as the way to achieve our goals. From an operations standpoint, I had all the information I thought I needed. Your questions and insight helped me ask new questions and look for new answers in places that I had not previously been looking. I found that to be an eye-opening experience.

"One of the first actions we took, based on your recommendations and comments, was to hire an outside consulting firm to assist us. Our goal was to forge a better understanding of how we were delivering value to our customers.

"The model the consulting firm used looks like this…" Jack reached into a portfolio and extracted the following chart.

Brand Value = Tangible Attributes + Intangible Attributes − Price.

"Internally, we simply call this the BVM. This simple brand value model was the key to helping us understand how we were delivering value, and how we could improve that value proposition. And without stealing anyone's thunder, it's the intangible attributes of this model that we failed to understand, and we have come to find out that those are the real source of value creation for our firm.

"Tangible attributes are the bundle of performance-based attributes of the brand. Intangible attributes are the bundle of emotional-based attributes of a brand—the brand's equity. These bundles are available at a price; the relationship between all three variables determines perceptions of brand value or worth. Of course, we expanded this model to isolate more specific areas, such as individual product performance attributes, service support attributes, and channel attributes. But it's this basic model that provided the insight and direction we needed. It showed us what our customers valued.

"With the help of the consultants, we executed a baseline BVM survey of customers and other buyers in the categories we operate in. This allowed us to find the key drivers to value within each of our major market segments and determine what we needed to do to improve our value proposition in alignment with our core beliefs about this company and what we stood for.

"With the consulting firm's help we learned the following:

"In terms of our customers and prospects, we found out that one of their values cut across most food service segments. It was their belief that a flavor or taste profile product that met specs was table stakes. In other words, most of the companies in our industry could manufacture and deliver a spice and flavorings mix that met the criteria for a given flavor or taste profile. There was no differentiating value in this performance-based attribute. That lack of differentiation, of course, put downward pressure on prices.

"When we probed deeper, we found that they also believed that there was a real need for menu innovation. To many food service operators, one of their core values is innovation. They wanted and needed help developing menu items that add value and attractiveness to their menus, hit their price points, keep their food and prep costs under control, stand up well operationally, and create satisfaction and repeat business for their customer base, all while attracting new customers eager to try the new menu items. This need extended even into the chains, especially the smaller chains, who—even if they had resources on staff for menu item development—often did not have the expertise to track industry trends, and quickly follow up on new items. They were looking for a resource that did not simply ask for the spice or flavoring mix order, but helped them create the menu item and set them apart from their competitors.

"We also determined that the belief that there was a real need for menu innovation was underserved. In other words, most of our competitors were chasing the 'specs and price' business, trying to compete for established menu items, as were we. And although there were opportunities to differentiate our offering, at least in the short term, based on distribution and logistical advantages, we seemed to be missing an opportunity in terms of menu item innovation.

"Also, in looking at our customers' consideration sets, none of our competitors was strongly associated with the belief in innovation—none of them had created that as a strong emotionally based attribute of their brand and of their offering.

"A strong belief that also cut across most food service segments was for consistency of product. We learned that consistency of product was key to meeting our customers' customers' expectations when they ordered a menu item. They wanted it to taste just like it did the last time they ordered it. No surprises here. But, no one was explicitly making that consistency guarantee. This was particularly important to multi-unit operators who wanted their customers to have the same experience at every one of their locations. This is a strong performance-based brand attribute.

"Another strong belief that came out of the research, and again cut across most food service segments, was a distaste for wasting food. Many food service operations waste a lot of food. Inclement weather and other reasons account for operators having prepared more food than they sell. The only recourse, most often, is to throw the surplus food out. But many people literally hate to see good food go to waste. They hate to see the fruit of their labor go into the dumpster. This attribute had both performance and emotional components. Initially, we didn't know what to make of this information, and we thought there was little we could do to address this issue.

"Another strong belief that was revealed is that food service operators do care about the health of their customers. There is a growing realization that addressing the health concerns of their customers is a way to differentiate their business, and that it's the right thing to do. So menu development was taking place with one eye on the health aspects of the menu, and how that impacted the perception of the restaurant's customers. This brand attribute had a strong emotional attraction to a very substantial segment of the population.

"Overall, our key finding was that our brand equity was not contributing very much to how customers valued us and our products. That is, our brand's value, as a percentage of our market value, was undistinguished when compared to competitors. With some exceptions, our brand did not enjoy a strong emotional bond with our customers. This, as we were told, does not bode well for customer churn. And as you recall, we were experiencing more than our share of churn.

"The good news, if you could call it that, is that the whole spice and flavor mix industry did not score well for brand attributes and value based on emotional attributes associated with innovation, partnering, creativity, and healthy foods. In a nutshell, in the business-to-business sector of this industry, branding and brand equities are weak across the board—and there was our leverage point. Since the industry seemed to be asleep at the switch, there was an opportunity to create a sustainable, competitive advantage. The bar was set low.

"I'm not going to go into the details of what we learned in terms of the BVM for our corporate and individual product brands. We did discover that there were intangible attributes related to innovation, relationships, and discovery that held potential value for some of our served market segments, but not others.

"We also did lost-customer surveys, which helped us to better understand why we didn't get certain orders, and why we lost share of customers, or their business entirely. In many cases our proposals were emphasizing elements that the customer did not consider to be important, while ignoring elements that were considered important. This provided further validation of the brand value model feedback. Our goal was to use this information to improve our sales conversion rate, and to gain share of customers' business.

"As you helped me to appreciate, the opinions of our customers and prospects, while vitally important, are not the only opinions that impact TasteRite's performance. So, we talked with other stakeholders.

"Again, our consulting firm helped us considerably in this area. We used Voice of the Stakeholder surveys combined with the BVM for key audiences to learn about their opinions and feelings regarding TasteRite compared to others in our industry.

"We learned, for example, that many of our employees got the most satisfaction and meaning from their job when they were working on new menu formulations. I'm not talking only about the food scientists and chemists in the R&D lab; I'm talking about everyone associated with product development and rollout, right down to the guy on the plant floor. They believed that new products were fun and exciting, and a way to show off their creativity and competence. Many of them wanted more involvement in the process.

"I remember one quote from an employee in the plant, who said 'Yeah, when I take my family to a restaurant that I know uses our products, it feels good to point out a new menu item that we helped develop. Then everyone orders it! And when they say it tastes good, well, that's a great feeling.'

"This information was part good news, part bad news. Good news from the point-of-view of 'here's something we can build on.' Bad news from an operational point-of-view: custom formulations, especially in smaller batches, created all sorts of manufacturing efficiency problems. That was a real barrier that we had to address.

"The other problem was that only a small group of people got to work on new product development. We needed to get more of the workforce involved in this exciting work.

"We also learned that many of our distributors found that cutting our products, or demonstrating our products against competitors' products did not offer them any clear-cut advantages over competitive products. So we were trying to maintain volume by offering too many of our standard SKUs on promotion, which put severe pressure on our margins. We needed a way to help them differentiate our brands to their customers, so we and they could maintain some pricing power.

"Some of our largest national distributors were demanding ever-higher slotting allowances and other fees to carry our products. They would threaten to replace our brand with their own private label brand if we didn't agree to their programs. This was putting added pressure on our margins.

"Well, that gives you some idea of what we learned. We shared this information with all members of the executive team during a three-day, off-campus meeting. After reviewing the information, I asked the team to answer this question: 'In the best of all worlds, what would great performance look like for TasteRite?'

"After much, much discussion, we agreed that it made sense to look very carefully at the stakeholders' values that came out of the research and see how they aligned with our values as an organization. First, there was food service operators' desire for innovative new menu items. Second was the 'high' employees got out of creating and producing new formulations and menu items. Finally, there was the need to differentiate our offering for our distributors.

"Since our corporate values encompassed the attributes of innovation, partnering, and creativity, we would use these key trust and image attributes to define our brand, what it stood for, and build our brand equity.

"After much more discussion, we agreed that 'great performance' would look like this." Jack reached into a portfolio case and held up a sign that said:

Mission:

TasteRite's proactive product ideation and flavor development resources serve innovative food service operators worldwide via great tasting new menu items.

"This statement captures many of the attributes that were identified in the brand value model for our key market segments. Some of you may have noticed the word 'worldwide' in our mission statement. We are mainly domestic right now; the 'worldwide' is something we aspire to at some point in the future.

"Bob Humphries, come on up here and tell what happened next."

Bob rose and walked up next to Jack. "This mission statement had profound implications for what marketing was saying and doing," stated Bob.

"The brand value model, or BVM utilities for trust and image attributes indicated that our former position and tag line were not optimum—in fact, it was hurting us. We learned that the attribute 'flavor' is not as meaningful an attribute as 'taste'. To understand why this is so, consider that 'flavor' is to 'drill' as 'taste' is to 'hole'—as in 'we're selling drills, the customer is buying holes.' Customers and employees are more attuned to what things actually taste like when used with other ingredients as part of a menu item, than in the flavor profile of a packet of seasonings. So, we needed to put the emphasis on taste, not flavor. We needed to stop talking in the language of the factory, and to start talking in the language of our customer, and our customer's customer.

"Furthermore, we found that service and other image attributes associated with partnering and innovation trump even taste. Taste differences are very important to our customers, but subtle and somewhat subjective for each customer. Innovation, creativity, and partnering are powerful concepts that customers seek from their suppliers. So this prompted us to change our company's position statement and theme from 'Get all the great flavor you deserve'—to this." Bob reached into the portfolio and extracted a sign that read:

Expect More Than Great Taste.

"'Expect More Than Great Taste' implied that there was a strong service component to our offering. It acknowledged that matching existing flavor profiles, whereas vitally important, did not add much value. It put the emphasis where it was most valued: on how things taste. It also implied that the services required to support innovation—creating new menu items with appeal because they looked, smelled, and tasted great, did, of course, add value.

"Once we had this position staked out, it created a promise that we then had to fully flesh out and deliver with no compromises.

"For example, the information from the BVM gave us tremendous insight into segment profitability, and led us to change our segmentation strategy. Combining information from the BVM with information from our CRM system and finance department, we found that the large chain business was not going to yield the pricing that would enable margin growth. In fact, we found that some of our largest chain customers were quite unprofitable, despite their high order volume.

"Somewhat counter-intuitively, we found that selected smaller chains and large independents with lower volumes offered us higher margin opportunities due to better pricing power and other advantages, along with greater lifetime loyalty potential. These folks were being underserved by our industry, yet they assigned more utility and value to attributes of innovation and partnering. They also met the five criteria for segmentation: effective, identifiable, profitable, accessible, and accountable.

"The key to our success with this new strategy would be to expand our sales and develop such a strong relationship with the smaller chains and independents, that it would offset a good portion of the volume we were selling to the large chains, and overall make us much more profitable.

"We used a hierarchy of effects model to see how, with this new position, we could move prospects from brand ignorance through the various stages of the funnel to brand advocacy. We compared our old performance to our expected performance with this new positioning. It indicated that our conversion rates, for carefully chosen segments, would dramatically rise. And that our customers' lifetime value to us in terms of share of customer and length of time we enjoy their business would also rise." A smile flickered across Nina's face.

"From a financial perspective, we needed to trade off volume for better margin, and more importantly, for more consistent and predictable growth.

"This is the dynamic business model we were looking for.

"This information also led us to reconsider how we were organizing our sub-brands' product and service offerings. We decided to more formally consolidate all operating brands under the TasteRite brand, creating a family of related brands. This revised brand architecture gave us the opportunity to put more emphasis on our 'authority brand'—TasteRite. This, in turn, led to a redesign of our packaging, labeling, and communications efforts.

"Overall, we saw a large margin opportunity in this new direction. For example, we discovered that many SKUs were no longer needed, and we greatly reduced their number. This, of course, had a positive impact on our inventory cost, especially among those segments that were least profitable.

"Among our communication efforts, was the design of a new extranet site to give our supplier and channel partners and our customers password-protected access to their programs. We used this site as a tool to support teamwork, and to provide instant communications on program status, development status, order status, shipping status, delivery times, and so forth. It has proven invaluable in eliminating errors, and in helping us to accelerate our performance. Kudos to Jonathan and Abdul and the other team members who made this possible.

"Finally, we created a customer relationship *marketing* system[1] so that we could continuously communicate with customers and potential customers in our targeted high-profile, high-margin segments who met certain criteria based on the BVM feedback. We communicate with these customers and prospects at least monthly, via provocative three-dimensional direct mailers, the Internet, outbound phone calls, and our inbound call center. We engage them in terms of their interest in new menu item development, share with them compelling case stories of our customers who have successfully developed new menu items, and invite them to explore how we could help them re-energize and grow their customer counts, check averages, and control costs.

"This program continues to produce excellent response in terms of high-quality, high-level contacts. In fact, Russ is meeting today with a company who responded as a result of this program. What's interesting is the president of the company is the one who first contacted us. This company is a high-profile prospect, and they were not being called on by our sales organization, who considered them to be a highly satisfied customer of a competitor. This speaks volumes to the difference between satisfaction and loyalty.

"Overall, these programs created a very strong story to tell our channel partners. Because we were beginning to enjoy more visibility and business with selected 'bell cow'[2] foodservice operators, we enjoyed more influence, thus leverage, with our distributor partners, and could show them that we were creating value for them in ways that our competitors were not. This helped them see that putting pricing pressure on us was not in their best long-term interest. Plus, returned goods requests and authorizations are going down rather dramatically—since we aren't trying to 'load' our dealers via promotions. It has put our partnering relationship with our distributors back on a more fair and equitable footing.

---

[1] We called this system "Nurture Marketing" based on a concept developed by Jim Cecil that he calls "Drip Irrigation Marketing." The premise is that often customers are lost due to "perceived indifference" and/or their current supplier is not in touch with them when they get a "spear in the chest," that is, an urgent need or opportunity.

[2] A "bell cow" account is of strategic importance to distributors in a local market due to their high volume, locations, or the types of product lines that they order. A bell cow is the cow that the rest of the herd follows from one pasture to another.

"This, in turn, led us to develop a 'Menu Masters' board, one each for customers from key segments, and for distributors. We invited a select group of customers and distributors to serve on each board, and called on them from time to time to get their opinions on key industry trends and developments. We invited the press to cover the event, and that generated great publicity for us in the trade press. We recognized our Menu Masters participants' at our national meeting for their service to us and to the industry. Again, it's a win, cubed."

Laura Regal spoke out, "Bob, what's going on with TasteRite's consumer product program?"

"Well Laura, that's a whole separate and huge topic in and of itself. Jack and I have discussed that, and agree that it's a topic for a meeting all its own. I can tell you we're making terrific progress on improving that program as well."

"Thanks Bob," said Jack, as Bob walked back to his seat.

"I'll stand in for Russ, and give the implications of the BVM findings and our new mission and position for R&D. This meant that R&D would switch from primarily a passive role, developing flavor formulations to meet customer specs, to a much more proactive role in partnering with selected accounts that met our criteria. We found that our current personnel had a terrific competence at menu-item innovation based on consumer trends. This was their passion, and our former operating style and major emphasis on operational efficiency had often put the brakes on in this area. They had repeatedly tried to communicate this, but no one was listening, including me.

"We also found that this passion for innovation existed outside of R&D. People throughout the company were excited by the idea of menu innovation.

"Morale, which had been low, began to improve due to our new position and the new-found respect we were getting from customers and distributors. In fact, morale throughout the company dramatically improved as we communicated our new position to the employees, and, perhaps most important, began to make it easier for them to deliver on this promise. This was something they really believed in.

"We created cross-functional teams devoted to menu-item development for selected target accounts. We used these teams in two ways: one, to develop ideas that our sales force could discuss with the client; and two, to work hand-in-glove with prospective and current clients' internal product development personnel, if they had them, as well as their operations, purchasing, and other key personnel to develop new menu items. This customer-focused team 'partnering' approach really appealed to prospective and current clients.

"We did not offer this service to just anyone, only to prospects and clients who met certain criteria in terms of their operations, growth rates, and commitment to innovation. We used an outbound call center, in follow-up to our three-dimensional mailings, to contact prospects and learn more about their values and needs. The intelligence from these calls went into our database, and was accessible via our extranet.

"We also partnered with outside product development and flavorings development firms to create a menu innovation network. They had no manufacturing capability, so we created a win-win for both parties.

"By applying a service mapping tool, we found that we had the competence to fast-track menu item development, so we worked with marketing, manufacturing, and IT to offer a special program that we branded the 'TasteRite® FastTrac℠' program. It promised menu development from ideation through finished benchmark product in 90 days. Of course, it cost more, but for food service operators desperate for new menu items that could reverse declining revenues, it was a lifesaver.

"We really found out how valuable the TasteRite FastTrac program was when the whole trans fat movement took place. Many food service operations were looking at alternatives to trans fats in their menus. Their health-conscious customers were demanding it, and, some municipalities were legislating it. The problem was, changing from trans fats to mono or unsaturated fats changed the taste of many menu items. Since consistency of taste is one of the core values of food service operators, and is demanded of them by their customers, this was a major issue. And a major opportunity.

"So Russ and his team took the initiative to contact key food service operators most at risk during this transition. They offered the TasteRite FastTrac program to them, and charged them for the consulting services. We then, of course, also had the opportunity to sell them the spice and flavoring mixes that achieved the right taste in their newly formulated menu items. Our conversion rate was very high. It was a huge win, cubed.

"Many of the accounts that we contacted were new to us, and met our profile for a highly desirable, high-margin new customer. We've been very successful at keeping their business, and in expanding our share of their business. They really appreciated our proactive approach to their business problems.

"We took what Russ and his cross-functional team learned and shared that with other teams we created. This helped us to leverage our reach into the market and accelerate our penetration rate for the FastTrac trans fat menu item replacement program.

"Barry, please come on up here and tell the folks how what we learned impacted manufacturing and purchasing."

Barry bounced up to the front of the desk and smiled. "My challenge was to go from a focus on relatively large runs, to a focus on a growing number of smaller batches. Since that was the direction the company was committed to, we were going to find a way to make it work. We located an enterprise resource-planning system that seemed to have the capability we needed. We experimented with various approaches in the factory, and found new ways to organize our processes. Working with Jonathan and his crew, we made the transition to the new system in less than six months. It was no cakewalk, but today we're much more flexible and agile than we were before we instituted this new system.

"In fact, we're more operationally efficient today than we were before. And we're learning every day how to work the system more effectively. The feedback we receive as a result of being part of the new cross-functional teams is invaluable in understanding the implications of smaller batch runs for the rest of the organization. The customers' expectations are what set the standard now for performance, that pull products through the system, and that define what quality is. The service mapping was instructive in understanding customers' requirements from their perspective. For example, they don't care about our ship date; they only care about the delivery date to their dock.

"One of the advantages of our new system and its extranet module is that it enables us to communicate with our suppliers in a manner that lets them do a better job of supplying us with just what we need, just in time for a production run. This results in a better quality ingredient, since there is virtually no storage time, and flavor degradation is held to a minimum. This has helped us to reduce our raw material inventory costs and our waste. It also enables us to upload information automatically to our extranet, so that everyone is getting real time information about what is going on.

"This helped marketing differentiate our offering, and it helped sales, R&D, logistics, etc. do a better job of communicating with our clients."

"Thanks, Barry. Now I'd like Matthew Gomez to come up here and give you sales' perspective on what we've accomplished. Matthew…"

"Thanks, Jack. Prior to this program, we were like many sales operations. We were chasing volume, and doing a good job of writing proposals, and, it seemed, a good job of closing deals. But we were not being strategic. With the insight and direction that this program has provided, we are doing a much better job of targeting segments, qualifying accounts before we call on them, and then committing considerable time and investment in converting our most strategically desirable target accounts into dynamic, high-performance customers. A high-performance customer is one who will get outsized benefits from our menu creation expertise, and other advantages, and therefore is willing to pay us accordingly—that is, pay us a premium.

"Another benefit of this new brand position is that we are attractive to precisely those companies that have the most aggressive growth plans. In a mature industry like food service, that's just where you want to be focused.

"The ongoing trans fat conversion program continues to be a major win for us. We worked hand-in-glove with R&D, making dual calls, and enjoyed great success. We've implemented a team selling approach that really aligns our personnel with their counterparts on the prospects' and customers' team.

"Our new program required new behavior on team members' parts. As a simple example, every team member was responsible for responding to a customer inquiry. We get back to a customer, even if we don't yet have an answer, within three hours, and let them know that we're working on getting an answer, when we expect to have the answer, and who will get back to them. We track and coordinate this activity on our extranet, so that all team members can see what's going on. We've developed an extensive FAQs database to serve as a knowledge and reference center for team members.

"This approach required that we change the sales organization's compensation package, and, working closely with Chris Russell in HR, we've been able to accomplish that. Sales used to be compensated by sales commissions. The major change is that sales personnel are now rewarded based on several criteria related to the desirability of an account from a sales revenue, margin, share of customer, and customer longevity perspective. By reducing customer churn, the sales force has enjoyed greater income on repeat business, and freed up time so they can do more careful pre-qualifying of accounts, and business development.

"The productivity of the sales department has improved since the company's new position and approach was incorporated into an action plan and kicked off about 14 months ago. For example, since we're doing a better job of targeting desirable accounts, our conversion rate on proposals has improved year to year by double digits, while the number of proposals submitted has also increased significantly. Improvements in both of those areas continue to accelerate. At the same time, we've seen a marked improvement in our ability to keep key segment customers' accounts. Although we haven't added any sales personnel, the effect is as though we've added about 20 to 30 percent more to our sales force. The bottom line results have been very gratifying."

"Thanks, Matt. Now I don't want everyone to think that this was as easy as we're making it sound. It wasn't. For example, during our first three-day, off-campus meeting, it became apparent that if we adapted this new position for our company and brand, there were some interesting implications. One implication was 'What do we do about the customers who don't meet our new target account profile?' You know, the customers who've been serving the same menu for at least the last five years, and have no interest in innovating. These 'transactional' customers were the ones who were putting the most pressure on us for great service and lower prices.

"I'm going to invite Pam Hill to come up here and tell us what happened with this issue, and to give you some overall results year-to-date on the action plan. Pam...."

"Thanks, Jack. We also worked with the outside consultant in concert with our marketing and sales departments, and when we did an analysis of our customer base, and segmented them according to our new criteria, we saw that we had two very different categories of customer, regardless of the food service segment they were in. Here's what that looked like." Pam reached into the portfolio and took out a chart.

TasteRite Account Segmentation (Baseline)

Category/Segment	Number(%)	Volume(%)	Profit(%)
Category I			
Sub-segment A	20	25	-
Sub-segment B	40	54	20
Sub-totals:	60	79	20
Category II			
Sub-segment C	10	6	12
Sub-segment D	20	12	60
Sub-segment E	10	3	8
Sub-totals:	40	21	80

"Category I was purely transactional in nature; they didn't want us to help them with developing new menu items. They knew what they needed and expected us to manufacture to their spec, deliver on time, and be competitively priced. This category, in turn, had two sub-segments.

Sub-segment A sent most of their orders out for re-bid. They often changed orders at the last minute. They also seemed to account for a very high share of returned goods. You get the picture. When we analyzed the profitability of this sub-segment, we saw that the majority of the accounts in the sub-segment were marginally profitable, or were losers. We were surprised to see that this sub-segment accounted for 20 percent of our accounts, and 25 percent of our volume, and flat to negative profits. In other words, they took up a lot of resources but gave no return.

"Working with marketing and sales, we immediately put these accounts on a program where we gave them the opportunity to work with us in a manner designed to lower our costs of doing business with them, and/or pay us higher prices. Many of them decided to take their business elsewhere. This put a real hit on our volume and top-line revenues last year. The impact on bottom-line profits was negligible.

"Sub-segment B, although transactional in nature, was easier to deal with. They were much more stable than the sub-segment A, and less demanding. When we analyzed their profitability, we found that they accounted for 40 percent of our accounts, 54 percent of our volume, and about 20 percent of our profits. Working with sales, we created a transition program for these customers. We would try to move them from being transactional to being more 'relationship' in nature. If we couldn't move them, we would continue to serve them—if for no other reason than they were profitable, and many of them were also important to our distribution channel. We would also strive to become more efficient in how we handled their business, so we could improve our margins. Also, as a result of our marketing and sales efforts, they might one day see the light and engage our product development services.

"The other category, Category II, was made up of accounts that did value product development and menu innovation. They accounted for about 40 percent of our overall accounts, 21 percent of our volume, and 80 percent of our profits. They, in turn, were broken out into three sub-segments.

"Sub-segment C, although they used our menu development services, was not willing to pay for them above and beyond what they paid for their spice and flavorings mixes. They accounted for about 10 percent of accounts, about 6 percent of volume, and their contribution to profits was about 12 percent. Our strategy here was to do a better job of helping these accounts see the value of our menu development services, and/or adjust our pricing to them. Results have been mixed. Our other strategy was to improve our operations, so we could improve our margins.

"Sub-segment D of this category valued menu-development services and were willing to pay a price premium for them. They accounted for about 20 percent of accounts, 12 percent of volume, and their contribution to profits was about 60 percent!! They, of course, employed the services of our R&D group the most. They also valued menu solutions that would help them define new restaurant ideas and themes—they wanted holistic solutions to their marketplace opportunities and really valued our role in helping them to innovate to realize those opportunities. As you can see, this profile account offers TasteRite tremendous leverage in terms of margins and profits. But, we had serious historical problems with many of these accounts in delivering our consulting services in a timely fashion. Our new FastTrac menu development service was designed to address this issue.

"The third sub-segment in this category, sub-segment E—while they valued menu development services—had their own in-house group and seldom used outside services. They accounted for 10 percent of our accounts, 3 percent of our volume, and 8 percent of our profits. Our strategy here was to help convince these accounts that by working with us, they could leverage their in-house capabilities. The results to date are marginal.

"You can readily see where our business development efforts will be focused in the future. The good news is that sub-segment D, as a percentage of all food service accounts, is a significant sub-segment. We serve a relatively small percentage of the accounts in the food service industry that match sub-category D criteria. So there's lots of upside potential.

"The impact of our action plan over the last 14 months has been dramatic. We are making fast progress towards Jack's goal to increase profits 50 percent by the end of the next three years. We are more than halfway towards that goal, and should easily exceed it. We believe our plan is sustainable, and will allow us to continue to show excellent double-digit profit growth for the foreseeable future.

"Finally, we also took a look at how we were doing compared to other competitors in our consideration set. We use a balanced scorecard that measures four broad areas: financial, customer, internal, and innovation.

"The short version of the story is that we are showing strong improvement in moving towards being the leader in our industry in terms of how productively we use our marketing resources. Our sales per dollar of enterprise marketing expenses have dramatically improved relative to our competitors. This indicates that our focused segment investment strategy with an emphasis on high margin services is working.

"Our enterprise marketing efficiency ratio, a measure of enterprise marketing costs compared to share of revenues, is less than 1, meaning that we are spending our resources efficiently. Our gross margins as a percentage of our sales revenues are growing. And our cost per point of share is nearly equal to our profit per point, which means that we are maximizing our earnings. We are balancing profitability with growth, short term with long term, and centralized control with decentralized authority.

"I'd like to thank my fellow executives, especially Bob, for their help in developing this information. Thank you for your kind attention…"

Jack interrupted, "Pam, before you leave, briefly tell our guests how you rearranged our financial reporting system to capture the impact of these new initiatives."

"I'll be brief. Basically, the BVM showed us that a considerable amount of our value as a company lies in the intangible attributes—the trust and image attributes of our brand. And we were not accounting for that, nor were we tracking it. The great majority of expenditures we were making in our repositioning and the new value-building initiatives were being expensed as required by FASB guidelines.

"But I knew, and the BVM model was telling us, that we were really investing in building the asset value of our brands. So, what I did was really rather simple. I started tracking and reporting our market capitalization, broken out by net tangible assets, that is book value, and intangible assets—the remainder once we subtracted the book value.

"Then, based on the BVM, our internal sales data, and our customer tracking program, I broke out the intangible values by brand, by channel, and by customer segment. I reported these monthly, using simple line graphs.

"What this revealed was that those expensed items were really paying off—starting about nine months ago, we began seeing sustained monthly increases in the company's brand equity. That is, as our stock price and total market capitalization increased, the majority of that increase was due to brand equity, not just booked profit, reflecting investors' expectations for our future prospects and performance.

"The Board of Directors reviews these charts on a monthly basis and has taken a great interest in monitoring our brand assets.

"One other thing—Jack is in my office on the fifth of every month to see these graphs as they're hot off the printer—I think he's using them as his personal scorecard."

"Ah, Pam, my secret is out. Thanks. That should give you a rough idea of some of what we did to follow-up on our initial two meetings. We've used the idea of values-driven brand and feedback from the BVM to reshape our mission and purpose, and have used the concept of brand integrity to re-examine and change much about how we go to market and serve our clients.

"During our first three-day, off-site planning meeting, there were times when everyone was getting a bit frustrated, and we didn't know where this effort was going. As we reviewed the BVM results, and compared them to our then-view of the market, it soon became apparent where we needed to focus, and how we had to change our approach. Once we knew our values as encoded in our mission, everything else became so much easier, at least in retrospect.

"There were many bumps along the way. But as we went along, more and more people within the company began to see what we were all about, and they began to get on board. Each department head did a great job of continuously explaining our mission, our new position, and the implications for their department and the company to their personnel, which we continue to do today, and will continue to do forever. I'm very proud of the way the people of TasteRite dealt with all the changes that we've gone through.

"Again, thanks to each of my group's members for your invaluable questions, insight, and suggestions that made this possible."

Frank stood up. "Jack, thanks to you and to your staff for a very insightful and informative presentation. I speak on behalf of the group when I say that hearing about what you've done and your success is very gratifying. Sort of like 'chicken soup for the soul'. Now, let's open the floor to questions. Anyone have any questions or comments to make to Jack or to his staff members? OK, Nan, go ahead…"

"My congratulations to each of you for the remarkable progress you've made over the last two years. I'm very impressed. I'd like to ask Chris Russell what impact this all has had on the HR function, outside of what you've already shared with us about your sales personnel."

Chris stood and replied, "The impact has been profound. It has changed most of the job descriptions within the company. It has changed how we define most of our roles, policies, procedures, and rules. It has changed who we recruit, what we look for, how we interview, and what we ask. Previously, we first looked for people who had direct industry experience. Now, we look for people who have certain values, depending on their department and role. For example, in research, if people can't demonstrate values that include innovation and creativity, self-starter, teamwork, sharing, etc., they don't make it through the first round.

"Each department has interpreted the overall BVM feedback to reflect their own perspective. Overall, we continue to fine tune it so that all the parts fit together.

"I'm also pleased to say that we have a backlog of highly qualified applicants looking to work at TasteRite. That's quite a change from two years ago. This has made it easier for us to interview more applicants for each job opening, and as a result of greater choice, to make better hiring decisions. This has been especially effective in hiring new personnel for the R&D department.

"Does that answer your question, Nan?"

"Yes, it sure does. Thank, Russ."

David Solomon raised his hand. "Yes, David?" said Frank.

"That's a very interesting reply. But what does that mean in terms of how people are treated, day to day?"

"Who's that question directed to?" asked Frank.

"Whoever wants to answer it."

Pam Hill, after a quick exchange of glances with her fellow officers, stood up. "I'll take a crack at that," she said. "Here's an example. Before we instituted the action plan we had tight controls on all discretionary spending. However, no one knew where those controls came from or why they existed, or why the policies were what they were. After reviewing all policies and controls in light of our corporate brand's new position, it soon became obvious that we needed to allow people dealing with our Category II customers, especially sub-segment D, the latitude to show initiative in developing programs on fast timelines.

"That necessitated that we provide 'seed money' for program development and left it up to the team members to best decide how to allocate that money to promising customers. Now, the discretionary money we spend on new menu item development is directed to the correct sub-segment, and the team members spend it wisely. New product idea-to-benchmark-to-launch timelines have dramatically improved, increasing our customer's positive perceptions of our company and people. This was especially essential to the success of the TasteRite FastTrac program. The results to date have more than justified our confidence and trust in our personnel."

"Thank you, Pam. That's a great explanation," said David.

"Any other comments or questions?" asked Frank.

"Yes," said Larry Labovitz. "Jack, how does your company's current performance impact your new performance-based contract?"

"You know, Larry, my performance contract is on public record, and all members of my staff have revised contracts of their own that echo the key provisions in my contract. I'm glad to say that we all are on track to benefit greatly from the improved performance of TasteRite. And that these benefits have accrued proportionally to the benefit of all employees.

"When I had my meeting with the family to explain our new initiatives and proposed my 'skin in the game' contract ideas, they had no problem approving it. We decided as part of our action plan and new position that we would run an 'open book' company, and we share key financials with the employees appropriate to their department and our shared mission, except for individual salaries. This has fostered a spirit of trust, sharing, openness, and communication on the part of everyone. All employees can see our key performance indicators, and know what it means for them, and for their compensation.

"The family is very pleased with our progress to date, and the investment community is tracking our performance closely. Our stock price has improved, and we expect it to continue to improve in line with our forward-looking statements and guidance. Our PR agency has done an excellent job of communicating our new position and the improved outlook that we have. And the churn rate in our stock has dropped, with more and more shares held longer and longer by institutional investors. This has positively impacted our beta rating."

"But Jack," interjected Chris Kalapolos, "aren't you concerned that your competitors will read about your new position and strategy and do the same things?"

"Well, Chris, the interesting thing about our approach is that we discovered that we had some people on staff with competence and creativity in this area, and they were frustrated that they could not easily get done what they wanted to get done without having to jump backwards through hoops of fire. We made it extremely difficult for them to be effective. It's taken some real work on our part to change things up around here so that we can execute our action plan and 'pay off' our new position.

"What I'm saying is this: I can watch Tiger Woods swing a golf club all day, but that doesn't mean I can play golf like Tiger. Competitors can read all they want about our new strategy, but unless they're willing to do the tough work to change things in their company, all the big things and the just-as-important little things, they will fail at copying our plan. And besides, since they have a different culture, values, and context than we do, our strategy is probably not appropriate for them. So blindly copying our plan would be a recipe for failure.

"In the meantime, we have a two-year head start on building our competences, on building and maintaining key customer relationships, on learning how to best drive values and the brand attributes that create value for us in focused segments, and we don't intend to slow down.

"OK, one last question—we're just about out of time for this agenda item," said Frank.

Stan May stood up. "Jack, are you having fun?"

Jack laughed, "You bet. Let me tell you a story. One of the values that we learned our employees had was 'service to the community.' I guess it could also be described as 'giving back' to the community. So we polled our employees on ideas they had on how TasteRite could be proactive in giving back to the community. We also shared some of the information from our BVM with our employees. Some of them put 2 and 2 together and came up with a 10. They suggested that we work with some of our key customers to help them address the issue of surplus or wasted food—food that was wholesome, but that the restaurant could no longer use. They wondered if the food could be repurposed and used in programs designed to get needy people basic nutrition, for example, children, senior citizens, shelters, etc.

"They even identified a not-for-profit organization called America's Second Harvest that consists of more than 200 food banks and food rescue programs that distribute donated food through 50,000 charitable agencies to hungry Americans. Their network serves all 50 states. For those of you interested in checking them out, their URL is www.secondharvest.org.[3] Second Harvest has several key programs currently underway.

---

[3] Although this chapter is a parable, Second Harvest and all the information about their programs is real.

"The BackPack Program is designed to meet the needs of hungry children at times when other resources are not available, such as weekends and school vacation.

"The Kids Café programs provide free meals and snacks to children of low-income families through a variety of existing community locations where children congregate, such as Boys and Girls Clubs, churches, or public schools.

"We're particularly proud of our participation in Second Harvest's Community Kitchen program. There are currently 30 Community Kitchen programs in operation. Nationwide, the program graduates over 770 students each year, and boasts a 66 percent job retention rate over 6 months. Students serve about 4.5 million meals a year. There were 1,292 students enrolled in the program in 2005.

"We have been working closely with Second Harvest to donate surplus spice and flavorings mix products for their use, and to develop information for their curricula that they can use to teach their students about the use of spices and flavorings, and their impact on taste, shelf life, and the overall appeal of menu items.

"It's a very positive program for us, because it supports our core values while supporting a worthwhile organization and cause. We now include material about their mission in most of our marketing communications programs. We're hot-linked to their Web site from our Web site. We try to work with our food service customers and channel partners in communities where Second Harvest graduates students to help them get placed in jobs. And of course, we work with our stakeholder network to help make everyone aware of Second Harvest, so that they can donate surplus food and used restaurant equipment to them. Everyone at TasteRite and our various stakeholders is very proud of our role in working with Second Harvest.

"We know, as an example of our extended impact, that our effort in support of Second Harvest helps over 9 million children each year. This may be the most gratifying outcome of our efforts to date. And it makes all of the hard work and effort that much more fun."

As all the Vistage members smiled approvingly and applauded, Frank stood up and said, "Jack, the last two years have been quite a journey of discovery and accomplishment for you. We all congratulate you, your staff, your organization, and your network of stakeholders on a job well begun. Best of luck as you continue your journey.

"Okay folks, our next agenda item is…"

Don Rogers raised his hand. "Frank, before we go on to the next agenda item, I have one last question of Jack. Do you still have the three envelopes?"

Jack smiled a little smile, and slowly shook his head, "No."

Jack's Top Ten List of "Ways To Improve Your Company's Performance":

#10. Interrogate reality (Find your values and your markets' values)

 #9. Employ the Brand Value Model (Define value for key stakeholders)

 #8. Understand how values create value via brand integrity

 #7. Create an Action Plan to build brands with integrity

 #6. Communicate: create shared understanding and expectations

 #5. Communicate: so people know what it means to them personally

 #4. Measure the right things, with the right frequency

 #3. Communicate the successes and inevitable setbacks via stories

 #2. Learn, share, adjust, improve

 #1. Give others credit for progress towards Brand Integrity

Bonus: Have some fun along the way

Overview of the Brand Value Model

We believe the total value of a brand in a given product/service category is composed of three parts.

1. The physical and readily identifiable features of the brand that deliver specific, tangible benefits to the purchaser, thus impacting purchase choice. We call these the **tangible product features** or **performance features.** These features may be delivered by the product or service itself or may be delivered through the channel in which the product is available.

2. The perceived intrinsic value associated with the brand name due to such things as trust, the image transferred to the purchaser, longevity in the marketplace, social responsibility, consistent performance, and so forth (i.e., the intangibles). We refer to this set of intrinsic values as the **brand's equity.** Generally, we classify the brand equity drivers into two sets—trust attributes and image attributes.

3. The **price** of the product. Price may include the initial purchase price, maintenance and support costs, or any other real costs relevant to the product or service category.

Thus, the total value (or utility) of a product or service is a function of its physical, tangible, and deliverable features; its brand equity; and its price. See Figure 1.

In addition, we believe that a brand's value is directly related to customer loyalty. That is, if a particular brand maintains a significantly higher perception of value to a purchaser than any other brand in the category, that consumer will consistently purchase that brand and consistently recommend that brand to others. Conversely, as brands in a category become less differentiated in terms of both tangible and intrinsic features, price becomes the major differentiator of value, and thus, there is little loyalty.

The Brand Value Model, shown in Figure 1, makes the following assumptions:

1. The **value** someone attributes to a particular branded product or service is equivalent to the total utility (in the economic sense) that person assigns to the product or service. Brand value will vary from consumer to consumer.

319

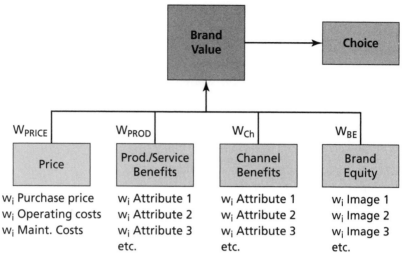

Figure 1

2. **Brand value** to a purchaser in the category is the **sum of the utilities** of
   a. Product Performance Features: the bundle of tangible and readily identifiable product features/attributes delivered by the branded product or service and/or its channel.
   b. Brand Equity: the bundle of intrinsic features/attributes delivered by the branded product or service.
   c. The **price** of those two bundles of features/attributes.
3. **Brand equity** is defined as the bundle of intrinsic features/attributes delivered by a branded product or service. It is measured as the price differential someone is willing to pay for a particular branded product or service over an identical product or service that is unbranded. Alternatively, this definition can be recrafted to state that brand equity is the difference in utility between two products or services that are perceived to deliver an identical set of tangible benefits at the same price.
4. We use a combination conjoint and discrete choice models to uncover brand value and brand equity. Thus, we make the following normal assumptions in all conjoint/choice models:
   a. Consumers are rational and attempt to optimize utility (value) in the process of choosing a product or service.
   b. Utility is summative.
   c. Price has a negative utility. That is, the higher the price, the lower the utility.

We observe that people trade off price against the combined bundle of tangible product features and brand equity to optimize total utility or total value. Thus, an unknown brand laden with features the purchaser desires and selling at a reasonable price may be given more total value than a familiar and well-respected brand that does not have as many features and/or is more expensive.

We also note that the intrinsic part of a brand's value, brand equity, may be positive or negative, meaning that a brand name can be used to increase overall utility of a choice, or may detract from the overall utility of a choice. Said differently, positive brand equity allows a marketer to charge a premium in the marketplace over the value of the bundle of tangible features alone, or over the value of an unbranded product/service. And, some branded names in a particular category could have such a negative value among some purchasers such that the brand's equity could be below that of an unbranded, or baseline, product/service.

SDR's Procedure for Modeling Brand Equity

Overview

The following is an overview of the procedure we have used most often for measuring brand value and brand equity. There are viable alternative approaches for getting to the same end.

We administer an electronic survey (either on the Internet or using a computerized survey on a disk or downloaded to the user's computer) to a representative sample of purchasers in the product or service category under consideration. Procedurally, the survey typically has the following flow:

1. Confirm the respondent is a category user and establish the frequency and/or volume of purchases by brand.
2. Establish brand purchased last, brands purchased within some reasonable time period, and any other brands the respondent is familiar with.
3. Establish the brand, cost, channel, and level of performance for each performance attribute of either the normally purchased product/service or the last product/service purchased, whichever is most appropriate for the category under study. The performance attributes and performance levels must include all of the attributes and performance levels that are in the second conjoint design, discussed below.
4. Conjoint tasks: Have the respondent go through the first conjoint task and the second conjoint task as discussed below.

5. Choice tasks: Within the survey program, calculate importance for each attribute in the second conjoint task. Then select the four most important attributes for this respondent. Select the brand with the highest utility that is NOT the purchaser's normal brand, or the brand they purchased last, as appropriate. Select the price attribute. For each of these six attributes, present the price with the highest utility (normally the lowest price), and each of the four performance features with their highest utility levels, and the brand with the highest utility (that was not their last or normal brand) to the respondent and ask if they would switch to this product/service on their next purchase opportunity. If the respondent says "no," stop. If the respondent says "yes," take the least important attribute and change its performance level from highest utility to the level with the lowest utility, and ask the question again. If the respondent says "no," stop. If the respondent says "yes," take the next least important attribute and change its performance level from the highest utility to the level with the lowest utility, and ask the question again. Continue this procedure until the respondent says "no." Record the profile of the bundle of performance attributes, brand, and price for which the respondent said they would not switch.

6. Next, let the respondent rate the brand they purchased last or brands they have used within a reasonable time period on the set of image and trust attributes, using a 0- to 10-point scale.

7. Collect demographic/firmographic information and other information as appropriate.

Analytical Procedures – Overview

The general form of the model is as follows:

$$\text{Total brand value (utility)}, U_t = U_{pr} + U_p + U_e.$$

This is a typical conjoint model and all of the cautions and caveats that go with designing and deriving these models are in play. Yet, for all of the discussion over the last 25 years, these models have proven to be very robust and highly predictive when correctly designed and analyzed.

First, we use conjoint models to estimate utilities. The respondent goes through two trade-off tasks.

1. Task 1: Brand/Price trade-off
2. Task 2: Brand/Features/Price trade-off

The rationale, methods, and procedures for doing these two conjoint tasks are explained in the next section. We merge results of both tasks at the respondent level and rescale utilities to make them comparable. The purpose is to get an accurate estimate of price utility.

Task 3 is the choice task. The respondent then goes through a choice task that is based on their conjoint results. The respondent is asked if they would switch to, or purchase next, their highest rated conjoint profile. If yes, we ask about another (lower) profile and so on until they would not purchase or switch. The purpose of this task is to measure barriers to switching and estimate the amount of utility required for this respondent to switch to another brand.

Task 4 decomposes brand equity into its component parts. Each brand in the competitive set is also rated (0–10 scale) on its imagery, by those who have used the brand or are familiar with it. For example:

- A brand I can trust
- A brand that I want to be seen in my home
- A company that will fix any problems I may have with their product

Ratings are then regressed against the rescaled derived brand equity from the conjoint exercise to get the relative weight of each image driver. Since these ratings are typically highly correlated, we use a ridge regression, Kruskal regression procedure, or some other "key driver" model that overcomes the problems with intercorrelations within the attribute set. The beta coefficients or weights from the regression (or similar models) reveal the key drivers that are most associated with each brand's utility (derived brand equity).

Brand Equity Valuation: By setting to equal the product features of all brands in this model, you can calculate the price differential between brand equities for which a respondent gives equal total value (utility) to each brand. This is done by adjusting prices to the point where the respondents give equal utility to all the bands. Thus, you can calculate the relative price premium each respondent is willing to pay for each brand, at the unit level, relative to an unbranded product or a "store" brand that was included in the trade-off design.

By calculating brand equity value at the unit level, you can also calculate total brand equity value at the business level by multiplying the unit equity price by total units sold. This provides a market-oriented total value, in dollars (or whatever currency was used), for a brand name in a single category.

Changes in brand equity can be tracked over time.

The utilities are embedded in a market simulator that allows you to construct a set of competitive products and determine either share of preference (when the calculated switching barrier is not included) or share of choice (when the calculated switching barrier is included or a discrete choice model is used).

Calculating and Rescaling Utilities

We estimate the utilities of tangible product features, brand equity, and price on an individual level by subjecting each respondent in a market research study to two conjoint tasks. The first conjoint task uses all relevant brand names in the category and a set of possible prices across those brands. From this task we estimate total product utility (U_t), price utility (U_{pr}), and product utility (U_b) for each brand and price level. In the first conjoint task, we assume that the brand name represents the sum of the utilities of both the tangible and intangible features/attributes ($U_p + U_e$). That is, the brand name represents consumers' perceptions of the total bundle of tangible and intangible attributes, as they are currently perceived in the marketplace.

It should be noted that one of the main reasons for this first conjoint task is to obtain an accurate estimate of the utility of price. When price is included in a conjoint task with many other features, its utility tends to be understated, highly so in some cases. On the contrary, there is significant evidence that in a straight brand/price conjoint exercise, as we describe in the first task, price may be overstated. We split the difference between the utility of price in the first conjoint exercise and the second conjoint exercise.

Also, a straight brand/price conjoint exercise allows us to derive the utilities of a relatively large number of price points—usually five or more price points centered and equally spaced across the typical price range for the category. By using this many price points we can better understand the form of the pricing function. That is, whether it is linear, curvilinear, or some other form.

We next subject each respondent to a second conjoint task that includes individual tangible product features and levels of features that tend to drive purchase choice, price, and brand name. This is typically a fractional factorial, main-effects, full-profile design conjoint. However, adaptive conjoint analysis (ACA) can also be used when the number of key features exceeds an efficient design for full profile conjoint models. In this second conjoint, price is usually collapsed to a three-level attribute, encompassing the end points and the midpoint of the same price range used in the first conjoint.

From these data, we derive utility estimates for each of the individual, tangible, product features u(u_i's) and brand equity (U_e). For a given product attribute profile, the sum of the u_i's describing that product equals the utility of the product's tangible features (U_p). This second task also gives us an estimate of the utilities for brand names, U_e, after we have taken into account the utility of the tangible features and price.

We then combine the results of the two conjoint exercises at the respondent level to properly allocate the utilities of price, performance attributes, and brand equity. Figure 2 illustrates how the model works.

The procedure is as follows:

1. Total utility (U_t) from the first conjoint is set to an arbitrary value, say 1000, and each respondent's derived utilities are rescaled such that the sum of the price and product utilities sum to that arbitrary value.

2. Total utility (U_t) from the second conjoint is set to the same arbitrary value, and each respondent's derived utilities are rescaled such that the sum of the price attribute utilities, the performance attribute utilities, and brand utility sum to that arbitrary value.

3. Importance for price and brand are calculated from the results of the first conjoint in the normal manner. That is, the absolute difference between the highest and lowest utilities of each attribute is divided by the sum of the absolute differences for all attributes.

4. Importance for price, product attributes, and brand equity are similarly calculated from the results of the second conjoint in the normal manner. That is, the absolute difference between the highest and lowest utilities of each attribute is divided by the sum of the absolute differences for all attributes.

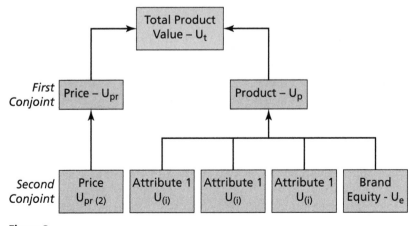

Figure 2

5. Price importance from the first conjoint is averaged with the price importance from the second conjoint to arrive at a new estimate for price importance.

6. Now, the remainder of importance values (1.00 minus the averaged importance of price) is reallocated to the importance of each performance attribute, and brand equity such that the sum of them all, including price importance, equals 1.00.

7. Finally, the utilities of price, performance attributes, and brand equity are rescaled such that the relative importance of price, performance attributes, and brand utility for each brand is preserved.

8. The result is a new data file containing the importance of each attribute and the rescaled utilities of each level of each attribute.

Choice Task

Recall that within the survey program, we calculate importance for each attribute in the second conjoint task. We then select the four most important attributes for this respondent. We also select the brand that has the highest utility that is not the purchaser's normal brand, or brand purchased last, as appropriate. And we select the price attribute. For each of these six attributes, we present the brand with the highest utility (that was not their normal or last brand), the price with the highest utility (usually the lowest price), and each of the four performance features with their highest utility levels and ask if they would switch to this product/service on their next purchase opportunity. If the respondent says "no," stop. If the respondent says "yes," take the least important attribute and change its performance from the level with the highest utility to the level with the lowest utility and ask the question again. If the respondent says "no," stop. If the respondent says "yes," take the next least important attribute and change its performance level from the highest utility to the level with the lowest utility and ask the question again. We continue this procedure until the respondent says that no, they would not switch. We then record the "no switch" profile in terms of brand, price, and the performance levels of the respondent's four most important performance attributes.

Few, if any, respondents will say "no" to the first product profile they are presented with because we have presented them with an acceptable brand, with the lowest price, and the best performance levels of their four most important attributes. For those who do say "no," it is assumed that they did not understand the conjoint task, and they are excluded from the analysis.

We next find the total utility of the "no switch" profile by adding the brand utility, the price-level utility, and the utilities of the four most important attribute-level utilities. We also calculate the total utility of the brand this respondent normally purchased or purchased last, the utility of the price they paid for that purchase, and the utilities of the performance levels of those four most important performance attributes of their normal/last purchase. The difference between these two total utilities represents an estimate of the amount of utility the respondent would need to realize for them to switch to a competing offer—the switching barrier. When this additional utility is added to the simulator, it converts it from a preference simulator to a choice simulator. That is, given a respondent's total utility for their current brand and it's performance attributes and price, and the additional utility it would take for them to switch, then we can reliably predict whether a competing brand, with a given set of performance levels and price, would offer sufficient utility for the respondent to switch, or not switch, on their next purchase occasion.

Choice Simulator

The choice simulator allows us to test changes in price or product/service performance levels and observe changes in choice among the respondents who have completed the conjoint and choice tasks.

We first form an Excel-type, fixed-field database where we record the following information:

1. Each respondent's rescaled utilities for each level of each attribute, including the levels of the price attribute and the utilities of the individual brands
2. The utility of the switching barrier
3. The calculated importance of each attribute
4. The performance levels and price of the respondent's normal/last purchase
5. The total utility of the respondent's normal/last purchase
6. The slope and intercept of the price attribute (see below)
7. The ratings for each of the brands the respondent rated on image and trust attributes
8. Any other respondent data that help describe the respondent, such as demographics/firmographics, current usage volume, and so forth

Normally, for the vast majority of respondents, price is monotonic and mostly linear. If that is the case, then we calculate the slope and intercept of that function so that we can easily estimate the utility of prices that fall between the price levels that were explicitly used in the conjoint design. If price does not appear to be linear for a significant number of respondents, then we build a subprogram that will estimate the utility between any two points explicitly tested in the conjoint exercise. We normally assume that the price function is linear between any two adjacent points and calculate the intercept and slope between those adjacent points on the fly for each simulation.

Then we develop a set of Excel commands, or alternatively write a Visual Basic program to conduct simulations of choice behaviors.

Let us assume that there are four brands in the market. Each brand has a particular level of performance on each performance attribute, and a price. For each of these brands, we can add together the utilities of the performance levels, the utility of price, and the utility of the brand name for each respondent. Then, by finding the brand/price/performance combination with the highest utility out of the four, for each respondent, we can be reasonably sure that it is the brand the respondent would choose, if those four products or services were available. Looking across all respondents, we can determine the share of choice for each brand as it is currently configured and priced by simply adding up the number of respondents that chose each brand.

Sometimes, when we run an initial simulation with the products set up as we believe they currently exist in the marketplace (that is, at their current price and their current performance levels), the results will vary significantly from known shares in the marketplace, or the reported shares from the survey. If this happens, some diagnostics and adjustments are called for.

1. First, check the sample of survey respondents to reassure yourself that it is representative of the category purchaser population. If not, then the sample should be weighted on the basis of demographic/firmographics of the population of category purchasers, and those weights should be included in the database and accounted for in the results of any simulation runs.

2. If the sample is not the problem, or if it has been weighted properly, and the simulator results are still at significant variance with reported usage shares, then determine if there are significant variances in volume of purchases within the set of respondents. If so, then weight each respondent on the basis of volume usage. Those weights should be included in the database and accounted for in the results of any simulation runs.

3. The described model relies on a "first choice" decision process. That is, the brand/price/attribute combination that has the highest utility

gets 100% of the choice even if there is only a very small difference between two or more products in terms of total utility. This may not be how your marketplace works. See the following section for some alternatives.

4. If all of these adjustments fail to bring the predicted shares in alignment with known shares in the marketplace, that is an indicator that there are likely distortions in the marketplace, typically due to awareness or availability issues. At this point, you have a choice of how you want to handle that issue:

   a. You could weight respondents such that their predicted shares (from the simulator) align with their reported shares in the survey.

   b. You could assume that the predicted shares represent the "real" situation in the marketplace once distortions in awareness and availability are corrected.

Now, suppose that Brand A changed a performance level, and/or its price. We want to know how share of choice would change. We repeat the process as before, adding together the utilities of the performance levels, the utility of price, and the utility of the brand name for each of the four brands. Then for each respondent, we find the brand with the highest utility. If this brand is different from the respondent's normal/last brand purchased, plus the utility of the switching barrier, then, we can be reasonably sure that the respondent would switch to the new brand. Looking across all respondents, we can determine the new share of choice for each brand by simply adding up the number of respondents that chose each brand. Furthermore, we can examine who switched brands.

In this manner, we can use the simulator to test variations in product performance and or price for any of the brands that were addressed in the conjoint and choice exercises.

First Choice vs Proportional Choice

As we previously described in the section "Choice Simulator," we stated that the brand that had the highest total utility, given its price and performance levels, would be chosen even if there is only a very small difference among two or more products in terms of total utility. Although this type of first-choice model has been shown to be the most accurate in several academic and practitioner studies over the years, there are some circumstances where a proportional choice or modified proportional choice model does a better job.

In a purely proportional choice model, the total utility for each competing brand/performance/price combination is divided by the sum of the utilities of all the brands at the respondent level. Then these proportions are averaged across all respondents to arrive at share of choice.

In a modified proportional choice model, the designer usually develops a heuristic for allocating the proportion of choice a brand receives. A typical heuristic would work like this:

a. If the brand/price/performance bundle with the highest utility is more than X utils greater than the next highest bundle, that brand gets 100% of the choice.

b. If the total utility of the two highest brands is less than or equal to X utils of each other, assign each a share of choice of 50%.

c. If the total utility of the three highest brands is within X utils of each other, assign each a share of choice of 33.3%.

d. If the total utility of the four highest brands is within X utils of each other, assign each a share of choice of 25.0%, and so on.

e. X can be an absolute number of utils or could be some other value based on statistical variances between the utilities of the brands, such as the standard deviation.

The proportional choice or modified proportional choice model is often more appropriate for categories where purchasers buy or use multiple brands in frequent purchase or usage situations, such as credit cards, restaurants, or some consumer packaged goods. In the event that the first choice model does not align with known shares in the market, after appropriate weighting, as discussed previously, then we test whether the proportional choice or modified proportional choice model does a better job.

Decomposing Brand Equity

Recall that in the survey, we asked respondents to rate their current/last brand and other brands that they had used or were familiar with. These brands were rated on a set of specific image and trust attributes, usually using a 0- to 10-point scale.

To decompose brand equity into its individual trust and image attributes, we use the derived and rescaled brand equity estimates from the conjoint exercise as the dependent variable and regress ratings of that brand against the utility of that brand. Since these ratings are typically highly correlated, we use a ridge regression, a Kruskal regression procedure or some other "key driver" model that overcomes the problems with intercorrelations within the independent attribute set. The beta coefficients or weights from the regression (or loadings from similar models) reveal the level of contribution each attribute is making to explain each brand's utility (derived brand equity).

In this manner, we can understand the key attributes that are associated with driving the equity of each brand and each competing brand. These key image and trust attributes tend to vary considerably from brand to brand.

More important, we can discover the image or trust attributes that are depreciating brand equity. This process alone should not be the only analysis to explore the key drivers of brand equity. You will also want to use additional analyses like perceptual mapping techniques and penalty–reward analysis to explore these issues in depth.

If brand equity has a low utility across the board (that is, the derived importance of "brand" generally is less than 10% across the vast majority of respondents), this procedure often does not work very well because there is too much random variation in the estimate of the utility of brand. Thus, it is more difficult to understand why brand equities are so low. One of several things may be in play. Going back to examine the Brand Value Model will normally reveal why this is happening. Possibilities include the following:

1. The category has become "commoditized." That is, purchasers perceive little difference between the competing brands in terms of product performance or brand equities; thus, price becomes the dominant differentiator. In this case, the vast majority of respondents will show very high importance for the "price" attribute.

2. The category is so new, or so dynamic, that brands have not had the opportunity to establish their equities. Typically, this will be a category undergoing major changes in technology or rapidly introducing new performance levels. If this is the case, you will see that the importance of the performance attributes, as a group, will be very high—70–90% of total importance, and price and brand will show much less importance.

3. If most of the brands show low equity, but one or two show significantly higher equities among some purchasers, then it is likely that brand has achieved a uniqueness that highly differentiates from the others. It is important to explore why that has happened and what distinguishes those brands from all the others in terms of image or trust attributes.

Design Considerations

In the design for both the first and second conjoint, it is important to make sure that the range of prices encompasses the full range of current prices in the marketplace and any anticipated short-term price changes.

When it comes to deciding on the product attributes to include and exclude from the design of the second conjoint, the rule of thumb is, the fewer the better. If an attribute is not a key driver of choice, then it should not be included. Use previous research and focus groups to find out. If all brands are performing at about the same level on some attribute that is basic to the category, then it should not be included unless there is an obvious opportunity for you or a competitor to significantly improve your performance and make that attribute a key differentiator between brands. For example, in PCS phone services, having an attribute like "Clarity of the Monthly Invoice" typically does not differentiate competitors, nor is it that important to most people in making the choice on which PCS provider to choose.

When developing the performance levels for each attribute, you should consider the performance levels that exist among all of the competitors in the category, as well as those you think may become available in the near future. Performance attribute levels should be stated as objectively and specifically as possible. For example, in a study of electric utilities service, avoid a level of reliability that says "highest reliability available." Instead, say something like "less than three outages of more than 5 minutes annually."

Furthermore, it is important to have the levels of the performance attributes organized in an ordinal fashion as much as possible. That is, the levels should be stated ranging from a lower level of performance to a higher level of performance. This will greatly assist in the value-based segmentation because we can use the derived importance for the attributes instead of the individual utility estimates for each level of the attribute in the clustering procedure.

The estimate of brand equity is relative to the other brands in the study. Therefore, to obtain an estimate of absolute brand equity, we recommend that the study include an unbranded product, a store brand with known low equity, or a dummy brand name, whichever is most appropriate for the category. This provides the base price point for estimating brand equity in terms of its absolute dollar value.

In considering price, if there are significant maintenance costs or costs for expendables, be sure to include those as separate attributes. Sometimes, these can be combined. For example, in a medical testing device category, you might craft the initial price levels as five levels ranging from $100,000 to $300,000, and then have a separate price attribute with test strips ranging in price from $200 per 1000 to $400 per 1000. Or you could have one level stated as "initial purchase price = $100,000 with the cost of test strips at $400 per 1000" and another level be "initial purchase price = $200,000 with the cost of test strips at $200 per 1000."

Results

The Brand Equity model allows us to provide the following information:

1. Obviously, we can estimate overall brand equity, U_b, for each brand and the average per unit price premium that equity is worth at the market level or within defined market segments compared to all the other brands in the study. Given accurate volume estimates, the per unit premium can be projected to a total value of the brand's equity in a particular category.

2. We can conduct simulations to estimate share of choice, given each brand's equity coupled with a known or contemplated product feature profile and a particular price and the utility of the switching barrier. Thus, we can observe the effects on share of choice for price changes and changes in tangible attribute levels for any brand or brand combination. A series of simulations whereby we only vary price allows us to develop estimates of price elasticity and cross-elasticities for a brand or brands at the total market level or within any market segment.

3. In a similar fashion, this methodology can be used to test and evaluate the extension of a known brand name into a new product/service category and to evaluate the equity transfer of the brand name into the new category.

4. Longitudinally, we can observe the effects on brand equity and share of choice due to changes in the marketing mix or investments in brand building for any brand or combination of brands.

5. Given self-explicated ratings of brands on the intrinsic features of a brand (e.g., a brand that enhances my self-image, quality of advertising, contribution to the community, social responsibility, protecting the environment, etc.), we often are able to relate brand equity to particular activities of the firm using regression techniques or "key driver" model techniques.

EXAMPLE

Following is a simplified example of how the model works. We use the home bread maker product category mentioned in Chapter 7. The first conjoint uses only brand and price attributes as shown in Table 1. Each brand is allowed to be associated with each price.

In this first conjoint exercise, each brand is associated with each price using a fractional-factorial, main-effects design (or a randomized design as in ACA). Each respondent ranks (or rates) the brand/price combinations in terms of preference.

The analysis of these data yields a set of derived utilities, or values, for each brand and each price, plus a derived overall importance of brand and price for each respondent. For example, one respondent's utilities and importance may look like those shown in Table 2.

If the current market prices were as shown in Table 3, this respondent's total utility (value) for each brand/price configuration would be as shown in the column labeled "Utility," which is simply the sum of the respondent's utility for the brand and the current price.

Since this respondent places the highest utility on the Oster bread maker at $139, they would prefer that brand/price combination over all those others available.

Table 1

Level	Brand	Price ($)
1	Oster	129
2	Braun	139
3	Sears	149
4	Acme	159

Table 2

Level	Brand	Utility	Price ($)	Utility
1	Oster	22.34	129	44.35
2	Braun	64.25	139	26.64
3	Sears	27.46	149	15.34
4	Acme	59.13	159	55.65
Total importance		123.38		100.00
Percentage of importance		55.2%		44.8%

Table 3

Brand	Market price ($)	Utility (value)
Oster	139	$(22.34 + 26.64) = 48.98$
Braun	149	$(64.25 - 15.34) = 48.91$
Sears	139	$(-27.46 + 26.64) = -0.82$
Acme	129	$(-59.13 + 44.35) = -14.78$

At this point, brand name is assumed to be the sum of both tangible and intangible attributes. The second conjoint is designed to let us separate those out.

The second conjoint includes the tangible product features that drive choice. For simplicity, we have only chosen two, capacity and loaf configuration, as shown in Table 4.

In this second conjoint exercise, each respondent ranks (or rates) brand/feature/price combinations in terms of preference. We do not need to show the respondent all 36 possible combinations because we can use fractional-factorial, main-effects-only designs.

The analysis of these data at the respondent level, using standard OLS regression, MONANOVA, or LINMAP yields a set of derived utilities or values, for each brand and each feature, plus a derived overall importance of brand, capacity, and loaf configuration, and price for each respondent. For example, our respondent's utilities and importance values are given in Table 5.

The importance of "Price" from this second conjoint is averaged with the importance of "Price" from the first conjoint. That yields a price importance of $(44.77\% + 25.28\%)/2 = 35.02\%$. Given that, we now rescale all the utilities from the second conjoint to this change to get the following adjusted model for this respondent.

Here, the importance of brand, capacity, and loaf are adjusted to be comparable with average importance of price from both conjoint exercises. We see that Braun has the highest brand equity, followed by Oster. Also, this respondent has a high preference for a 1.5 lb capacity and is fairly ambivalent

Table 4

Level	Brand	Capacity (lb)	Loaf
1	Oster	1.0	Round
2	Braun	1.5	Square
3	Sears	2.0	Rectangular
4	Acme		

Table 5

Second Conjoint

Level	Brand	Utility	Capacity (lb)	Utility	Loaf	Utility	Price ($)	Utility
1	Oster	10.22	1.0	−30.62	Round	5.86	129	21.33
2	Braun	32.04	1.5	20.15	Square	1.09	139	11.38
3	Sears	−14.86	2.0	10.47	Rectangular	−6.95	149	−12.42
4	Acme	−27.40					159	−20.29
Abs. diff.		59.44		50.77		12.81		41.62
Importance		36.10%		30.84%		7.78%		25.28%

about loaf configuration. Also note that this respondent is very price sensitive, especially for any price above $139.

The remaining task is to use these data to determine the brands' value in dollars.

We will assume that the Acme brand is our baseline. The question we wish to answer is, At what price for Acme is this respondent indifferent between an Acme bread maker and a Braun bread maker, all else being the same?

We see from Table 6 that the spread between the brand equity of Braun and Acme (the base brand) is $27.86 − (−23.83) = 51.69$ utils. This case assumes that the price function is linear. Thus, we start at the utility of the highest price ($159), which is −28.11, and add 51.69 utils, which equals 23.58. Using a simple linear regression, we find that the price value of 23.58 utils for this respondent is $133.66. So, for this respondent the value of the Braun name is $159.00 minus $133.66, or $25.34.

Table 6

Rescaled Second Conjoint

Level	Brand	Utility	Capacity (lb)	Utility	Loaf	Utility	Price ($)	Utility
1	Oster	8.89	1.0	−26.63	Round	5.10	129	29.55
2	Braun	27.86	1.5	17.52	Square	0.95	139	15.77
3	Sears	−12.92	2.0	9.10	Rectangular	−6.04	149	−17.21
4	Acme	−23.83					159	−28.11
Sum		0.00		0.00		0.00		0.00
Abs. diff.		51.69		44.15		11.14		57.66
Importance		31.40%		26.82%		6.77%		35.02%

If the price curve for a respondent is not considered linear, we can still easily find the corresponding value of brand by assuming that the price function is linear between any two adjacent price points. The change in utility from $159.00 to $139.00 is 43.88 utils. That leaves $51.69 - 42.88 = 7.81$ utils to account for in the change of utility from $139.00 to $129.00. The total utils for that price difference is 13.78. The ratio of $7.81/13.78 = 0.5627$, which represents the value of $129.00 + 0.5627 \times \$10.00$, which equals $134.63. That answer is very similar to the one where we assumed the entire function was linear.

Summarizing, if Acme offered a bread maker with a 1.5 lb capacity, making a round loaf, and priced at $134.63, it would have the same total utility of a Braun with the same capacity and load configuration, priced at $159.00. And that total utility is 22.37 units of utility, or utils, for either.

From Braun's point of view, this respondent is worth $159.00 - \$134.63 = \$24.37$ because that is the amount she is willing to pay for the Braun name on her bread maker, compared to the baseline Acme nameplate, when all the performance attributes are equal. Obviously, these same calculations could be made for the Sears or Oster brand names.

Note that the value of the brand is not absolute. It is relative to the other brands in the category. When we use the Brand Value Model to derive the economic value of a brand's equity, we typically include a store brand or a nonexistent brand to establish a baseline to which we can compare all of the other brands in the category.

Obviously, we can make these calculations for every respondent in the survey and report averages for total market or any market segment. If the sample is projectable to the total market, then we can easily estimate the total value of a brand name by multiplying the average brand equity value by total unit sales.

In addition, the calculated utilities and importance values from Table 6 can be used as a basis for segmenting the market into such groups as "price-sensitive," "feature-sensitive," "brand loyal," and so forth. Then we can calculate brand equities in each segment and optimize a brand's pricing scheme across segments. See the next section "Value-Based Segmentation," for more discussion on this topic.

We build a market simulator to estimate share of choice for each brand name with a known or contemplated attribute profile and a particular price. Thus, we can observe the effects on share of choice for price changes and changes in features for any brand or brand combination or, for the introduction of a branded product extension. A series of simulations whereby we only vary price, holding features constant, allows us to develop estimates of price sensitivity for any brand at the total market or any market segment.

It should be obvious that this modeling approach can also be used to determine how much of a brand's equity can be initially transferred into another product or service category.

Finally, we can monitor a brand's equity over time through a series of market studies. The results of experimentation with the marketing mix or investments in brand building can be easily monitored in this manner.

Although we have used a very simple illustration of the Brand Value Model, these models can be designed and used in just about any product or service category. However, the designs can get very complex.

The advantages of the modeling approach described in this addendum, using external surveys are as follows:

1. The model is not dependent on internal financial data.
2. It is relatively fast and easy to execute using proven research methods.
3. It can be executed at any time in the business cycle. That is, it is not dependent on internal cyclical accounting changes.
4. It takes into account all major relevant brands in a defined product/ service category.
5. It measures brand equity relative to other current and potential brands in the category, including unbranded items when they exist in the category.
6. It can be used to measure the transfer of a brand's equity into another category.
7. It recognizes that value of any one brand's equity can be defeated in the marketplace by competitor pricing strategies, at least in the short run.
8. It allows calculation of total brand value and brand equity over alternative pricing scenarios and volume scenarios for total market, or within defined subsegments.
9. It allows the firm to assess price elasticity and cross-elasticities of their own brands and competitor brands in a category.
10. Results can be projected to estimate the total value of a brand name under alternative sales projections. Thus, this modeling approach can be used to evaluate the total dollar value of a brand name for purposes of evaluation and acquisition.
11. If self-explicated ratings of the components of brand equity are acquired from the same respondents, brand equity can be further decomposed into specific equity-building activities.

Caveats and Cautions:

1. As in all conjoint models, the attribute set must include those features that are relevant to the purchase decision for all major market segments. If a major decision-driving attribute is excluded, it will be confounded with the estimate of price or brand equity.

2. This model works well for both products and well-defined services. However, it does not work well across categories (i.e. for a brand family). That is, the equity of a brand family (e.g., Honda automobiles, motorcycles, generators, outboard motors, etc.) is very difficult to measure simultaneously. Each category needs to be addressed separately. Also, the narrower the product category is defined, the more accurate the estimates.

Value-Based Segmentation

In value-based segmentation, we use the derived importance for brand, price, and each performance feature to segment the sample into relatively homogeneous benefit groups such as price-sensitive, service-sensitive, brand loyal for an individual brand, brand-combination loyal, and attribute importance groups. We can then calculate brand value and brand equities for each segment, and even break out results from the choice simulations by these segments. This assumes, of course, that there is sufficient sample size to make the segmentation reliable.

Depending on the complexity of the product or service category, you can expect to derive somewhere between 5 and 10 distinct segments.

As we stated in the Section "Design Considerations," it is important to have the levels of the performance attributes organized in an ordinal fashion as best as possible. That is, the levels should be stated ranging from the lowest level of performance to the highest level of performance. This allows us to use the derived importance for price and the attributes instead of the individual utility estimates for each level of the attribute in the clustering procedure.

We also initially use the importance of "brand" in the segmentation scheme. Then we break out the segment that places high importance on "brand" into individual brand, or brand combination groups.

We start this procedure using the same data file that we formed for the choice simulator, discussed earlier.

The basic procedure for forming the segments is as follows:

1. The first step is to inspect the database of utilities and attribute importance and make appropriate adjustments:

a. Inspect the utilities of each level of each performance attribute across all respondents. For the vast majority of respondents, these should be monotonic. That is, the lowest performance level should be given to the lowest utility, the highest performance level should be given to the highest utility, and utilities should increase as the performance level increases across levels.

b. In cases where the utilities for a particular performance attribute are not monotonic for a particular group of respondents, determine whether that attribute is important. If it is not important, then no adjustments are necessary because it will not have a significant impact on the clustering except to designate the attribute as not important for that group.

c. In cases where the utilities for a particular performance attribute are not monotonic for a particular group, and the attribute is important, we need to break apart that attribute and form two new attributes. For example, let's say a performance attribute for a PCS phone, "music download capability," has three levels—"none," "yes, with a $5.00 per month fee," and "yes, with no fee." Some people put high utility on "yes, with no fee." Others put high utility on "none." Yet this variable shows up as important to both groups, but for different reasons. You would form two new performance attributes. The two new attributes would be "prefer no music download capability" and "prefer music download." Importance on the first new variable, "prefer no music download," would be the importance for the original attribute for those who place high utility on "none" on the original attribute and zero for everyone else. These same people would have an importance of zero on the second new variable, "prefer music download." And, those who placed higher utility on either one of the music download levels would be given the same importance as was calculated for the original attribute.

2. Next, the data should be subjected to a cluster analysis to form those groups with similar importance profiles. Cluster analysis is a generic term for a set of algorithms that are widely available to marketing research professionals. Primarily, the various algorithms cluster together those cases or respondents that respond similarly to a set of basis questions, in this case the calculated importance of the various attributes. Some clustering algorithms are more

appropriate for marketing research than are others. In addition, some clustering programs may provide inconsistent or unstable results. At SDR, we prefer a Howard–Harris partitioning procedure. It is extremely important to thoroughly check segments that are generated by clustering procedures. Methods for doing this include the following:

   a. Use split samples, or holdout samples, to verify the results of the initial clustering.

   b. Rotate the order of the data, recluster, and determine if the results are nearly identical.

   c. Use several different clustering procedures and determine whether the results converge to a single solution.

   d. Use "boot strapping" procedures to test for convergence of results.

3. Typically (but not always) you should see the following segments emerge from the clustering:

   a. One or more segments that put very high importance on price or pricing/financing options.

   b. Several segments that put very high importance on different sets of performance attributes. For example, in the electric utility category, you might see attribute groups such as

      i. High reliability and minimum power interrupts

      ii. High levels of service support

      iii. High levels of responsiveness when there are outages or other problems

   c. A segment that puts high importance on brand. This group should be further broken out by the brand or brand set on which this group of respondents place the highest utility.

4. It is a good procedure to subject the cluster results to a multivariate discriminant analysis to thoroughly test whether the clusters (segments) are truly different from each other and to explore the attributes that are most contributing to differentiation between the clusters. This is done by designating the cluster membership as the dependent categorical variable and the importance of all the attributes as the independent variables. Specifically, you should inspect the following:

   a. The matrix of multivariate F statistics between all pairs of clusters. All of these should be highly significant.

   b. The reclassification matrix of cases, based on bootstrapping holdout procedures. In SPSS, that is the "leave out one" option.

    c. The significance of each attribute in differentiating between clusters and note those as key drivers of differentiation.

5. Produce and preserve the Fisher classification equations from the discriminant analysis in step 4 for use in the next step.

6. Once the clustering is completed and you are satisfied that you have arrived at your best solution, it becomes necessary to report the results of subsequent marketing research studies or from other customer information by market segment. To do this adequately, it is appropriate to develop a set of classification schemes, or scoring models, from the baseline survey. If developed correctly, a set of standard questions can be included in every subsequent marketing research study or customer inquiry, such that the answers to those questions will allow the researcher to classify respondents into their appropriate market segment with a high degree of accuracy and confidence. In this case, these classification equations are developed from the calculated importance of the attributes. You may want to rerun the discriminant analysis as described in step 4 in a stepwise fashion to eliminate nondiscriminating attributes.

7. In the case where we are trying to predict segment membership from a larger database, such as a transaction database or a customer file, with limited segmentation information, the typical steps are the following:

    a. Merge all of the database elements with the survey data.

    b. Cross-tab all the database elements against known segment membership from the survey data.

    c. Search for significant differences among the database elements using ANOVA or Chi-Squared statistics as appropriate.

    d. Use variables that show significant differences as the independent set in discriminant analysis, CHAID analysis, and/or logistic/logit regression to develop a classification algorithm to score cases in the database into their appropriate segments.

    e. This procedure requires a lot of time and patience and may yield only marginal results. An alternative procedure is to use an artificial neural network (ANN) to develop the scoring model. The application of ANNs for the development of segment-scoring models of transaction databases has met with considerable success, mainly because ANNs are not dependent on assumptions concerning data measurement and functional form.

8. Describe the resulting segments in detail. As a minimum, you will want to describe the segments in terms of
   a. The size of each segment and their purchase volume in the category.
   b. Your share of sales or volume for each segment, as well as competitor shares and volumes.
   c. What is most important to each segment and what is not important to them in terms of the performance attributes, price, and brand.
   d. Any demographic or firmographics differences.
   e. Any other pertinent information you collected in the survey or you can glean from matching respondents to customer data on your internal database or from secondary sources such as Cluster Plus or PRIZM.
9. Perceptual mapping is also a good technique for visually displaying how the segments differ on key performance attributes.

GLOSSARY
Brand Terms and Definitions

The beginning of wisdom is to call things by their right names.
—Chinese Proverb

Assets　An entity you own or borrow with the ability to create future positive cash flows; claims on future benefits.

Brand　A Quality Assurance Device that's an intangible asset.

Brand Architecture　How a company employs its brand offerings in discrete market segments for competitive advantage.

Brand Awareness

- The % of the market that mentions the Brand Name when the Brand Category is mentioned. Known as Unaided or Top Of Mind Awareness (TOMA).
- The % of the market that mentions the Brand Name when competitive Brand Names are mentioned (Aided Awareness).

Brand Category　Industry/market 'set' in which your brand competes.

Brand Development　Process of creating brand value.

Brand Descriptor　A short phrase that captures the Brand Essence and/or defines the Brand Category.

Brand Essence　A written description that captures the most dominant characteristic that best differentiates the Brand and creates positive expectations in the market's mind.

Brand Extension　Beyond product category or product form, eg., extending the Arm & Hammer baking soda brand beyond the baking category to the air freshener category for refrigerators.

Brand Equity　The perceived value of a bundle of image attributes associated with a brand by a specific market's members.

Brand Identity　What you'd like people to think when they hear brand name.

Brand Image　What people think about when brand name is mentioned.

Brand Integrity　When the performance of the organization/product/ service meets or exceeds the expectations of stakeholders.

Brand Loyalty When users continue to purchase your brand despite competitive offers.

Brand Name What you call yourself, your company, product, service.

Brand Personality The human characteristics associated with a brand.

Brand Promise (also can be called Brand Pull) A set of expectations created by your Brand Identity.

- Part of the Value Proposition.
- To be actively communicated to your market.
- Creates a unique set of expectations (differentiates).

Brand Strategy Why you change Brand Image to achieve Brand Identity.

Brand Value The value of a corporate, product or service brand: BV = TA (tangible attributes) + IA (image attributes) − P (price).

Branding Application of tactics and performance to achieve Brand Image.

Co-Branding The use of two or more brands to create mutual advantage.

DCF Future free cash flows discounted to reflect the cost of capital. Arrives at a net present value used to compare potential investment opportunities.

Economic Value Added NOPAT less the cost of capital = EVA.[1]

Goodwill Goodwill is the premium an acquiring firm is willing to pay for another company's assets in order to gain expected benefits of economies of scale, etc. It is the amount paid *above* fair market value.

Market Value The value of a firm expressed as: MV = TA (book value or tangible assets like real property, real assets less liabilities) + IA (intangible assets such as knowledge, brands, relationships, ideas, processes, etc.) Value is assigned when investors buy or sell shares of stock with price per share X # of shares outstanding = MV. (Also known as Market Capitalization.) Price per share divided by earnings yields P/E ratio, which is an estimate of future cash flows that can be compared to competitors in an industry.

Mission Answers the question: "What business are we in, and why do people pay us?" Similar to Purpose.

NOPAT Net Operating Profit After Tax measures earnings unleveraged by debt.

Position/Brand Position How you (brand) are perceived in the minds of customers, in relation to competition, in a category.

Pull   Values create 'pull' (or demand, motivation, inspiration, desire, meaning, etc.) which then elicits action and behavior.

Purpose   Why you do what you do, from an internal perspective, based ideally, on core values. Similar to Mission.

Strategy   How you achieve objectives and accomplish your mission.

Tactics   Elements, tools you use to execute your strategy.

Value   Perceptions of worth: economic value, financial value, investment value, market value, esthetic value, etc. Value assigns an estimation of current or anticipated worth in monetary terms.

Values   Beliefs, ideals, and principles: social values, family values, political values, workplace culture, etc. All ethics are values, not all values are ethical. Morals deal with values that society judges "right" or "wrong."

Values brand   A Brand that reflects the values of the chosen market set.

Values brand*ing*   A leadership process and management practice that aligns Brand Strategy with market and organization values.

Vision   Your view, ideally based on your customers, employees, other stakeholders and company's core values, of where you want to be in the future.

---

[1] Trademark of Stern, Stewart & Co.

INDEX

About TEXERE

Texere, a progressive and authoritative voice in business publishing, brings to the global business community the expertise and insights of leading thinkers. Our books educate, enlighten, and entertain, and provide an intersection where our authors and our readers share cutting edge ideas, practices, and innovative solutions. Texere seeks to cultivate, enhance, and disseminate information that illuminates the global business landscape.

About the typeface

This book was set in 10.5 point Bembo. Bembo was cut by Francesco Griffo for the Venitian printer Aldus Manutius to publish in 1495 *De Aetna* by Cardinal Pietro Bembo. Stanley Morison supervised the design of Bembo for the Monotype Corporation in 1929. The Bembo is a readable and classical typeface because of its well-proportioned letterforms, functional serifs, and lack of peculiarities.

Library of Congress Cataloging-in-Publication Data

Neal, William D. (William Douglas), 1943-
  Value creation : the power of brand equity/
  William D. Neal, Ron Strauss.
    p. cm.
  Includes index.
  ISBN 1-58799-204-3
1. Brand name products—Valuation.   2. Intangible property—
Valuation.   3. Brand loyalty.   4. Branding (Marketing)—
Management.   I. Strauss, Ron (Ronald), 1943-   II. Title.
  HD69.B7N36 2007
  658.8'27—dc22

                                            2007050294